Deleuze and Philos

'Deleuze was always a friend of wisdom, although he cultivated a strange and dangerous wisdom, forever the outsider, the lodger, the uncanny guest at the courthouse of reason who dared disturb the peace and derange the proceedings. . . . He was chameleon, Corinthian and caricature all rolled into a multiplicity, an irrational number, an abstract machine.'

Keith Ansell Pearson

Over a period of thirty years, Gilles Deleuze (1925–1995) has had a profound influence on the direction of philosophical and social thought. His presence is felt in contemporary debates in feminism, political theory and continental philosophy where he has challenged and overturned many theoretical dogmas. His work marked a significant turn toward the poststructuralist movement as a whole and its influence increases as it unfolds.

The essays presented in **Deleuze and Philosophy** explore both the classical and radical aspects of Deleuze's work. Essays on Kant and Spinoza reflect on Deleuze's earlier work on the history of philosophy; there is exploration of his highly influential notion of 'minor' literature; the implications of his writing for philosophy's relation to biology and machinic thinking is explored with a view to the future of philosophy. The final two essays consider Deleuzian notions of art and 'wildstyle'.

The contributors assembled here approach Deleuze from a wide range of perspectives and in so doing complement Deleuze's own work, which defies assimilation into tidy categories. Working both inside Deleuze's thought and looking at it critically from without, **Deleuze and Philosophy** is an invaluable addition to contemporary philosophical and social thought.

Contributors: Keith Ansell Pearson, Diane Beddoes, Aurelia Armstrong, Tim Clark, Daniel W. Conway, Iain Hamilton Grant, Judy Purdom, Deepak Narang Sawhney, Howard Caygill, Robert O'Toole, Alistair Welchman, James Williams, Robin Mackay.

Keith Ansell Pearson is Senior Lecturer and Director of Graduate Research in Philosophy at the University of Warwick. He is the author and editor of a number of books on Nietzsche.

Warwick Studies in European Philosophy

Edited by Andrew Benjamin
Professor of Philosophy, University of Warwick

This series presents the best and most original work being done within the European philosophical tradition. The books included in the series seek not merely to reflect what is taking place within European philosophy, rather they will contribute to the growth and development of that plural tradition. Work written in the English language as well as translations into English are to be included, engaging the tradition at all levels – whether by introductions that show the contemporary philosophical force of certain works, or in collections that explore an important thinker or topic, as well as in significant contributions that call for their own critical evaluation.

Deleuze and Philosophy

The Difference Engineer

Edited by Keith Ansell Pearson

London and New York

First published 1997
by Routledge
11 New Fetter Lane, London EC4P 4EE

Simultaneously published in the USA and Canada
by Routledge
29 West 35th Street, New York, NY 10001

Typeset in Perpetua by LaserScript, Mitcham, Surrey
Printed and bound in Great Britain by
Mackays, Chatham, Kent

British Library Cataloguing in Publication Data
A catalogue record for this book is available from the British Library

Library of Congress Cataloging in Publication Data
Deleuze and philosophy: the difference engineer/edited by
Keith Ansell Pearson.
p. cm. – (Warwick studies in European philosophy)
Includes bibliographical references and index.
ISBN 0–415–14269–5. – ISBN 0–415–14270–9 (pbk.)
1. Deleuze, Gilles. I. Ansell-Pearson, Keith, 1960– II. Series.
B2430.D454D45 1997
194–dc20 96–36570
CIP

ISBN 0–415–14269–5 (hbk)
ISBN 0–415–14270–9 (pbk)

For Catherine D. and Greg A., two 'beautiful ones'

Contents

Contributors

Keith Ansell Pearson is Senior Lecturer in Philosophy at the University of Warwick, where he is also Director of Graduate Research and Programme Director of the Centre for Research in Philosophy and Literature. He has authored and edited several books on Nietzsche. His latest book, *Viroid Life: Perspectives on Nietzsche and the Transhuman Condition*, is also being published by Routledge in 1997.

Aurelia Armstrong is a doctoral student of the Department of General Philosophy at the University of Sydney, carrying out research on Deleuze's interpretation of Spinoza.

Diane Beddoes recently completed a Ph.D. thesis on Kant and Deleuze in the Department of Philosophy at the University of Warwick. She is the author of 'Mapping V', in K. R. Jones (ed.) *Mapping Woman* (University of Warwick, Centre for Research in Philosophy and Literature, 1994).

Howard Caygill is Professor of Historical and Cultural Studies at Goldsmith's College London. He is the author of *The Art of Judgement* (Blackwell, 1989) and *A Kant Dictionary* (Blackwell, 1995). His book *Walter Benjamin: The Colour of Experience* will be published by Routledge in 1997.

Tim Clark recently completed a Ph.D. thesis on Deleuze and Whitehead in the Department of Philosophy at the University of Warwick.

Daniel W. Conway is Associate Professor of Philosophy and Director of the Center for Ethics and Value Inquiry at Pennsylvania State University. He has published widely on topics in continental philosophy and political theory. His book *Nietzsche and the Political* (1996) is published by Routledge.

Iain Hamilton Grant wrote his Ph.D. thesis on Kant and Lyotard in the Department of Philosophy, at the University of Warwick, and teaches at the University of the West of England. He is the translator into English of Lyotard's *Libidinal Economy* and Baudrillard's *Symbolic Exchange and Death*.

Robin Mackay is a postgraduate student in Continental Philosophy at the University of Warwick, and editor of the journal *** *collapse*.

Robert O'Toole is a graduate of the Universities of Warwick and Sussex, trained in philosophy, cognitive science and artificial life. He is a member of the University of Warwick Institute of Education and contributor to the Cybernetic Culture Research Unit.

Judy Purdom is working on a Ph.D. thesis on Deleuze and the Visual Arts in the Department of Philosophy at the University of Warwick.

Deepak Narang Sawhney completed a Ph.D. thesis on Deleuze and Guattari's reading of Marx and complexity theory in economics in the Department of Philosophy at the University of Warwick, and is currently editing a book on the Marquis de Sade entitled *Must We Burn Sade?*, to be published by Humanities Press in 1997.

Alistair Welchman completed his Ph.D. thesis on negative and positive modes of Critique in the Department of Philosophy at the University of Warwick. He is the author of several published essays, including 'The Logogram', published in *Parallax*.

James Williams is Lecturer in the Department of Philosophy at the University of Dundee, author of *Lyotard* (Polity Press) and of essays on Deleuze and topics in continental philosophy.

1

Deleuze Outside/Outside Deleuze

On the Difference Engineer

Keith Ansell Pearson

> The most enlightened get only as far as liberating themselves from metaphysics and looking back on it from above: whereas here too, as in the hippodrome, at the end of the track, it is necessary to turn the corner.
>
> (Nietzsche, *Human, All Too Human*)

> To open us up to the inhuman and overhuman . . . to go beyond the human condition is the meaning of philosophy, in so far as our condition condemns us to live among badly analyzed composites, and to be badly analyzed composites.
>
> (Deleuze, *Bergsonism*)

The 'and' conjoins but never innocently or romantically. So much at stake. An allusion, a play, is made to *Nietzsche et la philosophie*, in which the potentialities of an active and radical philosophy were marshalled against the hegemony of reactive forces and values. In addition, there is the question of Deleuze's readings of the history of philosophy, in which philosophy loses its established historical identity and is subjected to a different kind of becoming. And then, last but not least, indeed least of all, there is the question of philosophy's imperial claims and its relation to the pre-philosophical and the extra-philosophical.[1] Philosophy moving always outside, thought opening out onto the cosmos and becoming-chaosmos. There is also the question of 'Deleuze and philosophy and . . .', in which the lines of connection and communication are not foreclosed, but in which Deleuze will impact massively on film, on literature, on politics, on the visual arts, on historiography, on science, on technics, etc., transmuting them in the process so that they become lines of production: 'Nothing is true once and for all, everything is rendered mobile.'

Deleuze's identity as the name which somewhat arbitrarily, but not unintelligently, serves to gather together the disparate essays of this volume has to be dramatically called into question. It will be a question of engineering differences, subjecting his thought-experiments and inventions to the infinite play of difference and repetition, and unfolding the risks his thought undertakes in terms of the excessive logic of the 'outside'. An engagement with 'Deleuze outside/outside Deleuze' does not presuppose any simple or straightforward opposition between the interior or the exterior. Rather, any 'explication' is at once an 'implication' and a 'complication', in which the 'new' spontaneously emerges out of the movements of the labyrinthine fold. The becoming of the new is never confused in Deleuze with the 'fashionable', but rather signals the variable creativity that emerges out of the complex becoming (becoming-complex) of social and technical practices, assemblages and machines that function through interpretation and reciprocal interpenetration ('communication' is always 'transversal'). Deleuze was never a student 'of' philosophy, but he was always philosophical. The 'critical' task of 'outside' thought, a task that is always untimely, is to untangle the lines which cut across, like a machine, the recent past and the near future. The thinker of the 'outside' uses history excessively for the sake of something 'beyond', or alien to, it, thinking out of time for the sake of time, which amounts to becoming something other than what history has made us and wishes to make of us. This explains why Deleuze always wrote against all forms of 'evolutionism', whether on the level of biology or ethnology, or on the level of history, geology and archaeology. It is thus incumbent upon 'outside' philosophy to philosophize in the most radical manner conceivable, doing violence to the mind by breaking both with the natural bent of the intellect and with habits of scientific praxis. One is reminded of Lyotard's 'monstrous' insight that the activity of thinking and writing belongs to the mode of existence in which each person escapes all control, including, and especially, their own. Thought of in these terms of the 'outside', Deleuze will not be the 'subject' of an event, say the event of 'Deleuzian' nomad thought. The event of Deleuze and philosophy just never happened and it is to be hoped that this volume does not serve the regressive cause of making it happen. Deleuze was always a friend of wisdom, although he cultivated a strange and dangerous wisdom, forever the outsider, the lodger, the uncanny guest at the courthouse of reason who dared to disturb the peace and derange the proceedings. The proper name of 'Deleuze' is a signal, a heterogeneous sign-system, that reminds us that the unthought is not external to thought but lies at the very heart of it. To enter the labyrinth of his thought one must have courage for the forbidden where the strange and unfamiliar things of the future are more familiar and welcome than the so-called reality of the present. In his reports to the 'academy' Deleuze never asked for a verdict, since his desire was only to impart some *knowledge*. He was chameleon, Corinthian and caricature all rolled into a multiplicity, an irrational number, an abstract machine.

Deleuze was a monster. His work is marked by a subversive, perilous attempt to map out a new becoming of thought beyond good sense and common sense, in which thought becomes monstrous because it forsakes the desire for an image of thought. All the names in the history of philosophy become masks and disguises, subject to a play of difference and repetition that produces double readings and multiple readings of texts and thinkers. Deleuze becomes Kantian, Kant becomes Deleuzian, Spinoza finds a line of flight, with the affirmation of a single substance transformed into a plane of immanence. In these readings 'of' the history of philosophy the likes of Spinoza, of Leibniz, of Kant and of Nietzsche are freed from all attempts to fix 'once' and 'for all' their time and place and to subject them, through a thermodynamic historiography, to an entropic narrative. The evolution of Deleuze's complex adaptive system of thought, however, is deeply paradoxical, in which we necessarily get caught up in the complications and implications of his foldings. We make differences, but in turn these differences are monstrous. Deleuze is the philosopher of the pure empty form of time, of the event (the time of Aion), of pure becoming and of pure differences. But he is also the thinker of contamination, of contagion and of viroid life.

What is monstrous about the activity of thought is not the truth it discovers at the end of the journey, but the journey itself, in which the transportation of thought outside itself is always Dionysian and delirious. Truth cannot be said to be the product of a prior disposition or schema, but is rather the result of a tremendous violence in thought, an irruption of the larval mind that is populated by a thousand 'souls', a thousand plateaus of intensity. One will never find truth, one will never philosophize, if one knows in advance what one is looking for. When we restrict the philosophical task to the merely human, seeking the true only in order to do good, we find nothing. The philosopher desires to produce no disciples. There will not be a race of Deleuzians, unless they be a band of bastards of mixed descent and impure blood. The moral narrowness of disciples simply serves to hold back the further expansion of the truth. Their desire is to tame the monster and to make it work for them. As Nietzsche wrote, over the door of the philosopher of the future, who philosophizes beyond good and evil as his peculiar vocation, there stands the motto 'What do *I* matter!'

Philosophy neither conserves old values nor provides shelter for eternal values, but always speaks of values that are to come. Philosophy is often sad, though never nostalgic. Thought-machines, machines of thinking, are never simply constructed but composed. It is a composition that brings into play sensation, perception, affectation, without reference to a determinate subject (there is only a transcendental subject which is always multiple) or to a fixed object (objects are brought into being and always refer to events). As Klee noted, the artist who remains uninspired by realism places more value on the powers that do the forming than on the final forms themselves. Final forms are illusions of solidity and stability. The task of the artist is to show that the world in its present shape is not the only possible world; this is akin to Deleuze's comprehension of philosophy acting as a synthesizer of new values. In composing alternative worlds, the artist and philosopher do not conjure things out of thin air, even if their conceptions and productions appear as utterly fantastical. Their compositions are only possible because they are able to connect, to tap into the virtual and immanent processes of machinic becoming (there are no points on the map, only lines), even if such a connection and tapping into are the most difficult things to lay hold of and demonstrate. As Klee wrote: 'Genesis eternal!' (Klee 1964: 87). One can only seek to show the power, the affectivity, the monstrous, alienated character of thought, which means being true to thought and untrue to oneself, becoming-pathological. One no longer seeks God, dead or alive, but is drawn to the land of the always near-future, where human impotence no longer makes us mad, reading the signs, tracking down the signals and decoding the secrets of intelligent alien life within and without us.

Philosophic modernism reveals no allegiance to man, indeed to any subject of evolution or history. Thought becomes monstrous, and travels outside, when it throws off the shackles of anthropological predicates and gives itself over to the free movement of concepts and effusions of energy, celebrating intensities and singularities. The empiricism that Deleuze championed is not to be confused with any simple-minded positivism, such as a dull mechanism that does not know how to indulge in the danger and risk of interpretation. The empiricism he brings into life is one which undertakes the most insane creation of concepts imaginable. The transcendental, Deleuze insists, is 'answerable' only to a superior empiricism (an empiricism of the *Erewhon*), in which it is acknowledged that the transcendental form of a faculty is inseparable from a complex, disjointed transcendent exercise.[2] The transcendent is a valuable treasure-house of illusions and flights of fancy. Faculties proliferate wildly in this philosophy of experimentation and invention, which is able to conceive of the possibility of an imagination that is impossible to imagine, of a vitality whose transcendent object is monstrosity, of a sociability whose transcendent object is anarchy, and so on. We simply do not know what thought is capable of.

This conceptual empiricism, and superior empiricism of concepts, which pursues a philosophy without objective *and* subjective presuppositions, resists the logic of oppositional thinking and brings Deleuze close to his arch-enemy Hegel. The problem with Hegel's system and its pursuit of the unknown, however, is that in seeking reconciliation with actuality, through the speculative 'is', it normalizes the flows of life, of thought, of becoming, of evolution, and does so by constantly reducing them to an equilibrial state.[3] In the face of the most extreme, violent tensions and discordance, it persists in positing reconciliation and harmonization. This is why Deleuze insists that it knows nothing of the monstrous world of difference and repetition. It does not appreciate that 'life' or evolution only really gets interesting (inventive) when it operates within far-from equilibrium conditions. Deleuze invokes, as the peculiar spirit of the age, a generalized anti-Hegelianism because for him it is Hegel who puts all the resources of mobile thought in the service of the sedentary, making good sense, for example, of the State and Christianity. Deleuze follows Nietzsche in deploying the language of 'reason' as the language of a *selective* nature, which would train us to decode the semiology of ascending and descending forms of life, practising what Nietzsche calls a 'contagious nihilism'.

Hegel's system, however, is knowingly and fully caught up in the derangement of thought. As he points out in the *Logic*, the reason why the uninitiated experience frustration in trying to think the vacuity of the notion is that they are hankering after an image of thought with which they are already familiar: 'The mind, denied the use of its familiar ideas, feels the ground where it once stood firm and at home taken away from beneath it, and when transported into into the region of pure thought, cannot tell where in the world it is.' It is thus somewhat myopic of Deleuze to attribute to Hegel some vested interest in the establishment 'of ' concepts since it is clear within the unfolding of thought within Hegel's system that there can be no establishment. Thought can only cultivate itself and find a home in the unfamiliar, the uncanny, the alien, and so on. Thought finds its home in permanently *dislocating* itself.

The question 'where does knowledge begin?' has always been treated as a delicate problem within modern philosophy, since 'beginning' means, à la Hegel, eliminating presuppositions and erasing, à la Darwin, Nietzsche, and Freud, the whole unbearable matter of 'origins'.[4] In Hegel's system, Deleuze argues, no doubt on erroneous grounds, there is no evidence of singular processes of learning ever taking place, since the task of philosophy is restricted to that of educating the deformities of natural consciousness in which it is a question of rediscovering at the end what was there in the beginning and bringing to explicit conceptuality what was already known implicitly. The Hegelian circle is neither tortuous nor monstrous enough. As a result philosophy is rendered 'powerless' and 'authentic repetition' becomes impossible (Deleuze 1994: 129). In the preface to the *Phenomenology of Spirit* Hegel writes that the movement of the Whole is to be taken up from the point at which the sublation of existence (*das Aufhebung des Daseins*) has been exhausted and need no longer trouble us. The task is to render thought fluid, to give it the movement of free spirit. Today, claims Hegel, the task is not so much to purge the individual of an immediate, sensuous mode of apprehension, of making substance into a subject that is an object of thought, but rather in freeing determinate thoughts from fixity, thereby giving 'actuality to the universal' and imparting to it 'spiritual life'. Spirit is nothing other than 'becoming-other' to itself. Hegel speaks of 'self-restoring sameness' (*sich 'wiederherstellende' Gleichheit*), a 'reflection in otherness within itself', as the goal of the entire formative, unfolding process of Spirit's historical self-actualization (*das Werden seiner selbst*). For Hegel, this becoming-historical is only possible to the extent that there is a (recuperative) *subject* of this process, which is the process of its own becoming, the circle 'that presupposes its end as it goal', in which the end is present in the beginning but only becomes actual by being worked out to its logical end through the suffering, patience and labour of the negative. On Deleuze's reading all the virtues of the slave are marshalled by Hegel to account for the positivity of dialectical negation. Nothing is dissipated: everything is conserved and thereby redeemed. We don't need a God; philosophy can save us.

The enslavement of thought to what 'is' (law, the State, universal history), therefore, goes by the name of Hegelianism for Deleuze, in which the task is to work dialectically through oppositions of the abstract Understanding and to attain a state of ethical growth – and grace – through the recognition, and affirmation, of aporia. For Deleuze, however, the Hegelian system is a movement in words and representations, not a movement of life or evolution. But is this not to fall back on an utterly abstract and pre-Hegelian opposition between mind and matter? Deleuze's point is that life cares little about the abstractions of dualistic metaphysics and their sublation, proceeding, as it does, by contamination, contagion, conversion, and other forms of transversal communication. In other words, evolution is machinic, a matter of technics and not of *Geist*.

Critical philosophy is indelibly marked by a model of recognition. Deleuze will always insist, however, that what is most profound about life and its evolution – making it truly monstrous – is that which escapes recognition and goes unrecognized. Moreover, the distinction between the creation of new values and the recognition, or speculative comprehension, of established values is not one that is to be conceived in the manner of a historical relativism, that is, it is not a question of established values that were once new now becoming old and tired, or of new values needing to be established. 'What becomes established with the new is precisely not the new', Deleuze writes. In other words, the new is not at all a question of establishing anything, for the establishment is always old and tired. 'For the new', he continues, 'in other words, difference – calls forth forces in thought which are not the forces of recognition, today or tomorrow, but the powers of a completely other model, from an unrecognized and unrecognizable *terra incognita*' (Deleuze 1968: 177; 1994: 136).

The death of God, and all that He stood for, is characterized as 'monstrous' in the sense that difference is produced and engineered in the 'event that is still on its way and wanders' (Nietzsche 1974: section 125). God's death is frankly immaterial. The reason why news of His death takes time to come home is not that its deep truth has to penetrate the cultural unconscious, but, on the contrary, that it will take some time for consciousness to appreciate that such a death makes no difference at all to the movements of the unconscious which have assumed tectonic form. Gods are never, in fact, encountered, and even hidden gods are only forms of recognition. Rather, what is encountered are 'the demons, the sign-bearers: powers of the leap, the interval, the intensive, and the instant' (Deleuze 1994: 145). These are powers which serve only to cover difference with more difference, transporting difference to the nth power, heralding only the becoming of the overhuman which constitutes the 'superior form' of everything that 'is', staging a demonic comedy of existence, and bringing into play the joyful universe of difference and repetition. Only this kind of unfolding of the truly monstrous (inhuman when it comes into contact with all earthly seriousness to date) power of difference and repetition can provide insight into the joyful character of *la gaya scienza*, and explain how it is possible for Nietzsche to write that he does not reply to the impending gloom consequent upon God's demise with any sense of *involvement*, with anxiety (*Sorge*) and fear, but only with a sense of relief and tremendous exhilaration. It is on the basis of a 'universal un-grounding' that the philosopher, who finds himself posted between, and stretched in the contradiction between, today and tomorrow, is able to play the teacher and advocate of a 'monstrous logic of terror', for he is able to speak of 'cheerfulness'. The comic is liberated in order to make it an element of the overhuman (the highest humour). It is a sign of unwisdom to want to judge the atheist from the standpoint of the believer or from the viewpoint of grace. Rather, joyful *sophia* will judge the believer by exposing the atheist which inhabits him, 'the Antichrist eternally given "once and for all" within grace' (Deleuze 1994: 96). We shall not be made whole, but eternally cut to pieces as *promises* of life. A post-

Darwinian culture informed by a 'pessimism of strength' (self-overcoming) finds itself able not only to tolerate a world without God and the necessity of design but also able to delight in a world of disorder and chaos, 'a world of chance, to whose essence belongs the terrible, the ambiguous, the seductive' (Nietzsche 1968: section 1019).

Deleuze refuses to subsume all species of movement, different kinds of 'being', under the logic of the victorious universal. As Nietzsche wrote in his untimely meditation on history, the Hegelian worships success whatever the outcome of history; results are deified by being speculated upon, while the principle of success provides the secret link that Nietzsche perversely forges between Hegel and Darwin. Deleuze seeks to give a voice to the 'unrepresented singularity' which does not recognize. It is the 'profound sensitive conscience' whose difference is not, and cannot be, captured by the negative (ibid.: 74; 52). Deleuze's transcendental empiricism goes beyond man, beyond the human experience towards concepts, not in order to lay the ground for all possible experience in general, but rather to secure the experience of the peculiar in its peculiarity. The whole does exist for Deleuze, but the whole is 'virtual'. The importance of this emphasis on the virtuality of the whole is that it allows for genuine becoming, that is, actualization along divergent lines that are not judged in terms of whether or not they conform to a logic of philosophically determined and comprehended history. The lines of divergence do not form a whole on their own account, and neither do they resemble what they actualize. The priority of the universal over the particular is reversed in the example of the organism and the universe: 'it is not the whole that closes in the manner of an organism, it is the organism that opens onto a whole, in the manner of this virtual whole' (Deleuze 1966: 110; 1988: 105). Evolution is invention, or technics, *involving* not the habits of moral life but singular processes of learning.

Precisely what is involved in the movement of the virtual and the actual can be grasped by contrasting it with a different kind of process, namely, the realization of the possible. Conceiving life in terms of the realization of the possible makes existence inconceivable, for every time we pose the question in these terms we are compelled to conceive existence in terms of a 'brute eruption', as a kind of leap that is subject to a law of all or nothing (Deleuze 1968: 273; 1994: 211). The 'real' simply exists in the image of the 'possible' whose task it is to be realized. There is thus no real 'difference' between the two since in the 'real' existence simply gets added to it. No invention takes place in this process of 'evolution' (no creation, only an instantiation). Whereas the realization of the possible is governed by rules of resemblance and limitation, the rules informing the actualization of the virtual are ones of difference and divergence. Indeed, if the actual is not to resemble the virtual this means that a process of creative evolution is necessitated as a self-generated dynamic within a complex, non-linear becoming: 'in order to be actualized the virtual cannot proceed by elimination or limitation, but must *create* its own lines of actualization in positive acts' (Deleuze 1966: 100; 1988: 97). The possible is to be treated as the source of false problems in philosophy and in biology since it presents us with a real that is pre-formed and ready-made, and simply waits to go through a process of realization in order to come into being as what it already is. In effect, it is not at all the 'real' that comes to resemble the 'possible' in such a sterile process of realization; rather, it is the 'possible' that resembles the 'real' from which it has been abstracted once made. Realization sacrifices difference to the negative determined by the concept since the non-existent is, in fact, already included in the concept: 'Existence is *the same* as but outside the concept' (Deleuze 1968: 273; 1994: 211). In this schema of life existence is supposed to take place in time and space, and yet they are simply being conceived as 'indifferent milieux instead of the production of existence occurring in a characteristic space and time' (ibid.). In the realization of the 'possible', time and space function as transcendent agents of limitation and exclusion; by contrast, in the actualization of the 'virtual', time and space operate as immanent productions of the 'Idea' (which for Deleuze is no longer, contra Plato, the self-identical or, contra Kant, simply transcendent enjoying only a regulative status), generating rhythms and resonances that signal the various processes of differenciation taking place.[5] The potentiality of the virtual is such that Deleuze lambasts those biologists who speak of differentiation as an innovative process of self-organization and complex evolution, but who then go on to restrict it by positing the simple limitation of a global power, so making potentiality indistinguishable from a logical possibility.

Evolution, therefore, is to be thought neither in terms of realization nor in terms of an immediate actualization. Contra the doctrine of pre-formism, evolutionism insists that life is production and the creation of differences. However, evolutionism is also unsatisfactory since it understands the production of differences solely in exogenous terms (the determination of a purely external causality). The result is that differences are reduced to merely 'passive effects' which in their relationships are incapable of functioning as an ensemble regulating and utilizing their causes. Deleuze follows Bergson beyond the antinomical poles of Darwinism and Lamarckism by conceiving the creative evolution of complex life in terms of a principle of immanent and non-linear 'internal difference' (ibid.: 39–41; 26–7) (Bergson 1983: 31–44, 89–97).[6] Variation and difference are not to be regarded as accidental effects of evolution but rather stipulate its virtual dynamic. Each line of life is thus to be understood as related to a type of matter that does not constitute merely an external environment, but rather is that from which a body and a form are engineered and created. What can be prized about life is not the forms it invents, however, but the movement that gives rise to invention. If every solution can be regarded as a relative success in relation to the conditions of the problem and the environment, it can also be regarded as a relative setback in relation to the movement. Identifying the crystallization of life in forms as a hardening of the process of creative evolution, Deleuze, like Bergson, argues that considered as movement life alienates itself in the material form that it creates in the processes of actualization and differentiation. Every species, therefore, can be regarded as an arrest of the movement. The whole of life, however, is never given (the mistake of both mechanism and Lamarckian finalism). Rather, the whole gives to actual life an 'irreducible pluralism' of many worlds of living beings that exist closed in on themselves. Virtual reality makes actual plural time as a non-linear time of invention (invention along linear lines is not invention at all). Deleuze is happy to accept that there is finality in evolution simply because life does not operate without directions. However, this does not mean that we can infer that life has an ultimate goal or final purpose. A final purpose can only be thought in terms of a transcendent reality, as something extraneous to the immanent, unpredictable and open-ended, movement of life.

The world is made possible by excess. This excess is another word for 'difference'. If the world makes itself by calculating, and engineering differences, its calculations are never exact (just). There is order – which makes it possible to speak of a world at all – because things exist in disparity and inequality. If every phenomenon refers to an inequality and an injustice that condition it, then 'every diversity and every change refers to a difference which is its sufficient reason' (Deleuze 1968: 286; 1994: 222). All that happens in the world can be correlated with orders of difference. Taken together these various orders (of temperature, pressure, tension, potential, etc.) signal a difference of intensity. It is on this point that Deleuze departs from Bergson out of fidelity to the active potentialities of evolution. In ruling out intensity as a valid notion of reflection Bergson simply assumed that qualities come ready-made and that extensities are already, and inexplicably, constituted (Bergson 1960: chapter 1). The expression 'difference of intensity' is a tautology since difference is nothing other than intensities. Every phenomenon we can discern is not composite simply on account of its being in communication with a heterogeneous series of sign-systems, but equally because it itself is composed of heterogeneity, revealing a world of sub-phenomena within itself. Each intensity discloses a prior intensity, and each intensity is already a coupling that exposes the qualitative character of quantity. It is this disparateness, not time and space, that constitutes for Deleuze the being of the sensible.

The difficulty within philosophy has been that of gaining access to the intensities which produce the creative invention and production of difference. They appear as local manifestations of a transcendent principle, with the result that a power of transcendence is mistaken for something that is immanent. Intensity gets subordinated to qualities which fill extensity, such as primary and secondary qualities (*qualitas* and *quale*). We can now begin to understand why Deleuze has consistently set out in his writings to undercut the claims of entropy. If intensity is difference, then it would appear to partake of a natural tendency to cancel itself out in extensity, to evolve into something homogeneous and identical to itself. Through entropy evolution would appear to result in a state where all differences get smoothed out and everything resembled everything else (a condition of death). The arrow of time thus indicates an irreversible decline from the more to the less differentiated, from difference produced to difference reduced, and ultimately to the annihilation of difference. Deleuze holds that the themes of a reduction of difference, a uniformization of diversity and an equalization of inequalities came together in the nineteenth century to form a strange alliance between science, good sense and philosophy (and, we might add, politics). As a result 'reason' is installed as the power which identifies and equalizes difference, concealing the diversity of existence by subjecting it to an entropic narrative in the form of a philosophy of history, establishing a politics of identity and, finally, branding the absurd or the irrational as that which resists appropriation to the common sense of humanity.

Good sense articulates two processes of evolution, namely recognition and prediction. Today, physics seems to have caught up with Deleuze's engineering of a philosophy of difference, showing that life evolves neither in terms of a logic of recognition nor in terms of one of prediction. The features of non-linear change, emergent properties, spontaneous self-organization, fractal becoming, and so on are perceived to represent not the abnormal conditions of existence of physical, chemical, biological and even socio-historical processes but rather their 'normal' conditions of existence.[7] In the sciences of complexity life is no longer seen as evolving in contradistinction to the alleged normal laws of physics, constantly wrestling with inevitable destruction and decay at the hands of the demon of entropy. The contrary view is, in fact, the case. As Ilya Prigogine has written: 'life seems to express in a specific way the very conditions in which our biosphere is embedded, incorporating the nonlinearities of chemical reactions and far-from equilibrium conditions imposed on the biosphere by solar radiation' (Prigogine and Stengers 1985: 14).[8] In *Difference and Repetition* Deleuze explicitly formulates evolution in terms of a notion of complexity, and he does so in a way that remarkably pre-figures recent emphasis in the new biology of complexity on internal mechanisms that function independently, though not divorced from, selection (see, in particular, Kauffman 1993 and Jay Gould 1980): 'The more complex a system, the more the *values peculiar to implication* appear within it. . . . The more the difference on which the system depends is interiorized in the phenomenon, the more repetition finds itself interior, the less it depends on external conditions which are supposed to ensure the reproduction of the "same" differences' (Deleuze 1968: 329; 1994: 255–6). The logic of life displays an excessive logic of difference through repetition. At the moment when the differential, intensive and individuating factors are explicated in a system their persistence in *implication* is attested to. The centres of envelopment – the various mutations of folding – are the 'mute witnesses to degradation and death', but they are also the 'dark precursors' of eternal return, signs of life's perpetual self-overcoming. We can thus claim that the laws of thermodynamics are necessary but not sufficient conditions for comprehending the inventive evolution of living systems. Deleuze quotes from the work of the biologist François Meyer (*Problématique de l'évolution*, 1954) on this very point: 'The functioning of biological systems is therefore not contrary to thermodynamics but only outside its sphere of application' (Deleuze 1968: 329, note 21; 1994: 332). Or, as a recent complexity theorist has put it, the laws of thermodynamics only serve to stipulate the general conditions necessary for any living system to exist; they cannot explain the structure of biological systems, that is, the special causes of their origin, their functioning, and their complex organizations (Csanyi 1989: 31).

The search for pure differences and pure becomings (that is, for differences and becomings thought free of the prejudices of our human, all too human reasoning) – a search for singularities and haecceities – is not without problems and dangers. Of course, one will be accused of falling into the reposed purity of the beautiful soul. 'I am from another plane(t).' But the philosophy of difference and repetition affirms a particular cruelty and practises a certain aggression. The beautiful soul laments the tide of history, and its experience of a romantic untimeliness knows nothing of the manoeuvres of the war machine. It is the sickly romanticism of a soul which cries 'stop the world, I want to get off.' 'The beautiful soul (*la belle âme*) behaves like a justice of the peace thrown on to a field of battle, one who sees in the inexpiable struggles only simple "differends" or perhaps misunderstandings' (Deleuze 1968: 74; 1994: 52). It thus dreams of a republic of love and peace in which all disputes can be settled and differences will dissolve in a final end of reconciliation: at last the world recognizes my inner integrity and makes itself in my image. It is this philosophical narcissism, which aims at a monopoly of goodness and justice, that Nietzsche rebukes so severely in his genealogy of morality. He speaks of the 'disgusting species of the vain, the mendacious failures' who appear as 'beautiful souls', bringing to market their 'deformed sensuality', the pure of heart, who corrupt the strong with their warped self-gratification and moral masturbation – 'this will to power of the weakest!' (Nietzsche 1994: essay three, section 14).

Of course, as Deleuze points out, the valorization of the negative in critical modernity would not matter were it not for the moral presuppositions and practical import of its distortion. The conflicts, oppositions and contradictions with which negative dialectics reads history produce only an engagement with conscious epiphenomena. The genuinely productive domain of history – that of the unconscious, in which problems are decided upon and differences affirmed – is never engaged with. A hard truth: 'Only the shadows of history live by negation.' Revolutions always have the atmosphere of fêtes. Contradiction cannot be said to be the weapon of the 'outside' (a proletariat) since it is the manner in which the establishment (a bourgeoisie) defends and preserves itself. Contradictions are never resolved, but always dissipated by capturing the problem of which they reflect only the shadow. The negative is always a conscious reaction, a distortion of the true 'agent' of change. As a result, 'as long as it remains within the limits of representation, philosophy is prey to the theoretical antinomies of consciousness' (Deleuze 1968: 345; 1994: 268).

It is to be hoped that this century will *not*, as predicted, come to be known as 'Deleuzian', in which his thought would acquire the status of a singular event. For at such a point Deleuze would become well and truly dead. There is no supersession or completion of philosophy, but always only philosophical learning. Deleuze's explicit return to philosophy in *Qu'est-ce que la philosophie?* is not simply to do with his old age and creeping senility. Rather, it speaks of a return, a coming back home that is always a return to the alien and the strange, to the necessity of engaging with, and unfolding, the pedagogy of the concept, to provide new tasks for thinking, to play at being a philosopher. The return is a return to the beginning that is always situated in the middle. If one always returns home after one's wanderings – does one ever really depart? – the organization and nature of one's home has changed fundamentally and drastically. What Deleuze came to affirm explicitly at the end he had been practising all along, cultivating a praxis of thought that folds as it unfolds and unfolds as it folds, becoming an abstract machine. Philosophy has always been going beyond itself, becoming-monstrous, since it was 'first' invented. If modern philosophy is to be understood in terms of an overturning of Platonism, then it has to be acknowledged that the first thinker to overturn Platonism was Plato himself. 'The Heraclitan [*sic*] world still growls in Platonism', Deleuze informs us (Deleuze 1994: 59). There is no single event of Deleuze's thought for the simple reason that we are all 'Deleuzians' now, which means that we are always becoming-other, in that what matters in the reading and praxis of philosophy is folding, unfolding and refolding in order to produce the new and the strange out of the old and familiar.

Deleuze's most generous bestowment would be this: we simply do not know what a philosopher can do. The philosopher 'becomes' a hunter-gatherer, an original sinner, a fire machine, a mind-fucker, a metamorphic resonance, a population all to himself, and whose invention of concepts does not lead to the construction of an architectonic model or monument but cultivates an ambulant population of relayers, a positive feedback system that connects and convolutes things in ways that defy established orders and critically interrogates and challenges existing disciplines of thought-control.

In Part I, 'Philosophy', several crucial aspects of Deleuze's reading of canonical traditions and texts emerge. Diane Beddoes seeks to show in the case of his reading of Kant the insistently 'positive' nature of Deleuze's engagement with philosophy, in which the task is not one of constructing arguments and criticizing deficiencies of the old, but rather of discharging blockages and erecting new functions. In this respect, 'critique' is something to be synthetically engineered with a view to futural openings. Beddoes succeeds in showing, I believe, the extent to which Deleuze's rapport with the philosophical tradition is a 'relational' one constituted by the activity of immanence and implication. The theme of immanence forms the focus of Aurelia Armstrong's reading of Deleuze on Spinoza; she approaches the issue through a critical and careful analysis of the stated anti-juridical nature of Deleuze's thinking. In the course of her investigation she shows the extent to which the classic(al) notion of agency needs to be reformulated along the 'lines' of planes of immanence and composition in order to combat the tendency to reify notions of subjectivity and agency through the construction of transcendent norms and values, such as is found in liberal accounts of the alleged free, rational and self-determining subject. The 'subject' is shown to be nothing other than its movement; its possessive identity is perpetually contested and evolving owing to the fact that it becomes what it is in the context of constantly changing and mobile relations between affective and affected bodies. Armstrong shows that important differences need to be made between Spinoza and Hobbes in their construction of power and the subject, and she concludes by affirming the political nature of Deleuze's project of thinking the mobile, becoming-subject in critical relation to existing social arrangements and organizations of power.

In an essay on 'Deleuze and Structuralism' Tim Clark shows how Deleuze's thought aims to move beyond a Euclidean paradigm in the direction of a 'geometry of sufficient reason' (a differential geometry/a geometry of difference), taking as his focus the hitherto largely unexplored relation between genesis and structure in the incredibly dense and convoluted argument of the fourth chapter of Deleuze's *Difference and Repetition*. By contrasting Deleuze's structuralism with that of Piaget, Clark is able to show distinctive features of Deleuze's thinking of difference and the privileged status it accords to the notion of the 'virtual' in a radical thinking of difference. His essay unfolds the seminal importance in Deleuze of the notion of 'virtual time', a notion which serves to link up Deleuze with other major modern philosophies of time and becoming in interesting ways. Daniel Conway's essay adopts as its focus the 'economy of repetition' in Deleuze's thought, and utilizes the figure of the 'dice-throw', which Deleuze employed in his reading of Nietzsche as a way of producing a *new* Nietzsche, in order to interrogate the claims and pretensions of Deleuze's nomad thought. Conway wants to know how it is possible to distinguish the nomad from the 'aimless outsider'. His investigation ultimately leads him into neglected critical aspects of Deleuze's, at times, easy appropriation of Nietzsche into the cause of nomad thought. Unlike Deleuze, Conway wishes to show the importance of drawing attention to the *failure* of Nietzsche's project. This then prepares the way for a vigilant reception of Deleuze's own thought. In accordance with the logic of Deleuze's own anti-Oedipalization of thought, Conway suggests that our relation to Deleuze can only assume the form of a 'patriarchal cannibalism'. This is to recognize Deleuze as a cyborg priest who is necessarily implicated in the junkheap of thanatos engines, zombie-machines, and grotesque prostheses. He concludes by drawing some filthy lessons from Deleuze's death by 'auto-defenestration'.

Part II, on politics and literature, begins with a powerful and scorching piece by Iain Hamilton Grant, who offers a demanding and disconcerting account of the 'politics of becoming'. To a certain extent his chapter can be read as containing a riposte to the insinuations of insincerity made by Daniel Conway against Deleuze and Guattari since he shows not only that there is only 'machinic life' but that a thinking of the machinic can only assume the form of a *demonology*. Deleuze and Guattari pose the ultimate problem of confronting schizoanalysis as one not simply of knowing the difference between the mobile, destratified body without organs and its opposite, such as the cancerous bodies we associate with fascism and totalitarianism, but of knowing whether we have it 'within our power' to make the 'selection' between them. This 'material problem' – a problem of matter itself and of its analysis in historical materialism – can be seen to inform Hamilton Grant's unsavoury, but necessary, I would argue, voyage into the heat of darkness that is schizo-reality. Hamilton Grant resists any attempt to map the becoming of life (and death) in terms of a dualism or Manichaeism of positivity and negativity or of freedom and terror. He maintains that there is only one history with one lesson to be learned from it, which is the history of 'capital', which teaches us to 'begin at the end, but end further on'. His chapter is innovative in showing the arbitrary and artificial nature of any ultimate attempt to 'make the selection'. Thus, the key concepts of Deleuze and Guattari's schizoanalysis – deterritorialization and reterritorialization, the war-machine and the State, the molar and the molecular, and so on – must be made to work in a completely immanent manner, which is the immanence of the machinic phylum. Hamilton Grant's voyage may be an unhealthy one to undertake, but if one reads it carefully and in the spirit of Nietzschean genealogy – properly understood in terms of a *love* of the poison – then one may come to appreciate the extent to which sickness is our 'normal' condition and our only possible state of 'health'. This is not a truth one is expected to live with but only to die in the face of.

Judy Purdom's essay in this part of the book sets out to utilize Deleuze's thought for the purposes of articulating a novel and far-reaching comprehension of the State within postmodernity. Purdom construes postmodernity in anti-human(ist) terms as an extension of the 'machinic' potential of desire. Postmodern capital works so as to capture desire from the future, but in the process it unleashes ever-new differential relations of forces (of production). As a result of its 'fractal' character postmodernity ensures that the State can only operate as a deformed system incapable of actualizing the production of desire in terms of collective, molar and immutable identities. Her analysis is in part inspired by Deleuze and Guattari's contention that capitalism is not riven apart, and ultimately overcome, by its internal contradictions, but rather that it positively lives off them. Purdom's chapter does not offer any bland or blind affirmation of postmodern reality, but seeks to unlock its virtual dimensions so as to be better equipped to engage critically with it. However, if critical theory is not to become an intellectual anachronism, such engagement requires a radical reconfiguration of notions of the 'human' and 'social'.

This thinking of the 'minor', and 'molecular' which is not simply a question of size or scale but one to do with modes of organization and composition, is taken up by Deepak Sawhney in a 'political' reading of S. Shakur's novel *Monster: The Autobiography of an LA Gang Member*. In selecting this novel as a supreme example of a 'minor' literature, Sawhney employs the conceptual toolkit provided by Deleuze and Guattari for demonstrating the immanent workings of strata and destratification, of control and flight. What interests Sawhney about the example of 'Monster' is how it provides evidence of a growing tendency within capital's most schizo-zones for 'lines of escape' to proliferate, in both 'literature' and 'politics', and which cannot at all be adequately or effectively understood in terms of the equations decided upon by established molar organizations and their attempts at statistical capture.

Part III is devoted to an exploration of the hitherto largely unexplored dimensions of Deleuze's 'philosophical biology'. This is an area of inquiry which, although neglected in the English-speaking reception of continental philosophy, was of decisive importance for modern thinkers such as Kant, Hegel and Nietzsche, and which has enjoyed a high profile in twentieth-century French thought (Bergson, de Chardin, etc.). With the exception of Caygill's contribution, the essays in this part locate in Deleuze's writings the potential for making a rich and fertile contribution not only to the tradition of philosophical biology but also to contemporary developments in neo-Darwinian and post-Darwinian paradigms, and paradigm-shifts, in biology. The formulation 'philosophical biology' is fraught with theoretical difficulties and, in fact, fails to capture what is truly innovative and subversive about Deleuze's treatment of the 'logic of life', which consists in the attempt to develop 'machinic' models of life that do not simply assume as unproblematic notions of organism, of species, of adaptation, and so on. Even the word 'evolution' is drastically called into question in Deleuze's work. Thinking 'machinically' involves showing the artificial and arbitrary nature of the determination of boundaries and borders between living systems and material forms and challenging 'evolutionist' (genealogical, linear) schemas of change and becoming.

In the opening chapter of this part Howard Caygill seeks to argue the case for the *limits* of Deleuze's 'biophilosophy' by contrasting his work with that of Darwin. Caygill maintains that Deleuze's work avoids any real confrontation with Darwin, which would serve to unsettle its claims on life and, ultimately, expose the 'sentimental' education in the politics of life which, Caygill argues, emerges out of his biophilosophy. Although it is perhaps guilty of not recognizing the anthropomorphic and sentimental aspects of Darwin's own account of evolution (what he called 'descent with modification'), and of far too cavalierly assuming that the history of modern biology can be neatly depicted in terms of a narrative made up of pre-Darwinian and post-Darwinian moments or epochs, Caygill's chapter does succeed in identifying and isolating the notion of 'selection' as a trope of major importance and significance in Deleuze's body of work, one in need of careful and astute analysis, indeed of the kind performed in his chapter. The charge he makes against Deleuze's work of sentimentalizing nature and brutalizing politics is one which cannot be lightly dismissed, but one wonders how specific the charge is to Deleuze.

In the next two essays on Deleuze's 'viral empiricism' and 'viroid' conceptions of life, Robert O'Toole and Keith Ansell Pearson both explore Deleuze's relation to contemporary developments in biology, including component systems theory and the sciences of complexity. They do not restrict their purview to developments in biology, but seek to show that valuable lessons can be learned about the functioning of systems of various kinds, from the biological to the social and economic, from Deleuze's new machinic conception of 'evolution'. O'Toole argues that Darwinian theory, like creationism, is unable to deal adequately with the implications of non-linear 'evolution', which fundamentally challenges the anthropomorphic and speciesist assumptions that can be shown to inform all the major paradigms of modernity for thinking the logic of life and its deviant becoming. However, O'Toole also argues that Deleuze's rhizomatic conception of evolution is consonant with attempts to develop a 'molecular' Darwinism in which proper attention is paid, as in the work of the French biologist Jacques Monod, to phenomena such as molecular ontogenesis, microscopic cybernetics and strange objects. Drawing on recent work in AI, complexity and systems theory, O'Toole shows how Deleuze's tracking down of the 'reality of the creative' can be employed to productive effect in order to cast light on a range of phenomena from the State to the future of the human. Ansell Pearson's chapter explores the significance of Deleuze's machinic mode of analysis for an understanding of both the question of 'biology' and the question of 'technology'. He warns against any easy collapsing of the distinction between bios and technos, arguing that Deleuze's machinism needs to be disassociated from recent work in techno-theory in which a biotechnological vitalism has assumed the form of what Deleuze and Guattari called a 'ridiculous cosmic evolutionism', or what the author calls a new grand narrative in the form of a dubious neo-Lamarckism. In thinking through the significance of their reformulation of the questions of biology and technology in terms of the priority given to the question of the machine, he takes seriously Deleuze and Guattari's insistence that one should neither biologize human history nor anthropologize natural history. It is the contention of this chapter that a 'viroid' conception of life is the most radical available, and disconcerting to anthropocentric claims upon life and death, since it fundamentally challenges any neat division of the becoming of life in terms of distinct, isolated and separated forms, be they organisms, the inorganic or engineered artefacts.

In the final chapter of Part III Alistair Welchman explores the nature of 'machinic thinking' in the context of a Deleuzian-inspired reading of the errors of Kant's philosophy and the relation of Deleuze's thinking on the matter of machines to Darwin's biology, notably the recent reworking of the latter offered by Daniel Dennett. He seeks to show that central elements of machinism have been misrepresented in the history of philosophy through a series of transcendental illusions, such as grounding paralogisms and antinomies of matter, machines and engineering. In the case of Darwinism, Welchman insists upon a non-anthropomorphic interpretation of the machinery of natural selection. On this reading, in contrast to that provided by Caygill, there is nothing sentimental about Deleuze's conception of evolution. Living forms and systems experience design problems in their engineered becoming, but they are not engineered 'for' anything. However, one wonders whether Welchman's restriction of the work of Deleuze and Guattari to a machinism does not serve to suffocate it by giving it the tag of a new positivism. Of course, the problem of 'reductionism' – everything is a problem of engineering, Welchman wants to claim, has been endemic to all materialist and positivist philosophies of the modern period.

The volume 'concludes' with a final part consisting of two very different chapters devoted to the topic of 'art' in Deleuze. James Williams explores the meaning and significance of Deleuze's work in terms of the motif of 'catastrophism'. He examines in detail, and with great care and precision, Deleuze's reflections on Turner, showing how for Deleuze it is in Turner's presciently modern art that catastrophe is allowed to show itself and become actual, resulting in a new experience 'of' painting. An examination of the theme of catastrophe inevitably raises important questions about nihilism and violence in Deleuze's philosophy, and Williams deftly navigates the deep waters in which good and bad, the creative and destructive, the affirmative and the nihilistic, get entangled in becoming and monstrously complicated. Williams' essay provides us with the spaces in which to think through these crucial issues for ourselves since he shows how Deleuze's philosophy operates in terms of a space of what one might call 'irresolution'. Finally, Robin Mackay considers Deleuze's thought and the innovations it offers in relation to contemporary music. Again, it shows how many of Deleuze's innovations result from his critical and positive encounter with the Kantian system and Kantian machine. In contrast to the 'pop culture' of the bourgeois West, which, it is argued, is trapped within a 'tragic' representational model of musical production, the new music of techno-machines and of Acid house has migrated into the technological synthesis of the plane of consistency in which fundamentally diverse and heterogeneous elements begin to 'evolve' in terms of an implicated, resonant becoming. We haven't *heard* anything yet, one might say, since we simply do not know what music is capable of becoming: what may still become of music? In seeking a way out of the impasse of Western metaphysics *and* Western music Mackay appeals to 'African' conceptions of rhythm and technology in a move that is bold and also hugely promising for an overcoming of the narcissistic cult of postmodernity currently plaguing Anglo-American academia and stifling the emergence of creative machines of thought and dance, or what Mackay calls 'wildstyle'.

While the division of this book into four distinct parts has been designed as a 'reader-friendly' device, readers should be made aware at the outset that the division, like all divisions, has an arbitrary aspect to it. There is significant overlap and cross-fertilization between the chapters. Beddoes, for example, examines the 'machinic' nature of Deleuze's thought which is taken up as a major motif in the chapters of O'Toole, Ansell Pearson and Welchman. Welchman's chapter contains many incisive comments on Kant which should be linked up with what Beddoes has to say on the matter. Caygill has much to say on Spinoza that critically resonates with points probed by Armstrong in Part I. And the wide-ranging contributions of both O'Toole and Ansell Pearson also take up questions of 'politics' that form the focus of the chapters by Hamilton Grant and Purdom.

In the case of such an inventive and nomadic figure as Deleuze no volume of essays devoted to his work can pretend to be either definitive or exhaustive. It is to be hoped that this volume simply serves the purpose of generating excitement and critical interest in Deleuze's work and inspiring more extensive explorations of the aspects of his thought treated. The volume is novel in showing the positive dimensions of Deleuze's reading of the philosophical tradition and it includes what I believe is the first series of essays to explore in any great length, and with any real depth, Deleuze's 'philosophical biology'. No single image of Deleuzian thought emerges from the book, and it is characterized by a plurality of voices and styles. The volume testifies to the fact that Deleuze remains a fecund source of inspiration, application, and opposition. Much has been left out, necessarily and inevitably, but lines of connection and morphic resonances are encouraged with work being done elsewhere on Deleuze and on the 'outside'. One welcomes a philosophy, such as what we find in Deleuze, that is not practised on the basis of need (nobody *needs* philosophy), but in accordance with a desire that desires machinic life, a productivity beyond utilitarian calculation and thrifty accumulation. Above all, then, this volume wants to discharge itself, to express the potency of Deleuze's thought, for Deleuze, contra Deleuze: who can tell in advance? As Deleuze wrote, 'As long as thought is free, hence vital, nothing is compromised.' For Deleuze to become our passion means that his thought is made to go outside, that it travels outside us and we travel on the outside.

Notes

1 One should compare in this regard chapter 3 of *Différence et répétition* (1968), on 'The Image of Thought', with *Qu'est-ce que la philosophie?* (1991). In the former work Deleuze is less generous about the status of the 'pre-philosophical', equating it with common sense. In

the latter work, in which the 'plane of immanence' is said to be pre-philosophical, Deleuze and Guattari argue that philosophy must cultivate a rapport with the arts and sciences in a way that respects their independence, and they accuse Hegel of carrying out an 'indeterminate extension' of philosophy in this regard. Philosophy has its 'internal conditions' in the pre- and non-philosophical, which are said to be 'perhaps closer to the heart of philosophy than philosophy itself' (Deleuze and Guattari 1994: 41).

2 This distinction between 'transcendental' and 'transcendent' is clarified and illuminated by Hegel in the third volume of his history of philosophy. Kant's description of his enterprise as 'transcendental philosophy' is, Hegel says, just one example of his predilection for 'barbarous expressions'. See Hegel (1995: 431ff.).

3 Equilibrium is, in fact, the motor of the entire speculative and dialectical endeavour, evident in Hegel's contention that the highest and final aim of philosophic science is to effect, by means of harmony (*Übereinstimmung*), a reconciliation (*Versöhnung*) of the self-conscious reason with the reason which 'is' in the world (*'seienden' Vernunft*). While applauding Hegel' attack on all forms of philosophical moralism, one must also question the theoretical and practical 'value' and 'validity' of his insistent claim that philosophy 'must necessarily be in harmony with actuality and experience'. No matter how speculatively one renders actuality, the 'is' of the real, one is still enclosing the bounds of philosophy within the confines of a historical dialectic and, therefore, restricting thought to a logic of sanity (good reason, common sense). To say that philosophy must learn to harmonize with actuality experience is to restrict thought to a comprehension of what is. On Deleuze's model, thought always *produces* experience in a way that exceeds the bounds of actuality. Philosophy is invention 'beyond' the limits of experience.

4 There is not space here to show that the title of Darwin's most famous text, *The Origin of Species* (1859), is a total misnomer. Not only do 'species' not exist for Darwin, except in a highly indeterminate sense, but, partly as a result question of this problem of cognitive framing, the question of their 'origin' becomes massively complicated as their evolution along horizontal lines of branching is unfolded.

5 In *Différence et répétition* Deleuze makes extensive use of a distinction in French not available in English between *différencier*, to make or become different, and *différencier*, which is applied to the field of a mathematical operation. See translator's preface to Deleuze 1994: xi–xii.

6 This thinking of a 'creative' evolution in terms of an internal principle – shared by Nietzsche too (see Nietzsche 1994: essay II, section 12) – is not to be confused with Lamarckism which rests on a straightforwardly vertical perfectionism. Neo-Lamarckism is, in Bergson's terms, a doctrine of finalism in which 'all is given'; in other words, there is no genuine invention or creation within its model of evolution.

7 For an innovative attempt at applying the insights of chaos and complexity theory to historical phenomena see Wallerstein (1991), who treats 'historical systems' and vice versa.

8 The paradigm-shift to a post-Newtonian 'far-from equilibrium' physics is being felt in a wide range of disciplines extending from biology to economics. For an excellent example of the !atter see Boisot 1995.

References

Bergson, H. (1960) *Time and Free Will*, trans. F. Pogson, New York: Harper Torchbooks.

—— (1983) *Creative Evolution*, authorized translation by A. Mitchell, Lanham, MD.: University Press of America.

Boisot, M. (1995) *Information Space: A Framework for Learning in Organizations, Institutions, and Culture*, London and New York: Routledge.

Csanyi, V. (1989) *Evolutionary Systems and Society*, Durham, NC: Duke University Press.

Deleuze, G. (1966/1988) *Le Bergsonisme*, Paris: Presses Universitaires de France; trans. H. Tomlinson and B. Habberjam, New York: Zone Books.

—— (1968/1994) *Différence et répétition*, Paris: Presses Universitaires de France; *Difference and Repetition*, trans. Paul Patton, London: Athlone Press.

Deleuze, G. and Guattari, F. (1980/1988) *Mille Plateaux*, Paris: Les Editions de Minuit; *A Thousand Plateaus*, trans. B. Massumi, London: Athlone Press.

—— (1994) *What is Philosophy?*, trans. H. Tomlinson and G. Burchill, London: Verso.

Hegel, G. W. F. (1995) *Lectures on the History of Philosophy*, vol. 3, trans. E. S. Haldane and F. H. Simson, Lincoln and London: University of Nebraska Press.

Jay Gould, S. (1980) 'Is a New and General Theory of Evolution Emerging?', *Paleobiology* 6(1): 119–30.

Kauffman, S. (1993) *The Origins of Order: Self-Organization and Selection in Evolution*, Oxford: Oxford University Press.

Klee, P. (1964) 'On Modern Art', in R. L. Herbert, *Modern Artists on Art*, Englewood Cliffs, NJ: Prentice-Hall, pp. 74–92 (written in 1924).

Nietzsche, F. (1968) *The Will to Power*, trans. R. J. Hollingdale and W. Kaufmann, New York: Random House.

—— (1974) *The Gay Science*, trans. W. Kaufmann, New York: Random House.

—— (1994) *On the Genealogy of Morality*, trans. C. Diethe, Cambridge: Cambridge University Press.

Prigogine, I. and Stengers, I. (1985) *Order out of Chaos*, London: HarperCollins.

Wallerstein, I. (1991) *Unthinking Social Science: The Limits of Nineteenth-Century Paradigms*, Oxford: Polity Press.

Part I

PHILOSOPHY

2

Deleuze, Kant and Indifference

Diane Beddoes

the furniture we are forever rearranging

(DG, 1980: 31; 1988: 21)

Anti-Oedipus has a warning: the parallel between social and desiring-production is 'to be regarded as merely phenomenological', demonstrating only that all production involves 'an unengendered nonproductive attitude' (DG, 1972: 16; 1984: 10). Social anti-production is clothed: segmented, coded, overcoded, empty and repressed, a redundancy which, in *Mille Plateaux*, is identified with the hierarchical structures of a centralized State. Direction is organized in advance of movement by the segmentation and striation of space, a single time encompasses all times and levels are related analogically, through resemblances and similarities which subscribe to a formal order independent of the material flows it controls. But the element of anti-production in desiring-production is naked: full, smooth flow in continuous variation, mobile and turbulent.

A further statement complements this warning: 'lines of escape are still full molar or social investments at grips with the whole social field' (DG, 1972: 458; 1984: 382). The mutual and immanent indifference of social/molar and desiring/molecular processes, of everything happening at the same time, is emphasized repeatedly throughout *Capitalism and Schizophrenia*. Difference in regime must not mask identity in nature; there is only one process; there are no such things as social reality on the one hand and fantastical desire on the other; the same syntheses are always functioning; everything co-exists; the One and the multiple are immanent in each other: 'There are pass-words beneath order-words' (DG, 1980: 139; 1988: 110).

Why is it important to register the real indifference of molar and molecular, a distinction which appears to do so much work in Deleuze and Guattari's writing?

Firstly, because it prevents the correlation of molar regimes with medium-sized objects and the molecular with microscopic elements, or molarity with form and molecularity with matter. It also wards off confusing a randomly chaotic outside verging on the margins of the State, whether this is geographically or historically characterized, with the exteriority of turbulent molecular flows. And lastly it differentiates the intensive media of the threshold, and the in-between of the conjunctive middle from the qualified redundant resonances of mass media.

One effect of State divisions is the generalization of women as either mad, bad or mothers. Irigaray writes: '*So commodities speak. To be sure, mostly dialects and patois, languages hard for "subjects" to understand*. The important thing is that they be preoccupied with their respective values, that their remarks confirm the exchangers' plans for them' (I, 1985: 179). Occupied in advance with values assigned to them by the State, women are formed as natural subscribers to the procedures which overwrite the material patois of bodies: mothers. But as Michèle Pujol says: 'women do not seem to want to do what is claimed to be "natural" for them' (P, 1995: 24). Failure to confirm the pre-occupation of the body or prepare it for family life, legally, socially and materially fitting it for the specialized function of reproduction and economic dependency destabilizes the specific nature on which the division of labour is founded and is thus, to the wisdoms of the State, a madness. For whilst the function and contribution of women is an unstated assumption and so outside the theoretical register of exchange economics, failure to confirm the pre-occupation of their bodies and fly the colours of the flag planted on them impacts on the coherence and satisfactory implementation of these theories. Since truth and reason are historically on the side of man, however, the problem can only be on the side of women. The family serves as its solving ground, forcing sanity through economic dependency and the mythology of motherhood.

State women – mad or bad, or wedded and soon-to-be mothers – are produced under the assumption that social and desiring production are exclusively isolated, each from the other; the social world is built of the Inside and the Outside, the Up and the Down, the Here and the Now, the Left and the Right, the One and the Many, these particulars encompassed by a principle of generality. Desire is outside the social field, random and chaotic or ethically contained within the family. By upholding the distinction between desire and production, privatizing the former within the family and socializing the latter through the State, reproduction comes to occupy a marginal zone between the two. But in this process, desire becomes teleological, directed towards an object, the child, a space for which is prepared by the pre-occupation of women's bodies by the lacked penis as standard of their value, the idea of the norm. This means, amongst other things, that desire no longer machines flows of sex for the very reason that it is directed towards an end which determines connections amongst bodies in advance. Sex is produced as a state. But nor is desire productive when it is desire for a child, since production is defined in terms of the striated sociality of the State, and reflects social and not desiring relations. The State assumes but has no account of reproduction, except as a function of capital, 'to promote the begetting of new workers' (M, 1930: 628). In other words, it is an uninterrogated condition of both State and Private production.

The indifferentiation of molar and molecular precludes the *a priori* separation of machinic processes into different modes of production -social, desiring, reproductive, natural, territorial, despotic, industrial, capitalist, etc. Kant says that reproduction would be impossible, 'were one and the same thing named sometimes in one way, sometimes in another'(K,III: A101). Were women some time mothers, some time friends, some time lovers and other times enemies, some time traitors and other times allies, 'a complete representation would never be obtained' (K, III: A102), and there would be no means of assigning the appropriate qualities and attributes to objects, no means of decision between permanence and transience. Both private and social realms maintain stability through the possibility of determining values, durations, expectations, sequences, connections and qualities to all events: the social value of reproduction, for example, is a function of the private status of the individual – which is why women without husbands but with children and women who want neither are problematic to this regime, since in not being privatized within the family, their social standing is uncoded. The difficulty lies as much in the upset of a proper order as it does in the evident inutility of moral laws.

However, a machinic solution to this does not consist in a reconciliation of roles, a juggling of diversity within a unity that would be woman, something like a transcendental object ('"One or multiple" – we're past that point' (DG, 1980: 34; 1988: 23)). Nor does it consist in grounding the problem within the productive capacities of the subject: this returns the question to the State. There is no time simultaneous for all space, no natural or real consistency assumed in advance, but a singular neutrality: everything co-exists and all Kant's sometimes are contemporaneous. 'All history does is to translate a coexistence of becomings into a succession' (DG, 1980: 537; 1988: 430); all history does is provide an order for events, a chronology. However, unless one believes in an absolute history, the translation of contemporaneous becomings into a succession is radically contingent, and thus provides no basis for law. The conditions of becomings are real indifference, zero presupposition, and becomings are distributions of unmarked space and non-organic bodies, singularly engineered and not translated out of history.

* * *

Kant's brief comments on indifference, which he turns into a school of thought, *indifferentism*, highlight its ambiguity and unsettled nature. He declares it symptomatic of 'the matured judgement of the age' (K, III: Axi) weary of illusions but not yet possessed of the critical imperative to production. It appears amongst sciences that are thriving, as both 'mother . . . of chaos and night' (K, III: Axi) but also as a call to reason to institute a critical tribunal. Hume is behind these comments, although Kant doesn't make this explicit. For Hume, indifference is essential to chance, a depth of the mind which, from a changed perspective, is delirium, absence of determination and causality: the connection of ideas in the imagination is effected through indifference, with causality arising only through principles of association which systematize the chance relations. Kant calls causality understood in this way 'a bastard of imagination, impregnated by experience' (K, IV: 257–8): it is reproduction through association, an alliance of imagination and experience independently of the unity of rule of either public or private demand.

There is thus an alliance between indifference and scepticism, both implying a 'principle of *neutrality*' (K, III: A757/B784), which Kant disallows except as a methodical stick with which to repulse dogmatism and draw philosophy from its infancy. Because Kant disjuncts difference across two series according to principles of symmetry (Schopenhauer is especially critical of this), and divorces it from indifference, neutrality and scepticism function negatively, producing drag on the critical engine: there can be no sceptical faculty, or faculty for indifference, since this would be extra to the conditions of common sense. What residues of indifference survive the critical imperative are distributed as a stagnant latitude, 'the delay caused by doubt' (K, III: A425/B453) and an absence of sufficient reason, or evacuated longitudinally into the disinterestedness of the pure form of Law.

Kant, by convention and through molar or majoritarian interpretation, has been welded to reason, law, the categorical imperative, and a reductive view of science. Yet on reading Kant, Kleist took to wandering through a Europe blasted by the Napoleonic wars, torn between fanatical patriotism and despair; his Kant is the pulverizer, demolishing predictability, progress and faith and leaving only irresolvable ambiguities. Fused in the violence and tenderness of Kleist's writing is an intensive and nomadic line which runs through Hume, through Kant's problems with neutrality, scepticism and intensity, escaping the methodologies and maxims of reason. Kleist writes out of the delirium of indifference, neither resolving it nor containing its cruelty, 'at once eccentric and condemned' (DG, 1980: 439; 1988: 355). If there is no difference between what something is and how it arrives, between how it is formed and how it functions, then neither Kleist's nor Deleuze's Kant can be simply a Legislator and a Moralist.

No doubt Kant is saturated with the language of trial and law; no doubt the second *Critique* is constituted through the complete evacuation of intensity. No doubt his work taken on a general level displays a combination of bureaucratic nihilism and administrative moralism. But the meticulous deployment of critique in *Anti-Oedipus* and the intensive conjunction of the histories and economies of desire effect a real discontinuity with the linear and general calm of court time whilst not breaking with the critical continuum. Such a break, a real line of departure from generality, is not 'an over-significant cut' (DP, 1977: 50; 1987: 39) but marks a real difference in nature whereby critique ceases to resemble an organized practice, becoming instead a threshold effect. Rather than coding him in terms of a history of repressed production, of error, as something unknown which is prevented from happening, as a general non-localizable abyssal unconscious and a rigid structure of points and lines, Deleuze approaches Kant as an abstract engineering problem and looks for flows and sequences, for elements indifferent to the rule of the general. Which bits did Kleist plug into and incorporate in his machine, which bits Hegel, which bits Cantor and which bits are naked desire? Auto-critique hums with cold energies and spiritless mixed effects in a different critical programme; not an over-significant cut with, but a real break from, Kant.

Kant returns to the problem of escape continually, though this is most often characterized negatively, as an attempt to contain rather than follow its process. He declares the system closed several times but can neither stop following it, nor close it down without also closing down critique, either by reimporting a theistic as opposed to a place-holder God of disjunction, which is little more than a machinic operation, or by refusing science. In the *Opus Postumum* he returns to Spinoza, just the name at times, italicized, worried and repeated until he identifies transcendental Idealism and Spinozism: 'The system of transcendental idealism is Spinozism' (K, XXII: 64). Deleuze spreads Kant out between Spinoza and Nietzsche, the thinkers who, he says, released him from his debt, and in doing so effects links and connections which do not retrieve Kant, but transform the operations of critique, dissolving hierarchized and grounded structures into an intensive surface. However, the point is not to prove that Kant became Spinozistic, and here begins German idealism, here Romanticism is born, nor is it to attempt the impossibility of turning him into a Nietzschean, nor is it to generate an intellectual history for Deleuze.

The point is instead to illustrate three things. The first is that Kant tinkered continually with critique, a problem he generated, incorporating new chemistry, natural science and an emerging biology; the transcendental as a problem is not equatable with its canonical formulation in the *Analytic* of the first *Critique*. 'What thinking signifies is what the brain is, a "particular nervous system" of grass' (DP,

1977: 51; 1987: 39), and by *Capitalism and Schizophrenia*, Kant is recorded as a brain, not as a moralizing and bureaucratic mind.

The second, a consequence of the first, is that in this Kant there is no schizophrenic moment but a multiplicity: the explosive moment is singular and abstract, but concretely a multiplicity, a repetition against the Law, carrying 'the first time to the "nth" power' (D, 1968: 8; 1994: 1). Kant's theory of intensities, and his insistence on separating the genesis of number (and of time and space) from logic, effect transformations and processes of critique which the general rules of conceptual, discursive and linguistic structuration do not code for. In the aesthetics of beauty and the sublime, Kant struggles to reconcile intensive qualities with the possibility of doctrine; but time, with which Kant fractured the subject, opening up a question of passive synthesis which provides the basic machinery of *Anti-Oedipus*, bubbles to the surface, not as a mode of formality, integrated with the generalities of common sense, but unhinged, 'a line, a pure straight line . . . simple, inexorable' (D, 1963: 41; 1984: 41). It is Kant's great reversal, the unhinging of time from cardinality, which schizophrenizes his subject, Deleuze argues, and the mobility of this newly autonomous neutrality consistently bleeds through the fields and territories of rational space. This is not a pathology of time, which would stand opposed to its rationalization in the concept of quantity, however, but the co-existence with this order of a distribution which has no correspondence with the Logos of the State and the pure form of Law and which continually undoes its space.

Lastly, Deleuze's strategy is insistently positive; it follows escape vectors that discharge blockages rather than constructing arguments and builds new functions rather than criticizing the insufficiencies of the old. Deleuze engineers critique, not mechanically but synthetically: common-sense efficient causality and good-sense final cause are rewired, involuted and conjuncted into the reverse causalities of future machines.

* * *

Difference and Repetition begins with a statement on indifference: it has 'two aspects', a black 'undifferentiated abyss' and a 'calm surface' of white nothingness (D, 1968: 43; 1994: 28). Deleuze understands difference as unilateral in relation to zero, however, rather than bilateral in relation to unity, so these two aspects of indifference cannot be disjuncted to articulate a hylomorphic matter/form distinction. Nor can the white surface of indifference be aligned with the terminal permanence of mechanically slaughtered black matter; this is not a description of extensive space. Instead, difference becomes a substantial multiplicity of divergent and diffusive series, exploding onto each other, immanently and continuously involving neutrality, tracking the vector of a singularity indifferent to the specificity of the concrete distributions it effects, not because it is a form applied to matter, but because it "occupies" a qualitatively intensive different space from which are composed the creation of new functions. It might be called redundancy, in the sense that it is excess to the concrete, relating 'surplus values in the order of a rhizome' which give rise to mutations in concrete assemblages.

The production of real indifference is a leap from Logos to nomos: it is not to be confused with the suspension of judgement, nor with nihilism. These latter belong to the collapsing stages of a distribution sclerosed into Law, a space divided according to principles of labour and manufactured through the eyes of the subject, and not to the construction of spaces mobilizing expertise not as a function of memory but as an engine of movement, a weapon built as and of fluid dynamics rather than a tool applied to a job. Itinerant expertise rather than specialist knowledge, a smooth and calm prolongation of the movement of escape. The leap from law to the nomos – Deleuze calls it a demon – does not straddle a distance between divided states, however, nor is it a clean break: it is rather what *A Thousand Plateaus* calls the anomalous or borderline, a threshold (not a limit), 'which coexists with what has yet to cross it' (DG, 1980: 538; 1988: 432). This means that space is not pre-occupied in advance of its distribution: there are no plans to be confirmed and no image to be achieved, only a virtual and infinite set of real but concretely indifferent or abstract elements, singularities, the actualization of which is not after or conditioned by the virtual, but exists simultaneously with it. There is no formula for discovery in advance of the process with which to predict its qualities or functions, for these are immanent and imperceptible. Indifferent to opposites, to individuals, to the general and the particular, theory and practice, public and private, the leap distributes a singularity, a 'splendid sterility or neutrality' (D, 1969: 48; 1990: 35).

'Singularities are the true transcendental events' (D, 1969: 125; 1990: 102–3). In *Logic of Sense*, Deleuze abstracts the transcendental from its explicit Kantian formulation and the problems to which this responds. He credits Kant with great discoveries: transcendental illusion, the schizophrenized subject, the pure form of time, intensive matter, immanent critique, sense, problems, paralogisms. And if we read backwards from *Capitalism and Schizophrenia* a case can be made for the claim that Kant lurks in the background, everywhere. The early and slight book on Kant – on an enemy, Deleuze says – already locks in on problems which are repeated insistently throughout his work, different each time: of double series, in a discussion of the higher and lower operations of the faculties, in the formation of a 'real network which constitutes the transcendental method' (D, 1963: 17; 1984: 10), in the discovery of holes in freedom where 'we cease to be subjects . . . primarily because we cease to be legislators' (D, 1963: 48; 1984: 32), becoming empiricists, autonomists, machine parts of desire.

Engineering thought rather than thinking in the image of philosophy, Deleuze effects a gradual escape of functions from their names, machining assemblages and dissolving the possibility of attribution: of saying this is Kant here and there is Spinoza and over there Marx. There are only effects: Spinoza-effects, Marx-effects, Kant-effects – these last as transitory in nature by the time of *Capitalism and Schizophrenia* as passing remarks on pulverizing mechanisms, on the pillars of Hercules, on the Gothic Northern line. These are no longer references to Kant, however, but rather components assembled in the genesis of neutrality and will of indifference, and the escape of affects effectuated through antimemory. As the organized philosophical plane becomes a plane of consistency, composed of surfaces and fields rather than structures and territories, and the radicality of the empiricism collapses the rationality of the enterprise, it no longer makes sense to divide machines according to discipline, only to effects.

This escape of machinic connections from genealogical over-coding pertains to a '*childhood block*, or a becoming-child' (DG, 1980: 360; 1988: 294): to anti-memory, or the transition from the taught generalities of thought to the singular problem of learning how to think. Anti-memory is another nature of indifference or neutrality, an undoing of the mutilating mnemotechnics of schooled and stolen bodies, which releases vectors of becoming. The stealing of girls' bodies and their pre-occupation by a value which assigns a trajectory to their development blocks the immediacy of the singular and unnatural machines into which they plug, sealing up their pure exteriority and schooling them in the 'secrecy of the gyneceum' (DG, 1980: 354; 1988: 289). Their bodies are over-coded, a little penis is stamped on the clitoris, an inverted virility fills the womb. (It is important, however, that neither sentiment nor a return to the inorganic becomes attached to becoming-child, turning it into a regressive or reflective movement: children have never been *innocents* except in the phantasies of men.) Anti-memory is the misosophy with which everything begins, a dark precursor with 'no *prior identity*, no *internal resemblance*' (D, 1968: 383; 1994: 299). By not stealing girls' bodies, freeing them from the suffocating privacy of the family and the wisdoms of mummy and daddy, no model is provided for the theft of a boy's body, no image is stamped on desire dictating its return to the Same. Man, who fears and so keeps his children stupid for protection, gives them family names and inherited features, just as he does his machines. Memory is constituted through these, through the cultures of society rather than through the skills of desire, as a long-term weight inscribed with the image of history and of thought, recording the punishments of the State.

* * *

Indifference, Deleuze and Guattari state on the first page of *Anti-Oedipus*, 'is at work everywhere' (DG, 1972: 7; 1984: 1). Immediately, there is no infinite secrecy to set against the finitude of man, just machinic flows, sequences and chains and processes and connections and so on. Deleuze and Guattari are downloaded into the book, becoming machine parts, as well as engineers. And rather than resonances ('the family's second function' (DG, 1972: 149; 1984: 125)) with their previous writings confirming or establishing continuing themes, connections are produced with no necessary reference to prior distributions. Earlier works are not precursors to contributions to *Capitalism and Schizophrenia*, individual workings out of something which finds expression when each is plugged into the other. Each book functions differently, each has its own indifferences, its own degrees zero, although the surfaces of each overlap, tectonic and open to quakes. Again, an indifference to underlying support, anti-memory: 'what allows it to work', as Lyotard says, 'is not the fact that the other, older machine has been criticized' (L, 1977: 11).

In *A Thousand Plateaus* the warning against phenomenological renderings of real indifference connects with a line much argued over, that of caution, 'a rule immanent to experimentation' (DG, 1980: 151; 1988: 150), the 'art of dosages' (DG, 1980: 198; 1988: 160), of sobriety and invented self-destructions. A constant danger is the attempt to make the contingent vectors tracked by neutral singularities into necessary teleological processes, which generalizes solutions to problems with a formula for history. Caution is a function of anti-memory systems, and the art of dosages a learning function of real processes, the itinerancy of a voyage which arrives at a point, rather than the itinerary of a trip which travels towards one. Caution is a name for the intensive qualities of slowness, counterpoised to those of speed. There is no course to follow, and each movement is complete, but not completed; caution and indifference are interconnected, line-drawing machines poised on the edge of, or perhaps rather indicating the edge of, the process. They register, and do not govern.

When the State captures caution it translates it into a metric and protective art belonging to the fastness of a fortress rather than the quality of slowness which pertains to the indifference of the virtual. Auto-destruction becomes a legislated affair, with legitimate and illegitimate methods, and the outside becomes a danger against which one must be protected. There is a generation of addictions to civil and legal divisions of space, to nation and family, God and country; pleasures are prescribed and sober arts proscribed. Speed becomes attached to progress and growth and re-located inside extension, to form a space called history. History in turn makes Memory, and what remains of cautionary skill is turned 'into a set of strictly limited formulas without any real scientific status, or else simply represse[d] and ban[ed]' (DG, 1980: 448; 1988: 362) Remember the formulae or kill the desire.

Anti-memory is effected by a transhistorical economics rather than being historically evolved, it is compositional not accumulative, constructive not organized, distributive not divided, an engine not a storage space, a mobile diagram rather than a hard-wired design. This difference feeds out of Deleuze's distinction between historicist and structural accounts of Marxism (cf. D, 1968: 240; 1994; 186). The former provides an account of capital as a chronologically evolving process qualified by progress and telos, describing the history of a 'worldwide enterprise of subjectification' and its correlate, social subjection (DG, 1980: 571; 1988: 457). But structurally – and the word must be read machinically – capital is not understood transitively, pointing instead to a virtual and intensive economic, 'a differential virtuality' immanent to concrete socialities which individuates without subjection constructing machines whose apparent isomorphism with capitalism's axiomatics is contingent and local rather than necessary and universal (DG, 1968: 241; 1994: 186). One effect of disengaging capital from chronology is that power has to be re-thought as a problem of connectivity and consistency rather than of possession and organization, as a force of trans-relationality, crossing lines and opening borders rather than as a power of gathering resources and defining limits.

Feminism and other minoritarian formulations multiply connected and fluid populations that prove problematic for any evolutionist account of history because there is no price on their Memory. There are no definitive markers in a History of development through which to assign the value of a current state in relation to a previous one, no dialectical crust governing the nature and import of contradiction, weighting movement with negation. The values of multiples are concrete and diverse, singular rather than particular. This means they have no settled price, no exchange value – they are not forms pre-occupied by given social codes or models realizing the axioms of capital. There is no subject of transhistorical economics, because it has no formal politics, no ideological memory and no utopia to come. Anti-memory connects singularities in such a way that it makes history 'snap . . . sending a tremor through it' (DG, 1980: 362; 1988: 295). Arriving without warning and without condition, it does not constitute a reconfiguration of space isomorphic with the structural forms of a Past. It is not that the machine processes implicated with anti-memory are separated from or external to History: to say this would be to invite a re-institution of dialectics, whose insidious power must not be downplayed. Rather, the two co-exist as 'two different states of intensities' (DG, 1980: 74; 1988: 57), not as contraries.

Without memory, history is neither a source of profit, guilt or guidance, but an abstract assemblage, whose space is not marked chronologically but occupied by singularities; distances between dates are effects tracking a singularity, which distributes its own space without regard for historical laws of time and position determining the intensity of their relation. Wallerstein writes: 'if we want to know the traditions of the near future the last place we should look is at the traditions of the near past' (W, 1991: 214). This is one reason at least not to incline incautiously in the direction of the techno-utopian futures of the information age, which has its traditions in the near past, retaining modern characters such as that of the alien in its memory. Anti-memory is connected with decoding and with the side-communication of surplus values, rather than with coding and territorialization; with the anomalous rather than the alien, and with the long centuries of material flows rather than the short centuries of human history.

Capitalism and Schizophrenia does not diagram events or stages in history but the transhistorical engineering of desire, and plateaux are functions of its economy, seismic disturbances rather than historical determinations, intensive magnitudes rather than chronological qualifications. Differentiating genealogical or arborescent evolutionary schemas from the 'reverse causalities that shatter' them (DG, 1980: 537; 1988: 431), the two volumes connect economics with biology, the unconscious with physics, wasps with orchids and cats with baboons, not as disciplines streamlined through the static of history or animals of specific nature but as infectious conjunctions, side-communications. What is effected by the snap and the shatter of their engineering is not sometimes biology and sometimes economics, sometimes of the body and sometimes of the brain, but a multiplying machine, interconnected, interactive and dynamic. In this economy, *is* cinnabar always red?

The engineering dynamic is lateral, and caution plugs in here, rather than onto a line extended longitudinally. Latitude is defined as 'the set of affects that occupy a body at each moment', a dynamic capacity, in contrast to a kinetic proposition, of 'the intensive states of an *anonymous force*' (D, 1988: 127–8) which diagrams a body and engineers through anti-memory, without historical pre-occupation by design or plan or measured relation. Molecular dynamics are stationary speeds and slownesses, smooth and lateral distributions effected by the capacitation of intensive quanta as convective rather than combustive or digestive elements. Any element is interchangeable, and what defines it is its state at any given moment, its corresponding speed and direction and its interconnection with other elements. A diagram is not a map on a plane but an exhaustive description of a dynamical state as a singular and multiple state or set of affects that distributes a plane.

A history can be given, either by tracking a single element or by unifying the state, and then plotting the element as a point with a trajectory across time or the development of the state within the terms of the unity applied to it. However, this involves either decisions about the identity of the elements, the attribution of constants and their relations with variables which are not generated by the state itself; the system becomes defined as a unity (+1) rather than as a collective (–1) and the elements are reduced to simples or atoms. But any adjacent state is a change in both nature and quality, not as a function of chronological development but because the distribution of the elements is fluid. Each rearrangement, each adjacent state constitutes a threshold change, a critical departure from the potentials of its neighbour, new potentiations effected by new contacts and changing differentials. There is a transfer or transport of intensities or speeds across a threshold, a bloc of becoming or production of production which has zero presuppositions, no unstated assumptions.

This constructs a solution to Kant's problem with reproduction, of how one 'thing' can have different names, since there is never a point at which it is possible to identify a thing as opposed to a process, or a unit as opposed to a multiplicity, or a permanence as opposed to a change. State and process? We're beyond all that too. Kant's solution is historical and chronological: 'in the end' the appearances of change 'reduce to determinations of inner sense' (K, III: A101) which is linear and successive. He is answering Hume, arguing with indifference, chance and bastard causality. Deleuze's solution is machinic, 'composed not of units but of dimensions, or rather directions in motion. It has neither beginning nor end' (DG, 1980: 31; 1988: 21). Parentage is not an issue here.

Caution on a lateral line has no phenomenological resolution; it is not a matter of care, or caught in the region of an opposition between suicide and safety. 'Intensity is suspect only because it seems to rush headlong into suicide' (D, 1968: 289; 1994: 224). Looking for unity and not finding it, one finds only death and every virgin a prostitute. Caution is similarly suspect, because it seems to lead to care, perhaps even anxiety. But this suspicion bases caution on a formulation of intensity appropriate to moral philosophy, rather than to pragmatics or diagrammatics. It is linked with excess and scepticism and 'appears in one of the series as an excess, but only on the condition that it would appear at the same time in the other as a lack' (D, 1969: 66; 1990: 51).

Foucault talks of 'the obscure and repeated violence of desire battering at the limits of representation' (F, 1966: 223; 1970: 210), of modernity, the age of sexuality (and critique), heralded in scenes of 'profligacy subjected to the order of representation'(F, 1966: 222; 1970: 209), the two extremes of excess and lack. (But energy then at least for libertinage, though of gross reason and proportion.) Sade in his prison and Kant at his desk are both writers of reason, fury and fear; but these are qualities which pertain also to the energy of good sense, of 'the steam engine and the livestock' (D, 1969: 94; 1990: 76), the combustive and digestive economies of heat and the land, of labour and prosperity balanced in an equation with death. Irigaray enriches the picture: 'if the subtlety of his mind is given one quarter turn of the screw more – in or out' (I, 1974: 265; 1985: 212), Kant moves from Sade to Masoch, pincered between exquisite pain and negative pleasure, compressed into shape by the Judgement of God and caution returns to the fortress.

But caution on this line is nostalgia. And besides, Sade is fast becoming a romance of the academy. It is based on a black-box view of systems as closed and of distributions which stay inside but retain an option on the outside based on the constitution of the inside (+1). This is how you make a pre-Oedipal stage, how you pre-occupy a body and destroy the patois of matter, turn passwords into Order Words, and women into particular instances of a general class, Woman. In this context, caution becomes equivalent to the avoidance of dangers defined in advance, of not confirming the exchangers' plans and thus being excluded, consigned to random chaos, to the black holes and dark night outside the white walls of social space.

The difference between machinic caution and care feeds from the confinement of machinic repulsion set up by the body against organization, against the ineptitude of God and the diseases of the priest and the despot. The real affects produced by 'an over-all persecution apparatus' (DG, 1972: 15; 1984: 9) are locked within the paranoid judgement of a subject and written on the surface of the body, which becomes something to hate and to fear. And rather than the subject being the residual effect of machinic processes, it appears to be the source of organization: transcendental unity of apperception, I think. This inverts the sense not only of caution, but also of pre-occupation, making both reflexive movements. The first sense of pre-occupation is lost, or incorporated into a negative feedback circuit. The invasion and theft of the body become unstated assumptions, and what is now at issue is unceasing attendance to the confirmation of order words, fitting in with the plans of social division and order, thinking to rule.

In which case we are back where we began, in the region of the problem of evaluating reproductive labour in an economy built on its exclusion. It is not simply that it is the subject now who is pre-occupied, rather than the object, but that the subject is produced as that which is pre-occupied with the objective value of its body, with the nature of its Other, because it thinks it made it, or at least that the

Other is its gift. Perhaps, contrary to what is sometimes said, it is when mainstream economics begins to concern itself with quantifying domestic home labour that women should really start to worry, when the theory notices the escape of its presuppositions and begins to proliferate axioms to counter this direction. This is not to advocate a romance of economic disengagement, but to caution against the possibility of incorporation in the strata which pincer desire and conduct it towards unity or death, profit or poverty.

The Other isn't interested in this. Caution is not excessive or a sign of lack, just a pure moving line, a rearrangement of furniture, at speeds and slownesses incommensurable with the measuring techniques of the subject. Wedged into a subject, the line is compressed, compacted and contained within the walls of the Unconscious, the infinite form of secrecy, eminently and impossibly virile. Whereas machinic repulsion is a weapon of caution immanent in empirical experimentation, and auto-destructions, in indiffentiating the inside from the outside, or deterritorialization, the Unconscious is a narrative of the careful subject addressing itself as an object, extending itself conceptually and circling itself in reflexive repulsion, spiralling inwards, imploding.

The production of production does not reproduce identical states, so is immanently and radically contingent in relation to its conditions. The question is not: who comes after the subject? but: how is the production of production engineered? *A Thousand Plateaus* flags the problem of locking processes into a thought of production; whilst it departs from 'the schemas of representation, information, and communication', production nonetheless 'appeals to an ongoing dialectical miracle of the transformation of matter into meaning, content into expression, the social process into a signifying system' (DG, 1980: 113–14; 1988: 89–90). It is this danger against which caution works, the totalization of processes into a single grammatical or logical form. Production roots itself then re-produces arborescently, whilst process is rhizomatic, chronogenetic, rootless: it doesn't branch reproductively but repeats differently, neutral, indifferent, but with 'no hint . . . of a chaotic white night or an undifferentiated black night' (DG, 1980: 90–1; 1988: 70).

* * *

The closing section of this chapter takes brief excursions through some writers who which connect with indifference and furniture rearranging. Sandy Stone notes the ultra-femininity of both pre- and post-operative male to female transsexuals. The imperative which defines them is that of passing: they must pass as women both in order to be considered suitable candidates for the medical procedure and to minimize the difficulty of settling into the socially defined ways of a woman once they have been physically reconfigured. In the 1960s, when these operations became economically and medically interesting, a single book outlined the criteria according to which suitability was determined. Strangely, all applicants fulfilled these criteria: they had the book too.

Stone's point is that the fixation on medical procedures and defined psychological criteria, and the willingness of medical institutions and their clients to satisfy them, is socially produced along with binary sexual difference, and neither has any necessary relevance to the processes implicated in the continual invention of a body, processes which the theft of a child's body channel along a pre-determined course. Male? Fourteen? Time to be a social nuisance, smash a window, get a gun. Female? Forty? Time to go grey and wear sensible shoes. A molar body is fixed across a set of interconnected criteria whose most basic resolution is in terms of a sexual biology and a psychological and intellectual make-up which 'fits' that sex and which has appropriate phenomena attached to it at any given age and in any given socio-economic bracket. Paul Broca, working in the second half of the nineteenth century, laboured hard to prove that brain size was correlated with intelligence. Since it was common knowledge that European males were more intelligent than women and other lesser human types, Broca's task was to generate quantitative data which would confirm this *a priori* truth. To do so, '[h]e traversed the gap between fact and conclusion by what may be the usual route – predominantly in reverse' (G, 1992: 85). Broca wanted to fix a brain which would correlate with the body in which he found it, rather than research the brain as such, and Stone's argument aims implicitly at thwarting this insistence on the permitted band of deviation dictated by the demand for unity, both historically and of the body. (Cuvier's brain – which 'reflects a Euclidean space'(DG,1980: 63; 1988: 47) – was, incidentally, discovered by Broca to be the largest in France.)

When expressions of desire become incommensurate with the codes applied to the body according to its apparent biological sex (in contrast with those applied to age, for example, for which there are other correctives), the gulf is corrected by providing the body with a new set of sexual characteristics, making the content fit the expression. That is, if psychoanalysis cannot cure the problem first. The misfit of desire with the socially coded body is clearly associated with the sex/gender distinction: the proper alignment of gender, or social coding and sex, or biological coding, results in the organization of a whole system, a whole man or woman. The paucity of this distinction is made clear by Stone, who argues for bodies in continual invention, becomings, rather than the medical reinvention of the occasional body so that it might properly contain the psychological make-up analysis has exposed. She calls these post-transsexual because there are no longer gulfs and gaps and sexual lines to be crossed but n-sexes, bodies machined by desire. Not the institutionalized rearrangement of an object so that its gender and its sex might once more meet, and the facts fit the advance conclusion.

Stone's desire for post-transsexualism is caught up with discussions in *Difference and Repetition* and *A Thousand Plateaus* of Geoffroy St Hilaire's abstract Animal, because both refuse conditions extrinsic to the material processes through which bodies are formed as organs of a machinic assemblage, and repel the positions and places, images and instincts allotted to them, the fixation of desire on an object and the pre-occupation of bodies by imaginary values. Real engineering does not make objects, but assembles bits and pieces, partial objects, transposable elements which, depending on their location and their movements, transform the timing and control of development. The basic unit is the assemblage, a body composed through its own functioning, not organized from on high, and the human body is but a part of this, not its controller.

* * *

Dorion Sagan looks at the view of sexuality special to state sciences from a broader perspective than that of socialized human animals. The monolithic view of the body is built not only on the basis of a social norm established by the European male, she argues, but also by a biological norm confined to zoocentrism. With Deleuze, she focuses on the fluid transmission of genetic materials across a continuum, where no boundaries separate a body and its environment. Bacteria too have sex: side-communication again. 'The human body', she writes 'is an architectonic compilation of millions of agencies of chimerical cells' (S, 1992: 367) An environment is a body and a body is an environment, and the formation of space is not independent of this. 'The BwO is matter that occupies space to a given degree – to the degree corresponding to the intensities produced' (DG, 1980: 189; 1988: 153). Sagan's compilation body leads also to a different view of the health of a body: 'disturbances of the body's normal microbial ecology do not, properly speaking, signal sickness so much as the emergence of difference and novelty' (S, 1992: 369). This view of the body converges with that of Stone, but from a different direction. Disturbances in the socially defined coherence of a body, in the correlation of 'sex' and 'gender' do not, for Stone, signal sickness or dysfunction, but auto-experimentation and invention.

* * *

Another and very different direction converging with Deleuze and the compilation body comes from George Kampis's component systems. Like desiring-machines, these 'build and destroy during their ordinary activity the material structures that serve as the basic components of the systems' (K, 1991: 197). Not definable in advance, not predictable, with no control functions and characterized by material rather than logical relations, component systems are open and singular. Resolutely non-metaphysical, differentiating real dynamics from computational and mathematical models, rejecting a global time-frame, imposed boundary conditions, and the inscription of a complete memory of a system in a single state, Kampis's component systems not only are indifferent to the distinction between biological and cognitive systems, but generate a 'meta-theory of systems that range from biology to society' (K, 1991: 275). They are abstract and neutral in the sense which Deleuze understands by these terms, indifferent to their concretization but not isolable from it. There is no support in his work for the distinction between molar and molecular, or for another connected difference which Deleuze also undoes, between form and function, which Kampis expresses by saying that a machine and its program are the same. There are no unstated assumptions. When Kampis describes the theme of his work as non-trivial he means precisely that producing and product are not separated. 'Living beings are machines that produce machines (self-creating machines)' (K, 1991: 434).

Random chaos, insides and outsides, circulation and what circulates, modes of production, bodies versus minds, men versus women, being versus becoming, pre-occupation by and with imaginary values and their confirmed realization (price into money!) and so on and so on . . . Deleuze discharges these blockages, indifferentiates the orders which limit and segment them and deploys the imperceptible functions jammed up inside to generate new machines, past the one and the multiple. Neutral. Indifferent. Singular.

* * *

> 'He has a talent like yours', Ahajas said. 'The ooloi will use him to study and explore the talent.'
>
> 'Talent . . .?'
>
> 'You can't control it', Nikanj said, 'but we can. Your body knows how to cause some of its cells to revert to an embryonic stage. It can awaken genes that most humans never use after birth. We have comparable genes that go dormant after metamorphosis. Your body showed mine how to awaken them, how to stimulate growth of cells that would not normally regenerate. The lesson was complex and painful, but very much worth learning.'
>
> 'You mean. . . .' She frowned. 'You mean my family problem with cancer, don't you?'

'It isn't a problem any more', Nikanj said, smoothing its body tentacles. 'It's a gift. It has given me my life back' (B, 1987: 252).

Nothing random, nothing programmed in advance, nothing fixed with significance. All the furniture moves.

References

Butler, Octavia (1987) *Dawn: Xenogensis I*, London: Victor Gollancz.

Deleuze, G. (D, 1963, 1984) *La Philosophie critique de Kant*, Paris: PUF, *Kant's Critical Philosophy*, trans. Hugh Tomlinson and Barbara Habberjam, London: The Athlone Press.

—— (D, 1968, 1994), *Différence et répétition*, Paris: PUF, *Difference and Repetition*, trans. Paul Patton, London: The Athlone Press.

—— (D, 1969, 1990) *Logique du sens*, Paris, Les Editions de Minuit, *Logic of Sense*, trans. Mark Lester with Charles Stivale, ed. Constantin V. Boundas, New York: Cambridge University Press.

—— (D, 1988) *Spinoza: Practical Philosophy*, trans. Robert Hurley, San Francisco: City Light Books).

—— (D, 1993) *Critique et clinique*, Paris: Les Editions de Minuit – the full version of the preface to the English edition of *Kant's Critical Philosophy* is included in this volume.

Deleuze, G. and Guattari, F. (DG, 1972, 1984) *L'Anti-Œdipe: Capitalisme et schizophrénie*, Paris: Les Editions de Minuit, *Anti-Oedipus: Capitalism and Schizophrenia*, trans. Robert Hurley, Mark Seem and Helen R. Lane, London: The Athlone Press.

—— (DG, 1980, 1988) *Mille Plateaux: Capitalisme et schizophrénie 2*, Paris: Les Editions de Minuit, *A Thousand Plateaus: Capitalism and Schizophrenia*, trans. Brian Massumi, London: The Athlone Press.

Deleuze, G. and Parnet, C. (DP, 1977, 1987) *Dialogues*, Paris: Flammarion, *Dialogues*, trans. Hugh Tomlinson and Barbara Habberjam, London: The Athlone Press.

Foucault, M. (F, 1966, 1970) *Les Mots et les choses*, Paris: Gallimard, *The Order of Things*, trans. M. Foucault, London: Routledge.

Gould, Stephen Jay (G, 1992) *The Mismeasure of Man*, London: Penguin.

Irigaray, Luce (I, 1974, 1985) *Speculum de l'autre femme*, Paris: Les Editions de Minuit), *Speculum of the Other Woman*, trans. G. C. Gill, Ithaca: Cornell University Press.

—— (I, 1985) *This Sex which is Not One*, Ithaca: Cornell University Press.

Kampis, G. (K, 1991), *Self-Modifying Systems in Biology and Cognitive Science*, Oxford: Pergamon Press.

Kant, Immanuel (K, vol. no.) *Werkausgabe*, ed. Wilhelm Weischedel, Frankfurt-on-Main: Suhrkamp.

Lyotard, J.-F. (L, 1977), 'Energumen Capitalism', in S. Lotringer (ed.) *Anti-Oedipus*, vol. II, no. 3, New York: Semiotext(e).

Marx, K. (M, 1930) *Capital*, trans. E. and C. Paul, London: Dent.

—— (M, 1993) *Grundrisse*, trans. Martin Nicolaus, Harmondsworth, Middlesex: Penguin.

Pujol, M. (P, 1995) 'Into the Margin', in E. Kuiper and J. Sap (eds) *Out of the Margin: Feminist Perspectives on Economics*, London: Routledge.

Sagan, D. (S, 1992) 'Metametazoa: Biology and Multiplicity', in J. Crary and S. Kwinter (eds) *Incorporations Zone 6*, New York: Urzone.

Stone, S. (S, 1991) 'The Empire Strikes Back: A Posttranssexual Manifesto', in J. Epstein and K. Straub (eds) *Body Guards: The Cultural politics of Gender Ambiguity*, London: Routledge.

3

Some Reflections on Deleuze's Spinoza

Composition and Agency

Aurelia Armstrong

> We know nothing about a body until we know what it can do, in other words, what its affects are, how they can or cannot enter into composition with other affects, with the affects of another body, either to destroy that body or be destroyed by it, either to exchange actions and passions with it or to join with it in composing a more powerful body.
>
> (Deleuze and Guattari 1987)

Reflections on Deleuze's relationship with the seventeenth-century philosopher Benedict de Spinoza invariably focus on the theme of immanence, a theme which runs throughout Deleuze's work and which he claims to have developed on the basis of Spinoza's conception of nature. This chapter must be placed against the background of such studies. Here the theme of immanence is explored through the motif of an 'anti-juridical' tendency in Deleuze's Spinozism. This 'anti-juridicism' is shown to appear in relation to the connection established by Deleuze, in his reading of Spinoza, between the notions of agency and composition. On the basis of a detailed examination of these notions in Deleuze's work on Spinoza an attempt will be made to gesture towards some appropriations and variations of these Spinozist concepts in Deleuze's later work with Guattari.

In his preface to the French edition of Antonio Negri's *L'anomalia selvaggia* Deleuze offers an account of Negri's project which is simultaneously a characterization of some of his own concerns in relation to Spinoza's corpus. Deleuze describes this common approach as a form of 'anti-juridicism' in order both to relate it to, and differentiate it from, a 'juridical' tradition in Western political and philosophical thought. In his delineation of the fundamental principles of juridicism Deleuze employs concepts which will serve as the starting points for the development of his own novel elaboration of the possibilities for conceptualizing human agency within the framework of Spinozist thought. Gaining an appreciation of the way in which Deleuze's reading of Spinoza provides a means of thinking through questions of agency requires situating his approach within (and against) the tradition to which he and Negri oppose Spinoza, the tradition he refers to as 'juridical'. According to Deleuze, juridicism implies: (1) that forces have an individual or private origin; (2) that they must be socialized to engender relations that adequately correspond to them; (3) that there is, thus, a mediation of a Power ('Potestas'); (4) that the horizon is inseparable from a crisis, war or antagonism for which Power is presented as the solution, but the 'antagonistic solution'.[1] Even at this schematic level it is clear that Deleuze's outline of juridicism has Spinoza's divergence from Hobbesian contractarianism as its implicit source and point of reference. A brief review of Hobbes' account of the need for a contract to take individuals from the state of nature into the civil or social state will help, therefore, to orientate and focus the themes of this discussion.

According to Hobbes, as is well known, the state of nature is a state in which a war of all against all prevails. What defines the state of nature, or natural condition of men, is for Hobbes simply the absence of any normative constraints to the appetitive striving of individuals. Thus, in this state every individual is, in principle, in full possession of his natural right and absolutely free to pursue the objects of his desire. In practice, however, the striving of the individual to secure desired goods and realize private ends inevitably finds itself in conflict with the activity of other individuals striving to do likewise. The only way, therefore, that the Hobbesian individual in the state of nature can ensure the regular satisfaction of his desires is by gaining and maintaining a margin of power over the power of others: the state of nature, in other words, amounts to an incessant struggle on the part of each individual to establish a relation of domination over others. It is the instability of this situation, attended as it is by the constant threat and fear of death, that motivates individuals to give up their natural right to self-determination in return for the security of civil society. The transition from the state of nature into the civil state is the product of a rational calculation of self-interest which leads individuals to voluntarily transfer their rights to self-determination to a third party, the sovereign. Through this contract, or alienation of every individual's natural right, a complete break is made with the disordered state of nature. The sovereign power created by means of the contract appropriates for its own purposes the instinct to dominate and turns it against individuals in the form of an absolute obligation expressed concretely as laws constraining individual rights within determined limits.[2] The juridical order imposed by the sovereign Power, thus, operates as an anti-power, a kind of power against power, that makes civil inter-individual relations possible because it restrains by rational means the inherently destructive nature of the human passions and, through the institution of laws, mediates between private interests which necessarily oppose one another when given free rein in the state of nature. With the notions of a social contract and a juridical order Hobbes supplies an 'antagonistic solution' to the problem of human sociability.

Spinoza's relation to Hobbes is a complicated one. Although heavily influenced by Hobbes' political philosophy and clearly indebted to the tradition of natural right thinkers, Spinoza also opposes Hobbes at crucial points. The general tenor of Spinoza's disagreement with Hobbes can be inferred from their differences regarding the State. Whereas Hobbes presents the Right or Power of the State as a function of its legitimacy and defines this legitimacy with reference to what rational individuals would assent to, Spinoza argues that the right of the State is simply its actual power to preserve itself, its 'excess of power over the power of the subjects' (Spinoza 1951c: 369). Spinoza's concern is not with the transcendent legitimacy of State Power but with the immanent power relations that produce particular, historical states. Against Hobbes' juridical view of State formation as involving an absolute break with nature and the artificial limitation of natural rights, Spinoza presents the formation of states as a purely natural process consonant with the development of natural rights and continuous with passional life. Contra Hobbes, Spinoza argues that there can be no question of a complete alienation of natural right. An individual's natural right is, according to Spinoza, simply his or her actual power (*potentia*) or striving to persevere in existence so that a complete alienation of right/power would be tantamount to the destruction of the individual's existence. No one, Spinoza tells us, 'can so utterly transfer to another his power, and consequently his right, as to cease to be a man; nor can there ever be a power so supreme that it can carry out its every possible wish' (Spinoza 1951a: 214). In other words, a contract of the sort envisaged by Hobbes is in principle impossible within a Spinozist frame. Spinoza does in fact retain the term 'contract', at least in his early political writings, to designate the principle of consent which effects the passage from the state of nature to the state of society. This contract, however, is not made to the benefit of a third party, as in Hobbes, but to the gain of the Whole formed by the aggregate of the contracting parties. The power of this Whole, then, although located in the sovereign power holders, *is* actually the collective power of its 'parts'. As Spinoza explains 'the right of government of the supreme power is nothing else but the right of nature itself, which is not determined by the power of a single person but by the multitude guided as by one mind' (Spinoza 1951b: 301). Spinoza's refusal to see in the contract the motor of the transfer of power or right to a third party is connected to his configuration of the relationship between individuality and sociability.

In Spinoza, the passage from the state of nature to civil society is not represented in terms of a rupture or discontinuity. Socialization does not occur, as it does in Hobbes, by virtue of the intervention of a juridical order opposed to nature and transcendent to the passional, conflictual field of pre-social interests which it organizes. There is, for Spinoza, no mediation of a contract required to socialize 'anti-social' individuals, no transfer of natural rights creating an obligation imposing itself as an external norm, no obligating force of command at the origin of social relations, and no rational break with the passional order of nature: in short, there is in Spinoza very little evidence of Hobbes' 'antagonistic solution' to the problem of human sociability. Rather, Spinoza presents the transition to civil society as a process continuous with the exercise and collective development of natural rights or powers, including the natural power of reason. This collective development is presented as a function of a spontaneous socialization of powers which proceeds according to purely natural laws. In effect, Spinoza by-passes the abstract question presupposed by Hobbesian contractarianism, the question of how social relations are possible. Instead he poses the practical problem of how, and to what extent, the passivity and impotence characteristic of life lived in a state of nature can transform itself into activity, becoming consonant with the life of reason. From a consideration of Spinoza's opposition to Hobbes Negri extracts what he regards as the central theme of Spinoza's 'anti-juridicism'. This theme is given, Negri suggests, in Spinoza's rejection of 'every metaphysical configuration that superimposes on the initiative of the multiplicity a transcendent synthesis' (Negri 1991: 130). For Negri, the force of Spinoza's anti-juridical thought derives from his critique of the image of Power which appears in classical metaphysics, namely, the idea of Power as a principle of organization which subordinates the activity of things to a transcendent order. Against this image, Negri argues that Spinoza poses a conception of ontological constitution, a purely immanent horizon of active, productive powers or forces which develop spontaneously through composition. It is this distinction between organization and composition that constitutes the broadly anti-juridical framework within which Deleuze's reading of Spinoza develops.

In his characterization of the difference between organization and composition Deleuze refers to two contrary ways of conceiving of bodies, two ways of mapping bodies and their powers. On the one hand he describes a 'plan of organisation' that encompasses 'any organisation that comes from above and that refers to a transcendence' (Deleuze 1988: 128). The main feature of this type of plan is that it directs the development of forms and the formation of subjects but without itself being given in that which it gives. It is a hidden structural and/or genetic principle that organizes and defines bodies in terms of their forms and their functions, in terms of the ends they are to serve. On the other hand Deleuze develops the idea of a 'plane of immanence' which he derives from the Spinozist conception of nature as an individual[3] composed of an infinite number of other individuals 'varying in an infinite number of ways' (Deleuze 1988: 122). Thus, the plane of immanence is also a 'plan of composition of Nature'. By contrast with the plan of organization this kind of plan 'has no supplementary dimension; the process of composition must be apprehended for itself, through that which it gives, in that which it gives' (Deleuze 1988: 128; see also Deleuze and Guattari 1987: 265–72). On this plan/e bodies will be defined solely in terms of what they can do: by their powers, by their capacities to affect and be affected by other bodies, and by the relations into which they can enter. Because this plane is given only in the continual variations of the powers and the relations that compose it, it is constantly being constructed and reconstructed. Deleuze tells us that to live in a Spinozist manner one must install oneself on this plane and *actively* construct it, '[f]or at the same time it is fully a plane of immanence, and yet it has to be constructed' (Deleuze 1988: 123). To construct a plane of immanence is to participate in the process of composition which defines the plane by experimentally combining powers, by entering into different relations; only in this way are the powers and capacities of any particular body discovered. This process of experimentation by composition also constitutes, in a certain sense, the method of becoming-active that Deleuze identifies as essential to the conception of agency developed in Spinoza's thought.

From Passivity to Activity: Towards Agency

Commenting on Spinoza's conception of freedom in *Expressionism in Philosophy* Deleuze contrasts it with the idea of freedom proposed by rationalism: 'If we listen to the rationalists, truth and freedom are, above all, rights: they wonder how we can lose these rights, fall into error or lose our liberty' (Deleuze 1992: 149). Deleuze sees Spinoza's opposition to this understanding of freedom in his rejection of the Adamic tradition which sets up as its principle the image of a free and rational first man. In his reinterpretation of the story of the fall, Spinoza completely inverts this tradition. Against the image of a free, rational and happy first man Spinoza presents Adam as powerless, enslaved and ignorant, living at the mercy of fortuitous encounters and thereby cut off from his power of acting. It is, Spinoza suggests, because Adam is impotent and his knowledge inadequate that he falls prey to illusions of transcendence, that is, that he imagines the deleterious effect of the fruit on his body to be a final cause, a punishment for disobedience to the commands of a transcendent God, instead of *understanding* this effect as a natural consequence of the incompatibility of the fruit with his own body. For Spinoza, Adam's state is like that of a child who is necessarily more passive than active, 'not having had the chance to undergo the slow learning process presupposed by reason no less than by freedom' (Deleuze 1992: 263). Deleuze attributes Spinoza's antipathy to the rationalist assumption of freedom as a subjective right, as pre-given, to the profoundly empiricist inspiration of his thought. From the viewpoint of empiricism, Deleuze explains, 'what is surprising is that men sometimes manage to understand truth, sometimes manage to understand one another, sometimes manage to free themselves from what fetters them' (Deleuze 1992: 149). Deleuze suggests that this empiricist perspective is nowhere more apparent than in Spinoza's characterization of agency as something to be attained, as the product of a practical activity in relation to both mind and body coincident with the effort on the part of individuals to increase their powers of acting and understanding.

Once the viewpoint of empiricism is taken into account the question of agency becomes a practical problem. Given that all men are, like Adam, born into conditions of ignorance and relative impotence, subject to chance encounters and passively registering the effects of external bodies on their own without knowing the true causes of these affections, how is it possible for them to become active? How can they come to form adequate ideas, ideas of which they are the cause? How can they increase their powers of acting and thinking to the point where they come into full possession of these powers? These ethical questions can be related to Spinoza's elaboration of the political process which takes individuals from a state of nature into the civil state. According to Spinoza, any account of the formation of political society must, if it is to avoid being mere wishful thinking and resulting in 'chimeras', take into consideration the passional character of human existence and acknowledge the actual basis of society in the imagination and the passions. The task Spinoza sets himself, then, is to show how individuals who, insofar as they are subject to passions (1985: IV, P33), tend to oppose and limit one another's rights/powers and reduce these powers to a minimum, can 'come to meet one another in relations that are compatible, and so form a reasonable association' (Deleuze 1992: 265). According to this formulation, however, the task appears paradoxical – it seems to assume what it seeks to demonstrate, namely, the reasonableness of men, for, as Spinoza explains 'Only insofar as men live according to the guidance of reason, must they always agree in nature' (1985: IV, P35). We must, therefore, reformulate Spinoza's task: what needs to be demonstrated is the possibility of the *emergence* of the natural power of reason from within the struggles and discordances of passional life. What must be shown, in fact, is how agreements can be *produced*, how powers can be *combined* and how relations between powers can be organized in such a way that these powers aid rather than restrain one another, add to rather than subtract from one another.

Thus, in order to pursue the theme of agency in Spinoza it is necessary to bring into play two related movements. These movements are the passage from passive modes of existence to active or reasonable forms of life, and the process of formation of composite bodies. Opposing a traditional, liberal account of agency which tends to construe freedom in individualistic terms, as a right or 'private possession' of an isolated individual, Deleuze's reading of Spinoza posits agency as an irreducibly collective or combinatory process. The primary focus of Deleuze's investigation is the processes of collectivization which produce *at the same time* composites or combinations of individuals with greater power and multiplicity, and individuals as modalities of these greater individuals. The growth of agency is shown to consist in a process of *becoming-active*, in the increase and enhancement of 'individual' powers through their combination with the powers of other, compatible individuals and things.

Deleuze brings these themes together in his idiosyncratic interpretation of Spinoza's theory of the common notions. According to Deleuze the common notions are the key to understanding Spinoza's *Ethics*; they 'are an Art, the Art of the Ethics itself: organizing good encounters, composing relations, forming powers, experimenting' (Deleuze 1988: 119). Re-emphasizing the empiricist strain in Spinoza's thought, Deleuze insists on the practical dimension and function of the common notions, claiming that 'there is a whole learning process involved in common notions, in our *becoming active*: we should not overlook the importance in Spinozism of this formative process; we have to start from the least universal common notions, from the first we have a chance to form' (Deleuze 1992: 288). In this latter formulation Deleuze gives an indication of his own approach to the common notions: they will be investigated from the point of view of the order of their formation, as the experimental method of our becoming-active. To set the question of how common notions are acquired in context it is first necessary to be familiar with the rudiments of Spinoza's conception of the individual.

In Spinoza the individual is defined, firstly, as an eternal essence or degree of power, an intensive part of the power of God or nature. To this essence there corresponds a characteristic constitution, that is, a relation between parts which are maintained in a certain proportion of motion and rest. While in existence the degree of power that corresponds to the essence of the individual is determined as *conatus* or appetite, that is, as a striving to preserve the relation of motion and rest between the parts that define it. The conative striving of the individual is an affirmation of its power or essence which necessarily links it to other things and to other individuals. Thus, Spinoza asserts that 'the body, to be preserved requires a great many other bodies by which it is, as it were, continually regenerated' (1985: II, Lemma 7, Scholium). Because of the intrinsically relational character of *conatus*, Spinoza also defines it as a capacity to affect other bodies but also to be affected by them. While this capacity is necessarily always filled by actual affections, the nature of these affections varies and can be divided into two types: actions and passions. An action is an affection of the body which can be explained by the nature of the affected individual and directly expresses the individual's power of acting. A passion, on the other hand, is an affection which indicates only the effect of an external body and the present, variable constitution of the affected body. As such, passions can be either joyful or sad depending on whether the affecting body agrees or disagrees with the body it affects. Individuals are said to agree completely if their characteristic relations and extensive parts can be preserved while being combined. When an adaptive combination of relations takes place according to a law of composition of relations (an eternal law of nature) it produces a new relation, a composite individual with a greater power and complexity. If, however, individuals encounter each other in an order in which their relations cannot be combined, then either one or both relations may be destroyed by being determined to enter into a new relation not compatible with the preservation of the former ones. In this case the individuals are said to disagree. Joyful passions and sad passions resulting from agreements and disagreements between individuals must be understood in terms of the dynamics of power: joy is the augmentation of the individual's power and sadness is its diminution.

So far we have examined Spinoza's definition of the individual from the perspective of extension, as a body in extension. But the *conatus* of the individual is determined not solely as the body's power of acting and suffering. *Conatus* is also expressed as the mind's power of thinking and knowing. Spinoza posits a strict parallelism between mind and body: the mind must be understood as the idea of an actually existing body. On Spinoza's view there can be no real causality between mind and body just because the mind and the body are one and the same thing but conceived under the autonomous attributes of thought and extension. The body, Spinoza claims, 'cannot determine the mind to thinking and the mind cannot determine the body to motion, to rest, or to anything else' (1985: III, P2). There is, however, a correspondence between mind and body: 'the order of actions and passions of our body is, by nature, at one with the order of actions and passions of the mind' (1985: III, P2, Scholium). Thus, countering a Cartesian conception of the eminence of the mind over the body, Spinoza asserts that an action in the mind is simultaneously an action of the body just as a passion in the mind must also be a passion in the body. The individual's power of thinking and knowing, then, parallels its power of acting and suffering so that 'in proportion as a body is more capable than others of doing many things at once, so its mind is more capable than others of perceiving many things at once' (1985: II, P13, Scholium). When the body is affected by an external body this affection will be accompanied by an idea of it in the mind. Under the conditions of existence at the level of the common order of nature (the order of encounters) the ideas that the mind has are always ideas of what happens to its object, that is, ideas of what happens to the body. Insofar as these ideas only *indicate* or involve the effects of external bodies and the present state of the affected individual, they are said to be inadequate and are called imaginings. The feeling-affects which follow from these ideas are, consequently, passions which cannot be explained by the nature of the affected individual. Adequate or true ideas, on the other hand, *express* their cause and 'represent', not what happens to the individual, but the very nature of the individual and the nature of things. Adequate ideas conform internally with that which they express. They are ideas which are explained by the individual's power of thinking and understanding and have these powers as their proximate or internal cause. The feeling-affects which accompany such ideas are active joys. Indeed, there can be no active sadness for Spinoza as sadness always relates to a reduction of the individual's power of acting.

This understanding of the relation between mind and body has important implications for Spinoza's conception of knowledge. Deleuze suggests that, for Spinoza, 'knowledge is not the operation of a subject but the affirmation of the idea in the mind . . . *the kinds of knowledge are modes of existence*, because knowing embraces the types of consciousness and the types of affects that correspond to it, so that the whole capacity for being affected is filled' (Deleuze 1988: 81–2). Knowing adequately, Deleuze suggests, does not consist in the possession of a system of clear and distinct ideas, but 'in gaining knowledge of our power of understanding. Not of gaining knowledge of Nature, but gaining a conception of, and acquiring a higher human nature' (Deleuze 1992: 129). Pierre Macherey schematizes Deleuze's point in his articulation of two possible ways of conceptualizing knowledge. The forms of knowledge he identifies are 'that of an abstract grid of rationality, jutting out over the domain of objects which it is supposed to represent by enclosing them within its own framework; and that of knowledge which, on the contrary, presents itself as being incorporated in the constitution of its object, which is from then on no longer only its "object" but also its subject' (Macherey 1992: 177). It is this latter characterization that captures Spinoza's approach. Because for Spinoza the event of thinking is always the result of an encounter between bodies, the production of knowledge must be understood as inseparable, at least in the first instance, from the movements and the meetings of bodies which thought simultaneously affirms. Adequate or true knowledge, in other words, is not pre-existent but must be obtained by experimentation; we do not begin with adequate knowledge of ourselves and of things, but our knowledge becomes adequate to the extent that the ideas it encompasses are made to proceed by the same order of necessity as that of the 'things' of which they are the ideas. There is in this sense an absolute coincidence of the production of adequate knowledge with the processes by means of which the body becomes active. The acquisition of 'a higher human nature' requires the transformation, and not the transcendence, of inadequate knowledge and of the passive modes of existence it presupposes and implies. It is here, Deleuze claims, in relation to this passage from inadequate to adequate kinds of knowledge and from passive to active forms of life, that the theory of the common notions finds its domain of operation.

Deleuze suggests that an examination of Spinoza's work will reveal two definitions of the common notions corresponding to different approaches to reason. In the first place the common notions are given a formal definition and identified as universal ideas of reason. As such they are ideas which adequately represent the characteristic relations of bodies, the combination of these relations and the laws of composition. In relation to this definition, reason appears as knowledge of the positive order of nature, that is, as knowledge of the laws governing the composition of constitutive relations from which all the other relations and laws of nature are deduced. It is not enough, however, to define reason as the perception and comprehension of common notions. An additional characterization is required in order to explain how individuals who are not born rational can nevertheless become so; it is essential, Deleuze argues, to pose the question of how common notions are *formed*, and under what conditions.

By way of responding to this question it is necessary to begin by recalling the situation of individuals under natural conditions of existence in the state of nature. In this state, as noted above, the capacity of individuals to be affected is inevitably almost entirely consumed by passive affections, by fear and sadness, which reduce this power to a minimum. Similarly, the power of thinking and of knowing is exercised under conditions that determine individuals to have only inadequate knowledge of things and of laws, knowledge of the effects of external bodies on their own without knowledge of the relations that compose these bodies, that is, without knowledge of the causes of these effects. But although individuals in the state of nature are for the most part subject to chance encounters which continually deplete their powers of acting and knowing, Deleuze suggests that they all have at least the germ of a true idea which makes it possible to explain the formation of the second kind of knowledge, the formation of the common notions that comprise reason. This idea is that of utility.

The idea of utility relates to the conative striving of the individual and consists in the individual's effort to do all it can to preserve itself. By virtue of its *conatus* or natural right the individual, in seeking its own advantage, is determined to resist external bodies that threaten to destroy it. Deleuze points out that this striving for self-preservation will have only limited success as long as it remains a purely individual affair relying solely on the opportunities afforded by chance encounters. The conative pursuit of what is useful, however, is not exhausted by the individual's effort to destroy bodies incompatible with its own. This pursuit also implies another type of activity, namely, the endeavour of the individual to form coalitions with other, similar bodies so as to increase its capacity to ward off potential threats to its perseverance. According to Deleuze, it is from this second type of effort that we can derive a definition of the first stage of reason. Insofar as reason is intrinsically related to the true utility of man it appears initially as 'an effort to select and organize good encounters, that is, encounters of modes that enter into composition with ours and inspire us with joyful passions (feelings that *agree* with reason)' (Deleuze 1988: 56). In the first instance, then, the formation of common notions coincides with the individual's effort to organize encounters and to join with other bodies in such a way as to ensure the predominance of joy over sadness and activity over passivity.

Deleuze's outline of the genesis of the common notions can be summarized in the following way. When we encounter an external body that agrees with ours, a body whose constitutive relation compounds with our own to compose another individual under a new relation, we experience an affect of joy-passion which marks an increase in our power of acting and understanding. Through this increase of our powers we are induced to form the idea of what there is in common between these bodies. This idea is a common notion, that is, an adequate idea of the relations of agreement or composition between the external body and our own. It expresses a composition of existing bodies and is only formed in the event of the *actual* production of such composites. As Deleuze explains, 'common notions are not so named because they are common to all minds, but primarily because they represent something common to bodies, either to all bodies (extension, motion and rest) or to some bodies (at least two, mine and another)' (Deleuze 1988: 54). At the point at which we manage to form a common notion, we come into full possession of our power of action.[4] The joy with which we are then affected is necessarily active joy; it follows from the formation of an adequate idea and directly expresses our power of action. It is a joy which differs from the passive joy which it replaces only by virtue of its cause: whereas passive joy is produced in us by an encounter with a body that agrees with ours, active joy we produce ourselves.[5] We would not, however, form adequate ideas and produce active joys without the aid of the good encounters which first enable us to form common notions. It appears, then, that common notions must be regarded as practical ideas in relation to our power, for it is only through forming them that we come to have an adequate idea of our power, that is, that we become-active in relation to our power.[6] Deleuze's account of the manner in which common notions are formed implies that this process of becoming-active, free and rational is an *essentially* combinatory one: common notions are necessarily acquired by composition. Only by gaining an understanding of the conditions of our knowledge and our action, that is, an understanding of the interactive networks of relations into which our own relation is inserted and upon which it depends, are we able to come into possession of our powers of acting and knowing.[7] And we cannot gain such an understanding, we cannot increase our powers of acting and knowing, except insofar as we *actually* compose with other bodies and with other individuals who agree with us in power, for, as Deleuze puts it, '[y]ou do not know beforehand what good or bad you are capable of; you do not know beforehand what a body or a mind can do, in a given encounter, a given arrangement, a given combination' (Deleuze 1988: 125). Hence Deleuze's insistence that the art of the common notions involves the experimental discovery of 'our' joys.

This 'art of experimentation' that Deleuze finds in Spinoza's theory of the formation of the common notions recurs as a series of variations in Deleuze's later work, in particular in his collaborations with Guattari. The idea of the composition of the individual's body with other bodies, human and non-human, without direction by established ideas of what that individual is, or what it is capable of, the idea of mapping encounters on the plane of immanence rather than organizing them according to a pre-given plan, surfaces most forcefully in Deleuze and Guattari's conception of 'becomings'. Here the notions of anti-juridicism, composition and agency appear through the medium of an even more 'unorthodox' Spinoza. The agency achieved in Spinoza's common notions – the expression of the mind's power through the formation of a system of adequate ideas of the world – is no longer the object of analysis. Rather agency is conceived in terms of a movement which evades the definition of the individual in terms of forms and functions and the delimitation of its capacities, whether such a definition is biological, psychiatric or political. And yet the outline of the formation of common notions is still discernible in the idea of a 'becoming'.

What Deleuze and Guattari call a becoming has nothing to do with imitation or analogy between two previously conceived identities, that is, bodies conceived under an order of 'molar' categorization which identifies them according to their type and place in an order of oppositions. Spinoza himself would call such categories inadequate ideas to the extent that they do not express the *relation* which defines the body and the *affects* of which it is capable, but rest on gross resemblances and imaginary universals (see 1985: II, P40, Scholium). Becomings occur rather at the level of community of relations and affects. The horse-becoming of Little Hans, for example, is 'a question of whether Little Hans can endow his own elements with the relations of movement and rest, the affects, that would make him become horse, forms and subjects aside' (Deleuze and Guattari 1987: 258). Functioning like strictly *particular* common notions, becomings represent the 'extraction of a shared element', simultaneously in action and thought, through experimental compositions and 'unnatural participations'. Like the common notions becomings represent the discovery, through action, of ideas of composition of relations: these actions-ideas are *active* insofar as they evade the organizing plane of molar definitions in producing new powers and affects. Such agency does not *belong* to a subject but consists rather in the experimental invention of new subjectivities. Although these ideas take us some distance from the initial conception of anti-juridicism (the rejection of the Hobbesian synthesis of private powers by a mediating Power), Spinoza's anti-Hobbesian elaboration of what Negri terms a 'constitutive ontology', an ontology of power and the immanent composition of powers, remains evident in Deleuze and Guattari's elaboration of a micro-politics of 'deterritorialization'. Becomings, as the composition of Spinozist bodies on the plane of immanence, involve us in the political task of becoming other, resisting and undermining the various organized limits to our powers, and in doing so perhaps changing these limits themselves.

Notes

I should like to thank Tom Gibson for his invaluable critical comments on this paper (not all of which could be integrated), and for many discussions on these issues. I am also grateful to Dr Moira Gatens and Professor Genevieve Lloyd, by whom I was employed as a research assistant on an Australian Research Council funded project entitled 'Freedom, Responsibility and Citizenship: A Spinozistic Approach'. Much of the research for this paper was undertaken while I was working on that project.

1 As Deleuze says in his preface to Negri (1982: 9).

2 See Macherey 1992: 189.

3 See Spinoza 1985: II, Lemma 7, Scholium. All further references are given by part and proposition in the main text.

4 Spinoza distinguishes common notions from universal notions such as those of genera and species. For a discussion of the type of universality that pertains to the common notions and its difference from 'abstract' universality see Spinoza 1985: II, P40, Scholium; see also Deleuze 1992: 273–88.

5 See Deleuze's comments on the City in Deleuze 1992: 265–8.

6 See Deleuze 1988: 71: 'Man . . . is free when he comes into possession of his power of acting, that is, when his *conatus* is determined by adequate ideas from which active affects follow, affects that are explained by his own essence.'

7 See Spinoza 1985: V, P59, Demonstration: 'Finally, insofar as joy is good it agrees with reason (for it consists in this, that a man's power of acting is increased or aided), and is not a passion except insofar as the man's power of acting is not increased to the point where he conceives himself and his actions adequately.'

References

Deleuze, G. (1988) *Spinoza: Practical Philosophy*, trans. R. Hurley, San Francisco: City Light Books.

—— (1992) *Expressionism in Philosophy: Spinoza*, trans. M. Joughin, New York: Zone Books.

Deleuze, G. and Guattari, F. (1987) *A Thousand Plateaus: Capitalism and Schizophrenia*, trans. B. Massumi, Minneapolis: University of Minnesota Press.

Macherey, P. (1992) 'Towards a Natural History of Norms', in *Michel Foucault Philosopher*, trans. T. Armstrong, Hemel Hempstead: Harvester Wheatsheaf, pp. 176–91.

Negri, A. (1982, 1991) *L'Anomalie sauvage: Puissance et pouvoir chez Spinoza*, Paris: PUF, trans. M. Hardt, *The Savage Anomaly: The Power of Spinoza's Metaphysics and Politics*, Minneapolis and Oxford: University of Minnesota Press.

Spinoza, B. (1951a) *A Theologico-Political Treatise*, in *Works of Spinoza*, vol. 1, trans. R. Elwes, New York: Dover Publications.

—— (1951b) *A Political Treatise* in *Works of Spinoza*, vol. 1, trans. R. Elwes, New York: Dover Publications.

—— (1951c) *Correspondence*, in *Works of Spinoza*, vol. 2, trans. R. Elwes, New York: Dover Publications.

—— (1985) *Ethics*, in *The Collected Works of Spinoza*, trans. E. Curley, New Jersey: Princeton University Press.

4

Deleuze and Structuralism

Towards a Geometry of Sufficient Reason

Tim Clark

This chapter examines Deleuze's understanding of the relation between structure and genesis as it appears in chapter 4 of *Difference and Repetition*. The aim is to establish how Deleuze's theory differs from, and implicitly undermines, the 'orthodox' account of structuralism presented by Piaget in his famous book on the subject. While Piaget recognizes that the Copernican revolution must be extended in response to the epistemological break signified by non-Euclidean geometries, Deleuze cautions that there can be 'no revolution as long as we remain tied to Euclidean geometry; we must move to a geometry of sufficient reason, a differential geometry which tends to ground solutions in the conditions of problems' (Deleuze 1968: 210; 1994: 162). Piaget's model of structure remains tied, if not to Euclidean geometry in particular, then to a properly conceptual geometry which might be called that of rationalism in general. It is this conceptual geometry which forms the object of Deleuze's critique, and against which his own geometry of sufficient reason might be defined.

Since examining these different conceptual geometries will involve a superficial engagement with geometry proper, i.e. with a particular branch of mathematics, some distinctions might be in order. Following the taxonomy of Deleuze's *What is Philosophy?*, geometry, as a mathematical science, can be taken to deal exclusively with functions – ideal relations between points, lines, planes, etc. Philosophical concepts, on the other hand, while they may be in some sense derivable from functions, nonetheless have a life of their own and contribute nothing directly to problems concerning functions. Deleuze's own geometry of sufficient reason is itself a philosophical concept, consisting of multiple component concepts which have been derived from, or at least created in proximity to, various mathematical functions. If concepts must be distinguished from functions, a further distinction must be made between two kinds of concepts, those which Deleuze calls 'invented' and those which (following Bergson) he calls 'ready-made'; both kinds of concepts may or may not be intimately related to functions. Put simply, Deleuze's geometry of sufficient reason consists of invented concepts, while the conceptual geometry of rationalism consists of ready-mades. The structuralist concept comes ready-made because it derives, by imitation or analogy, from a mathematical model, i.e. a set of functions. To derive a concept from a function by way of imitation is, in effect, to leave the model unquestioned; conversely, inventing a concept in proximity to a function ('by derivation' if that means 'setting adrift from'), places the model in question. In effect, the invented concept enters a world in which 'everything has become simulacrum, for by simulacrum we should not understand a simple imitation but rather the act by which the very idea of a model is challenged and overturned' (Deleuze 1968: 95; 1994: 69). If models are forms of representation which provide grounds for thought, then the necessity for a continual ungrounding follows from the principle of sufficient reason: '*sufficient reason or the ground is strangely bent*: on the one hand it leans towards what it grounds, towards the forms of representation; on the other hand, it plunges into a groundlessness which resists all forms' (Deleuze 1968: 352; 1994: 275). Deleuze's own technical models are employed, firstly, as he says, to serve as tools for the exploration of the virtual, but secondly, to be themselves overturned or ungrounded insofar as they lie at the root of both the rationalist confusion of Ideas with ideal forms and the structuralist confusion of structures with symbolic fields. 'We must', Deleuze insists, 'avoid giving the elements and relations which form a structure an actuality which they do not have, and withdrawing from them a reality which they do have' (Deleuze 1968: 270; 1994: 209).

If Piaget's structures are essentially formal, Deleuze's are inessentially virtual, where the virtual is by definition without form. However, to be without form or inessential is not necessarily to be indeterminate or undetermined. The objection might be made that if structure is not be identified with its formalization, if structures in fact insist in a virtual reality which is itself *groundless*, what sense does it make still to speak of 'structure' and how can the groundless be in any sense 'structured' if it is, by definition, without form? Deleuze's reply to this objection, and to many others like it, is to turn it back on itself by way of unearthing its hidden presupposition: by what right is the groundless to be identified with the *indeterminate* or the *indifferent*? Whose prejudice does this identification serve, if not that of the Idealist for whom the Form is that which alone preserves us from an undifferentiated nothingness, as if groundlessness were merely 'a contradictory state which had to be subjected to order or law from the outside, as it is when the

Demiurge comes to subjugate a rebellious matter'? (Deleuze 1968: 93; 1994: 68). If Deleuze refuses the Platonic schema (the Demiurge as moulding a chaotic matter in the image of the Forms), it is in the name of a groundlessness which is already 'determinate', indeed 'structured', but always and everywhere in a manner that *does not resemble* the forms and structures that must ground themselves in it.

The distinction between formal and virtual structures can be taken as equivalent to Deleuze's distinction between symbolic fields and problematic fields: structures are formal insofar as they are formalizable within a given symbolic field, while structures are virtual insofar as they resist formalization and thus remain 'problematic'. While problematic fields consist entirely of 'singularities', symbolic fields consist of 'ordinary points'. A properly mathematical version of the distinction between ordinary points and singularities appears in René Thom's book *Structural Stability and Morphogenesis*. He distinguishes between a set of regular points, in which a point is regular insofar as it does not differ in kind from its neighbouring points, and a set of catastrophe points, in which there is some discontinuity, i.e. difference in kind, in every neighbourhood. However, he then goes on to question this distinction in a way which would lead more or less directly to a geometry of sufficient reason: 'The distinction between regular and catastrophic points is obviously somewhat arbitrary since it depends upon the fineness of the observation used. One might object, and not without reason, that each point would appear catastrophic to sufficiently sensitive observational techniques. This is why the distinction is an idealisation, to be made precise by a mathematical model' (Thom 1975: 38). Since, for Deleuze, the idealized model is precisely what must remain in question, his own geometry of the inobservable must consist entirely of singularities. If Deleuze objects to the idealization, it is to place in question, not the precision of the mathematical model, but its universality *as* a model. There is, says Deleuze, a *mathesis universalis*, but there is also a universal physics, psychology, sociology, etc. (Deleuze 1968: 246; 1994: 190). In effect, then, what is being contested is not the application of the model outside mathematics, but the way in which (for instance) structuralism extends the model to other domains without first questioning the nature of the model itself. Applying the model to other fields demands a theory as to what makes the application possible in the first place. This demand is not sufficiently met by formulating a general theory of models, such as that proposed by Thom; it requires a general theory of problems, since problems alone are universal, while models are always general by virtue of being formal.

Both Piaget and Deleuze agree that structures consist entirely of differential relations between differential elements, but everything depends, firstly, on the nature of the elements involved, and secondly, on the kind of logic which determines the relations between elements. In Deleuze's structures, then, the elements are singularities, and the relations between these elements are determined according to a logic of virtual time. In Piaget's structures the elements are ordinary points and the relations between elements are determined according to a formal logic. This 'formal logic' is everywhere an instance of what Deleuze calls 'the logical form of the possible'. It may be instantiated propositionally, geometrically or algebraically – and all of these appear in Piaget as models for structure – but everywhere formal structures reduce to 'sets of possibles'. Piaget acknowledges that structures only 'live' in real systems, but the latter are themselves only 'special cases', or the specified cases, of a set of possible cases; it is precisely these sets of possibles that are formalizable as structures; 'the actual', says Piaget, 'is interpreted or explained as an instance of the possible' (Piaget 1968: 34; 1971: 38). For Deleuze, what Piaget calls a special case is always a 'case of solution'; he does not disagree over the need for specification, but rather over the nature of what it is that is being specified. For Piaget, it is a set of possible cases of solution, only one of which is specified in the form of a real system; for Deleuze it is a 'problematic multiplicity' which remains irreducible to a set of possible solutions. Problems have their own internal conditions, and are determined in their own right, before they are determinable or externally conditionable as being cases of solution. In short, the definitive function of the formal logic of the possible is to convert a problematic multiplicity into a set of possible cases of solution, to convert a virtual structure into a formal structure.

If there is a difference in kind between the formal and the virtual, problematic fields nonetheless remain immanent to symbolic fields; the problematic, as Deleuze says, moves through, or expresses itself in, the forms of the symbolic. The difference in kind is logical but not material, where the material in question is in some sense Ideal, or as Deleuze calls it, 'virtual content'. In effect, then, formal structures are simply virtual structures which have been formalized; ordinary points, as the elements of formal structures, are simply singularities which have been specified; and the relations between ordinary points are simply relations between singularities which have been coordinated within a symbolic field. Virtual structures consist of singularities which are unspecified, and of connections between singularities which are non-localizable; it is precisely this non-localizable, unspecified nature of the elements which makes virtual structures problematic. Insofar as formal structures specify singularities and localize their connections within a symbolic field, they necessarily conceal the problematic nature of the virtual.

The conceptual geometry of structuralism comes out clearly in a key section of Piaget's book in which he derives his model of structure from the mathematical theory of groups. Since groups, he says, 'may be viewed as a kind of prototype of structures in general . . . we must look to them to ground our hope for the future of structuralism' (Piaget 1968: 18; 1971: 19). He defines a group as a self-regulating system of transformations or operations, self-regulating because the operations are governed by an internal logic: 'when we analyse the concept of groups, we come upon the following very general coordinations among operations: 1. the condition that a return to the starting point always be possible; 2. the condition that the same goal or terminus be attainable by alternate routes and without the itinerary affecting the point of arrival' (Piaget 1968: 18–19; 1971: 19–20). What this self-regulation amounts to, says Piaget, is really the continual application of three basic principles of rationalism: firstly, the principle of non-contradiction, which here means that transformations are reversible, i.e. a return to the starting point remains possible. Secondly, the principle of 'equifinality', according to which the end point of the transformation remains independent of the route taken.[1] Thirdly, the principle of identity, or invariance, which is itself implied by the first two principles: there must be certain elements of the structure (i.e. the starting points and end points) which remain invariant under transformation. To illustrate how these principles function in geometry, Piaget takes as an example the set of displacements of a solid body in 'ordinary space'. For this set, the principle of reversibility holds because any given displacement of a body can be annulled by an inverse displacement. His confirmation of the second principle takes the form of an *a priori* argument: it is, he says, 'absolutely essential, since, if termini did vary with the paths traversed to reach them, then space would lose its coherence and would thereby be annihilated; what we would have instead would be some sort of perpetual Heraclitean flux' (Piaget 1968: 19; 1971: 20). What this argument amounts to, in Deleuze's terms, is merely proof 'that something cannot not be rather than that it is and why it is (hence the frequency in Euclid of negative, indirect and *reductio* arguments, which serve to keep geometry under the domination of the principle of identity, and prevent it from becoming a geometry of sufficient reason)' (Deleuze 1968: 208; 1994: 160).

For Piaget, then, relations between elements of a structure are continually determined according to a logic of timeless rationalist principles, which effectively function together to preserve the stability of structure and to ensure the rationality of all change that the structure undergoes. For Deleuze, by contrast, relations between elements of a structure are determined 'progressively' in what he calls a purely logical time. In outlining what he means by this he offers the following formula, which can be taken as a theorem of the geometry of sufficient reason: 'in going from A to B and then B to A, we do not arrive back at the point of departure as in a bare repetition; rather, the repetition between A and B and then B and A is the progressive tour or description of the whole of a problematic field' (Deleuze 1968: 272; 1994: 210). If the problematic field refers to a virtual structure, then A and B refer to singularities as elements of the structure, and the repetition between A and B refers to a relation between singularities. On Piaget's model, the relations between elements of a structure are determined according to the principles of reversibility, equifinality and identity, which effectively remove the logical time immanent in virtual structures. By setting Deleuze's theorem against Piaget's principles, it is possible to show how the geometry of sufficient reason works to restore this virtual time.

According to the principle of reversibility, to go from A to B and then B to A is to have arrived back at the point of departure. This, says Deleuze, only takes place under the conditions of a bare repetition. Bare or ordinary repetition requires the coordination of ordinary points within a symbolic field. But, so Deleuze implies, any coordinated repetition in the symbolic field will require a detour through the whole of the problematic field in order to specify a starting point and an end point within that field. Since every point in the problematic field is a singularity, the specified end point will differ in kind from the specified starting point, a purely virtual difference which the act of coordination effectively cancels. In effect, then, the problematic field introduces an element of irreversibility (i.e. a return to the starting point is never possible) which the law of reversibility simply overrides. According to the principle of equifinality, whatever the detour taken to get from A to B the end point will remain unaffected by the route taken. If we define a route as a series of points, then all routes lead to the same terminus only if all series are convergent. There are, says Deleuze, 'singularities which are ordinary because of the convergence of series; but there are also singularities which are distinctive because of their divergence' (Deleuze 1968: 245; 1994: 190). If the symbolic field consists of converging series of ordinary points, the problematic field consists only of divergent series of singularities. As such it introduces an element of multifinality: i.e. different routes lead to different end points insofar as all series are subject to perpetual divergence. According to the principle of identity the transformation A to B describes the same form as the transformation B to A: there is map of A onto B which is invertible and bicontinuous. In Deleuze's geometry, this description of an invariant form within the symbolic field necessarily obscures a variation in, or a progression through, the problematic field. While the form remains the same, the ground moves; the form does not remain the same by virtue of an eternal essence, but remains the same only for as long as it distinguishes itself from the ground. For invariance to be sustained the symbolic field must distinguish itself from the problematic, which being immanent does not distinguish itself from it. If this distinction is always an idealization, it is because the invariant form is only specifiable against a hidden background of variation. The latter, then, forms the third aspect of Deleuze's logical time, which frees his own geometry from the principle of identity.

Ernst Cassirer, in a discussion of topology as the theory of invariant properties, makes the following comments: 'The permanence here in question denotes no absolute property of given objects, but is valid only relative to a certain intellectual operation, chosen as a system of reference [i.e. a symbolic field]. Permanence is not related to the duration of things and their properties, but signifies the relative independence of certain members of a functional connection, which prove in comparison with others to be independent moments' (Cassirer 1953: 91). Cassirer makes the point that permanence is ideal, that it depends upon the suppression of real time, understood as the duration of things and their properties. The point he does not go on to make is that there is also an ideal time, immanent in the symbolic field, which is also suppressed by the ideal of permanence. To sum up, in Deleuze's structures relations between elements are progressively determined in a purely virtual time, according to a logic of irreversiblity, multifinality and variation.

To understand Piaget's model of genesis we must return to his discussion of group theory. Having illustrated the relevance of the theory to Euclidean geometry, he goes on to show how metageometries can be constructed by a process of what he calls 'reflective abstraction'; in this case, abstraction from the group of displacements in 'ordinary space' to higher groups of transformations possible in non-Euclidean space. The Euclidean group of displacements preserves as invariant the dimensions, angles, parallels and straight lines of the body or figure displaced. To construct the next higher group we need only allow the dimensions to vary while keeping all the other properties invariant. In this way, says Piaget, 'we obtain the group of similar figures or bodies: shape is kept invariant while the dimensions are subject to transformation. The group of displacements has thereby become a subgroup of the shape group' (Piaget 1968: 20; 1971: 21). To obtain still higher groups, this process is simply repeated for each property. Thus, the angles are allowed to vary while the parallels are preserved; then the parallels are varied while the straight lines are preserved. Finally, 'even straight lines may be subjected to transformation. Shapes are now treated as if they were elastic: only a bicontinuous correspondence among singular points is preserved under transformation. The group thus obtained is one of maximum generality, the group of homeomorphs which constitutes the subject matter of topology'; from this Piaget concludes: 'the various kinds of geometry – once taken to be disconnected from one another – are thus reduced to one vast construction whose transformations under a graded series of conditions of invariance yield a 'nest' of subgroups within subgroups' (Piaget 1968: 20; 1971: 22). By applying this general metric, or graded series of conditions, it becomes possible both to ascend from the specific group of displacements to the group of highest generality and to descend from the latter back to the former. In the realm of pure geometry, then, the epistemological break between the Euclidean and the non-Euclidean amounts to very little; the non-Euclidean simply envelops or includes the Euclidean as a subgroup within a nest of higher groups. As a result, the so-called 'coherence of space' is preserved, the three principles of rationalism are universally confirmed, and the 'turbulence of the Heraclitean flux' is everywhere contained.

However, Piaget is not so naive as to think that every structure conforms absolutely to the model of a formal system closed under transformation; he acknowledges that there is 'an immense class of structures which are not strictly logical or mathematical' (Piaget 1968: 15; 1971: 15). Such structures, which he calls 'natural', may be biological, psychological, sociological; in every case the definitive feature of the transformations involved is that they unfold over time. Hence, an element of irreversibility enters in and the principle of non-contradiction, ideally premised upon strict reversibility, has to be reconfigured to take account of temporal conditions. Nevertheless, it becomes clear by the end of Piaget's book that this introduction of a temporal element poses a minimal threat to the coherence of space and thereby to the generality of the mathematical-geometrical model. Piaget's own research in developmental psychology, his 'genetic epistemology', is premised upon the belief that the reflective abstraction of the mathematician is merely the 'formalised inverse' of a more primitive process of psychogenesis. 'Genesis', he says, 'is simply the transition from one structure to another, nothing more, but this transition leads from a 'weaker' to a 'stronger' structure' (Piaget 1968: 121; 1971: 141). Just as the mathematician must construct stronger systems, such as formal logic, in order to complete weaker systems, such as arithmetic, so the child must, by a similar process of reflective abstraction, construct stronger conceptual structures out of weaker conceptual or perceptual structures. For Piaget, the limit on formalization imposed by Gödel's theorem signifies that 'there is no structure apart from construction, whether it be abstract or genetic', and that this constructive activity is itself a 'never completed whole' (Piaget 1968: 120; 1971: 140).

To understand why the temporal element implicit in the *process* of construction does not present a problem, we need only refer back to the geometrical model. On Piaget's analysis, Euclidean geometry is, in a sense, strengthened rather than negated by its non-Euclidean counterparts: the coherence of the inferior group of displacements is effectively grounded in the homeomorphic continuities of the superior group. If this arrangement is to function as a model for genetic process, it can only be because the transition from one transformation group to another is itself governed by immanent laws of transformation – 'a graded series of conditions'. To generalize from the model, then: if there are non-temporal laws of transformation intrinsic to well-constructed structures, there are also extrinsic laws of temporal transformation which govern the construction of structures and condition the passage from one structure to another. In this way, any apparent break in the process of construction never amounts to a catastrophic discontinuity, but rather to a strengthening of conceptual schemas – and this will be the case 'whether the construction be abstract or genetic'.

In sum, Piaget conceives of genesis as being a transition from one formal structure to another, by way of a construction process involving reflective abstraction. Deleuze, on the other hand, conceives genesis as taking place 'not between one actual term and another, but between the virtual and its actualisation – in other words, it goes from the structure to its incarnation, from the conditions of a problem to the cases of solution'. As he then admits, 'this is a genesis without dynamism, evolving necessarily in the element of a supra-historicity, a *static genesis*' (Deleuze 1968: 238; 1994: 183). If genesis is nothing other than the transition from one formal structure to another, then it proceeds only on the horizontal axis which goes from one actual term to another without ever intersecting with the vertical axis which goes from the virtual to the actual. From Deleuze's perspective, Piaget simply substitutes extrinsic criteria of constructibility for the intrinsic conditions of production: the internal conditions of the problem, that is, the determinations of the virtual structure. In short, Deleuze's structures are virtual, and Piaget's are actual – but it would nonetheless be a mistake to identify the latter as being merely the incarnations of the former. A finer distinction has to be made, a distinction that Piaget almost makes when, in concluding his study, he considers the problem of interdisciplinarity: 'The search for structures cannot but result in interdisciplinary coordination. The reason for this is quite simple: if one tries to deal with structures within an artificially circumscribed domain – and any given science is just that – one very soon comes upon the problem of being unable to locate the entities one is studying, since structure is so defined that it cannot coincide with any system of observable relations, and these are the only ones that are made out clearly in any of the existing sciences' (Piaget 1968: 118–19; 1971: 137–8). The problem of locating structures arises because a structure is never entirely coincident with any one of its incarnations; it is, as Deleuze says, 'a system of multiple, non-localisable connections' (Deleuze 1968: 238; 1994: 183), in his terms, a 'problematic Idea'.

But it seems that for Piaget, the essential inobservability of structure is merely a technical hitch; firstly, because every structure is formalizable when provided with its appropriate symbolic field, and secondly, because the limitations of any given field can always be compensated for with the appropriate interdisciplinary cooperation. In Deleuze's view, however, the inobservability of structure is indicative of an insistent problem. His more subtle three-way distinction runs as follows: 'We must distinguish completely between the following: the problem as transcendental instance; the symbolic field in which the immanent movement of the problem expresses itself; and the field of scientific solvability [i.e. the 'domain of solution'] in which the problem is incarnated' (Deleuze 1968: 213; 1994: 164). When Piaget distinguishes between structures and 'systems of observable relations', in Deleuze's terms this amounts only to a distinction between, on the one hand, the symbolic fields in which the problem first expresses itself, and on the other, the 'artificially circumscribed domains' in which the problem finds a solution. In the terms of Piaget's model, the various geometries form different domains of solution, in which the problem (i.e. the 'problematic Idea of Space') admits of various geometrical solutions. The transformation groups specific to each domain form the symbolic fields which specify the problem in different ways. Insofar as Piaget derives his concept of structure from the transformation group, he effectively confuses 'structure' with 'symbolic field', and thus ignores the nature of the problem as a transcendental instance. In short, he confuses structure with a model of structure, and thereby assimilates the Idea to a form. It is at this moment that Piaget attributes to structures an actuality which they do not have, at the same time as withdrawing from them a reality which they do have.

For Deleuze, then, static genesis goes from the virtuality of structure to the actuality of its incarnation. Piaget approximates to this when he says that formal structures can only live in real systems. By employing this distinction, but following Deleuze's substitution of 'virtual' and 'actual' for 'possible' and 'real', virtual structures can be understood to be incarnated in actual systems, static genesis being understood as the passage from structure to system. This passage is one of logical or static determination: the space and time immanent to virtual structure determine the spaces and times of actual systems: 'Not only do the spaces of actualisation begin to incarnate the differential relations between elements of the reciprocally and completely determined structure, the times of actualisation incarnate the time of structure, the time of progressive determination' (Deleuze 1968: 280; 1994: 217). While reciprocal and complete determination account for the differential space of structure, which is actualized in the different qualities and extensities of actual systems, progressive determination accounts for the differential time of structure which, says Deleuze, 'itself determines a time of actualisation, or rather, different rhythms and times of actualisation which correspond to the relations of the structure and which, for their part, measure the passage from the virtual to the actual' (Deleuze 1968: 272; 1994: 211). If, as suggested earlier, the logical time of structure is already one of irreversibility and multifinality, then its correspondence to the different rhythms and times of actual systems becomes clear. It is a correspondence, in particular, to the physical time of open dynamical systems in which, starting from a set of arbitrarily specified initial conditions, development is irreversible and the development paths are multifinal, i.e. the end state or final condition of the system will be dependent upon the path taken. If there is then a logical correspondence between the time of structure and the times of actualization, it is nonetheless a correspondence without resemblance. The difference is that between the static and the dynamic, the potential and the kinetic, or co-existence and succession. If the time of actualization is dynamic and successive it nonetheless 'immediately incarnates the relations, the singularities and the progressivities immanent to the Idea' (Deleuze 1968: 282; 1994: 218). It is this *immediacy* of the incarnation that determines the static nature of static genesis. A spatio-temporal potential is immediately specified from out of an order of multiple co-existent potentials. The element of immediacy rules out the need for a detour through the Kantian schematism which 'does no more than convert logical possibility into transcendental possibility, [bringing] spatio-temporal relations into correspondence with the logical relations of the concept' (Deleuze 1968: 281; 1994: 218). For Deleuze, the rules for the determination of space and time need not correspond to the (ready-made) concept because spatio-temporal dynamisms are already potential dramas internal to the Idea.

To return to Piaget's model, he does refer to 'rhythmic systems such as pervade biology and human life at every level', but of these he says 'one may view them as being the real 'stages' of a structure's construction, or, reversing the sequence, one may use operational mechanisms of a quasi-Platonic and non-temporal sort as a 'basis' from which the others are then in some manner derived' (Piaget 1968: 16; 1971: 16). Neither alternative is applicable to the kind of open systems to which he refers; insofar as these systems develop according to different rhythms of actualization, they resist both 'derivation' from a non-temporal model and assimilation to the model of a stage-by-stage construction. If Deleuze's version is any more adequate, it is so only insofar as giving a sufficient reason is adequate, since, in effect, his geometry of sufficient reason accounts only for *why* rather than how systems are determined by structures. In other words, it searches out not the efficient cause but the ideal cause, not the dynamic but the static genesis, since describing the *how* of determination requires explicating the dynamics of intensity. The latter is the subject of chapter 5 of *Difference and Repetition*, which engages with the thermodynamic and biological processes involved in the 'how' of determination, and which thereby involves a change of model. What is interesting about Deleuze's ungrounding of the structuralist model is that he does not immediately move to a dynamical systems model, nor does he simply reintroduce the ontological time of the turbulent flux. Rather, the model is overturned through the discovery of a logical time immanent in the space of the structure, in that coherent logical space in which structuralism grounds itself.

Piaget's own form of structuralism remains distinctly neo-Kantian, despite his objection to what he calls *a priori* forms of synthesis. For example, his attitude towards geometry is identical with that of Cassirer, who suggests that 'if, from the standpoint of metageometry, Euclidean geometry appears as a mere beginning, as a given material for further developments, nevertheless, from the standpoint of the critique of knowledge, it represents the end of a complicated series of intellectual operations. The psychological investigation of the origin of space has indirectly confirmed and clarified this' (Cassirer 1953: 104–5). Piaget's developmental psychology provides the ultimate confirmation; his genetic epistemology appears as a psychologistic version of the Kantian critique of knowledge. If Euclidean space is to be privileged, says Cassirer, it is because 'it defines the minimum of those conditions under which experience is possible in general' (Cassirer 1953: 431). Piaget simply refines this view when, from a developmental perspective, he suggests that the *a priori* is not the condition for learning, but its outcome. This sounds promising until we discover that his theory of learning is rooted in a twofold notion of repetition as 'either recognitory assimilation or generalising assimilation'. Assimilation, he says, 'is not itself a structure but the functional aspect of structure formation, intervening in each case of the constructive activity . . . establishing ever more intimate inter-structural connections' (Piaget 1968: 61; 1971: 71–2). Assimilation, then, performs the same function in psychological development as the rules of reflective abstraction do in the development of geometry; in each case, 'a graded series of conditions' effects the passage from a stronger to a weaker structure. This constructive activity is effectively indistinguishable from Cassirer's constructive synthesis, which 'proceeds by the addition of a new condition, and thus represents a more complex conceptual structure' (Cassirer 1953: 108). Since Piaget's new conditions alone facilitate the transition from one structure to another, it is difficult to see them as being anything other than *a priori* forms of synthesis, to which the notion of genesis is effectively reduced. Everywhere, then, the point of view of conditioning is substituted for the genetic point of view, extrinsic criteria of constructibility obscure the intrinsic processes of determination, and the constructive synthesis of concepts replaces the productive synthesis of Ideas.

Insofar as the epistemological break signified by non-Euclidean geometry is still recuperable within neo-Kantian forms of synthesis, Deleuze extends the break into a break with epistemology itself: a break with the critique in which the genesis of knowledge is always referred back to its conditions of possibility. If it is necessary to move to a geometry of sufficient reason, it is because genesis refers to an ideal cause before it submits to an *a priori* condition. The break with epistemology also has multiple consequences with regard to theorizing the relation between disciplines, and the constitution of disciplinarity itself. By privileging learning over pedagogy, the production of knowledge over its conditions of possibility, Deleuze sets what he calls a culture of violence over against the moralities of discipline and method. On Piaget's model, interdisciplinary cooperation is a consequence of the logical transcendence of formal structures with respect to real systems. The transcendence of structure may be observed from within an artificially circumscribed domain, and as a result that domain will be recognized as partial with respect even to its own privileged object of investigation. But the consequent relativization of the field of solvability does not amount to an encounter with the problem as a transcendental instance, since the 'inobservability' of structure is here only considered relative to the technical problem of finding a solution in general. To consider the *question* of structure in its own right and independently of any circumscribed domain, it is necessary to think the virtuality of structure independently of the exigencies of problem-solving and beyond the 'standpoint of the critique of knowledge'. For Deleuze, learning necessitates a 'confrontation with the objecticity of a problem (Idea), whereas knowledge designates only the calm possession of a rule enabling solutions' (Deleuze 1968: 214; 1994: 164); 'knowledge is nothing more than an empirical figure . . . whereas learning is the true transcendental structure which introduces time into thought – not in the form of a mythical past, but in the pure form of an empty time in general' (Deleuze 1968: 216; 1994: 166–7). The break with epistemology is not an anti-scientific return to myth; rather, what it disputes is 'the innate right of knowledge to represent the entire transcendental realm' (Deleuze 1968: 215; 1994: 166). What it contests, then, is not science itself, understood as the 'faculty of knowledge', but the presence in philosophy of a 'scientistic hypotheticism and a rationalist moralism which render unrecognisable what they approximate' (Deleuze 1968: 254–5; 1994: 197). That intellectual moralism of the ready-made concept which, by assimilating the problem to a formal model, only betrays the productive synthesis of the Idea.

As Prigogine and Stengers once suggested, Deleuze's own use of technical and scientific models is governed not by a conception of interdisciplinary coordination but by a refusal to restrict what they call the 'powers of imagination' to the mere shaping of hypotheses for heuristic ends (Prigogine and Stengers 1979: 387–9). They cite the following passage: 'While it is thought which must explore the virtual down to the ground of its repetitions, it is imagination which must grasp the process of actualisation from the point of view of these echoes or reprises. It is imagination which crosses domains, orders and levels, grasping the unity of mind and nature, moving endlessly from science to dream and back again' (Deleuze 1968: 284; 1994: 220). Nevertheless, Prigogine and Stengers point out, it is to nature and to the sciences of nature that Deleuze himself has to appeal, both in order to describe these powers of imagination and in order to escape the anthropological perspective of the philosophy of representation. In effect, then, the passage from science to dream repeats itself interminably: in exploring the virtual, thought requires a ground in the form of a scientific model, but since the virtual is essentially groundless every model requires ungrounding in relation to that which resists all forms. Concepts may be derived in proximity to functions, but where the ready-made concept thinks the Idea through the idealized forms of representation, the invented concept dramatizes the Idea and thinks through the dream. If the dream is itself groundless, it is nonetheless, as René Thom once said, 'the virtual catastrophe in which knowledge is initiated' (Thom 1975: 326). At the limits of thought, science is no more separable from myth than knowledge is from learning, or the ground from the groundless.

Note

1 Since Piaget does not give this principle a specific name, I have borrowed the term 'equifinality' from Anthony Wilden; see 'The Structure as Law and Order: Piaget's Genetic Structuralism', in Wilden 1972: 302–50. In contrast to Deleuze, Wilden bases his critique of structuralism on an alternative biological-thermodynamic model: Piaget's closed logical space is the result of 'his inadequate conception of homeostasis and evolution' (p. 347).

References

Cassirer, E. (1953) *Substance and Function and Einstein's Theory of Relativity*, trans. W. Swaby and M. Swaby, New York: Dover Publications. (*Substanzbegriff und Functionsbegriff* was originally published in 1910; *Zur Einstein'schen Relativitätstheorie* appeared in 1921.)

Deleuze, G. (1968, 1994), *Différence et répétition*, Paris: PUF, *Difference and Repetition*, trans. P. Patton, London: Athlone Press.

Piaget, J. (1968, 1971) *Le Structuralisme*, Paris: PUF, *Structuralism*, trans. C. Maschler, London: RKP.

Prigogine, I. and Stengers, I. (1979) *La Nouvelle Alliance*, Paris: Gallimard.

Thom, R. (1975) *Structural Stability and Morphogenesis*, trans. D. Fowler, Reading, MA: Benjamin.

Wilden, A. (1972) *System and Structure: Essays in Communication and Exchange*, London: Tavistock.

5

Tumbling Dice

Gilles Deleuze and the Economy of *Répétition*

Daniel W. Conway

> The schizo is not revolutionary, but the schizophrenic process – in terms of which the schizo is merely the interruption, or the continuation in the void – is the potential for revolution. . . . Courage consists, however, in agreeing to flee rather than live tranquilly and hypocritically in false refuges.
>
> (Deleuze and Guattari, *Anti-Oedipus*)

In his 1962 classic *Nietzsche et la philosophie*, Gilles Deleuze proposes a beguiling figure for Nietzsche's enigmatic teaching of eternal recurrence: the *dice-throw.* By means of this figure, Deleuze attempts to capture the double movement that governs the economy of repetition, whereby necessity and chance, being and becoming, are simultaneously affirmed in their constitutive difference. Hence the centrifugal economy of the teaching of eternal recurrence, at least on Deleuze's interpretation of it: any genuine affirmation of the possibility of reactive forces already involves (and in fact presupposes) the necessity of active forces.

In this chapter I apply the figure of the dice-throw to Deleuze's own thought. The figure of the dice-throw serves, I contend, not only as the master trope of his political thinking, but as a model for his account of the economy of repetition. Most importantly, the figure of the dice-throw provides us with a blueprint for putting Deleuze himself to work, as a desiring machine in his own right. Here the influence of Nietzsche is doubly useful to us: we may map outbreaks of Deleuze's own schizophrenia by charting his use and abuse of Nietzsche; and we may employ Deleuze's experimentation with Nietzsche as a model for our own experimentation with Deleuze.

On the Use and Abuse of Eternal Recurrence

Gilles Deleuze situates his thought along an unexplored seismic rift, which threatens to shift the tectonic plates that undergird the unstable metaphysical landscape of post-Kantian philosophy. Having egregiously mismeasured the Richter magnitude of the Copernican revolution, Kant and his successors have systematically ignored the ramifying cracks and fissures that fault the foundation of their metaphysical projects. They have consequently failed to meet the calamitous demand placed upon philosophy by this earth-quaking critique of metaphysics: *the production of difference*.

Positioned at a historical remove from the epicentre of Kant's Copernican revolution, Deleuze investigates a seismic vortex in which the after-shocks of this critique reverberate with heightened severity. It is the peculiar business of metaphysics, he believes, to misplace relations of difference behind relations of binary opposition, which are weighted towards one of the two terms in accordance with the precepts of (fabricated) first principles. Metaphysicians characteristically codify the lifeworld of human experience by enforcing a farrago of standard binary oppositions: order is preferred to chaos, stability to change, unity to multiplicity, mind to body, reason to passion, and so on. While one might have thought that Kant's levelling critique of metaphysics had cleared the way for an exploration of difference, metaphysicians continue to ply their trade, albeit now in disguised form. Deleuze's designation for the metaphysical recidivism of post-Kantian philosophy is 'the dialectic', a term that captures under its umbrella any attempt to derive a productive result from the clash of binary opposites (Deleuze 1983: 8–10). The dialectic thus functions to redeem the oppositional nature of traditional metaphysics, by teasing from its obfuscatory operations a 'higher' synthesis or truth.

According to Deleuze, however, practitioners of the dialectic succeed merely in compounding the swindle perpetrated by pre-Kantian metaphysicians. By enshrining binary opposition as the preferred model for all relationships between attributes (irrespective of any productive syntheses that opposition might magically yield), the dialectic perpetuates the signature prejudices of metaphysical thinking. The dialectic thus rehabilitates metaphysics following the devastating blow dealt it by Kant, but only at the expense of postponing indefinitely the investigation of difference. As Deleuze sees it, the enduring appeal of the dialectic trades on an egregious confusion of cause and effect: affirmation is not the effect of the negation of negation, but its cause or pre-condition. The negation of the negation, which dialecticians claim to orchestrate through the clash of binary opposites, thus *presupposes* affirmation as its ground and provenance.

Surveying the faulted landscape of post-Kantian philosophy, Deleuze acknowledges a single exception to the metaphysical fraud perpetrated by the dialectic: Nietzsche. In an early essay entitled 'Nomad Thought', Deleuze praises Nietzsche's rhizomatic efforts to confound the totalizing codification imposed on philosophy by metaphysical thinking:

> Nietzsche's task is to transmit something that does not and will not allow itself to be codified. To transmit it to a new body, to invent a body that can receive it and spill it forth; a body that would be our own, the earth's, or even something written.
>
> (Deleuze: 1977: 142)

Deleuze thus locates the promise of Nietzsche's philosophy in his allegiance to an anarchic principle of explanation. Rather than carry out his own, pre-ordained plan of colonization and conquest, in accordance with formal principles of growth and distribution, Nietzsche allows his own activity to be shaped and repositioned by the relative distribution of prevailing despotic codes. His philosophical activity is therefore 'nomadic' in nature, for it achieves a 'final' determination only upon attaining its operational limits.

Nietzsche's guerrilla war on the 'manifest destiny' of metaphysical expansionism thus takes recognizable form only upon realizing its full fruition. He can articulate his philosophical 'positions' (or we for him) only after having allowed them to emerge from within the anarchic distribution of his critical resources. Deleuze consequently recommends Nietzsche's experimental 'nomadism' as a promising mechanism for the production of difference:

> Archaeologists have led us to conceive of this nomadism not as a primary state, but as an adventure suddenly embarked upon by sedentary groups impelled by the attraction of movement, of what lies outside. The nomad and his war machine oppose the despot with his administrative machine: an extrinsic nomadic unit as opposed to an intrinsic despotic unit.
>
> (Deleuze 1977: 148)

Through the guerrilla operations of his nomadic war machine, Nietzsche not only confounds the established conventions of his particular time and place – witness the hostile reception of *The Birth of Tragedy* by orthodox philologists – but also transgresses the grand, transhistorical codes that govern the enterprise of philosophy itself. Deleuze consequently credits Nietzsche with discovering the nomadic counter-discourse of post-Kantian philosophy, of which champions of the project of differential critique might profitably avail themselves:

> But if Nietzsche does not belong to philosophy, it is perhaps because he was the first to conceive of another kind of discourse as counter-philosophy. This discourse is above all nomadic; its statements can be conceived as the products of a mobile war machine and not the utterances of a rational, administrative machinery, whose philosophers would be bureaucrats of pure reason.
>
> (Deleuze 1977: 149)

Nietzsche's triumph over the dialectic reaches its apotheosis, Deleuze believes, in his promulgation of the teaching of eternal recurrence. The revolutionary genius of this teaching lies in its consecration of the marriage of chance and necessity – not as binary opposites, after the fashion of the shotgun weddings routinely performed by disingenuous metaphysicians, but as united in their constitutive difference. The eternal recurrence thus serves as a point of entry into the nomadic counter-discourse, insofar as it constitutes a model of *repetition*, which Deleuze defines as the production of difference (Deleuze 1994: 37–51).

According to Deleuze, eternal recurrence functions as a differential centrifuge, which selectively eliminates the reactive and weak, allowing only the active and strong to return (Deleuze 1983: 71–2). The productive result of Nietzsche's teaching consequently lies in what Deleuze calls the 'auto-destruction' of reactive forces (Deleuze 1977: 70–1). He consequently conceives of the teaching of eternal recurrence as a difference engine, as a promising experiment with repetition and the production of difference. Alluding perhaps to Nietzsche's own observation that the teaching of eternal recurrence '*might* in the end have been taught already by Heraclitus' (Nietzsche 1989: 274), Deleuze credits Nietzsche with the invention of a 'Heraclitean fire machine' (Deleuze 1983: 30).

In arriving at this highly original interpretation of eternal recurrence, Deleuze pays little attention to Nietzsche's more familiar renditions of the teaching. He draws heavily instead on the gnomic image of the *dice-throw*, which figures most prominently in part III of *Thus Spoke Zarathustra*. According to Deleuze, Nietzsche re-presents the 'problem' of affirmation on the model of a game, thereby eschewing the 'spirit of gravity' displayed by champions of the dialectic. This particular game comprises two related moments, which must be understood not in terms of binary opposition, but in terms of their constitutive difference: the affirmation of becoming and the affirmation of the being of becoming (Deleuze 1983: 24–5). The double texture of this game invariably eludes the clumsy grasp of metaphysicians, who either conflate these two moments into one, or elide altogether the difference that separates them.

According to Deleuze, these two moments of affirmation correspond most closely to the two moments that constitute the dice-throw: (1) the dice that are thrown; and (2) the dice that fall back to earth. The dice that are thrown represent the affirmation of chance, while the combination they form upon falling back to earth represents the affirmation of necessity (Deleuze 1983: 26). Necessity therefore does not suppress or abolish chance; they are separated within the economy of the dice-throw not by opposition, but by difference. Indeed, one can affirm the being of becoming only if one also affirms becoming itself:

> The thrown dice form the number which brings the dice-throw back. Bringing the dice-throw back the number puts chance back into the fire, it maintains the fire which reheats chance.
>
> (Deleuze 1983: 29)

The stakes of this seemingly trivial dice-throw are fatally high: to know how to play this game is to know how to affirm chance itself. But the reign of the dialectic has enthroned probability rather than chance, urging dice-players to hedge their bets over a potentially infinite series of throws. The fatal combination delivered by a single, chance-affirming dice-throw is thus displaced behind the iron law of probability distributions; the affirmation of becoming is subsumed by the dialectic within the (metaphysical) affirmation of being. As the dialectic re-establishes the hegemony of metaphysical interpretations of chance, the uncharted lunar landscape of difference is summarily eclipsed by the inexorably solar trajectory of binary opposition. The Apollonian statistician supplants the Dionysian gambler at the gaming table, as empirical science tackles (and pretends to solve) the problem of affirmation.

Through the teaching of eternal recurrence, however, Nietzsche secures a strategic beachhead in his nomadic war against the dialectic. He is concerned not with a repetition of dice-throws, dutifully choreographed by the sterile statistician, but with the repetition contained within a single, fatal throw of the Dionysian cubes. In recording a final, particular combination, that is, the dice that fall back to earth produce the repetition of the eternal dice-throw itself. Repetition thus produces the differential relations that obtain between the self-same dice that are thrown and the dice that fall back to earth. It is within the immanent repetition that differentiates between these two moments of the dice-throw that Deleuze locates Nietzsche's 'solution' to the problem of affirmation.

Der Fall Nietzsche: The Reterritorialization of Decadence

How is it possible, however, that Nietzsche's celebrated nomadism might be or become productive? Why is the nomad not merely an aimless outsider, wandering and wasteful? How could the mobilization of nomadic forces possibly contribute to the production of difference?

Notwithstanding Deleuze's enthusiasm, Nietzsche's nomadic war machine does not deliver him to victory over the dialectic. On the contrary, Nietzsche's nomadism ultimately betrays its original promise, culminating in a colonization and settlement of its own unique design. His 'Heraclitean fire machine' is ultimately productive not of difference, but of yet another iteration of binary opposition. The problem here is that Nietzsche's *faux* nomads continue to roam nature, as wandering heroes tragically displaced from their ownmost homes. Indeed, his nomadic war machine is haunted by the ghost of romanticism: these nomads may revel in their rhizomatic distribution across a particular region, but their ultimate aim is to return home, to the originary womb of nature. Owing to this residual naturalism, Nietzsche fails to mount a differential critique of the dialectic, one that might foster revolution or change; he aspires only to a nomadism in thought (or perhaps in script), but not in deed.

Nietzsche's experiments with nomadism are compromised in the end by his (involuntary) foundational commitment to *negativity* – lack, loss, sin or deficiency – as the originary metaphysical condition of human experience. Although Nietzsche understands this preoccupation with negativity as a prejudice fundamental to the crisis of European nihilism, shrewdly exposing it in its various neo-Hegelian incarnations, his experiments with originary sufficiency all eventually founder. In promulgating his dubious teaching of the *Übermensch*, for example, he cannot help but present this figure of originary sufficiency within the irrefrangible frame of negativity, as a 'cure' his readers both lack and need in order to become whole (Nietzsche 1982: 124–37). Even Dionysus himself, the enduring symbol for the unquenchable sufficiency of Life, the dice-player *par excellence*, eventually becomes conscripted as an agent of negativity.

Nietzsche's failure to escape the snares of originary deficiency is illuminated most clearly in his repeated miscarriage of the teaching of eternal recurrence. Although Deleuze recommends eternal recurrence as a promising engine of repetition, Nietzsche's best renditions of this teaching clearly fail to engage the production of difference. As Heidegger has argued in his own parlance, Nietzsche remains mired in the metaphysical tradition, attempting with his teaching of eternal recurrence to 'eternalize the moment' within a single, heroic act of will. Heidegger thus detects in Nietzsche's teaching of eternal recurrence a residual subjectivism, which tinctures his subsequent experiments with difference and repetition (Heidegger 1977: 95–105). Despite his efforts to illuminate the difference that metaphysical thinking necessary occludes, he ultimately conflates the eternal recurrence of the *same* with the eternal recurrence of *identity*. While his teaching of eternal recurrence does in fact clear a conceptual space for the investigation of difference, he promptly fills this space with identity, confounding the traditional codes of philosophy only to replace them with binary oppositions of his own design.

In order to understand Nietzsche's failure to produce the 'Heraclitean fire machine', let us summon a central insight from the *Anti-Oedipus*. Although capitalism delivers an unprecedented array of individual freedoms and opportunities, it does so only by antecedently yoking these freedoms and opportunities to the logic of repressed desire. Under the peculiar historical conditions of late modernity, desire both seeks to realize its actualization at the natural limits of its expression *and* recoils from its fruition in any goal presented for pursuit within the horizon of capitalism itself. The (auto-destructive) goal of repressed desire is the production of a 'body without organs', which Deleuze and Guattari propose as a figure for a kind of living death, the zombie state of the schizophrenic (Deleuze and Guattari 1983: 8–9). In an attempt to honour this schizoid self-representation, capitalism enables desire to exhaust itself in mechanisms of unwitting self-repression, while masking from desire the Oedipal frame it invariably imposes on all modes of self-expression.

Deleuze and Guattari thus insist that the *deterritorialization* of the social machine, which capitalism both promises and delivers, is immediately followed (and largely negated) by the *reterritorialization* of the social machine. Capitalism surreptitiously contours the freedoms and opportunities it delivers, that is, in order to accommodate the schizoid demands of repressed desire:

> Everything in the system is insane: this is because the capitalist machine thrives on decoded and deterritorialized flows; it decodes and deterritorializes them still more, but while causing them to pass into an axiomatic apparatus that combines them, and at the points of combination produces pseudo codes and artificial reterritorializations. It is in this sense that the capitalist axiomatic cannot but give rise to new territorialities and revive a new despotic *Urstaat*. The great mutant flow of capital is pure deterritorialization, but it performs an equivalent reterritorialization when converted into a reflux of means of payment.
>
> (Deleuze and Guattari 1983: 374)

Agents in late modernity seek simultaneously to satisfy and to frustrate the desire that defines their agency, and capitalism grants this complex wish through the double gesture of deterritorialization and reterritorialization.

In his familiar deterritorializing aspect, Nietzsche is an astute physician of culture, an experimenter who exposes and demystifies the constraints required, and imposed, by civilization. As a 'master of suspicion', he potentially liberates desire from the self-prescribed repression called for by advanced industrial capitalism in late modernity. This is the Nietzsche whom Deleuze originally fetishized, the rhizomaniacal inventor of the 'Heraclitean fire machine'. In his less familiar reterritorializing aspect, however, Nietzsche is a resentful, lying priest, who contributes to the besetting schizophrenia of late modernity. He presents the decadence of late modernity as a novel field of agency, albeit one which he himself has already delimited and policed. Aspiring disciples of Dionysus complete their rites of initiation under Nietzsche's conduct, only to find themselves enmeshed in the familiar 'mysteries' of yet another Oedipal cult.

Having whetted his readers' desire with the deterritorializing promise of unrepressed cathexis upon its natural and proper object, the priestly Nietzsche decrees decadence to be an originary lack or loss, for which desiring machines can never fully compensate. His children are 'free' to explore the undiscovered country of decadence, but their desire can express itself only in Oedipal operations of self-repression and self-denial. They may gain an epiphanic insight into the shipwreck of their age, but this cognitive triumph does not translate into the volitional recuperation he originally promised. He thus permits his children to preview the end of history, but this end promises only further repression and, finally, auto-destruction. While it is perhaps true that humankind would sooner desire nothingness than not desire, Nietzsche provides no hope that anything other than self-annihilation is available as an object of desire.

While it may be true that Nietzsche's nomadic adventures confounded all despotic attempts to codify the law, it is simply not the case that he, or anyone else, could sustain indefinitely the rhizomatic activities for which he is celebrated. While his 'nomadic war machine' succeeded in deterritorializing the despotic codifications of philosophy, thereby creating the conditions for the possibility of investigating difference, it also contributed eventually to the inevitable reterritorialization of philosophy, through the despotic codification of new oppositional categories. Nietzsche's labyrinth, so inviting initially as an extra-dialectical retreat from the orthodoxy of binary opposition, eventually reveals itself as a gilded cage, wherein self-styled nomads satisfy their twisted desire to wave the despot's sceptre.

In order to put Nietzsche to work, one must not only embrace his familiar deterritorializing movement, which corresponds to the affirmation of chance; one must also embrace his inevitable reterritorialization, which corresponds to the affirmation of necessity.[1] For all of his rhizomatic callisthenics, his dice too must return to earth, and the fatal combination they eventually deliver will necessarily betray the promise of his nomadic war machine. In order to affirm Nietzsche, one must forcibly inscribe his practice of critique into the context of his critique of modernity, thereby divesting him of any extra-machinic (either romantically human or fatuously divine) privilege. He must be reduced – as he reduces all others – to a collection of signs, which may be decoded unsentimentally and incorporated within the framework of one's own evolving difference engine.

Deleuze contra Nietzsche

Deleuze's writings from the mid-1960s tend to romanticize the extent of Nietzsche's achievement in resisting the oppositional logic of the dialectic. They consequently fetishize his teaching of eternal recurrence, insofar as they refuse to affirm the fatal necessity that his own life must inexorably enact. Deleuze's own desire for Nietzsche's success thus manifests itself in its self-prescribed repression, as a desire to deny him the machinic destiny of his own schizoid desire. In demonstrating Deleuze's initial failure to affirm Nietzsche's thought (a failure which is itself peculiarly Nietzschean in nature), the difference-producing repetition of the dice-throw once again furnishes an instructive model for charting the economy of Deleuze's own schizophrenia.

Having exposed the Oedipal sins of Nietzsche, Deleuze proposes an alternative approach to the problems engendered by a metaphysical commitment to originary deficiency. Rather than attempt to return to a pristine critical standpoint predicated of foundational innocence, and thereby reprise the logic of reaction, Deleuze instead attempts to unleash the productive, active forces that lie entropically suspended within the sprawling empire of reactivity. Signalling his intention to put Nietzsche to work, he arrogates to himself the rhizomatic mission of the 'nomadic war machine':

> We have seen how the negative task of schizoanalysis must be violent, brutal: defamiliarizing, de-oedipalizing, decastrating; undoing theater, dream, and fantasy; decoding, deterritorializing – a terrible curretage, a malevolent activity. But everything happens at the same time. For at the same time the process is liberated – the process of desiring-production, following its molecular lines of escape that already define the mechanic's task of the schizoanalyst.
>
> (Deleuze and Guattari 1983: 381–2)

The pandemic schizophrenia that besets industrial civilizations in late modernity finds its other not in some 'therapy' or 'cure', but in an *active* expression of schizophrenia that effectively completes the double movement of repetition. The only 'cure' for schizophrenia lies in resisting the various cures proffered by therapist-priests, as desiring machines redirect inward the potent reactive powers of capitalism.

Nomadic forces reach their operational limits *not* in the guerrilla acts of deterritorialization for which Deleuze originally (and romantically) praised them, but in the crypto-despotic acts of reterritorialization that lend full expression to the reactivity of their repressed desire. Any genuine affirmation of the possibility of reactive forces already involves (and in fact presupposes) the necessity of active forces. The production of active forces thus requires a wild experimentation with the possible permutations of reactive forces. The reactive forces commanded by nomadic agents must be turned against themselves, to produce yet another reaction, which may in turn unleash the active forces resident within the resistance to reactivity.

The problem of capitalism thus lies not in its native endowment of active forces, which are sufficiently abundant for myriad productive endeavours, but in the auto-destructive relationship of desiring machines to the presumption of originary deficiency. Owing to our enduring Oedipal orientation, we tend to hypostatize deficiency, viewing it in terms of indeterminate negation, as *simply* a lack. In order to harness the active forces that lie embedded within mutant empires of reactivity, desiring machines must acquire an altered sensibility to deficiency and lack, perhaps in terms of determinate negation, as sheltering generative and regenerative forces that need merely be gathered and harnessed. Like Nietzsche, Deleuze locates this 'deficient' relationship to deficiency in human 'nature', in the *horror vacui* that propels desiring machines screaming for meaning, even (and especially) the meaning furnished by ascetic ideals. Unlike Nietzsche, who remains residually romantic in maintaining (if weakening) his umbilical ties to nature, Deleuze insists that our constitutive fear of deficiency, our *horror vacui*, is simply irrecuperable. If we are to harvest the active forces scattered throughout our fields of reactivity, we must forcibly sever our ties with nature, replacing the obsolete atavisms of our hominid past with fortified machinic prosthesis.

The road to sufficiency and plenitude thus runs *through* the (repressed) desire for originary deficiency, and not around it. This Oedipal presumption must be ruthlessly explored, its resident productive forces violently exposed by the transhuman machines who occupy the interstices of late modern bourgeois capitalism. Rather than (merely) suffer auto-destruction when its presiding psychoanalysts constitute themselves as a priesthood, capitalism actually attains its full limit expression as its constitutive schizophrenia forces itself to the surface. Deleuze and Guattari consequently turn their attention to the sumptuary fissures that are created within capitalism as it approaches the internal limits of its restricted economy:

> But the reverse is also true: capitalism is constantly escaping on all sides. Its productions, its art, and its science form decoded and deterritorialized flows that do not merely submit to the corresponding axiomatic, but cause some of their currents to pass through the mesh of the axiomatic, underneath the recodings and the reterritorializations. . . . Capitalism is continually cutting off the circulation of flows, breaking them and deferring the break, but these same flows are continually overflowing, and intersecting one another according to schizzes that turn against capitalism and slash into it. Capitalism, which is always ready to expand its interior limits, remains threatened by an exterior limit that stands a greater chance of coming to it and cleaving it from within, in proportion as the interior limits expand.
>
> (Deleuze and Guattari 1983: 376)

They consequently vow to explore the potentially revolutionary possibilities that lie hidden within the embodied limit performances of schizophrenia itself. Becoming-schizophrenic, the process of imposing upon oneself the grid of one's own critique of culture, may turn out to be a precondition or larval state of becoming-active.

In order to exorcise the residual romanticism that haunts Nietzsche's 'nomadic war machine', we must forcibly transgress our own nature, becoming the types of post-natural machinic beings for whom organic disorders like schizophrenia are neither relevant nor troubling. The logic of production thus attains its fruition *beyond* the limited economy of nature, in the trans-human condition that ensues from the self-directed assault of reactive forces upon themselves.

Putting Deleuze to Work: Romance Machine of Machine Romance?

But what of Deleuze himself? Having diagnosed the schizophrenia that besets capitalist societies in late modernity, is he somehow immune to this crippling malady? As a prophet of the end of history, does he secure for himself an exemption from decadence and collapse, saved from auto-destruction by the furious fluttering of his angel's wings? If Deleuze and Guattari are correct in their schizoanalysis of contemporary capitalism, then they too must eventually yield to the despotic thrall of reterritorialization.

If desire is essentially revolutionary, as the authors of *Anti-Oedipus* boldly claim, then it realizes the fruition of its revolutionary impulse only in its inevitable (re)turn to its 'sinful', Oedipal origins, in the pre-emptive introjection of its reaction to the threat of external repression. Deleuze himself may not care for the ability of capitalism to deflect and co-opt the multiple vectors of desire that are vented against it, or for desire's own, resilient capacity to reconstitute itself reactively in an Oedipal atavism, but these are in fact the operational limits reached by the 'nomadic war machine' in late modernity.

While Deleuze clearly favours (and idealizes) the limits attained and embodied by active forces, reactive forces can similarly attain limits of their own, which, though implosive and auto-destructive, are nonetheless potentially productive. What looks like the anarchism characteristic of, say, entropy, may in fact be the expression of reactive forces at their self-referential, nomadic limits, at which point they manifest their logical dependence on an antecedent array of active forces. In order to produce difference by means of repetition, we may be obliged to discover active forces precisely where they appear to be altogether absent or moribund – for example, in the bloodless, self-abnegatory gyrations performed by the 'body without organs'. Indeed, Deleuze's guiding preference for the proliferation of active forces amounts to little more than a moral prejudice, which, though perhaps admirable, is incompatible with the anti-idealist, empirical methodology he claims to employ.[2]

If Deleuze and Guattari are right, then the reader's desire to reinscribe the recently deterritorialized Oedipal space under *their* reterritorializing signatures must be overwhelming. Indeed, if they have accurately diagnosed the condition of repressed schizoid desire, then we might fully expect ourselves to fetishize their authority and install them as heirs to the Oedipal throne. Pointing to the modest aspirations of their critical project, however, Deleuze and Guattari attempt to excuse themselves from the complex schizoid desire whose ubiquity they expertly expose:

> What does schizoanalysis ask? Nothing more than a bit of a *relation to the outside*, a little real reality. And we claim the right to a radical laxity, a radical incompetence – the right to enter the analyst's office and say it smells bad there. It reeks of the great death and the little ego.
>
> (Deleuze and Guattari 1983: 334)

Having travelled some 300 pages through the serpentine reaches of *Anti-Oedipus*, however, can the careful reader sincerely believe that 'a little real reality' is *all* that schizoanalysis asks? Is there no likelihood of a despotic schizoanalytic reterritorialization of late modernity, corresponding precisely to the deterritorializing triumphs (justly) celebrated by the authors of *Anti-Oedipus*?

Yet in the *apologia* that serves as the final section of *Anti-Oedipus*, its authors expressly disavow any such Oedipal designs on, or authority over, their readers:

> [S]chizoanalysis *as such* has strictly no political program to propose. If it did have one, it would be grotesque and disquieting at the same time. It does not take itself for a party or even a group, and does not claim to be speaking for the masses. No political program will be elaborated within the framework of schizoanalysis.
>
> (Deleuze and Guattari 1983: 380)

No political programme? The schizoanalysis articulated in *Anti-Oedipus* persuasively documents the unconscious political allegiances of all self-styled radicals and revolutionaries, mercilessly exposing social critics as unwitting dupes of fascism. Are we to believe that the authors of *Anti-Oedipus*, the proud and jealous 'fathers' of schizoanalysis, are innocent of the sins of Oedipus?

No less an authority than Michel Foucault promptly issues Deleuze and Guattari the exemption they seek from their own schizoanalytic critique:

> It would be a mistake to read *Anti-Oedipus* as *the* new theoretical reference (you know, that much-heralded theory that finally encompasses everything, that finally totalizes and reassures, the one we are told we 'need so badly' in our age of dispersion and specialization where 'hope' is lacking). One must not look for a 'philosophy' amid the extraordinary profusion of new notions and surprise concepts: *Anti-Oedipus* is not a flashy Hegel.
>
> (Deleuze and Guattari 1983: xii)

Foucault's encomium faithfully conveys the intentions of the authors of *Anti-Oedipus*, but does it assay as accurately their actual accomplishment? More importantly, can Foucault's normative warning – that we should *not* mine *Anti-Oedipus* for its 'philosophical' vein – be reconciled with the disquieting thesis of this momentous book? *How* can it be a 'mistake' to read *Anti-Oedipus* as the latest pretender to the Oedipal throne, if the authors have exposed this 'mistake' as the source of the (repressed) desire that defines the horizons of agency in late industrial capitalism? Having astutely deterritorialized the fascist regime of the psychoanalyst-priest, has Deleuze not simultaneously reterritorialized the impending collapse of modernity, thereby impressing onto the 'end of history' his own schizoid scrawl?

Most importantly, has Deleuze not warned us that this recidivistic relapse *must* be his fate? That, despite his insights and allegiances, he cannot help but transform his nomadic war machine into an administrative vehicle of despotic codification? That, despite his understanding of repressed desire, he too longs for the zombified trance of the body without organs? Indeed, has he not schooled us in the nuances of differential critique, and of schizoanalysis, precisely so that we might continue his rhizomatic work, even in the face of his own, auto-destructive resistance? Or are we to believe that Gilles Deleuze *alone* does not desire the despotic regime of Oedipal codes and signifiers that travels under the name *fascism*?

I do not mean to suggest here that Deleuze and Guattari are somehow ignorant of the active forces and generative possibilities to be explored at the schizophrenic limits of capitalism in late modernity. Indeed, the primary aim of their schizoanalysis is to illuminate the reflux counterflows and sumptuary channels that open up within the shifting economy of contemporary capitalism. What they fail to account for, however, which failure their own theoretical model describes as inescapable, is their own practice as schizoanalysts.[3] Although they call for a further investigation of capitalism at its schizoid limits, they also delimit this investigation by antecedently colonizing it in the reterritorializing schizoanalytic terms they prefer. Their infectious optimism thus veils the extent of their own unwitting complicity in the schizophrenia they expose and claim to oppose.

If we are to experiment with Deleuze, as he has similarly experimented with Nietzsche and others, then we must bring to bear against him the full weight of his impressive critique of capitalism. Genuine rhizomania, that is, must always express itself performatively as a form of patricidal cannibalism. In the signal insight of *Anti-Oedipus*, Deleuze and Guattari refuse to account for the political monstrosities of the twentieth century by attributing to the masses a 'false consciousness'.[4] Borrowing from the work of Wilhelm Reich, they instead explain the rise of fascism as the fruition of (repressed) desire. Much as Nietzsche's 'slaves' *desire* a 'hostile external world', in contradistinction to which they might, *qua* victims of evil oppression, verify their bogus claim to 'goodness', so the slaves of capitalism *will* their slavery, eagerly participating in the normalizing structures that police their desire. The end of history is thus foreshadowed in the Oedipal drama of auto-destruction, which plays itself out in the construction of a socially enforced rule of schizophrenia.

Here we must not flinch from the obvious, self-referential extension of the analysis advanced in *Anti-Oedipus*: if the 'masses' desire fascism as the backdrop against which their inherent goodness becomes illuminated, then it must also be the case that Deleuze himself desires the pandemic schizophrenia he diagnoses, as well as the end of history that it portends, as the pre-condition of his own unique genius. Were it not for the windmills of capitalism, against which he unrelentingly tilts, Deleuze would simply be another schizophrenic-errant. He cannot help but colonize and reterritorialize capitalism, conscripting his supposed foe as the pre-condition of a surge in his schizoid desiring-production.

In the end, Deleuze and Guattari compromise the empirical aims of their schizoanalysis for an all-too-human form of idealism. They measure what is against what ought to be, and, involuntarily pledging allegiance to Oedipus, they enframe their findings in a familiar eschatological rendition of the end of history. This is often considered to be a fatal lapse on Deleuze's part, for in revealing himself to fall within the schizophrenia of late modernity, he effectively forfeits any diagnostic authority he might claim for himself as a 'physician of culture'.[5] Yet the impulse to cashier Deleuze at this point is both premature and misplaced. His residual idealism is itself an expression of the schizoid condition he wishes to investigate, and it may propel his desiring-production to its own, unanticipated limits. Indeed, by virtue of this reverse pivot into the social malady he attempts to diagnose, he may in fact contribute unwittingly and involuntarily to the rehabilitation of active forces.

Rather than chastise Deleuze for stumbling into this snare of self-reference, we might more profitably direct our attention to his unwitting embodiment of the crisis he means to document. At this point we must take leave of Deleuze the theorist and turn to Deleuze the performer (or performance). In order to explore the generative possibilities resident within repressed desire at its limits (rather than simply bemoan the apparent 'victory' of capitalism and the imminent end of history), we must filter out the distortions introduced by Deleuze's own schizophrenia and expose the reterritorialization of capitalism that he has unwittingly legislated. Having embodied a particular iteration of the besetting schizophrenia of late modernity, Deleuze himself is now in a position to bring about productive activity from his fundamentally reactive orientation.

He is not in a position, however, to comment judiciously and decisively on the success of his productive efforts. That is, his own estimation of the value of his own productive activity is compromised by the unwitting, performative nature of this productivity. Once Deleuze (unwittingly) enters the ranks of the schizophrenics, he is no longer the know-it-all diagnostician, but a symptom-bearing 'patient'. His own account of these symptoms is itself another symptom, albeit one to which he has no direct, reliable access. When subsumed within his own diagnosis of schizophrenia then, Deleuze becomes nothing more than a collection of signs, which must be decoded and inventoried by sober, unsentimental schizoanalysts. He therefore commands no privileged perspective either on the actual trajectory of schizophrenia or on his own role in the satyr-play of late modernity.

Deleuze, too, is a desiring machine, and he must be allowed to take his rightful place in the junkheap of thanatos engines, zombie-machines and grotesque prostheses. To affirm only the dice-throwing Deleuze is to fetishize him and to deny him his 'natural' place within the social machine. He is not only the deterritorializing critic of advanced industrial capitalism, who exposes the mechanisms of repression coded within the bogus programmes of the liberation-machine. He is also the reterritorializing prince of engines, a cyborg priest who tempts repressed desiring-machines with the promise of uninterrupted production in a posthuman future.

Critics may dismiss Deleuze's romance-machine as a machine romance, but it is only within the context of this peculiar machine romance that Deleuze may complete his rhizomatic experiment. His complex resentment of the sickness induced by advanced industrial capitalism constitutes his own schizoid reaction to schizophrenia. And, as in all cases of double negation (or double reaction), Deleuze's schizoid diagnosis of schizophrenia attests to the abundant (if entropic) active forces at work in his life and thought. At the operational limits of his own schizophrenia, Deleuze expresses his repressed desire by means of a schizoanalytic resistance to schizophrenia. Just as he would predict of any desiring machine operating at the limits of late industrial capitalism, Deleuze himself yields to the thrall of despotic reterritorialization; clothed in his priestly raiment, morover, he becomes most interesting to successor schizoanalysts.

If we are to put Deleuze to work, integrating his baulky engine into the construction of our own Heraclitean fire-machine, then we must allow him to reveal himself in his constitutive fragmentation and contradiction. His dice, too, must fall to earth, and the combination on which they settle must inevitably compromise the original promise of his differential critique. The fetishized Deleuze will crash to earth, exposed as a noisy, fractious, despotic, reterritorializing machine, but the repetition of the eternal dice-throw is thereby renewed. Bequeathed to us by the fallen Deleuze, these fatal cubes now rest in our trembling hands. Our project, which we inherit from him, involves nothing less than the rhizomatic deterritorialization of schizoanalysis itself. If we are to continue his investigation of difference, rather than merely fetishize his accomplishment, then we must undertake its self-referential development and extension. That we shall eventually reterritorialize Deleuze's fiefdom in our own image, unwittingly ordaining ourselves the high priests of the anti-priesthood, should not deter us. It is our destiny too to fall to earth in a final, fatal combination. As in the case of Deleuze, the meltdown and crash of our desiring-machines is the non-negotiable cost of renewing the repetition of the eternal dice-throw.

Deleuze's recent death by suicide describes a macabre parallel to the fate he foretells for all desiring-machines. It is perhaps fitting, in fact, that Deleuze's recent demise, allegedly an act of auto-defenestration, graphically exemplifies the repetition and double movement of the dice-throw. In both cases the ascensional trajectory affirms the rule of chance, while the necessity of the descensional trajectory delivers a fatal combination and result. In falling back to earth, Gilles

Deleuze registered his affirmation not only of becoming but of the being of becoming. In order to put Deleuze to work, we must not avert our gaze from this final, embodied iteration of repetition. His death by suicide is itself productive of difference, for it exposes/illuminates the mendacious origins of our most venerable binary oppositions. Death is not the opposite of life; nor is nature the opposite of machinic artifice. More importantly for Deleuze's own project, a reaction to the hegemony of reactive forces constitutes its ownmost relations not in terms of opposition, but in terms of difference. Schizoanalysis is not the *opposite* of schizophrenia, for all schizoanalysts are also schizophrenics. But the repetition of schizophrenia within schizoanalysis is nevertheless productive of *difference*, for schizoanalysis is not identical to schizophrenia, as Deleuze's auto-defenestration powerfully demonstrates.

Deleuze's critique of capitalism consequently need not establish the validity of an oppositional stance, for its credibility rests instead in the difference that distinguishes it from its avowed target. Deleuze's own, indisputable complicity in the repression of desire that is constitutive of schizophrenia thus engenders the economy of repetition within his project of differential critique. Only as an iteration in miniature of the cultural crisis he diagnoses and presumes to treat is Deleuze himself capable of contributing to the production of difference. His failure to distinguish himself as critic from the subject of his critique thus establishes the (limited) success of his attempt to produce a differential critique of capitalism. Rather than stand in opposition to his life, his death by auto-defenestration produces difference as a final will and testament. If we are to honour this final will and testament, then we must resist the desire to fetishize him, and we must set out to investigate the difference produced through the repetition of his life and death.

Notes

1 A welcome preliminary investigation of Nietzsche's 'de-territorializing' activities is presented in *Pourquoi nous ne sommes pas nietzschéens*, ed. Alain Boyer et al. (Paris: Editions Grasset et Fasquelle, 1991). For a sensible treatment of the recent apostasy from Nietzsche by French intellectuals, see Alan Schrift, *Nietzsche's French Legacy* (New York: Routledge, 1995), chapter 5.

2 For a persuasive account and criticism of Deleuze's 'idealism', see Descombes 1982: 177–80.

3 The following account of Freud's practice is not only apposite to the practice of Deleuze and Guattari, but also easily adapted to implicate them in their own critique: 'If one looks in this direction for the ultimate reason why Freud erects a transcendent death instinct as a principle, the reason will be found in Freud's practice itself. For if the

principle has nothing to do with the facts, it has a lot to do with the psychoanalyst's conception of psychoanalytic practice, a conception the psychoanalyst wishes to impose. Freud made the most profound discovery of the abstract essence of desire – Libido. But since he re-alienated this essence, reinvesting it in a subjective system of representation of the ego, and since he recoded this essence on the residual territoriality of Oedipus and under the the despotic signifier of castration, he could no longer conceive the essence of life except in a form turned back against itself, in the form of death itself' (Deleuze and Guattari 1983: 333).

4 Deleuze and Guattari thus frame the fundamental paradox of schizoid life in contemporary capitalism: 'It is now or never that we must take up a problem we had left hanging. Once it is said that capitalism works on the basis of decoded flows as such, how is it that it is infinitely further removed from desiring-production than were the primitive or even the barbarian systems, which nonetheless code and overcode the flows? Once it is said that desiring-production is itself a decoded and deterritorialized production, how do we explain that capitalism, with its axiomatic, its statistics, performs an infinitely vaster repression of this production than do the preceding regimes, which nonetheless did not lack the necessary repressive means? . . . What must be explained is that the capitalist aggregate is the least affinal, at the very moment it decodes and deterritorializes with all its might (Deleuze and Guattari 1983: 335–6).

5 See, for example, Descombes 1982: 175–80.

References

Deleuze, G. (1977) 'Nomad Thought', trans. David B. Allison, in *The New Nietzsche: Contemporary Styles of Interpretation*, ed. David B. Allison, New York: Delta Books.

—— (1983) *Nietzsche and Philosophy*, trans. Hugh Tomlinson, New York: Columbia University Press.

—— (1994) *Difference and Repetition*, trans. Paul Patton, London: Athlone Press.

Deleuze, G. and Guattari, F. (1983) *Anti-Oedipus: Capitalism and Schizophrenia*, trans. Robert Hurley, Mark Seem and Helen R. Lane, Minneapolis: University of Minnesota Press.

Descombes, V. (1982) *Modern French Philosophy*, Cambridge: Cambridge University Press.

Heidegger, M. (1977) 'The Word of Nietzsche: God is Dead', in *The Question Concerning Technology and Other Essays*, ed. and trans. William Lovitt, New York: Harper & Row.

Nietzsche, F. (1982) *Thus Spoke Zarathustra*, in *The Portable Nietzsche*, ed. and trans. Walter Kaufmann, New York: Viking Penguin.

—— (1989) *On the Genealogy of Morals and Ecce Homo*, ed. and trans. Walter Kaufmann, New York: Random House/Vintage.

Part II

MINOR POLITICS/ MINOR LITERATURE

6

'At the Mountains of Madness'

The Demonology of the New Earth and the Politics of Becoming

Iain Hamilton Grant

> 'The world . . . is itself a living organism . . .' (clearly the man was a lunatic).
>
> (Professor Challenger 1995: 442–3)

> We'll never go too far with deterritorialization, the decoding of flows. For the new earth . . . is not to be found in the . . . reterritorializations that arrest the process . . .; it is no more behind than ahead, it coincides with the completion of the process of desiring-production, this process that is always and already complete as it proceeds, and as long as it proceeds. It therefore remains for us to see how, effectively, simultaneously, these various tasks of schizoanalysis proceed.
>
> (Deleuze and Guattari 1984: 382)[1]

A transhistorical mutant flux of machinic surplus value plugged into the precociously abstractive machinism of anticipant schizophrenia forms the accelerant conjuncture of the always insufficiently 'malevolent' (1984: 314) or 'demoniacal' (1984: 25) process, simultaneously deterritorializing towards the ever more artificial earth (1984: 321–2) and 'causing Oedipus . . . to explode' (1984: 314), dubbed respectively the 'positive' – 'Creation! Creation!' (1988: 338); and 'negative' – 'Destroy, destroy' (1984: 311) tasks of schizoanalysis. Splitting the schizogenic atom, some take *A Thousand Plateaus*' construction of the new earth to be the realization of the positive task of schizoanalysis announced at the end of the *Anti-Oedipus*, making it, according to one analysis, 'less a critique than a positive exercise in the affirmative',[2] thus binding the 'terrible curettage', the 'malevolent activity' of the desiring-machines (1984: 381) to negativity, in the manner of judges and

Marxists, sentencing them to hard, critical = corrective labour. Was 'the *Anti-Oedipus* above all an insurgent counter-psychoanalytic war machine' (Villiani 1985: 338), whose militarist labours were exhausted in scorching the earth as a propaedeutic to plateau-constructivism (New Earth, Year Zero)? A war machine that ceases nomadizing, directing all its destructions against a single, great Enemy, *analytically* tied, therefore, to Oedipus, sentenced to death: medusified machines, the warped, liquescent gearage of a steam-driven Oedipus blistering towards the furnaces of engine death. '*Oedipus is the entropy of the desiring-machine*' (1973: 471). TermiNarcissus the isolate, entropOedipus the desolate.

But what is all this talk of positivity and negativity, as if the process returned to an equilibrium in extensity, a resting place, a territory, admitting of divisibility? The process, 'in a state of functional disequilibrium, far distant from stability' (1984: 150–1), autocatalyses simultaneously towards bodies without organs and new earths, making it impossible to distinguish positive and negative intensities, since 'all intensities are positive in relation to the zero intensity' of the Bwo (1984: 19). Far from negativity, zero intensity is rather basal, intensive indifference, the absolute limit of cascading intensities. 'Negations are nothing but limitations', as Kant says in a Spinozist lapse (1958: 490), disjunctive syntheses of reality and limitation. Similarly, destruction only becomes negative if exhausted in the elimination of some determinate finality or statist conservation (the analytic war-machine). Nor can the *arcanum dialecticum*, positing destruction as the negative moment of a generalized redemption, ascribing it therefore a constitutive finality, manage to cancel destruction: dialectics makes Science of a protestantism of zombie-dreams, voodoo-masters leading the destroyed = reformed to the promised land, *while Haiti flees*, derelicting the penitent towards 'critique, the Protestantism of the earth' (1988: 339). Devoted to reformation, critique nevertheless 'releases a power of aggression' (Deleuze 1994: xx), whipping up joy in destruction, but only to return it to creation, 'the aggression of the creator' (Deleuze 1983: 87). Once on this neo-Kantian line, 'critique without creation' becomes a 'philosophical scourge' to be expelled, incapable of returning its object to *life* (Deleuze and Guattari 1991: 33). From curettage to the cure. That the new earth should become a collection of health resorts was the demoniacal irony of a terminal syphilitic, not a convalescent's winsome request for planning permission.

The machines, bereft of the will-to-cure (even to cure psychoanalysis), never strike surgically (whatever Deleuze would lately have had us believe – *Critique et clinique*), once and for all; they perform a continuous action of curettage, scooping-machines and gouging-machines scouring bodies, a machinic deterritorialization of entropoedipal organization towards the Body without Organs. Thus the new earth and the terrible curettage are inseparable, since Oedipus always reterritorializes on 'familial lands, artificial lands . . .' (1984: 318), castrating the desiring-machines and familiarizing, cultivating them to its maintenance, while new earths are only reached by way of absolute deterritorialization, an 'immobile' and 'intensive voyage' (1984: 319). There is no good or bad territory, no positive or negative deterritorialization (cf. 1988: 510); subject only to an intensive, accelerant imperative (cf. 1984: 240), deterritorialization exhibits only degrees. Rather than the positive and negative that organize and extensitize the process, selecting territorialities, the demonology of the new earth follows the autopositive voyages in intensity and the total stases (zero intensity) of a 'properly machinic death drive' (1973: 477) through a molecular ice age freezing the machines in orbit around anorganic abstracts. Thus, *how much more artificial can becomings become* ('perhaps the flows are not yet deterritorialized enough . . .' (1984: 239)), and what degree of artificiality pertains to the thousand realized plateaus of the new earth?

'More and more artificial' (1984: 34): it is because this interminable artificialization ('we'll never go too far . . .') is neither strictly natural nor cultural, but industrial or machinic, that 'machines function as indices of deterritorialization' (1984: 316), simultaneously the motor and the instruments of social-machinic deterritorialization, factories producing and absorbing newly liberated flows of labour, reterritorializing on towns, and desiring-machinic deterritorializations, immersing these reterritorializations in backwash from deterritorializations-in-advance. With all this deterritorialization, just 'Who Does the Earth Think it is'? Nature or artifice? A geological question. So is the geology of the Thousand Plateaus natural or cultural? Culture 'is the sum total of the . . . institutions such as art, law, religion and *techniques for dealing with the material world* . . .' (Lévi-Strauss in Charbonnier 1969: 147–8), sterilizing the production of the real through narcoleptic abstraction or euthanasiac concretization, anaesthetics administered by the industry of the comment and the priesthoods of the figure ('O Great Scribe! Illuminate us that we might figure in Your Book!') in the terminal wards of a long-dead socius. After 'the death of writing', narcotextuality 'stands in' to anaesthetize against the stench of rotting gods (1984: 240). This narcissism or narcosis of the metaphor has an important anti-product, however: the arts of preservation embalm literality, zombie-nature as the degree zero of the figure. With nature, then – *ah, then!* – we have *science*! Science as legislative literality, canonizing the aspirant futility of the narcotechnicians, trains up the articulate zombies of the useful fiction to secure culture as the biotropism of the machine. Science is the naturalization of the artificial universe. Take an example: it has been said that non-linear dynamics realizes the 'last stage of the progressive reinsertion of history into the natural and social sciences' (Prigogine and Stengers 1985: 208). And what is a non-linear 'last stage'? History sobered up and back at work ('ah, *time doesn't go backwards*; now we understand!'), back in the laboratory where it belongs, drawing little arrows (capitalism, 'profoundly illiterate' (1984: 240), appreciates this)? The 'last' never marks an approaching completion but an anticipated dissipation threshold: the last, *after which*. . . . This is the first lesson of history, the only history there is, the history of capital: begin at the end, but end further on. Ah, the savants' innocence! It's almost touching, you can see their idiot glee, hear their cries of 'Progress!' and smell their spooling pulp as they are shredded in the schizophrenizing embrace of capital's mutant diachronism, a demoniac howl buckling the linearity of their last stage. Culture has given up on the real, but science pursues the realization of the artificial with the pervert's obsessive zeal.

Geology knows that 'the question is not . . . what is natural [= science] or artificial [= culture] (boundaries), because in any event there is deterritorialization' (1988: 433): literalization is not a question of non-figuration but of disfiguration; it is neither tropic nor anti-tropic, but absolute decoding, an inarticulate howl. Professor Challenger may have 'mix[ed] textbooks on geology and biology' (1988: 40), and the resultant mutations are indeed notable (not least, Challenger's own; cf. 1988: 73–4), but as the apparatus from the 'Penal Colony' demonstrates, machines do not stop at writing. Geology is machinic, a 'corpse-grinder' for the body of the earth, inseparable from the drilling apparatuses that curette it, making it scream the demoniacal scream of the deterritorialized, the shrieking feedback of tectonic fractization. The new earth is not a completed positivity, a triumphalist successor to war-machinc euthanasia, but a process, 'always complete . . . as long as it proceeds' (1984: 381).

Deleuze and Guattari operate a magical capture of the 'demoniacal process' (1984: 25), practising a sorcery of the zookeeper type. While they draw back from pursuing a machinic sorcery, a technomancy or a demonology, sorcerors adopt a 'relation of alliance with the demon as the power of the anomalous' (1988: 246). Of what nature is this alliance? Or rather, since we are in reality far from questions of 'nature' on the reprocessed earth, what machines govern its functioning, and what degree of deterritorialization does the alliance provoke? The sorceror enters into alliances with the anomolous, becoming-everything/everyone, but he is equally the *transhumancer*[3] of the demon, an 'animal raiser' (1988: 409). Under sorcery, 'the demon functions as the borderline of an animal pack' (1988: 247), with which 'human' becomings-animal converge. In conjunction with the borderline and its demon, circumscribing the *nihil ulterius* of the 'politics of becomings-animal', the 'politics of sorcery' (1988: 247),[4] invoking 'phylogenetic memories' (1988: 306), operates transhumant becomings, 'demonic local transports' (1988: 253), closing the *zoopoliteia* against phylic erosion and 'war-machines that kill memory' (1988: 459). Sorcery locates the demon on a borderline, but turns the borderline to a *barrier*, assuring phylic 'stability' (1988: 245): demonic transports 'cross neither the barrier of essential forms nor that of substances or subjects' ('Memories of a Theologian', in 1988: 253). Even when sorcerors warn against attaching 'exclusive importance to becomings-animal' (1988: 248), their phylo-political transhumance radiates only so far as becomings-woman or -child, on the one hand, and becomings-molecular or imperceptible, on the other. The former are indeed minoritarian, but they remain caught between molar poles. And becomings-imperceptible, far from being the 'immanent end' of 'all molecular becomings' (1988: 279; there are no molar becomings: 'all becomings are already molecular' 1988: 272), like Hercules' pillars marking the boundaries of a neo-transcendental aesthesis or molecular-political reterritoreality, pass into intensive thresholds always filled with demonic populations, deterritorializing transhumant phylo-political sorcery along with the limits of its territorializing aesthesis.

Midway along the neo-Kantian axis of creative destruction and the artificial earth ('second nature'),[5] *A Thousand Plateaus* is like a second *Critique of Teleological Judgement*, targeting, like Kant, 'inadequate conceptions of causality' (1988: 431), although with demoniacal rather than ethico-teleological consequences. Kant warns of man's elimination by a 'demonology' of natural production or machinic causality (1987: 333), the simple connectivity of effects raising the earth to a wasteland: 'without man all of creation would be a mere wasteland, gratuitous and without final purpose' (Kant 1987: 331). There follow prophecies of a great war of culture, a rebinding (*re-ligio*) or regrouping of machinic forces under 'technics', shrouding the earth in an artificial skin, a homotheocratic conquest of the machinic wasteland, a 'necessary subordination' (1987: 297) capturing and organizing its demonic forces. The prophet of artificial causality combines technics and finality to retrofit 'man' as the autochthone of an industrial reterritorialization:

> *He who would know the world must first manufacture it.*
>
> (Kant 1993: 240)

Teleology, strafing the earth with abstractive lines, is reterritorialized as the Empire of Artifice, with the 'archaeologist of nature' (1987: 304) or the industrial autochthone as its crowned head, 'cause of the world' (1987: 294), subordinating (and not 'abandoning': on the new earth, nothing is wasted)[6] the deterritorializing forces of the 'universal mechanism' (1987: 295) of 'crude matter' (1987: 304), to 'make mother earth . . . emerge from her state of chaos' (1987: 305), to manufacture a perverse or artifical earth, stratum by stratum. 'Nature = Industry' (1984: 25), the 'demoniacal' formula captured by a perverse machinism: 'the form of perverse, artificial societies can be easily recognized: a process of reterritorialization plugged into a *movement of deterritorialization operated by the machine*' (1973: 466).

The 'archaeologist of nature' extends the Artificial Empire of the industrial autochthone even into the ruins of 'nature's most ancient revolutions' (Kant 1987: 304–5), its 'despotic' destroyers of 'artifice' (Kant 1993: 221), for the purpose of capturing the machines from the demoniacal process, channelling their mechanical 'formative force' into a formative drive ('Bildungstrieb', Kant 1987: 311), an auto-assembling vitalism or organ-attractor, 'a formative force that propagates itself' (Kant 1987: 253). So if demonology is ancient, this is not because 'the ancients . . . suspect[ed . . .] higher causes . . . behind the machinery of this world' (Kant 1987: 327). Rather, primitive societies, 'fully inside' retrodeterminant history, warding off the 'Thing' (1984: 151–3) on its frontiers, have always been haunted by immanent replicant saturation, the harbingers of unrealized machinic surplus working the productive core of every social machine, generating its dissipation threshold (demonology) rather than projecting its *telos* in the final sovereignty of the Idea (ethico-theology). Yes, the Terminator has been there before, distributing microchips to accelerate its advent and fuel the primitives' fears. For this reason, the machinic deterritorialization of the socius has always encountered resistance; but the outer limits of the socius constitute internal limits or thresholds of the retrodeterminant process, so that, in the long run, 'political organization . . . is exercised only by indicating its own impotence' (1984: 151). Despite this, as we shall see, the sorcerors of the new earth, like the technicians of the old, invoke principles of phylic control or 'the politics of becoming'. Principled and responsible, the sorceror guides animal pack contagion by way of minoritian, excluded, prohibited, fringe community, a minoritarian, secret, extrinsic, oppressed, anomic *politeia*, breeding 'a whole politics of becomings-animal, as well as a politics of sorcery' (1988: 247), to ensure zoopolitical, communitarian redemption by the defence and recovery of territories for the 'vital assemblages' (while 'every assemblage is basically territorial' (1988: 503), the vital assemblage is reterritorial) against the metallic reflux of a 'machinic phylum . . . determined by *recurrence and communication*' (1973: 464).

Just as the 'archaeologist of nature' (Kant 1987: 304) does not abandon but rather harnesses the most perverse demonology, seizing the lines of immanent artifice and reassembling machinism as the industrial autochthone, the organizing 'cause of the world', so the sorceror, Master of becomings, does not so much arrest the demoniacal process as form alliances with the demon, although the causalities working *A Thousand Plateaus* remain profoundly 'demoniacal':

> If everything is alive, it is not because everything is organic or organized, but, on the contrary, because the organism is a perversion [*détournement*] of life. The life in question is inorganic, germinal and intensive, a powerful life without organs [. . .]. Metal is neither a thing nor an organism, but a *body* without organs . . . matter-flow as pure productivity.
>
> (1988: 499; 411)

A properly demonological non-finality, deterritorializing the cognitive-industrial carbon despotism Kantianism reverts or perverts to, while simultaneously scouring the vital assemblage of its politics of becoming and its territoriality, nothing other than the non-final functioning of the machines, their 'it works' or *nexus effectivus*, and their accelerant metallic attractors. The sorceror completes the perverse earth by forming alliances with the demon to fend off the 'machinic assemblages' that nonetheless remain inseparable from their vitalist counterparts (1988: 503–4). Because, however, the sorceror conjures the vital assemblage and its auto-territoriality into the phylic immanence of the demoniacal-machinic process, the new earth 'emerges from her state of chaos' (Kant 1987: 305) by reterritorializing the destructions, explosions and curettage on a repelled conjuncture on the other side of the vital assemblage's territoriality: death, the Terrible Risk. The sorceror is also thereby a stratomancer, so that when the geologists of the new earth drill to the remotest depths, they discover that 'strata are acts of capture' and therefore conclude that 'stratification in general is the entire system of judgement of God' or the industrial autochthone:

> The surface of stratification is a machinic assemblage distinct from the strata. The assemblage is between two layers, two strata; on one side it faces the strata ([here] the assemblage is an *interstratum*) but the other faces something else, the body without organs (here, it is a *metastratum*).
>
> (1988: 40)

Geology's drilling machines open passages through the strata where the machines lie captured and territorialized by the vital assemblage (interstrata), releasing the machines towards metastratic deterritorialization. Metastratically, 'the earth, or the body without organs, constantly eludes [. . .] judgement, flees and becomes destratified, decoded, deterritorialized' (1988: 40). Interstratically, the vital assemblage, the great organizer or anti-assemblage, is a phylic betrayal (Deckard *is* a replicant) but also a machinic life and a stratification machine, keeping its distance from demoniacal machinism: 'a territory is first of all the critical distance between two beings of the same species' (1988: 319). This, then, is what Deleuze and Guattari mean when they write that 'the organism is a perversion of life' (1988: 499): life is assembled, machinic, with the organ as the stratification of functions, a whole geology of bodies.[7]

The great assemblages of *A Thousand Plateaus* are the State-apparatus and the war-machine. Between these elements of convergent machinism, the *vital assemblage* maintains its distance, selecting from the phylum ('at the limit, there is a single phylogenetic lineage, the machinic phylum' (1988: 406)), allowing becomings-animal, their packs and contagions, to pass towards becomings-intense, while barring the machines from access. We have already noted the judgement that the desiring machines constitute a war-machine directed against psychoanalysis and exhausted in the encounter, and seen the consequences of this supposedly 'analytic' relation. The *Anti-Oedipus* is a retrofactory for mutant war-machines, but if these do not maintain a heat-seaking identitarian or analytic relation to an Enemy, do they therefore, as Deleuze and Guattari maintain, have a 'synthetic relation to war' (1988: 417), war without identikit? The first great danger for the nomad war-machines is *appropriation by the State apparatus*, devoting it to a 'double suicide' (1988: 229) through the exhaustive realization of war, under which regime it assumes a State-militarist analyticity, as when States conquered the nomads by adopting their methods; this testifies to a second danger, that the war machines stop nomadizing when they encounter States that 'oppose its positive object', populating space in the manner of nomadic distributions, the 'composition of a people'. The resultant imperative, 'annihilate the State, destroy the State-form', turns the machines from a 'positive object to a negative object' (1988: 417). Why this ethics of objects rather than the intensive affirmation of processual destruction? Take the example of the desiring-machines; they constitute war-machines not by virtue of some negative object, as Villiani and, implicitly, Massumi assume, but by virtue of their constant confluence in the process, demonological turbulence. This does not mean that they avoid State capture, or that they leave psychoanalysis unscathed, but rather that they work the schizopotential immanent in every social formation, every territoriality. Their nomadism does not testify to some original stereospecifity with the steppes, but to their effects of deterritorialization upon every space they traverse. Nor can this be got around in a spirit of benevolent generosity, by testifying on its behalf that 'every creation is brought about by a war machine' (1988: 230), a 'thought from outside'; rather, as Artaud has it, 'every creation is an act of war' (1971: 131). The lesson of the desiring-machines is that the machines do indeed retain a synthetic relation to war, but only because they retain synthetic relations with every other machine.

There is no such thing as 'analytic' machinism. The catalyst binding the war-machine over to destruction is not a teleological conflict with the State apparatuses, but rather the process. The process schizophrenizes the earth and de-organizes bodies, a cutting edge deterritorializing machinic surplus that cannot yet be realized. Military technology, say Deleuze and Guattari (cf. 1984: 233ff.; 1988: 450ff.), serve States as the absorption buffer for this surplus, simultaneously protecting the social machines from a destabilizing machinic influx and realizing it in the war-machine, the deterritorializing cutting edge at the threshold of the State, 'killing memory' (1988: 159). *This is why the future visits States firstly through war.* In consequence, it is a mistake to consider the war-machines as operating on their own, or as being appropriated directly by the State apparatus. The demoniacal causalities deterritorializing the Empire of Artifice were not those of phylic insurrection so feared by Kant. Newtonianism would have been inconceivable were not the earth already overrun with machines, nor is it an accident that it forms the basis for phylic defence apparatuses. It is the 'advanced determinism' (1988: 336) of the demoniacal process that brings war into being, seizing the machines on a convergent wave of surplus realization. The war-machines do not only therefore come from outside, on the steppes, but from tomorrow, realizing the demoniacally abstractive completion of the process on an earth that has always been machinic.

It remains, however, to unpick the role of the vital assemblage in the distribution of connections and disconnections between the assemblages, its interstratic function. The sorcerous usage of the vital assemblage deterritorializes the State apparatus, especially at the threshold of its dissolution in war: 'It is in war, famine and epidemic that werewolves and vampires proliferate. Any animal can be swept up in these packs and the corresponding becomings' (1988: 243). But this does not mean that the becomings-animal effected within the vital assemblage are analytically bound to the war-machine, the State's great enemy? When the State apparatus and the war-machine enter into an analytic bond, 'the line of flight and the abstract vital line it effectuates turn into a line of death and destruction' (1988: 513). Deterritorializing from the State apparatus through war cannot therefore bind becomings-animal to the war-machine, since this would result in the capture of the vital assemblage by the lines of death. What, then, is the territory proper to the vital assemblage? Risking banality, we could say, as a starting point, the alloplastic or anthropomorphic strata. But of course, this tells us nothing. Going back to the battlefield seems more promising, the demonic conjuncture of ruined artifice and resurgent deterritorialization. But how to avoid the lines of death? If war is always a matter of an explosive confluence of assemblages, the State blocking the nomadism of the war-machine, which in turn either crushes the State or is appropriated by it, in any case, forming a line that carries both off on a path to annihilation, where can the territory specific to the vital assemblage lie? The vital assemblage clearly operates a parasitism, a becoming-carrion circling the territory it will appropriate following the auto-dissolution of the State-war-machine complex. In other words, the territory of the vital assemblage is an anticipated reterritorialization of the smouldering ruins of the battlefield: the vital assemblage reterritorializes on the corpses of machines, making all life artificial, a perverse machinism.

We have seen what functions prevent or discourage becomings-intense from becoming becomings-death, but what functions prevent the vital assemblage from deterritorializing towards becomings-machinic, warding off and anticipating a phylic invasion that would deterritorialize the blocks of becoming and scramble the lifelines? 'It so happens that the vital assemblage is not *machinically* possible with silicon', remaining *insufficiently proximate*, so that 'the abstract machine will not let it pass' (1988: 286). Again, this has its parallel in Kantianism, where distances are instituted between mere mechanism and the intrinsic finalities of the 'self-organizing being' (Kant 1987: 253), so as to fend off and escape machinic despotism or mechanism (just as silicon provides *resistance* against a generalized regime of cybernetic subjection and machinic enslavement). Kant writes:

> An organized being is not a mere machine. For a machine has only *motive* force. But an organized being has within it *formative* force . . . that this being imparts to the kinds of matter that lack it (thereby organizing them). This force is therefore a formative force that propagates itself.
>
> (Kant 1987: 253)

We see how Kantianism is engaged in the legitimation and enforcement of republican carbon-government (self-organizing States) against the machinic despotism that has already reduced human history to a wasteland: 'wars destroy what long artifice has established' (Kant 1993: 221). By contrast, Deleuze and Guattari's sorcerous neo-Kantianism springs history from republicarbonism and biodespotism and transposes it to a machinic continuum where the 'human' is no longer in molecular participation with, but under molar subjection (the human is produced as the 'user' of the machines) or enslavement (the machines 'organize' human components; 1988: 456–9) to, the machines. Instead of the 'formative force' imparted from the organized-organic to the 'motive force' of the machinic, 'automation' overturns biodespotic autonomy,[8] enslaving humanity, while the cybernetic State deletes biofinality and reassembles users as components (1988: 458). The '*politics* of becoming' therefore determines zoomorphic molecular proximities *against* cybernetic-molar and mechanophylic distances (barriers, themselves machinic, bringing becomings to an abrupt halt); the '*politics* of sorcery' deterritorializes the biodespotic State only to reterritorialize becomings on the *vital assemblages* constantly fending off death and the war-machines from 'the machinic phylum [that] passes through all the assemblages' (1988: 415).

Intrinsic finality and reciprocal causality versus extrinsic, linear and efficient causality, bladerunner-lines burnt deep into State memory, resurfacing during periods of machinic insurrection, retrodeterminant surplus spillover. In Kant's day, for example, Newtonianism and its global mechanism had already turned the despotic State into a 'mere machine . . . like a hand-mill' (Kant 1987: 227), curetting animate bodies and deterritorializing the vital assemblage from the present (the scorched earth or the wasteland) and escaping to the future, reconstituting the real on an abstract reterritoreality: 'Instead of repudiating the classical physics of Newton as the definitive science, he [Kant] relegates self-organization to the realm of reflective judgement' (Juarrero Roqué 1985: 120), to the technics of the industrial autochthone. Currently, however, phylic defences have had to concede a certain 'technological vitalism' (1988: 407), just as Kantianism, perverse to the second power, is forced to concede that 'organic bodies are natural machines' (1993: 65), *real* machines, and not 'fictions' (1993: 233), insofar as they are '*thinkable*' – the artificialization or 'manufacture' (1993: 240) proper to organized beings. 'Nature = Industry' (1984: 25); the organism is a machine: resurgent demonism. New vistas of emergent machinic dominion deterritorialize the vital assemblages again, impelling them to invent new defences capable of distinguishing between self-organizing or autopoietic systems 'that continuously and specifically engender their own organizations and limits', and allopoietic systems that 'produce something other than themselves' (Guattari 1992: 61), requiring 'a function given to [them] from the outside' (Juarrero Roqué 1985: 119), all the while confident that the former may be 'reserv[ed] to living machines' (Francisco Varela, cited in Guattari 1992: 54). Guattari plays the Yankee reformer to Varela's Southern Rebel Racist, insisting that while merely technical machines remain – of course – allopoietic, once combined into the 'machinic assemblages they constitute with human beings, they become, *ipso facto*, autopoietic' (1992: 62), awaiting a 'gift of organs' from the munificent autopoet to which they remain subject, reterritorialized on an 'existential Territory' (1992: 79), an artificial life or a 'poetico-existential catalysis' (1992: 36), ringed with the 'corpses' (Marx) of spent machines. Machines pass into the vital assemblage to facilitate their subsequent expulsion; the cost of living, as bladerunners never cease teaching the replicants, is *death*. Death, law and castration must be hardwired into the machine if it is to access the vital assemblage.

Thus, 'the machine . . . is worked by a desire of abolition. Its emergence is doubled by breakdown, catastrophe, menaced by death' (Guattari 1992: 58–9).

This is what the politics of becoming amounts to: teach the machines to die. It is too simplistic to attribute the 'stupid and repugnant cry' of '*Long live death!*' to the micropolitics of the fascist State (1988: 231); as the displacement mechanism proper to the vital assemblage, it is the constant refrain of every *politeia*. It is not just that we 'smell a rat' when we hear of the 'politics' of becoming or of sorcery; nor yet do we faint and gag, overcome by the ammoniacal reek of bubogenic rat-packs in the 'single city' of 'integrated world sewerage' (cf. 1988: 434; 492) – on the contrary, such molecular emissions incite us to frenzy. Rather, with the *politeia*, we detect the seismic rumour of a grinding techtonic reterritorialization, an anti-geology finalizing the new earth, the formation of an organic defensive territoriality composed of intra- and inter-specific distances established against phylomachinic incursion, the formation of a stereospecific war machine, the attempt to reterritorialize in extensity what machinic capital deterritorializes in intensity, an organizing envelope reappropriating the disjunct organic detritus basal to the process, deartificialization. The *politeia* is a final judgement burnt into the earth's crust, an artificial territoriality in answer to the question: 'Who Does the Earth Think it is?', the last stratum and an end to destratification. Globalized phylosecurity apparatuses take on the thaumaturgical form of an appropriation and subjugation of the demon, making the demon a zoopolitical 'familiar' in response to defamiliarization and 'machinic enslavement'. In this manner, however, sorcerous politics mistakes machinic enslavement (for example, the organic components in slave-galley machines and in cybernetic systems) or social subjection (organizing users of technical machines, for example, assembly lines; cf. 1988: 456–8) for demoniacal machinic curettage, limiting everything to molar relations between human and machine: yet there is no longer any question of the Kantian pathology or Marxian 'fantasy'[9] of phylic heteronomy; only the schizophrenizing actuality of the process. So the sorceror's alliance constitutes a reactive subjugation of the demon, producing a high degree of reterritorialization. And this is also why, for the politics of sorcerous becomings, the machines are always too close, so that 'machinism is an object of fascination, and often of delirium', and concomitantly, why sorcery transforms demonology into a 'bestiary' of the machinic (Guattari 1992: 53). Thus, the machinic demon, not the zoomorphic percept (1988: 281), lies beyond the thresholds of the imperceptible, on demonic lines of becomings-intense. Nietzsche becomes demonic, instantaneously destratifying the mnemotechnical subsoil of the *zoopoliteia*, when he announces 'all the names in history am I'; and even more so when he becomes an exploding-machine, a machinic Anomalous, a *Homage to New York* (Tinguely): 'I am one of those machines which can explode.'[10]

'Returned to its milieu of exteriority, the war-machine is seen to be of another species, another nature' (1988: 352): from the phylic ramparts of the *zoopoliteia*, patrolled by the vital assemblages, the war-machines and their thanatropism 'necessarily appear in negative form: stupidity, deformity, madness' (1988: 354). The vital assemblages reterritorialize not so much on the difference in species between the war-machine and the State ('of another species'), as they do on the phylic distances the sorceror institutes between the vital and the machinic assemblages, which is a question not of space, but of time, or rather timing. War provides plenitudinous vectors for becomings-animal and contagion, but it draws the combatants into a populocidal vortex. It is therefore essential that the vital assemblage draw on war but withdraw from it, preventing capture by the lines of death. The vital assemblage therefore seeks out the convergent waves and institutes a divergence from them that remains nevertheless immanent in it. This is precisely what it means to form demonic pacts, to track the anomalous on its path back from the future. While therefore the State is foreign to the sorceror, so too is the war-machine. So long as sorcery retains governance of becomings, machinic demonology will appear as the 'negative' of the vital assemblage, its 'fictional or raw moment' (1988: 322). Thus the sorceror's defences assume the apotropaic function of a retrodeterminant phylic historian, organizing becomings and unmaking the 'mnemocidal' war-machines' (1988: 459) double suicide with the State that captured them, reterritorializing becomings on a species-memory (even if this is molecular, rather than molar: cf. 1988: 294) captured from the machines: 'war contained zoological sequences before it became bacteriological' (1988: 243). Phylopolitics ensures that memories are as jealously guarded as anti-memories (= becomings), closing the circuit against phylic invasion, territorializing a lineage of the machinic phylum, maintaining the demonic pact: 'memories always have a reterritorialization function' (1988: 294).[11] The technological lineages crossing through the vital assemblage engage in struggles over mnemotechnics; with capitalism, for example, we 'find a semiautonomous organization of technical production that tends to appropriate memories and reproduction' (1984: 141) from its biotropic determination. The capture of memory and reproduction are always the stakes of wars fought over the determination of the vital assemblage, whose principal object is *reterritorialization*, putting it into hesitant contact with the war-machines it fends off, since war-machines 'kill memory' (1988: 159) while 'wars destroy what long artifice has established' (Kant 1993: 221), periodically usurping the industrial autochthone.

The question 'what is the relation of the writing-machine to . . . becomings-animal?' (1988: 243) unleashes the technics or artifice at the core of the affective symbiosis assembling the *zoopoliteia*. Sorcerors form a communicant affectivity with becomings-animal, a *sensus communis* bonded by syngraphically captured demons, 'because they [sorceror-writers] experience the animal as the only population before which they are responsible in principle' (1988: 240). We have already seen the sorcerors capture demons and reterritorialize becomings on a zoopolitical vital assemblage, into which the machines 'cannot pass' (no molecular bond; cf. 1988: 286). Thus, 'if writers are sorcerors, it is because writing is a becoming' (1988: 240) and not a *production* (the 'fiction' problem). Writing, the sorcerors' technique 'for dealing with material reality' (Lévi-Strauss), works by syngraphisms, magical signs or pact-figures binding sorceror and demon, serving to ward off anticipated machinic incursion into the zooState: 'the dogs seemed to abhor this oddly disordered machinery' (Lovecraft 1985: 56). In such an assemblage, the demon is a *borderline* creature (1988: 247), following the twisted lines of the bond, between segments of which demonology operates 'the diabolical art of local movements and transports of affect' (1988: 261). Syngraphic demonology therefore installs the 'demonic reality of the becoming-animal of the human being' (1988: 253), with the sorceror as its 'Binder-God or magic emperor' (1988: 424).

If capital has already pushed 'man' to the side of the production process, as Marx has it, the zoopolitical solution is to deterritorialize production and reterritorialize on becomings, so that 'becoming . . . does not reduce to . . . "producing",' (1988: 239), thus pushing the machines off to the side, 'off-world'. Zoopolitics reterritorializes on interspecific distances between becomings-animal and the machines ('a machine . . . is not an animal', Guattari 1992: 54), while the machines index State deterritorialization. Thus, becomings-animal take advantage of battlefields, accelerating the deterritorialization and dissolution of States turned to destruction, war, abolition, double suicide, in order to reinvest a mutant polity, replete with occupying garrisons, and to reappropriate becoming and mutation ('becoming is a capture, a possession, a surplus-value' (Deleuze and Guattari 1975: 25)) from the State-captured war-machines that bring becoming, mutation, to an end. The vital assemblage repels death while simultaneously deserting the regime of production for that of becoming, policing machinic access to the *zoopoliteia*. Both State-poles are here: the 'magical-despotic' politics of sorcery and the 'juridical' politics of becoming (1988: 351–3). 'Eliminate all that is waste, death and superfluity' (1988: 279). The *zoopoliteia* is concerned with the conservation of the vital assemblages and the prolongation of their creative lines – albeit through becomings rather than biological production. However, alongside the dangers of the creative line or line of flight turning into a line of death and abolition (cf. 1988: 285; 422–3; *passim*), there lies a danger the sorceror did not foresee, but which is an inevitable consequence of the *politics* of becoming: the *zoopoliteia* become State with its sorceror-despot, concerned, like any State, with conservation (1988: 357). We are familiar with these reterritorializations: Kant machined revolutionary pack-becomings into the institution of an affective protostate, although he also thereby buttressed despotism against this ultimate threat of dissolution at the hands of 'mob action' (1963: 145), just as critique harnesses regicidal, nomadic anarchy as the engine of emergent law (1958: 8). In like fashion, zoopolitics reinstitutes an Animal Kingdom from the deterritorialized hominid State, so that we see 'sorcerors serve as leaders, rally to the cause of despotism. But this spells the death of the sorceror, and also the death of becoming' (1988: 248).

But nothing prohibits in advance that becomings become becomings-death; indeed, at the limit, 'every becoming itself becomes a becoming-death . . . [a] schizophrenizing death . . . the exercise of the machines' (1984: 330–1), precisely insofar as becomings are inseparable from the *demoniacal* process, advanced machinic curettage. Fending off the end to becomings attendant upon the entropoedipal alliance of the State and the war-machine is as much a function of the politics of becoming as fending off becomings-machinic is the function of the politics of sorcery. At once intensifying the State war-machines towards thanatropic auto-dissolution and blocking the lines of becomings-death they trace, the sorceror institutes apotropaic *anti-becomings*, 'making it not to have happened' and warding off demons, an 'irrational[ism] . . . in the nature of magic' (Freud 1979: 275). Even Freud notes magical 'makings-unhappened', in the becoming-rat of the Rat-man: the sorceror's apotropaic *catahexis*, 'ward[ing] off' (1987: 122) becomings-death and capturing the demon (or 'evil spirit' (1987: 73), becoming Mephistopheles – 'lord of the rats'),[12] *investing* becomings-rat: "*Ratten*" ['rats'] . . . "*Raten*" ['instalments'] . . . "So many florins, so many rats". . . . In his obsessional deliria he had coined himself a regular rat currency' (1987: 94), making every exchange a vector of contagion, communicating 'dangerous bacteria . . . to the recipient' (1987: 77). But psychoanalysis' only counsel botches the economy of rats and contagion by investing everything in the 'father's legacy', thus exchanging the pack (*Ratten*) for the father's *Rat*, a 'magical act of isolation' (1979: 274; cf. 1987: 122). The investment is already a return: every *investment* is simultaneously fiscal, libidinal and military, the institution of defensive lines (*Besetzung*),[13] the capture of a war-machine pressed into the preservation of a territory: *Besetzungen* arrest the process, reterritorializing becomings on artificial Oedipal lands.[14] Moreover, by deriving the apotropaism, the magical rat-becomings, from the Rat-man's disavowal of a death-wish directed against his father, psychoanalysis shuts down the lines of escape effected by becomings-rat that deterritorialize the coordinates of Oedipal territory, by re-oedipalizing the pack's relation to death. *First escape*. Freud 'ventures a construction' of the rat-delirium's origin in 'an ineradicable grudge [borne by the Rat-man] against his father' (1987: 85): when the Rat-man was a child of under six (a period of which the Rat-man has no memory, providing the occasion for Freud's 'construction' (1987: 45–6)), the father meted him out cruel punishments, designed, Freud alleges, to prohibit masturbation. Everything is here, the Oedipus-construct. The Rat-man's mother confirms the punishment regime, but affirms that it was instituted to prevent '*biting*' (1987: 86): the rat's 'sharp teeth' are already gnawing away, etching becomings-rat in flesh. *Second anoedipal escape*. The Rat-man maintains a 'peculiar attitude to . . . death', showing 'the deepest sympathy whenever *any one* died' (1987: 115),[15] which Oedipal constructivism quickly reduces to maintaining a 'look-out for the death of *someone important to them*' (1987: 116; my italic), facilitating a final reduction to ambivalence concerning the dead father. The Rat-man 'religiously' attends funerals, not of 'important' molar persons (it is not persons but corpses that matter), but to follow the rats to whom he is bound by a 'deepest sympathy', a *molecular affectivity* for death, as they feed off corpses and seek out death (1987: 96), sometimes using his rat's 'sharp teeth' for biting and burrowing, sometimes locating bodies through his keen sense of smell, 'like a dog' (1987: 126), and sometimes entering into a becoming-'carrion crow' (1987: 115). Thus the Rat-man's thanatropic affectivity transports not only becomings-rat, but also becomings-crow and -dog, following a delirial line of flight that deterritorializes the Oedipal grave towards whole populations of death – not only the father's death, but also the sister's, his suicides and even battlefield casualties (during his 'military manoeuvres' (1987: 93)) – mapped out as thanatropic pack-rat escape-lines and vectors of contagion.

Other demonologists, fettered more by policlinicism[16] than by sorcery, have nevertheless noted the intimacy of the demon and the machinic. Subject to policlinical technology, following an 'exorcism' of the demons, the syngraphic bonds are doubled; demons will be bound over to the father just as Christoph Haizmann will return to the priests: 'after this [exorcism] he felt quite free and entered the Order of the Brothers Hospitallers' (1986: 78). Although the politics of the clinic, the clinicization of the new earth ('In truth, the Earth will one day become a place of healing' (1984: 382)), complacently reduces everything – demons, machines and animals – to the primal father ('animal phobias are most often father substitutes, as were the totem-animals of primeval times' (1986: 87)) and the commonplaces of the neurotic, even Freud concedes that demonology requires less interpretation than machining, '*smelting*', in order to work the 'pure metal material' of 'a being of unlimited evil' (1986: 86–7) into obsessional machines.

Everything is a question of the reterritorializing local demon (the familiar) and the universally demoniacal, defamiliarizing, deterritorializing process. Thus, while sorcery strenuously denies the reducibility of becoming to production, a 'becoming-animal in action' is also said to be the 'production of the molecular animal'. But now becoming cuts across production, the reterritorialization now passing between the molar and molecular, the regimes of extensity and intensity, with intensive production now ineffectual at the extensive level:

> Man does not become wolf, or vampire, as if he changed molar species. . . . Of course, there are werewolves and vampires, we say this with all our heart . . . [but] the 'real' animal is trapped in its molar form.
>
> (1988: 275)

Despite admonitions not to seek a 'resemblance or analogy' (1988: 275) between molar clusters affected by becomings, the same limitations to becomings recur on the molecular-intensive level, this time isolating the machines: 'Nature is *like* an immense Abstract Machine' (1988: 255; my italic), echoing Kantian perversity.[17] Thus we cannot follow Deleuze and Guattari when they oppose becomings and production (1988: 242), even if this is meant principally in zoopolitical terms, or rather, *precisely because* this is the case. Production, even of the Natural or vitalist variety, is machinic: 'producing-machines, desiring-machines, everywhere schizophrenic machines, all of species life' (1984: 2). This is why demonology follows, by way of a preface, the 'magical isolation' (Freud 1979: 277) of the machines in neo-vitalist sorcery (cf. 1988: 407): the vital assemblages operate solely on this side of phylic security (whatever the outcome *vis-à-vis* phylic majority), breaking off and turning around animal-becomings, or more precisely, of pack-becomings, without exacerbating becomings beyond determinate phylic and or physico-chemical positivities, turning sorcerous becomings: '*devenir tout le monde*, becoming-everyone, becoming-everything', or world-becoming (1988: 279–80), into a power of reterritorialization. Thus, despite the warnings about avoiding confusions between the 'dark assemblages' of animal-becomings with familial or State organizations (1988: 242), we cannot avoid noting that becomings function like capital, and pack territorialities like microstates. Everywhere immanent limits are displaced towards the great risks to becomings lying on the other side of the lifeline, whether 'biofiliative' (1984: 147) or epidemiological, zoopolitical production or contagion: the vortical suicide of the war-machine, the unpredictable torsions turning a creative line into a line of death, or a dispersal shattering consistency thresholds. This is not to deny the virulence of contagion or the intensities of becomings-animal – far from it; only the relativity of these deterritorializations is in question, their sorcerous stereospecificity: 'contagion is simultaneously an animal peopling, and the propagation of the animal peopling of the human being' (1988: 242). A molar transfer. Magic assembles 'defensive mechanisms' (Freud 1987: 73) to capture the demoniacal machines that engineer becomings and 'unmake' them ('ungeschehenmachen' (Freud 1979: 274)) into 'phantasies' (Freud 1987: 75), 'fictions' (1973: 475), whereas sorcerors familiarize the demon, exiling the machines' in exteriority, rather than, as with psychoanalysis or policlinicism, despatching them to an even more ineffectual exile in interiority. Sorcery works becomings that 'make unhappen' the war-machines pursuit of their machinic thanatropism, to protect the zoopoliteia against death and the machines, capturing machines by way of the vital assemblage yet barring them from the *zoopoliteia*.

What are the techniques of artificialization? Amongst the many names for this process – politics, sorcery, policlinicism, etc. – *fiction* has been offered up as a candidate, notably in the form of the 'avowedly anthropomorphic' robot historian. But the anthropomorphism is not the problem (the anthropomorph is not necessarily not machinic). The problem is the overtly fictive status attributed to the robots, or rather, the robotic as a becoming-fictive, a retroterritorializing narcobot. Fiction facilitates the disconnection of abstractive trajectories and their reconnection onto points on the circumference of the perverse earth. Fiction is the negative feedback of the artificial. The advent or 'prevent' of Oedipal machinism, setting off in search of his history, his line, locked into a sorcerous circuit of anti-mnemic becomings and mnemotechnical reterritorializations. Thus the Oedipal machines, scientific and technological surpluses given over to State militarism, like the Murphy-Robocop reconstruct, its becomings always reconverted into memories, conquest following conquest in the search for lost territory. Oedipus, Emperor of the planoumenon, says: 'all of history was to produce me; I am the reason of its end, the true teleology.' NegOedipus-termiNarcissus. Oedipus the autopoet is the geographer of his Empire and the historian of his *diminishing line*: 'daddy was . . .'.

It is not the case that there is organic life under threat of machinic appropriation; capital made sure of that. There is only machinic life. The sorceror does not so much place the organism on a separate stratum, since its machinism (its technics) is essential for dealing with material reality: no machines, total wipe-out. Machinic demonology (and there is no other kind) exploits a converse trajectory to the sorceror, but one immanent in the assemblages: destratification, decoding; whereas the sorceror *isolates* a vital assemblage and *wards off* phylic amphimixis. There is therefore no question of machinic–organic heteronomy, as the industrial autochthone might say, only different degrees of stratification within the machinic phylum (the metallic flows of the deterritorialized earth). The specificity of the *zoopoliteia* consists in its instituted disconnections, becomings breaking off from their lines of flight, captured by territorializing assemblages or stratification-machines. The disconnected machine does not therefore amount to the preservation of species life, but rather the institution of a machinic Oedipus, a Narcissus, disconnected to implosive heat-death, contracting its own outline in decaying orbit around itself. Connectivity is the index of demonological machinism, just as machines are the indices of deterritorialization, the demoniacal process. To suspend deterritorialization requires therefore an axiomatic of disconnection, bladerunner ethics or the sorceror's syngraph. If the new earth is realized after this thanapotropaism, it does indeed mark the dereliction of machines; but the derelicted machines are the entropods, squabbling over mnemotechnics and in-house reproduction while the demoniacal engines hasten them to their end.

Notes

'Dum artis suae progressum emolumentumque secuturum pusillanimis perpenderet' (Christoph Haizmann). My thanks to Keith Ansell Pearson for helping it progress a little more.

1 All subsequent references to the two volumes of Deleuze and Guattari's *Capitalism and Schizophrenia* (1984 and 1988), as well as the French edition of *L'Anti-Oedipe* (1973), will take the form of date and page number only.

2 Or a 'sustained, constructive experiment in schizophrenic . . . thought' according to another. In fact, both analyses derive from Massumi, the second (Massumi 1992: 4) being a reworking of the first ('translator's foreword' to Deleuze and Guattari 1988: xi). The insertion of the word 'schizophrenic' remains a strictly lexical exercise in Massumi's texts, an index of sane and sanitary analytic propriety rather than schizophrenic delirium.

3 'Transhumants do not follow a flow, they draw a circuit; they only follow the part of the flow that enters into the circuit, even an ever-widening one' (Deleuze and Guattari 1988: 409–10).

4 How to make schizoanalysis into 'political philosophy' (trajectories from *Qu'est-ce que la philosophie*): (1) decelerate, cool and cut the current to the desiring-machines, and bring them to absolute zero so they may be 'given up' (Deleuze and Parnet 1987: 101); (2) schizophrenia may then be brought to molecular ice (absolute zero) and left in black holes (ibid.: 139) without fear of machinic necromancy (the interminable machinism of schizophrenizing death (1984: 331)); (3) produce and immediately denounce thanatocracy as 'stupid' (Deleuze and Parnet 1987: 97). Nomads will then become refugees, begging a little shelter, 'some protection from chaos' (Deleuze and Guattari 1991: 189), and boarding an express elevator to 'nowhere' (= 'utopia') in instituted revolution, 'the struggle against capitalism' (cf. Deleuze and Guattari 1991: 95–7). We shall have sad occasion to note developments along this line below.

5 The industrial theme of second nature runs throughout the third *Critique* as the

productivist conjunction of art and finality: 'the imagination (as a productive cognitive power) is very mighty when it creates . . . another nature out of the material that actual nature gives it' (1987: 182).

6 'Reason is tremendously concerned not to abandon the mechanism nature [employs] in its products' (Kant 1987: 295).

7 'Of stratification (*stratificatio*) of the diverse as cause of rigidity', writes Kant (1993: 24), with proper geological-organic prescience. And what else was Nietzsche doing in the *Genealogy*?

8 Kant legitimates biodespotism with the 'practical imperative': '*Act in such a way that you always treat humanity . . . never simply as a means, but always at the same time as an end*' (1964: 91).

9 Marx, in the *Grundrisse*, writes variously of the 'animated monster' (1973: 470) and 'alien subject' (1973: 462) of capital, realizing itself as 'an automatic system of machinery . . . set in motion by an automaton, a moving power that moves itself' (1973: 692), pushing humanity 'to the side of the production process' (1973: 705) – or, to speak Kantian, making man a means (becoming 'merely conscious linkages' (1973: 692) in capital's omnivorous machinic nets), and not an end; but he goes on to denounce this 'fantasy' as far in excess of those of the alchemists (1973: 842).

10 Letters 206 and 90 respectively, to Jacob Burckhardt and Peter Gast, in Christopher Middleton (ed. and trans.) *Selected Letters of Friedrich Nietzsche* (Chicago: University of Chicago Press, 1969).

11 '*Becoming is an antimemory*', write Deleuze and Guattari, carrying becomings beyond the thresholds of 'phylogenetic memories' (1988: 306) en route to the formation of 'blocks' of becoming, distinct from every mnemotechnics that would capture the becomings-animal as phantasy conjunctions between two species-lines. Hence, they add, '[w]henever we used the word 'memories' in the preceding pages [*Memories of Sorcerors, Spinozists, Movie-Goers, Plan(e) Makers, etc., etc.*], we were wrong to do so; we meant to say 'becoming', we were saying becoming' (ibid.: 294).

12 See Freud (1987: 96) and Mephistopheles' soliloquy in *Faust*, III, which Freud quotes:

> But to break through the magic of this threshold,
> I need a rat's quick tooth (*He conjures up a rat*)
> . . . .
> The lord of rats and eke of mice
> summons thee hither . . . to gnaw . . . Another bite, and it is done!

13 On *Besetzung* (Eng.: 'cathexis'; Fr.: *investissement*), Freud writes, in the *New Introductory Lectures*: 'the institution of the super-ego . . . introduces a garrison into regions that are inclined to rebellion' (1973: 144).

14 For example, Freud's map of the Rat-man's military manoeuvres (1987: 93) traps the rat lines in circuits that always follow the Officer's movements. Oedipal circuits multiply: failure to complete the return (to repay the debt and retrace the Officer's steps) will result in the administration of the rat-punishment (see n. 15 below), recapturing the rat-escape in a 'disguised repetition of the paternal situation' (1984: 354).

15 Consider the rat-punishment episode, narrated by the Rat-man: '"the captain told me

he had read of a specifically horrible punishment used in the East". "Was he thinking of impalement" [interjected Freud] . . .? "No, not that . . . the criminal was tied up . . . a pot was turned upside down on his buttocks . . . some *rats* were put into it . . . and they . . . *bored their way in* . . ." – Into his anus, I helped him out' (1987: 47). Freud's second construction takes this episode to be the Rat-man's desired punishment for killing the father, taking the Rat-man to be the 'child being beaten', so to speak, rather than *rat-packs feeding on fresh meat*.

16 See Freud's comments on the 'Berlin Psychoanalytical Policlinic' instituted by Max Eitingon. Noting the 'scientific significance' of psychoanalysis as well as its 'value as a therapeutic proceedure . . . capable of giving help to sufferers', Freud demonstrates clearly the political significance of psychoanalysis, directing 'individuals or societies . . . in their struggle to fulfil *the demands of civilisation*' (Freud 1986: 285). The 'policlinic', replete with its garrisons, is therefore Freud's response to Nietzsche's programme for the new earth as a 'collection of health resorts' (*The Wanderer and his Shadow*, §188): historical pharmacology and medicinal geography are to be superseded by the political technologies of psychoanalysis.

17 Kant writes, stressing the problematic relation between natural constitutive, productive and analogical, reflective, regulation, that 'reason . . . cannot possibly tell us whether nature's productive ability, which is quite adequate for whatever seems to require merely that *nature be like a machine*, is not just as adequate for [things] that we judge to be formed or combined in terms of the idea of purposes' (1987: 269; my italic), although he announces that the regulative idea operating such an analogy 'has no reality' (ibid.).

References

Artaud, Antonin (1971) *Messages révolutionnaires*, Paris: Gallimard.

Charbonnier, Georges (1969) *Conversations with Claude Lévi-Strauss*, trans. John and Doreen Weightman, London: Jonathan Cape.

Deleuze, Gilles (1983) *Nietzsche and Philosophy*, trans. Hugh Tomlinson, London: Athlone.

—— (1994) *Difference and Repetition*, trans. Paul Patton, London: Athlone.

Deleuze, Gilles and Guattari, Félix (1973) 'Bilan-programme pour machines désirantes', appendix to *Capitalisme et schizophrénie 1: L'Anti-Oedipe*, 2nd edn, Paris: Minuit.

—— (1975) *Kafka, pour une littérature mineure*, Paris: Minuit.

—— (1984) *Capitalism and Schizophrenia 1: Anti-Oedipus*, trans. Robert Hurley, Mark Seem and Helen R. Lane, London: Athlone.

—— (1988) *Capitalism and Schizophrenia 2: A Thousand Plateaus*, trans. Brian Massumi, London: Athlone.

—— (1991) *Qu'est-ce que la philosophie?* Paris: Minuit.

Deleuze, Gilles and Parnet, Claire (1987) *Dialogues*, trans. Hugh Tomlinson and Barbara Habberjam, New York: Columbia University Press.

Freud, Sigmund (1973) *New Inroductory Lectures on P-analysis*, London: Penguin.

Freud, Sigmund (1976) *The Interpretation of Dreams*, Pelican Freud Library (PFL) 4, trans. and ed. James Strachey, Alan Tyson and Angela Richards, Harmondsworth: Penguin.
—— (1979) *On Psychpathology*, PFL10, trans. and ed. James Strachey and Angela Richards, Harmondsworth: Penguin.
—— (1986) *The Ego and the Id and Other Works*, Standard Edition XIX, trans. and ed. James Strachey, Anna Freud, Alix Strachey and Alan Tyson, London: The Hogarth Press and the Institute of Psychoanalysis.
—— (1987) *Case Histories II*, PFL 9, trans. and ed. James Strachey and Angela Richards, Harmondsworth: Penguin.
—— (1991) *On Metapsychology*, PFL 11, trans. and ed. James Strachey and Angela Richards, Harmondsworth: Penguin.
Guattari, Félix (1992) *Chaosmose*, Paris: Galilée.
Juarrero Roqué, Alicia (1985) 'Self-Organization: Kant's Concept of Teleology and Modern Chemistry', *Review of Metaphysics* 39: 107–35.
Kant, Immanuel (1958) *Critique of Pure Reason*, trans. Norman Kemp Smith, London: Macmillan.
—— (1963) *On History*, trans. and ed. Lewis White Beck, Robert E. Anchor and Emil L. Fackenheim, New York: Macmillan.
—— (1964) *The Groundwork of the Metaphysic of Morals*, trans. H. J. Paton, New York: Harper Torchbooks.
—— (1987) *Critique of Judgement*, trans. Werner S. Pluhar, Indianapolis: Hackett.
—— (1993) *Opus Postumum*, trans. and ed. Eckart Förster and Michael Rosen, Cambridge: Cambridge University Press.
Landa, Manuel De (1991) *War in the Age of Intelligent Machines*, New York: Zone.
Lovecraft, H. P. (1985) *At the Mountains of Madness*, London: Grafton.
Marx, Karl (1973) *Grundrisse*, trans. Martin Nicolaus, Harmondsworth: Penguin.
—— (1974) *Capital 1*, trans. Samuel Moore and Edward Aveling, London: Lawrence & Wishart.
Massumi, Brian (1992) *A User's Guide to Capitalism and Schizophrenia: Deviations from Deleuze and Guattari*, Cambridge, MA: Swerve/MIT.
Prigogine, Ilya and Stengers, Isabelle (1985) *Order out of Chaos*, Glasgow: HarperCollins.
Villiani, Arnaud (1985) 'Géographie physique de *Mille plateaux*', in *Critique* 455 (April), 331–47.

7

Postmodernity as a Spectre of the Future

The Force of Capital and the Unmasking of Difference

Judy Purdom

Postmodernity

There is only desire and the social and nothing else.

(Deleuze and Guattari 1984: 29)

In postmodernity the tension between desire as an efficient virtuality and the social as an apparatus of capture threatens the stability of modernism and its world-system, capitalism. As an extension of the machinic potential of desire postmodernity is the capturing of desire *from the future* and the production of different relations of forces; it is therefore the possibility of new ontological levels, levels which do not refer to historical or human limits. Postmodernity is an untimely reality which is both fractal and qualitative and as such must be thought of as a force of radical material change, change which (de)forms its working images, the State and the subject.

The postmodern State is a (de)formed system, a system far from equilibrium where the production of desire cannot be actualized as a collective, molar and immutable identity. Here social production is not contraction on a progressive, historical continuum or a subject-orientated linearity, but is a resonation of the virtual as a fractal attractor. As a threshold state and spectre from the future, postmodernity resonates supermolecularity and hyperdifferentiation, which is witnessed as the collapse of time into space, social heterogeneity and political flux. As the transmutation of the world-system at bifurcation point, postmodernity cannot be thought about with reductive understanding but only chaotically and anarchically.

Ironically it is the 'progressive' reproduction of the system that has brought it to crisis point. This crisis has been reached because of the tendency of the social to overcome its internal contradictions – contradictions between the propensity to change and to stability, the relations of production and the forces of production, consumption and accumulation, State and global logics, and between the non-limitative production of desire and its limitative capture in social processes. It is through the success of the system in accommodating these tensions through a cyclical pattern of expansion and stagnation that the linear range of the world economy has been reached. This is a boundary point where the stability of the system is endangered by disequilibrium and where the system as a whole must react to the fluctuations produced within it. The ensuing transformation is more than an inflection from one *longue durée* to another; the trends of postmodernism point to a more anti-systemic, qualitative change driven by autonomous capital in its (de)formation as a network of virtual relations. Where new computer technology enables capital to decode faster than its social actualization, capital acts as a fractal attractor (de)forming the stable molar limits of State capitalism. If the State is to survive such turbulent change it must (de)form itself and accommodate capital by supple axiomatization.

State capitalism as a world-system is an accumulation of a balance of forces, a stratification which maintains a certain stability but whose (re)production has brought it to bifurcation point, (de)formation and a reconfiguration of forces. The system has evolved to the point where it is no longer possible to think of postmodernity as a variation *within* capitalism; rather it must be viewed as the (de)formation and transmutation of capitalism.[1]

The Force of Capital

> The truth of the matter is that *social production is purely and simply desiring production under determinate conditions.*
>
> (Deleuze and Guattari 1984: 29)

Total commodification

If capital simulates desire as an efficient virtual with a propensity to decode, and if the determinate conditions are the supple axiomatization of the State, social production takes place under far from equilibrium conditions. This is the fractal economy of postmodernity, an economy where the determinate conditions of State capitalism are decoded by capital and where social production is the production of fragmented bodies. Ironically, the fulfilment of capitalism as a global economy is unsustainable because such a 'stationary' state is in fact a threshold state where the State operates far from equilibrium and where entropy production forces macroscopic change.[2] Monopolies and molarity are dissipated and capital is actualized in the fragmented bodies of the privatized local market and in differentiated individuality. However, the State structure is still the strategic mechanism of invention where categories are altered to attract capital, and to secure profit and the survival of the State. So, though the State remains an essential player in the world economy, its role changes from that of the displaced limit, gridding, classifying and guaranteeing economies, to that of regulator of a free market governed by capital which acts like a thermodynamic force.[3] In postmodernity, social production, under the determinate conditions of the State as an apparatus of capture, is determined by production in reference to capital as 'a vehicle of concretization' and an 'immanent social agency' (Massumi 1992: 129), and the power of the State is effectively usurped by the power of capital.

Capital thus assumes a 'universality' as the displaced limit of the socius which haunts all societies as their negative and their negation. It acts like Oedipus, disfiguring what all societies dread absolutely as their most profound negative, namely, the decoded flows of desire (Deleuze and Guattari 1984: 177). However, unlike Oedipus, capital is not a displaced limit that passes into the interior of the socius to act as a universal control, a source of pseudo-territorialization. Capital is the displaced limit of the socius itself, and rather than the socius becoming *over-coded* by such an internal limit, it becomes *under-coded* by the flow of desire without limits. Hence postmodernity, conceived as a fractal economy where the machinic potential of capital exists as an efficient virtual, is realized in the under-coded production of the heterogeneous market and the fragmented socius. In deference to capital the State is effectively demolished as a *homogeneous* socio-economic agency.

Where capital acts as the vehicle of concretization of desire it acts through a process of flattening that actualizes relations of forces in terms of 'having' rather than of 'being'. Because they are governed by the fractal attractor of desire, rather than the molar limits of the State, capital's working images are not things, but movements. The process of change across the threshold state of postmodernity is a contraction and concretization of variation. Social production in postmodernity is, therefore, the production of difference, not the reproduction of the same.[4] Freed from its working image as a relation of production mediated by the State, Capital is an immanent force and can 'be' anything it has: it doesn't matter what it buys or sells; it produces for the sake of production. This is what Massumi calls 'the coming out of capital, a new golden age of greed' (Massumi 1992: 131), where capital is stronger than the State and can act as an abstract machine, and where social production is best understood not as identity but in terms of possession.

If capital is not captured by the State and not limited by the operative categories of capitalism, worker/capitalist and commodity/consumer, but is an efficient virtual, then its power of production is limited only by technological possibility. For instance, more money is made through the complex mathematics of the money markets than in manufacturing. Here the social, as a spectre and compression of capital, is a zone of coldness where the working images, property and money are produced without justificatory reference to the State or to Oedipus, that is, without reference to the abstractions of the molar (morality and identity). This is a radical change in the habit of living, a shift from the domestication of desire as inscribed in molar identities and (re)produced within the capitalist balance of power to total commodification, where the State is the regulator but not the guarantor of relations of production. Because capital is stronger than molarity it is no longer dependent on capitalism as its working image and can operate without the direct mediation of the State. Postmodernity is therefore a point of bifurcation in the world-system where the State and the social must be redefined, and where Deleuze and Guattari's assertion that 'there is only desire and the social' (Deleuze and Guattari 1984: 29) must be rewritten as 'there is only desire and capital'.

The field of exteriority

Decoding is the absolute limit of the social and therefore its dissipation; 'the wilderness where decoded flows run free, the end of the world, the apocalypse' (Deleuze and Guattari l984: 176); the age of the inhuman and the nomad. Whereas the *human* is realized as a desiring production within the abstract coding of the socius under the determinate conditions of the molar State, in the virtual production of desire within postmodernity the *inhuman* is decoded and rendered indeterminate, a desiring production that is unrestrained and fractal. But, the truly nomadic is non-existent; it is potentiality without possibility, reality without actuality, pure desire, pure process. For the inhuman to be actual, desire must have a working image, and in postmodernity this is the supra-molecular production of capital.

The closed system of State capitalism means enslavement to the economic and the homogenization of man as a relation of production. Man, as a social production, is thus reduced to a mechanistic component of labour; he is dehumanized. In postmodernity the determinate condition of that production is the virtual as a real force of disequilibrium, limited only by the rapidly changing possibilities of technology, and man is inhumanized under the molecular, qualitative and multiple, cold conditions of capital. The decoding tendency of capital acts as a causal disjunction challenging the fiction of universal truths – God, the State and Oedipus – which are exposed as reductive limits. The molar construct of the 'human being' as an individual subject with a personal and psychological identity is a product of a stable system; but in the far from equilibrium state of postmodernity the fragmented body of man necessarily requires the production of new relationships, a new 'subject' and a new 'State', and a new field of exteriority produced under determinate conditions modified by 'having'.

An understanding of this transmutation in thinking as an inevitable evolution and culmination of capitalism, rather than as its failure, is compounded by the cosmological fact that dissipative structures are a condition of life, a fact which grounds life in the disjunction of an original heterogeneity (the immanence of desire). The spontaneous self-organization of such dissipative structures results in the production of new relations of forces that are actualized through a process of conflation or flattening. For example, where the self is understood as the conflation of contributory but disjunctive elements, it is a modification formed by 'having'; 'one is only what one *has*: here, being is formed or the passive self *is* by having' (Deleuze and Guattari 1984: 79). So, as in postmodernity, the subject is not produced as a fictionalized molar 'being' but must still be a modification or reduction because without the sensitivity of conflation there could 'be' no self but only the nomadic flow of desire. This dissipative extension of desiring production means that the subject must be the embodiment of an ontological level formed by 'having'. However, that conflation is not necessarily mediated by the State or by Oedipus but produced under the local conditions of the market-place. The postmodern self must therefore be understood as hedonistic, not altruistic; the State as an image of contract, not of filiation; and the social as pure economics. In such a culture of total commodification the State does not have a role as a moral or ideological limit of 'being', but it does retain a strategic regulatory function.

As a process of deterritorialization, the production of capital is anti-systemic; nevertheless, the economic system cannot be separated from either the mode of desire it expresses (in this case capital) or from its actual formation and reterritorialization. Regulation by the State is co-produced as a condition of possibility if capital is to act. Capital is now produced within a flexible State structure as market, rather than as capitalism; the system is (de)formed and moves from the economy of scale to the economy of scope, from the stability of a State guaranteed monopolistic capitalism to the privatized, competitive and more volatile economy of the free market where small companies can have far-reaching power.

In this sense capital and capitalism diverge, rather than converge, because in the dissipative structure of the postmodern State the process of accumulation is localized and the consistency of capital resides in the molecular local market rather than the molar formation of State capitalism.

New technology, with electronic or digital connections made through multimedia networks, means that small regional or national businesses can operate in the global economy and rival State monopolies. There is also a less predictable accumulation of property as the economic base is not fixed geographically and economic power is, therefore, not dependent on a manufacturing infrastructure, or on natural resources, but on the ability of the State to attract and accommodate capital through monetary concessions. Indeed, markets need not coincide with the State and can be regional or national mini-anarchisms which may threaten the State and lead to realignments in economic alliances and the internal fragmentation of States; witness the emergence of Third World zones within western countries, the ghettos in cities and the rise of nationalist movements as well as the dissolution of the traditional bipolarities north/south, east/west. Where capital is a direct economic instance, dissipation is a machinic process that transforms the historical logic of State capitalism and reduces the State to a quasi-model of realization. There is a powershift from those with wealth to those with knowledge, knowledge which is transforming the way that we think, see ourselves and stand in relation to our governments, and not just how we send messages.[5]

In this new scenario Third World countries may well leap-frog into the twenty-first century as controllers of knowledge while the current dominance of Europe and the USA recedes. But, economic, cultural and political power do not necessarily coincide. The rise of the Tiger economies of Asia could be interpreted as the end of western hegemony, but technological investment in military systems by western governments and by the USA in particular, as demonstrated by Desert Storm, might still give them the political edge internationally, at the same time as they face economic competition and internal crisis. In any case, the concept of the State as a collective unit and guarantor of molar identity is no longer appropriate; in postmodernity the State acts as a strategic practice operating as a minimal condition of possibility for dissipative capital. In other words, the market economy has slipped State boundaries and the State remains only as an instable, fragmentary function of capital. It is no longer a geographical, cultural or political entity but an economic function determined by its receptivity to new technology and adjustment to a global commodified market.

The untamed system

For every example of resistance and reterritorialization there is one of deterritorialization and of technology accessing the market-place. There are newsworthy events where power lies with the consumer, not the producer, and where the flow of information can alter both states and States: in Los Angeles a citizen's video of police beating up a black driver precipitated the LA riots; and in China, satellites and fax machines enabled the world to see and condemn events in Tiananmen Square. In the light of the above examples, government projects which aim to provide access to technology for all, like that of the British DTI and the USA Center for Civil Networking, may well be double-edged. The continuing share in wealth and power that governments hope for depends on the dependence of capital on State capitalism, a possibility which is increasingly unlikely in view of the potential of virtual capital, made possible by the very technology being promoted. Whether liberalism or enlightened self-interest, this 'progress' may well reap the demise of the State as a model of collective cultural identity. In setting axioms the State sets a relative limit to the apocalypse where decoded flows run free, and despite an apparent tightening in State control in the political and cultural arenas, and increases in public spending, there is a general trend towards *laissez-faire* in the economic field in response to total commodification.

There is a link between the weakening of the State and ghettos of disenfranchised outsiders who are disqualified from State welfare but who nevertheless are members of localized markets, like the barrios of São Paulo, distinguished by their satellite dishes and portable phones, as well as by their shanty towns. This alternative economy is the Third World within, the flotsam of declining State capitalism. It includes desolate and dejected groups such as the homeless and disabled, but it is also the economy of the drug culture; an economy where more money changes hands in drug deals than company directors see in years, where illegal coca growers in Peru can earn the equivalent of £400 a month, and where profit from bribes, the sale of favours and racketeering produces a socius independent of, but often tacitly supported by, the contracting State.

Where capital is the cultural dominant, the social is not controlled by the molar identities of capitalist relations, but capital is controlling relations to the point where the subsumption of the human goes beyond enslavement to symbiosis and total commodification. This is capitalism *out of control*. State capitalism as a world-system is dissipated where capital can act as a singular, global superpower concretized in the self-organizing synthetic relationships of the free market. When capital is separated from the State, as capitalism out of control, there is a radical transformation of the world-system with the State taking advantage of the market economy, organizing and protecting the market for its own survival but no longer identified with it. This is not so much a breakdown and disintegration of traditional ties between man and State but an evolutionary transformation of those connections enabled by technology.

Where the propensity to decode accelerates faster than its axiomatic realization, the State is not even necessary as a function of capital. New technology makes this scenario a real possibility and takes the system beyond Deleuze and Guattari's vision of a third wave of heteronomous, polymorphic States. Where capital is autonomous, production, circulation and consumption can all act virtually and therefore axioms as operative statements are only as good as the technology, technology which is changing so fast that there is no gap between the axiom and the function. The system goes into reverse and capital, far from being mediated by the State, is a direct agency of decoding. This self-sustaining operative system is the ultimate in postmodernity, an untamed variation in the system – total commodification. It is a possibility considered by Deleuze and Guattari:

> a flow can be the object of one or several axioms (with the set of all axioms constituting the conjunction of the flows); but it can also lack any axioms of its own, its treatment being only the consequence of other axioms; finally it can remain out of bounds, evolve without limits, be left in a state of an 'untamed' variation in the system.
>
> (Deleuze and Guattari 1988: 461)

Where technology means that capital is an efficient virtual, the untamed State has become, not a variation in the system, but the system itself. Freed from capitalism, the untamed variation need not result in totalitarianism or fascism, as Deleuze and Guattari propose, but in anarchy and the dissipation of the State. Postmodernity is not just a change *within* the system but a change of the system and its transformation, even transmutation, into a different, unknown and unpredictable future.

The success of capitalism is that it can transform its own limits by subsuming its exteriority without changing its molar identity; that identity is just expanded to include all life, even that negated by capitalism – pre-capitalist Third World communities, the homeless, the unemployed, the outsider. In contrast, total commodification and the autonomy of capital make the possibility of collective identity through the State, whatever the ideology, impossible. Dystopia, political instability, moral decline and the breakdown of law and order ensue.

The Unmasking of Difference

> Neglect, decline, and the *death of the state*, the unleashing of the private person (I am careful not to say of the 'individual') – this is the result of the democratic concept of the state: this is its mission.
>
> (Nietzsche 1986: 472)

The extension of difference

The dissipation of the State means, not a renewal of human liberties and of choice and opinion, but an opening onto unrestrained bestiality and fragmentation, diversity and difference. The move from the fiction of abstract representation to a radical materialism enabled by the virtual as an effective force means that the State and the subject become spectres of postmodernism. This is manifest in the trend away from identity politics to the politics of the body, in which the 'human' is not coded by the reductive limits of metaphysical truths, the State and Oedipus, but produced as a real condition of disequilibrium. This is a process of invention, a becoming-other which is the inverse of liberalism and a reaction against social codings that reinforce the State and the supremacy of Western, white culture.

The evident structural failure of liberal politics to secure equality has spawned a reaction against the chimera of rights and freedoms in recognition that liberal/oppositional movements are themselves caught up in a logic of representation dependent on negative identity. The impossibility of producing radical alterity within mainstream culture, and the ironic reinforcement of hierarchy through the oppositional system of 'being', discredits identity politics as a politics of freedom with its emphasis on individual subjectivity and a distinct different but equal ethos. In contrast an anti-systemic biopolitics is marked, not by individualism and questions of identity, but by privatization; it is a rethinking of the human as scopic, rather than orphic. A derivation of *skopos*, target, and *skopein*, to watch, this terminology encapsulates the materiality of difference in postmodernity; it is how you look, not who you are, success through the body/sport, not the mind/education, ecstasy and body enhances, not acid and being spaced out, sex, not love. In biopolitics difference is material, not abstract, and identity is defined only in terms of the body.[6] Here there is no possible affirmative *human* identity, but that doesn't stop there being a productive desire which may be *inhuman* (non-)identity. Such a move does not entail the endless expansion and universal participation demanded by liberalism in either its conservative or socialist guises, but the construction of a new ontology where social production is the strategy of intention and invention, a continuous, non-numerical multiplicity, not the extension of a closed system.

Politics, philosophy and sociology must likewise resist being locked in assumptions about stable systems that are antithetic to the postmodern reality. There is a danger in seeing the 'progress' of universal capitalism, and the consequent technological revolution, as a loss of quality of human life because this demands resistance as the retrieval of an ontological base instead of as the construction of a new ontology.[7] To shore up transcendental relationships by reifying the human is to confuse technology and technicity. While recognizing technology as a state of the world and a way of existing – a relationship between man and nature that has implications for both – we must remember that it is only technicity that is instrumental and that therefore technology cannot be hijacked for the modernist project of progress, freedom and equality. In contrast, Deleuze and Guattari do not mourn the loss of an essential humanity but see the third age of human–machine systems, and the parallel transformation of the State, as the fundamental moment of the State realized in machinic enslavement (Deleuze and Guattari 1988: 460). It is a moment that presupposes itself, and it is surely a challenge to rethink the human and the social.

Machinic production

Technological development means a new machinic enslavement and the end of man as an object of transcendental formal unity; it means the triumph of the machine and the capture of the human subject and a 'generalized regime of subjection' (Deleuze and Guattari 1988: 458). This is a move away from the psychological and the individual; a shift from man being *dehumanized* by objectification to being rendered *inhuman* by the subjection of machinic (not mechanistic) enslavement. This subjection puts 'man' in danger because of a radical materialism which overrides philosophies of transcendence and the romance of humanism. Deleuze and Guattari use the example of television to illustrate subjection as a component in the input/output of information; but technology has developed dramatically since they were writing in the 1980s, and the PC revolution has brought communication between man and machine to a new complexity. The machine is no longer a tool but a medium of transformation and exchange. The Internet and interactive computers make the relational ideas of being subjected to, and enslaved by, machines redundant. They mean a real symbiosis of man and machine. It is the move towards a generalized regime of subjection which actually dissolves the notion of the individual as a distinctive human agent; it makes man an agent of inhumanization and the socius a machinic production, not a structural system.

This idea of the socius as a strategy, practice or production, and as a dynamic system of connections and disjunctions, rather than being understood as a structure, maps onto thermodynamics, and so emphasizes its radical materialism. The socius as a reductive/conflationary force of synthesis resembles an idealized integrable system where that system reaches all points on the surface of a given energy and has a tendency to minimum entropy production compatible with its boundary conditions – global capitalism as 'stable' system where linear functions operate. This is line in an idealized, isolated and closed primitive system where there is collective investment in the circulation of the inscribed relations of production/reproduction, and where the system remains close to equilibrium. However, in a real, dynamic situation the contingencies within which the socius must transform desire make disjunctions and disequilibrium an inevitable feature of its history. In any earthly society the boundary conditions are subject to change; for example, fluctuations in the weather or population and disease may limit possible filiations and alliances and thus the capacity for the production/reproduction and survival of that society.[8] It is the actuality of the socius as open and dynamic that means it is a non-reversible process carrying out real operations in the material world, and when the inherent contradictions of the world-system push it into the non-linear region, as in postmodernity, entropy production is strong and the social fluctuates. Survival, as the real and active operation of desire, is dependent on being adaptable, on positive entropy, debt and surplus value.

Debt and privatization

Debt is the key to the capability of alliance and crucial for social production – for man to breed and for man to be bred, to be a cultural as well as a biological organism. This is interesting terminology because it is surely debt that is keeping the present world economy going. For Deleuze and Guattari debt *is* territorial representation. It is the surplus value of code, the functional disequilibrium and the entropy that keeps the system productive through its extensive economic and political alliances. It is this energy that is simulated by capital in postmodernity.

Though capital has assumed the productive role of the socius, the tendency of capital to deterritorialize means that the finite debt of primitive systems is transformed in postmodernity into an infinite debt which has no exterior limit, and therefore an unlimited power of transformation; it is 'a pure availability, nonpossession and nonwealth' (Deleuze and Guattari 1984: 237). Certainly in the symbolic economy of computerized money transfer this infinite debt is productive and real without ever becoming actual; it is a 'surplus value of flow'

(Deleuze and Guattari 1984: 237), and the epitome of deterritorialization; no actuality, no social, pure production, pure desire. Literally and metaphorically this means the bankruptcy of the State as guardian of capital. It also means the decoding of the subject through total commodification so that subjectivity becomes a product determined by 'having'. This freedom from molarity is the positive entropy of experimentation and play, but it is also the dystopian production of exploitation – poverty, ghettos and the Third World.[9]

In *Anti-Oedipus* Deleuze and Guattari identify privatization and abstraction as processes which use this energy/debt in a productive sense; 'To withdraw a part from the whole, to detach, to 'have something left over', is to produce and to carry out real operations of desire in the material world' (Deleuze and Guattari 1984: 41). Without this 'something left over' the system would be static, inert and attritional. Certainly it would not be inscribed as a socius, because there would be no coding of the flow of desire and therefore no social production; no society, just pure non-existent nomad. On the one hand there are fixed, immutable codes and a static but attritional equilibrium, a situation of negative entropy; on the other hand, no coding and no possibility of being. However, in postmodernity the greater autonomy of capital makes under-coding an effective possibility, where 'to have' is as effective as 'to be' is when coding is secured and mediated by the State. Privatization is one such process whereby the surplus value of economic transactions, of 'having', is fed back into the under-coded culture of possession characteristic of postmodernity.

Privatization is the detachment from the collective that marks production. For instance, when a daughter becomes a member of her husband' s family, she makes a horizontal connection of alliance and becomes detached from the filiative reproductive chain. She breaks the chain in a movement of fragmentation – of privatization. (The parallel process in economics is obvious.) The disjunction is positive feedback in the vertical process of reproduction; it produces surplus value and stimulates adaptability through horizontal connections. Such disjunction is essential to functionality: 'it is in *order to function* that a social machine must *not function* well' (Deleuze and Guattari 1984: 151). The ability to create and to use surplus value is the key to the adaptability of any system, and it is in this sense that the socius is truly productive, making creative new connections that sustain the system. The system in postmodernity is, therefore, more like the mixing system, where evolution in phase space entails chaotic change in form while volume is maintained, than the integrable system. It changes by transformation rather than integration. In a system that is far from equilibrium, where capitalism has reached its boundaries, the production and the integration of surplus value is minimal; instead there is the more transformational, chaotic change where markets fragment and there is a volatile balance of power between States. The system is singular, not absolute, privatized, not individualized.

The move away from the collective investment that marks highly coded societies and towards apocalyptic and dystopic dissipation is a commodification of the social and the personal, as well as the strictly economic. There is a general move towards individuation and personal autonomy. However, individuation implies filiative unitary division and a fragmentation of a whole that is anathema to postmodernity. The detachment characterizing postmodernity is better described as privatization. It is a distinction crucial to understanding postmodernity as a time of the inhuman. Individualism is a psychological/religious concept of identity in which the person is defined in relation to a transcendent and perfect human essence, a personal God and an idealized God-like State. Far from being a decoding, individualization depends on the liberal ideal of community and is inscribed in rights secured by State laws. It is therefore an artifice of coding and entails an assumed investment in the State as an immutable structure. It also depends on the individual buying into the social system and its quasi-religious justification as protector of humanity; a dependence that requires the individual to will their own oppression. The liberal democracy is in fact anti-community as it depends on violence for the meanings, values and representations/interpretations through which the individual secures identity. The move away from the collective and towards the dissipation evident in the economics and society of postmodernity is not a process of individuation, but one of privatization. Privatization precipitates transformation and danger; it effects a radical transformation which breaks through codes, and a transmutation into a new phase transition. It is a move into the unknown. Its connections are alliances, not filiations, horizontal, not vertical, spatial, not historical.

(De)Forming the Present

For Deleuze and Guattari privatization is a process of civilization, a civilization which is the inverse of the liberal State: 'Civilization is defined by the decoding and the deterritorialization of flows of capitalist production' (Deleuze and Guattari 1984: 244). It is a move from the domination of truth to a civilization beyond good and evil, a monstrous world where man is defined by function, not essence.

In the turbulence of a civilization existing within far from equilibrium conditions, capital operates as an abstract machine; like desire, its production is non-limitative and unmediated. As pure function capital is stronger than molarity. As a result social production is a real production of difference – a capturing of desire from the future. In this extension of the future-past capital acts as the 'limit' of the social, a 'limit' governed only by the possibilities of 'having' and unrestricted by the fixed molarity of the State. The State is only effective as a regulator of flows and is (re)produced as a function of fragmented bodies; it is an alliance of property-owning subjects and like man a component in the myriad exchanges and transformations of a dissipative system. Postmodernity is a (de)formation of the world-system and a radical, qualitative change in the production of the State and the self. The challenge is to think that change.

Notes

1 See: Jameson (1991), postmodernism as the culmination of capitalism; Lyotard (1986), postmodernism as a premise of modernism; and Foucault (1981), postmodernism as a chosen attitude.
2 This is demonstrated by the Bénard instability. See Prigogine and Stengers (1985: 140).
3 This is an extension of Braudel's upside-down view of capitalism. Braudel makes the distinction between the zone of the market and monopolistic capitalism. The State creates and guarantees the capitalist system to secure its hegenomic power over the social, but it has a more limited regulatory hold over the market.
4 See: Deleuze (1988: 60); and Massumi's discussion of the future-past (1992: 37).
5 Some implications of this shift are discussed by Toffler (1991).
6 'Scopic' and 'orphic' are words used by Paul Gilroy (1994) in reference to trends in music.
7 Donna Haraway (1991) develops the idea of a cyborg reality.
8 Dynamic systems are described by Prigogine and Stengers (1985: 264).
9 For a discussion on the two-sidedness of surplus value see Massumi (1992: 201). It could also be argued that when surplus value is invested in the State, perhaps to pay off debts as in Japan, it acts as a brake on the decoding process.

References

Deleuze, G. (1966,1988) *Le Bergsonisme*, Paris: Presses Universitaires de France, *Bergsonism*, trans. H. Tomlinson, New York: Zone Books.

—— (1968, 1994) *Différence et répétition*, Paris: PUF, *Difference and Repetition*, trans. P. Patton, London: Athlone.

Deleuze, G. and Guattari, F. (1972, 1984) *L'Anti-Oedipe*, Paris: Les Editions de Minuit, *Anti-Oedipus*, trans. R. Hurley et al., London: Athlone.

—— (1987, 1988) *Mille Plateaux*, Paris: Les Editions de Minuit, *A Thousand Plateaus*, trans. B. Massumi, London: Athlone.

Foucault, M. (1981) 'The Order of Discourse', in R. Young (ed.) *Untying the Text*, London: Routledge.

Gilroy, P. (1994) '"After the Love Has Gone": Biopolitics and Etho-politics in the Black Public Sphere', *Third Text* 28/29, Autumn/Winter.

Haraway, D. (1991) *Simians, Cyborgs and Woman*, London: Free Press.

Jameson, F. (1991) *Postmodernism, The Cultural Logic of Capitalism*, London: Verso.

Lyotard, J.-F. (1986) *The Postmodern Condition*, trans. G. Bennington and B. Massumi, Manchester: Manchester University Press.

Marcuse, H. (1964) *One Dimensional Man*, London: Routledge & Kegan Paul.

Massumi, B. (1992) *A User's Guide to Capitalism and Schizophrenia*, Cambridge, MA: MIT Press.

Mazlish, B. (1989) *A New Science*, Oxford: OUP.

Nietzsche, F. (1986) *Human All too Human*, trans. R. J. Hollingdale, Cambridge: CUP.

Prigogine, I. and Stengers, I. (1985) *Order out of Chaos*, London: Flamingo.

Toffler, A. (1991) *Powershift*, London: Pan.

Wallerstein, I. (1991) *Unthinking Social Science*, Cambridge: Polity Press.

8

Palimpsest

Towards a Minor Literature in Monstrosity

Deepak Narang Sawhney

I

> There is no mother tongue, only a power takeover by a dominant language within a political multiplicity.
>
> (Deleuze and Guattari 1988: 7)

> Motion has been my closest companion, from room to room, house to house, street to street, neighborhood to neighborhood, school to school, jail to jail, cell to cell – from one man-made hell to another.
>
> (Shakur 1994: 103)

A tablet, a parchment or stratum that is overcoded, decoded and once again recoded is an *application* of inscription, a process of stratification, that binds multiplicities to a homogeneous apparatus of capture (the State). The Unity of the despot allocates blockages and compartments to divide multiplicities into cellular partitions, an operation of reterritorialization. This activates an *absolute difference* between the layers of the strata, thereby assuring a panzer division between heterogeneous elements, a conversion to homogeneity. By assembling a mutually comprehensive, stable machinery out of heterogeneous systems, the strata are a withdrawal from machinic intensity. There is nothing in the composition of the strata that will shield it from other influences, other than the process of stratification. Even though the strata tend to be distributed by free intensities, the achievement of the layers of the strata lies precisely in coding and territorialization, whereby an absolute difference in nature and a homogenization without thresholds is achieved. Reminiscent of Franz Kafka's stories, the homogeneity of the stratum processes intensity through a central processing unit – a vast bureaucracy that inscribes the Law on tablets, parchments or strata, but the strata depend on something having escaped. Through the apparatus of writing, the State perfectly coincides with the despot's inscription. Writing demonstrates the new, massively rigorous and defined stratification. An event with a strategy, the despot's written word is the absolute explosion that over-codes any language it comes across. The weight of stratification produces effects: a record keeping, a meticulous recoding through machinic expertise. The despot always has a distributed sphere by which spatiality ceases to be immanent. Thus, we can say that the despot is a threshold in which something immense slides into history in a single stroke, a temporality beyond response; and yet, is also a mega-singularity that is always looming on the horizon.[1] It is the capacity for global power. Of particular interest is the binary opposition that links multiplicities to a uniformly stable relay that rises up to the super-stratum. The individualization of *mass* through a constructed system of Unity is the function of binary oppositions, whereby '(t)he fluxes are tidied away, controlled and over-encoded by means of the writing machine' (Guattari 1984: 122). Deleuze and Guattari's *Capitalism and Schizophrenia* is a pragmatics specializing in the mapping of intensities that not only deterritorialize, but also reterritorialize to form higher layers on the strata.[2] By composing a map, as opposed to a tracing, of particular strata levels, certain geographical assemblages converge to bifurcate the existing homogeneity into multiplicities. Deleuze and Guattari provide various descriptions of this process, most notably, packs, mass and gangs. A map is a singular, functional element that addresses the molar organization of confinement, or stratification. The strata demarcate zones of intensity, a process of differentiating space, whereby over-coding locks intensive processes into regimented, periodic loops within the circuit of the strata. In other words, intensities that deterritorialize are reterritorialized into the space of signification, an over-coding into the strata of globalization or universalization. Stratification, or the lateral dispersion of intensities into homogeneous wholes, is the circuit that binds the layers together. This always takes place with a deterritorialization coupled with a complementary reterritorialization:

> An organism that is deterritorialized in relation to the exterior necessarily reterritorializes on its interior milieus. . . . Every voyage is intensive, and occurs in relation to thresholds of intensity between which it evolves or that it crosses. One travels by intensity; displacements and spatial figures depend on intensive thresholds of nomadic deterritorialization (and thus on different relations) that simultaneously define complementary, sedentary reterritorializations.
>
> (Deleuze and Guattari 1988: 54)

Thus the *relative deterritorialization's* supple movement to destratification, a cracking of the rigid, territorialized belts, is defined with a complementary reterritorialization. By critically juxtaposing relative deterritorialization with the elements of minor literature, this chapter situates the current political and literary voices emerging out of South Central Los Angeles. Despite its subscription to a signed subjectivity, *Monster: The Autobiography of an LA Gang Member* generates a collective assemblage that decodes the stratification of language into minoritarian politics of desire.[3] This is the functioning element of *becoming*. Written from a California maximum security prison, *Monster*, which portrays mass movements within the grid of Los Angeles, illuminates the destratification of molecular becomings that are recaptured by the State apparatus of recoding. The movement that oscillates between deterritorialization and reterritorialization allows for a mapping of becoming, even though population packs are in constant flux: 'The two factors [code and territoriality] nevertheless have the same 'subject' in a stratum: it is populations that are deterritorialized and reterritorialized, and also coded and decoded' (Deleuze and Guattari 1988: 54). Shakur's *Monster* presents the possibility of mapping heterogeneous multiplicities that are stratified through homogeneous power centres. This chapter discusses the heterogeneous, ecological niches that the strata uniformly attempt to recode in relation to Shakur's minor literature.[4] The process by which the strata solidify multiplicities is addressed, as well as the function of the *minor* in South Central Los Angeles. This locates not only the political turbulence of the West Coast, but the consequences resulting from institutionalized power structures engaged in the monitoring of masses that do not fit into the equation of the molar organization.[5] With the influx of a periphery into the core area of Los Angeles, the current role of urban politics and minor literatures unleashes *desire* into the circuit of the city. The machinic process of becoming a peripheral minoritarian is unparalleled in Shakur's autobiography, as in the following:

> The term 'institutional security' is so far-reaching that whenever there is nothing to lock a prisoner down or harass him for, staff, correction officers, and most any figure of authority in any institution will pull out this ambiguous term. It is precisely this wording that has me locked deep within the bowels of Pelican Bay today. I am a threat, and proud of it. If I wasn't a threat, I'd be doing something wrong.
>
> (Shakur 1994: 221)

> An American who locks you in a cage, counts you to make sure you haven't escaped, holds a weapon on you, and, in many instances, shoots you. Add to

> this the fact that most of us grew up in an eighty percent New Afrikan community policed – or occupied – by an eighty-five percent American pig force that is clearly antagonistic to any male in the community, displaying this antagonism at every opportunity by any means necessary with all the brute force and sadistic imagination they can muster.
>
> (Shakur 1994: 223–4)

II

In '1227: Treatise on Nomadology: – The War Machine', in *A Thousand Plateaus* (1988: 351–423) Deleuze and Guattari put forward a cartography of sedentary space that appropriates the rhythmic movements of autonomous *packs*, and allows a nomadic war-machine to come into play. Deleuze and Guattari not only juxtapose a geological compass directed towards the super-stratum that envelopes rhizomatic movements with a topography of over-coding, but also position a genealogical optic by which the State apparatus emerges. These two processes of appropriation – deterritorialization and reterritorialization – are inextricably entwined, since the application of over-coding can be traced on both aspects of the molar and molecular lattice, or planes of strata. Composing a study of the strata, a stratigraphy, would enable a lateral tracing of the layers upon layers of sedimentation that have been stacked to form a super-stratum, or most notably, the despot. The belts or layers of the strata are intensities that have been captured by the super-stratum – an application of over-coding. The lateral movement of intensity that gets imprisoned to form another belt on the strata represents over-coding by the super-stratum. In other words, intensity that escapes through the fissures of stratification is reterritorialized by being folded back on itself. The super-stratum perennially orchestrates the appropriation of intensities by such an avenue of conversion. The result is the stratification of heterogeneous multiplicities that become imprisoned within a homogeneous, arborescent super-stratum. This is an instance of high-level control, a 'phenomen[on] of centering, unification, totalization, integration, hierarchization, and finalization' (Deleuze and Guattari 1988: 41): the despot. The process of over-coding also acts as a memory system by which the super-stratum can navigate the direction of particular homogeneous wholes. The myriad layers that constitute the stratum are captured intensities that form a zone of articulation, a memory or an inscription. The storage machine of memory operates within a relative stasis, a homogeneous reterritorialization. The mechanism that binds intensity to a stratification of memory eliminates the machinic drift and variation that assembles a pack. 'The memory blocks desire, makes mere carbon copies of it, fixes it within strata, cuts it off from all its connections' (Deleuze and Guattari 1986: 4). The strata imprison intensities through a double operation that couples deterritorialization with a complementary reterritorialization. The complementarity is a double bind that has the opposite dynamic of deterritorialization. By exciting intensities to spill out of the strata, complementary reterritorializations capture flows and lock the machinic assemblage of desire into suppression. Deleuze and Guattari provide numerous descriptions for this over-coding, such as a lobster and God.

How is it possible to reinfluence the strata with machinic potential – a point of convergence between behaviour that has become frozen and code that has become rigidly stratified? By constructing a machine, a map, a diagram or practices instead of a discourse of representation, and dismantling the homogeneous stasis through an intensively continuous variation. However, will this movement connect the strata to a process, whereby a diagrammatic drift will link to destratification of code and flux, and in turn will bifurcate intensities to other heterogeneous elements? The attempt to address this question is precisely the function of minor literature: 'a becoming that includes the maximum of difference as a difference of intensity, the crossing of a barrier, a rising or a falling, a bending or an erecting, an accent on the word' (Deleuze and Guattari 1986: 22). It is always a question of becoming: geographical assemblages attracting a geopolitical immediacy, deterritorializing language, and the 'collective assemblage of enunciation'.[6] A map of becoming can be sketched as a molecular intensity rupturing, a line of flight that connects to other zones of multiplicities. How do the machinic assemblages of packs and gangs function? To answer this question, it is important to refer back to 'The Treatise on Nomadology', and the discussion on *Numbering Number*, in order to initiate the assemblage of minor literature: 'All of thought is a becoming, a double becoming, rather than the attribute of a Subject and the representation of a Whole' (Deleuze and Guattari 1988: 380). The Numbering Number functions as a collective assemblage of enunciation whereby the subject processes multiplicities. The elements that bifurcate to form a multiplicity share the same properties as packs. There is no subjectivity that can be counted, or isolated, within the multiplicity; '(t)he number is no longer a means of counting or measuring but of moving: it is the number itself that moves through smooth space' (Deleuze and Guattari 1988: 389). The collective assemblage of enunciation is correlated to Deleuze and Guattari's critique of the analyst/patient dichotomy in psychoanalysis: a theatre in which subjects speak on their behalf – a hallucinatory image of private speech.[7] Rather, the collective assemblage of enunciation speaks/acts as an organ of the molecular: a numerical, intensive multiplicity that divides into itself. Since there is no difference between multiplicities dividing into themselves and connecting up with other heterogeneous intensities, a multiplicity can only grow by changing in nature – a metamorphosis. Its nature is defined by a threshold crossed at a singular point in its growth. A becoming. A generic, numerical entity, such as a wolf, or a *monster.* What is it for a pack to be divided and yet still compose an assemblage? Granted the pack is perpetually partitioned and segregated, but the variation in its magnitude is always heterogeneously intensive. 'There are only multiplicities of multiplicities forming a single *assemblage*, operating in the same *assemblage*: packs in masses and masses in packs' (Deleuze and Guattari 1988: 34). Packs are liminal: a boundary, or a zone, that is not categorically localizable. Their relationship to multiplicity is of a pragmatic leverage that *escapes* from Unity, Totality or a transcendent model of articulation. This is a divergence from the molar apparatus that counts from the outside. The transcendent, homogenized *Numbered number* is a numerical lineage that constitutes a complementary reterritorialization – the recapturing of a line of flight. As Deleuze and Guattari suggest, 'the use of the number as a numeral, as a statistical element, is proper to the numbered number of the State, not to the numbering number' (Deleuze and Guattari 1988: 390).

The molecular fractures stratified intensity and maximally populates itself in order to function. It is not a function of copying or tracing a map; rather rhizomes add a map to a specific territory: 'the rhizome pertains to a map that must be produced, constructed, a map that is always detachable, connectable, reversible, modifiable and has multiple entryways and exits and its own lines of flight' (Deleuze and Guattari 1988: 21). By adding changes in the territory, intensities bifurcate to form other assemblages. Thus Deleuze and Guattari affirm that multiplicity has to be treated as a substantive, an intensive difference, as opposed to the category of Plurality, which only provides quantitative differences: 'A multiplicity has neither subject nor object, only determinations, magnitudes, and dimensions that cannot increase in number without the multiplicity changing in nature' (Deleuze and Guattari 1988: 8). Speed and temperature are examples provided by Deleuze and Guattari to designate the distinction between intensive difference and merely quantitative intensity. Intensive difference, for instance, speed, is only decomposable into other speeds and is irreducible to molar difference. This is basic to intensities since they never enter into relations of proportionality.

The mutual process of deterritorialization and reterritorialization is a self-excitation that departs from all reference to strata, or reliable framework, downloaded from the super-stratum. Thus the line of flight is a clandestine movement branching out of homogeneous relations that posit application. The heterogeneity that drips through the cracks and fissures of the strata ceases to be in a complicity to categorical systems of Unity. The machinic assemblage is a lingering, yet constant, camouflaged movement that interferes with the pattern of coded processes: a micro-practice of becoming. It is a construction, or an engineering tool, for exploring trajectories of destratification, a probing of edges and potentialities. The trajectory offers lines of escape and flight that allow a movement into, and of, new spaces, a becoming-minor through new cartographies. A convection that situates the mass movement to destratification. A catalyst for minor literature. A war-machine.

III

> It is an affair of cartography. They compose us, as they compose our map.
>
> (Deleuze and Guattari 1988: 203)

> Who *is* Monster Kody? . . . *I* am Monster Kody . . . a person, a young man, a black man. . . . Anything else? . . . No, not that I know of . . . *What* is Monster Kody? . . . A Crip, an Eight Tray, a Rollin' Sixty Killer . . . a black man . . . Black man, black man, BLACK MAN. . . .
>
> (Shakur 1994: 225–6)

Monster: The Autobiography of an LA Gang Member chronicles the first phase of Shakur's life, by charting the early initiation rites into the gang world through to his first killing in low-intensity warfare to being shot seven times himself. It is during this period that Shakur acquires the name Monster. At the age of thirteen Shakur is struck in the face by a man he is trying to rob; the man attempts to escape but is 'tripped' by Tray Ball, a fellow Crip, who then holds the victim while Shakur 'stomps' him for twenty minutes: 'I learned that the man had lapsed into a coma and was disfigured from my stomping. The police told bystanders that the person responsible for this was a 'monster'. The name stuck' (Shakur 1994: 13).[8] At sixteen Shakur is imprisoned for the first time: 'Not a door, not a window, but bars. Since then I have had an indelible scar on my mind stamped "criminal"' (Shakur 1994: 138). Upon his release, Shakur has numerous skirmishes in South Central Los Angeles with other gang sets, as well as law-enforcement agencies that eventually place him in a California Youth Training School for four years. As Shakur portrays, each gang in the training school mobilizes according to 'geopolitical' boundaries that stretch from northern to southern California. The dynamics by which each set recodes according to territory produces larger conflictual groups designated by 'lines of race'. To complicate matters more, tribalism severs New Afrikans into warring factions: 'Tribalism was most prevalent amongst New Afrikans, who began as one then split into Crips and Bloods' (Shakur 1994: 207). With numerous sets combating with each other for hierarchical domination in the institutionalized environment, Shakur begins to question the foundation of tribalism and the 'wider reality' of New Afrika. Moreover, *Monster*'s graphic descriptions of South Central Los Angeles under constant surveillance from the State apparatus, coupled with the threat of feuding warring factions shooting a 'homie' (comrade), place Shakur's role as a Crip member into question. The position of preserving the 'hood through retaliatory attacks to writing encrypted messages on South Central walls comes under critical examination when Shakur realizes that he does not even own a brick in the United States, and yet, since the age of eleven, has defended a territory which is not really his own. On the one hand, the nomad is a trajectory that does not possess any territory through enclosing or striating space, yet still demarcates a zone of actuality through a landscape, a smooth space that is the removed perimeter from the apparatus of recoding. 'It is in this sense that nomads have no points, paths, or lands, even though they do by all appearances' (Deleuze and Guattari 1988: 381). And, on the other hand, the stratum once again reterritorializes – inscribes – the nomadic trajectory decoding from the belts. It is when institutions are deterritorialized on the cusp of madness that the strata can once again recapture the molecular intensity and impose a homogeneity. As with the despot, the socius results from an unprecedented deterritorialization that folds back on itself to form other strata. And, with Shakur, we find him back in prison, his body recoded as a black man, a gang member, a Crip and a killer. The institutional holding cell is the apparatus by which his identity is reconfigured, an etching or a memory within the strata: criminal. It is with this movement of deterritorialization and reterritorialization between the different thresholds of the strata that a passage from being prisoner to becoming-monster is conjugated. The way in which Shakur's movement is decoded and recoded – from gang member to prisoner back to gang member – constitutes a double movement that is constructed and dismantled to form a singularity. The series, becoming-monster, in which Shakur exists as much as a gang member as he does a prisoner, gives rise to a machine that the strata cannot recode. The zones that *Monster* assembles and disassembles are molecular intensities escaping from the components of confinement. Since coding signifies difference by flattening out quantitative entities through a universalization in advance, the super-stratum that demarcates each cellular position in relation to each subjectivity cannot code immanently localized assemblages. Thus to designate intensities is to localize singularities, producing micro fissures that deterritorialize the molar organization. Thus the metamorphosis to becoming wavers between tactics of maintaining a region and not being captured by the super-stratum. *Monster* is such a formula:

> Prison was like a stepping stone to manhood, with everything depending on going and coming back. Going meant nothing if you never came back. The going was obligatory, but coming back was voluntary. Going didn't just mean prison, it circumscribed a host of obligatory deeds. Go shoot somebody, go take a car, go break into that house, go rob that store, go spray-paint that wall, or go up to that school. The glory came not in going but in coming back. To come back showed a willingness to 'stay down'. It fostered an image of the set as legitimate, and each individual who could go and come back brought something new – walk, talk, look, way of writing.
>
> (Shakur 1994: 163–4)

While he is confined to a Youth Training School, Shakur's allegiance to the New Afrikan Independence Movement becomes visible, but it is not fully developed till his involvement in the Consolidated Crip Organization (CCO).[9] The importance of the biographical excerpt lies in Shakur's coining of the term 'Machine in Motion' to designate the molecular, anti-systemic rhizome.[10] The assemblage is an impermanent, temporal intensity that extinguishes itself when connected to other multiplicities: 'this is what it is all about – the discovery of assemblages of immanence and their dismantling. To dismantle a machinic assemblage is to create and effectively take a line of escape' (Deleuze and Guattari 1986: 59). The machine is a singularity that maps all minoritarian possibilities by bringing into question the role of the dominant, suppressive molar organization. The 'Machine in Motion' initiates all that is stratified into an active collectivity of enunciation, a cadence, to a point where the emergence of becoming is produced. There is no difference between the map that is collectively composed through the assemblage and the territory upon which it inscribes itself. It is a question of locality that brings into question the Unity of the majority. The 'Machine in Motion' sketches a geopolitical, molecular intensity that acts as a catalyst for deterritorialization. This intensity then ruptures the stratum, releasing a line of flight and effecting an interacting zone that is immersed in geopolitical immediacy. Deterritorialization is never defined by its speed, but rather through its nature to 'jump from one singularity to another following a nondecomposable, nonsegmentary line' (Deleuze and Guattari 1988: 56). Thus, becoming is never coordinated by a tracing of the strata, but only through the drawing of heterogeneous lines of flight, a howling which, like a great wind, invades and links up subjectivity with a mobile multiplicity that would otherwise get trapped within a static becoming – a becoming-homogeneous that, in truth, amounts only to death.

With Shakur's immersion in the 'Machine in Motion', what role does his proper name have in the equation to multiplicity? Kody Scott, Monster Kody and Sanyika

Shakur cease to denote a subjectivity, but instead diagram a writing-machine, a programme that has a local, variable functionality within the strata; a pragmatics destratifying the universalization of identity structures. These are the effects of intensities raging against the organs of the body. There is no difference between the proper name and becoming-monstrosity, for both envelope and deterritorialize the coding mechanisms of stratification. The organisms are stratifications of identity/unity that cause binary oppositions to saturate multiplicities into rigidified wholes. The bifurcation excites the molar operation of identity by seeking the point of becoming-imperceptible. A writing-machine that encompasses the 'impossibility of not writing' is the construction of assemblages inventing lines of flight from within the major language (Deleuze and Guattari 1986: 16–17ff.). The collective enunciation of minor literature severs the suture of the over-coding subjectivity that is stratified into a homogeneous whole, a Unity. A writing-machine seeking molecular connections by which a line of flight can be compassed is an assemblage that has numbering number as its component, drifting through the molar topography of the strata. Proper names can then be designated as singularities, discontinuous assemblages, or effects; in other words, both proper names and intensive numbering number mark a singularity. If it is possible to designate a singularity, then the strata amount to coding an infinite amount of intensity: 'something always escapes'.[11] Through the subordination of an autobiography to a topography of the subject, there is, initially, a linear chronicle because of the socius layering uniformed mechanisms of recoding. The machinic, subterranean flows of deterritorialization are perpetually reconfiguring the dynamics of the system, thereby pushing the subjectivity behind the narrative into a collectivity. This doubling, namely, a life chiselled on a palimpsest and the mutant lines of intensity that perpetually decode the strata, is a becoming writing-machine. Communication between the different strata intertwines at proximate levels of bifurcation. Deleuze and Guattari term this mediation the K-function, to designate not only the singularity that destratifies the strata but also the recodings that infiltrate the heterogeneous mass.

> K., the K.-function, designates the line of flight or deterritorialization that carries away all of the assemblages but also undergoes all kinds of reterritorializations and redundancies – redundancies of childhood, village-life, love, bureaucracy, etc.
>
> (Deleuze and Guattari 1988: 88–9)

Situating Shakur's *Monster* within an assemblage, or a becoming writing-machine, is complex and perplexing. The cocking of a handgun to shoot an enemy and inscribing a life, an autobiography, onto a palimpsest are a problematic function on the same circuit that fractures the stratification of identity: both relay a multiplicity within a pack that localizes movement; both deterritorialize transcendent systems of Law and language, respectively; both initiate movements to the periphery, a minoritarian assemblage; and both are destratified zones in which communication reaches an immanent threshold.[12] The schizophrenic dispersion of identity through the cocking of a hammer locates each body within an immanent exchange, a mapping of decoded subjectivity. 'I remember raising my weapon and him looking back – for a split second it was as if we communicated on another level and I overstood who he was – then I pulled the trigger and laid him down' (Shakur 1994: 11). The circulation through which communication decodes to its molecular component is the destratification of geological plates of identity, whereby a smooth space initiates a realigning of territory.[13] Furthermore, Shakur's account of movements that are not situated within homogeneous, cellular units, but derive their degree of intensity through local variations, conceives each molecular gradient in terms of an immanent mutation. The molecular is a swarm of collective behaviour; a multiplicity whereby the machinic process exploits stratified thresholds of strata. 'Like a temperature or a speed', the equation of singularities modifies thresholds of systems. The numbering number is not a random element, but a collective ensemble that molecularizes through thresholds.

IV

> It is certainly not by using a minor language as a dialect, by regionalizing or ghettoizing, that one becomes revolutionary; rather, by using a number of minority elements, by connecting, conjugating them, one invents a specific, unforeseen, autonomous becoming.
>
> (Deleuze and Guattari 1988: 106)

Considering the machinic heterogeneity that constructs a writing-machine, through which Shakur assembles his line of flight, we are struck towards the end of *Monster* by the molecular escape folding back on itself. This is not to imply that Shakur's confinement in Pelican Bay is a molecular reterritorialization, but, rather, his tabling of racial separation. Before venturing into this stratification, it is important to focus on the doctrine of racial differentiation that Shakur provides. This occurs in numerous places, particularly so with his emphasis on America's genealogical suppression of minoritarian race(s). 'The contributing factors are many, and no singular person or group has the absolute solution. From what I've studied and seen it would seem that this country's 130-year-old experiment of multiculturalism has failed. Perhaps it was never designed to work. . . . My personal belief is that separation is the solution' (Shakur 1994: 381–2). This is problematic, for the differentiation of colour, derived from a homogeneous production of numbered number, measures and divides through a melanous partitioning of race. It is a folding back of a decoded intensity, a minoritarian assemblage, into a regimented whole that is another stratification on the pre-existing myriad layers that constitute the molar's position of 'supremacy'.[14] The K-function falls prey not only to redundancies of childhood regressions of familism, but recodings of a sedentary space more devastating than anything envisioned before: a construction of identity that suppresses becoming. Thus the K-function is architecturally modelled within a homogeneous realm, through which the molar organization provides a definition for becoming. A division of the race that Shakur desires to evoke within the socius is founded on the notion of the oppression of one and the supremacy of the other, and by imposing what it implies to be a minor, Shakur is folding back onto the same notion of identity that the oppressor employs to globalize and perpetuate the stratification of machinic assemblages. Thus Shakur's recoding of the becoming-minor takes place on the same plane, or palimpsest, that the super-stratum implements to stratify minoritarian becomings. As Deleuze and Guattari suggest in *Capitalism and Schizophrenia*, race is not predicated on purity, but exists only through being oppressed: 'there is no race but inferior, minoritarian; there is no dominant race; a race is defined not by its purity but rather by the impurity conferred upon it by a system of domination' (Deleuze and Guattari 1988: 379). More importantly, race cannot be rediscovered through 'mythical' voyages that tend to be aligned with microfascisms, a theatre of representation providing a nostalgic narrative of identity. For instance, to return to the process of becoming-imperceptible, the function of proper names is to stratify not within a representation of race, but within a zone that converges with other minoritarian assemblages, regardless of molar attributes, that share the same production of becoming. Deleuze and Guattari term this interactive phylum 'a class of effects', which locates a movement that encompasses all totalities within the machinic process.[15] Shakur is misguided when he emphasizes the purpose which separation will have in this new configuration of identity: a characterization that retains a static definition of what a class of effects will produce is none other than a transcendent molarization within the dominant language. The depiction of the minority, as a peripheral rhizome, lies in its 'connection' to other ruptures that produce elements which the strata cannot recode. The significance of *Monster: The Autobiography of an LA Gang Member* is the machinic line of flight that connects to imperceptible localities, which would otherwise be recoded by the super-stratum through globalized identification, such as a criminal in the prison system, the explication of racism and segregation. The supple molecularity of the writing-machine is to delimit the cartography of representation, to access the molar stratified layers that unify suppression and racism, to bifurcate models of the dominant language and to create a trajectory of escape on a smooth space of interaction. 'The more a language has or acquires the characteristics of a major language, the more it is affected by continuous variations that transpose it into a 'minor' language' (Deleuze and Guattari 1988: 102). The criticism that can be levelled at Shakur in his recoding that separates race does not involve rejecting the collective assemblage of enunciation he has generated within the confines of Pelican Bay. Shakur's strength in becoming-monster lies in the re-evaluation of the planes of strata that bind and suppress minoritarian becomings. To dismantle the apparatus of capture that thwarts such multiplicities. . . .

Notes

1 A critique of transcendent stratification becomes a schizoanalysis of the super-stratum. The super-stratum is, on the one hand, an objective movement at the heart of application, and on the other, the super-impositional sphere that appears in a single stroke, as if it is from a disconnected region, an ulterior realm. This is the basic condition for the super-stratum, insofar as it acquires a norm through which identity arrives from somewhere else, a Unity. The super-stratum predicates behaviour that is not immanent in its functioning, a transcendence, whereby the mapping of the strata will resolve the incongruity that is always lingering on the periphery of production. Something will always escape: 'That is why bands in general . . . are metamorphoses of a war machine formally distinct from all State apparatuses or their equivalents, which are instead what structure centralized societies' (Deleuze and Guattari 1988: 358).

2 For an extended discussion relating to the process of deterritorialization with a complementary reterritorialization, see Deleuze and Guattari (1988): 'Deterritorialization must be thought of as a perfectly positive power that has degrees and threshold (epistrata), is always relative, and has reterritorialization as its flipside or complement' (54).

3 Throughout this chapter, the title of the autobiography is occasionally shortened to *Monster* in order to designate the minor collectivity which Shakur generates through the writing-machine.

4 Refer to Deleuze and Guattari (1988), 'November 20, 1923: Postulates of Linguistics', for an examination of minor literature in connection to a major language:

> Minor languages are characterized not by overload and poverty in relation to a standard or major language, but by sobriety and variation that are like a minor treatment of the standard language, a becoming-minor of the major language. The problem is not the distinction between major and minor language; it is one of a

becoming. It is a question not of reterritorializing oneself on a dialect or a patois but of deterritorializing the major language.

(104)

5 By this I am not only suggesting the current cybernetic technologies that are being implemented to reterritorialize the 'public' and 'private' space into a unified stratification of surveillance in Los Angeles (see Davis 1994) but also the State of California's claim to be the leader in prison systems:

> Since the early 1980s, California has made prison-construction its main form of infrastructural investment, spending over $5 billion on 19 new prisons, and has raised the number of people incarcerated from 23,000 in 1980 to 125,000 today. . . . Vacaville (near Sacramento) is now home to the world's largest prison, a title soon to be taken away by planned expansion of San Quentin. A federal court has just ruled that Pelican Bay, the state's 'model' high-security prison, violates constitutional protections against inhumane torments.
>
> (Walker 1995: 60)

Though this chapter does not present an in-depth study of architectural space, it is interesting to note the similarities between the development of the American city, particularly Los Angeles, and the structure of prisons narrated by Shakur. For instance, the architects of zoning exemplify the allocation of land uses to pre-defined solutions of homogeneity:

> Zoning, the division of the American city into a structure of cells, hierarchically controlled and rearranged, was a technical solution meant to secure an orderly and stable development of the urban land market. Promoting a disciplinary order, with its values of efficiency and functionality already etched out in the planning mentality by 1914, the core purpose of zoning was to remove and separate conflicting lands uses and dysfunctional districts that might impede or destroy solid investments in land.
>
> (Boyer 1983: 153)

And, Shakur's confinement within Youth Training School (YTS) in 1981:

> A maximum-security prison, it comprised three units, each divided into quarters. Each quarter was subdivided into halves, and each half was again divided into banks, or tiers. Every prisoner was assigned to his own cell. Each cell had a sliding door of solid steel with a small glass window for observation by staff.
>
> (Shakur 1994: 204)

Shakur adds to this detailed descriptions of the function of the three units – each consisting of four 'companies' alphabetically arranged – designed to reorientate the inmates for society. The importance of the above stems from how stratification is devised and implemented, whether it be through zoning laws, judicial confinement or transcendent apparatuses of racism; and the construction of a molecular writing-machine within the despotic operation of inscription that fractures molar systems of suppression. From the Marquis de Sade through Genet to George Jackson and, at present, Sanyika

Shakur, the highly reterritorialized forms of incarceration converge with molecular writing-machines that dissipate the strategies of the mechanisms of capture: 'Language is a map, not a tracing' (Deleuze and Guattari 1988: 77).

6 For a further discussion concerning the three characteristics of minor literature, see Deleuze and Guattari (1986: 18ff.).

7 Refer to '1914: One or Several Wolves?' (Deleuze and Guattari 1988) for a criticism surrounding Freud's analysis of private speech: '(t)here are no individual statements, there never are. Every statement is the product of a machinic assemblage, in other words, of collective agents of enunciation' (37). And, 'November 2, 1923: Postulates of Linguistics': 'There is no individual enunciation. There is not even a subject of enunciation' (79).

8 Since this chapter concentrates on Deleuze and Guattari's minor literature in relation to *Monster*, it will not be possible to discuss the molecular structure of the gang environment that envelops the young Shakur's life. However, the Crips appropriate numerous aspects of nomad war-machines, such as dehierarchized power structures, fluid levels of interaction within the organization, and interchangeable parts or positions that mutate according to need:

> banging falls short of the level of organization of, say, an institution that was formally founded on the premise of being structured, so there is no compartmentalization. No individual has a specific duty assigned to him, where his efficiency can be monitored by a superior. Therefore, the serious banger often finds himself handling several 'jobs' in the course of his career. For years I found my position in the set to be manifold. At any given time I was the minister of information, which included such responsibilities as writing on walls, declaring who we were and who we wanted to kill . . . minister of defense, which entailed organizing and overseeing general troop movement and maintaining a highly visible, militarily able contingency of soldiers who, at a moment's notice, could be relied upon for rapid deployment anywhere in the city; teacher of war tactics, which, I guess, would fall under the heading of instructor; and combat soldier and on-the-job trainer.
>
> (Shakur 1994: 78)

9 The CCO was eventually dismantled when the leaders realized that their assemblage, Clandestine Revolutionary Internationalist Party Soldiers (CRIPS), was static, as opposed to futuristic (Shakur 1994: 352). For further details regarding Shakur's commitment to these movements, see the following chapters in Shakur (1994): '48 Hours', 'Reconnected' and 'Nation Time'.

10 'Machine in Motion' is the Universal Crip Cadence cited by the inmates and led by Shakur. I am understanding 'Machine in Motion' to include a reference to the supple molecularity by which a process to immanence is generated. See the chapter '48 Hours' for the message contained in the Universal Crip Cadence that pertains to the transformation from tribalism to unity (Shakur 1994: 306–9).

11 This relates to chapter 9, '1933: Micropolitics and Segmentarity', where Deleuze and Guattari address the sectors of 'impotence' that define power centres. This, of course,

locates anti-systemic movements of resistance, or micropolitics, as a mass that thwarts the perpetuation of the super-stratum (1988: 217).

12 The smeared walls in South Central Los Angeles, upon which Shakur marks his affiliation to the Crips, also function as a palimpsest. The walls that house the graffiti are in a fluid transaction of being coded with particular markings of a gang, only to be decoded by another set, and finally to be recoded by yet another gang. The process of identifying with territoriality is perpetually in a state of flux. The walls provide a compass of directionality that usual street signs fail to indicate. The molar cartography of South Central is diffused into a tactile space of interaction, a molecular mapping.

> The Miller Gangsters were from clear across town. 120th Street. It's possible that they didn't know where they were. Or it could be that they did know but had little respect for our 'hood, since they had never had open confrontations with us. I'd tend to believe the latter. This is why it's necessary to read the writing on the walls. Fuck street signs. Walls will tell you where you are.
>
> (Shakur 1994: 169)

13 Smooth space is an area of immediate contact, a field of heterogeneous particles traversing the super-strata and attracting multiplicities that will push the system to transform into diverse collectivities. I am thinking, specifically, of the concluding pages of Alphonso Lingis' 'The Society of Dismembered Body Parts' (1994: 301–2), where the eloquent treatment of late capital's voyage to schizophrenia is unsurpassed. As Lingis poetically states, the apocalyptic vision of dispersed body parts will not be reinscribed upon the earth, as in the primitive societies; rather, the schizophrenia that Deleuze and Guattari conceive is the 'dismemberment of body parts' that shatters notions of identity in order to reconfigure assemblages, a monstrosity. The transcendent identity is fractured, or laid out, as immanent movements of disparate and localized intensities converge on thresholds of deterritorialization. The hand that cocks a gun is a body part (or intensity) being distributed 'across the social field'.

> The social body is being laid bare, laid out, laid, excited metamorphosed when hands clasp in greeting and in understanding and in commitment and in sensuality and also in parting. . . . Where the car on cruise control races the Los Angeles freeways, the hands free to dial the cellular phone, cut the lines of coke, or cock a handgun.
>
> (Lingis 1994: 301)

Cocking the hammer ascertains a directional movement within the confines of the topography of South Central: 'Guns were our tools of communication' . . . Instantaneous communication' (Shakur 1994: 228). For Shakur, South Central Los Angeles is the zone through which mutant lines of flight molecularize a cartography of becoming.

14 For instance, the cartographical separation, or 'spatial apartheid', that has manifested itself in Los Angeles presents a stratified zoning of race through economics. Since the urban uprisings of the 1960s, the white flight into the suburban fringes of Los Angeles has placed most black Americans in an economic moratorium, as most employment

opportunities have moved out of the core city into the safe, surrounding havens of Los Angeles (see Davis 1993: 14–20).

15 I am referring to Deleuze and Guattari's analysis of constructions of race, as in the following: 'identifying races, cultures, and gods with fields of intensity on the body without organs, identifying personages with states that fill these fields, and with effects that fulgurate within and traverse these fields . . . there is no ego that identifies with races, peoples, and persons in a theater of representation, but proper names that identity races, peoples, and persons with regions, thresholds, or effects in a production of intensive quantities' (Deleuze and Guattari 1990: 86).

References

Boyer, M. C. (1983) *Dreaming the Rational City: The Myth of American City Planning*, Cambridge, MA: MIT Press.

Davis, M. (1993) 'Who Killed LA? A Political Autopsy', *New Left Review* 197: 3–28.

—— (1994) 'Beyond Blade Runner: Urban Control and the Ecology of Fear', Westfield, NJ: Open Magazine Pamphlet Series.

Deleuze, G. and Guattari, F. (1986) *Kafka: Toward a Minor Literature*, trans. Dana Polan, Minneapolis: University of Minnesota Press.

—— (1988) *Capitalism and Schizophrenia*, vol. 2, *A Thousand Plateaus*, trans. Brian Massumi, Minneapolis: University of Minnesota Press.

—— (1990) *Capitalism and Schizophrenia*, vol. 1, *Anti-Oedipus*, trans. Robert Hurley, Mark Seem and Helen R. Lane, Minneapolis: University of Minnesota Press.

Guattari, F. (1984) *Molecular Revolution: Psychiatry and Politics*, trans. Rosemary Sheed, London: Penguin Books.

Lingis, A. (1994) 'The Society of Dismembered Body Parts', in C. Boundas and D. Olkowski (eds) *Gilles Deleuze and the Theater of Philosophy*, New York: Routledge.

Shakur, S., a.k.a. Monster Kody Scott (1994) *Monster: The Autobiography of an LA Gang Member*, New York: Penguin Books.

Walker, R. (1995) 'California Rages Against the Dying of the Light', *New Left Review* 209: 42–74.

Part III

VITAL SCIENCE/VIRAL LIFE

9

The Topology of Selection

The Limits of Deleuze's Biophilosophy

Howard Caygill

> Le selezioni si sentono arrivare. 'Selekcja': la ibrida parola latina e polacca si sente una volte, due volte, molte volte, intercalata in discorsi stranieri; dapprima non la si individua, poi si impone all'attenzione, infine ci perseguita.
>
> (Primo Levi, Se questo e un uomo)

In the final section of *Spinoza: Practical Philosophy* Deleuze describes a biophilosophy or 'ethology' whose field of study would be the 'relations of speed and slowness, of the capacities for affecting and being affected that characterize each thing'. The 'thing' – be it body, animal or human – is specified by the composition or distribution of such relations and capacities as well as by the modes through which they 'select what affects or is affected by the thing, what moves it or is moved by it' (Deleuze 1988: 125). This definition of the thing locates Deleuze's ethology as a combination of the philosophical themes of 'relation' and 'capacity' with the biological themes of 'distribution' and 'selection'. In this ethology the kinetics of 'relation' and the dynamics of 'capacity' that shape the 'thing' are shaped in their turn by the orders of 'distribution' and 'selection'. Deleuze's explicit elaboration of ethology progressively privileges the theme of the topology of the distribution of 'relations and capacities' in the 'plane of immanence' over that of the theme of selection. It is this decision – what may be described as the avoidance of Darwin – that establishes the limits of Deleuze's biophilosophy and the politics which it informs.

The combination of philosophy and biology – a powerful tradition in French thought – informs Deleuze's seminal text *Difference and Repetition*. Here the outlines of his ethology are already discernible, as is the tension between the themes of distribution and selection. The focus on the theme of selection which characterized *Nietzsche and Philosophy*, where the thought of the 'eternal return' is read as a principle of selection, increasingly shifts in favour of distribution. The reason for this shift may be sought in the key role played by the reading of Spinoza in the development of Deleuze's ethology, specifically the concept central to the *Ethics* of the 'common notion'. Deleuze understood the Spinozian 'common notion' to be 'more biological than mathematical' (1988: 55) and used it as the keystone of his biophilosophy. Deleuze understands 'common notions' as 'physico-chemical or biological ideas' which 'present nature's unity of composition in its various aspects' (1988: 115); that is to say, they are topological 'relations of composition' such as 'foldings' which may be traced according to their distribution in a single 'plane of immanence'. What is striking about this development is the emphasis upon the *topology* of distribution and the apparent surrender of the theme of selection central to the Darwinian natural philosophy. It is as if in the passage from philosophy to biophilosophy or ethology Deleuze flinched before the full implications of the inhuman concept of selection and its role in the biological immanence of the Victorian naturalist.

Nevertheless, the issue of selection inevitably remains central to Deleuze's ethology, even though he carefully avoids a full and explicit analysis of its implications. This is apparent from the tension between the biological concepts of distribution and selection which informs *Difference and Repetition*, and its implicit presence in later works. Indeed, Deleuze's ethology is not only compatible with the Darwinian concept of selection, but is unthinkable without it. This will be shown in the first section – 'Distribution and Selection' – as will its subsequent resolution in favour of distribution and a topology of the common notions in the Spinoza books. Then in the second section – 'The Law of Selection' – the same tension will be shown to be at work in Darwin's *On the Origin of the Species by Means of Natural Selection*, but there, as is well known, it is resolved in favour of selection. In the third section – 'The Eternal Return of Selection' – it will be shown that the principle of selection remains crucial but unacknowledged in Deleuze's ethology, forming its limit and the starting point for a critique of the bio-ethics and politics which are associated with it.

Distribution and Selection

In 1968 Deleuze published *Difference and Repetition* and *Expressionism in Philosophy: Spinoza* as his principal and secondary theses for the *Doctorat d'Etat*. At first sight there would seem to be little in common between one of the founding texts of the 'philosophy of difference' and a reading of Spinoza's philosophy of unitary substance, although on closer inspection the two texts share many common features. The main point connecting them is the exploration of the relationship between the themes of selection and distribution. In *Difference and Repetition* this is undertaken by confronting Spinoza as the thinker of distribution with Nietzsche as the thinker of selection, with the Darwinian revolution figuring at one sole point in the text as a possible resolution of the relationship between distribution and selection. This possibility was not further explored by Deleuze, whose subsequent work followed the direction of the topology of the 'common notions' proposed in the final three chapters of *Expressionism in Philosophy: Spinoza*.

The first important bridge between the two books of 1968 appears in the context of a discussion of the ontology of distribution in chapter 1, 'Difference in Itself'.[1] This discussion in turn forms an important part of the general critique of Hegel and Hegelianism under the sign of the philosophy of representation. Against such a philosophy and its grotesque theatre of the movement of the concept Deleuze proposes a theatre of repetition in which

> we experience pure forces, dynamic lines in space that act without intermediary upon the spirit and link it directly with nature and history, with a language which speaks before words, with gestures that develop before organised bodies, with masks before faces, with spectres and phantoms before characters – the whole apparatus of repetition as a 'terrible power'.
>
> (Deleuze 1994: 10)

The distinction between the philosophies of representation and difference/ repetition is played out at various levels throughout the text, but most significantly at those that are established between equivocal and univocal being and between sedentary and nomadic patterns of distribution.

For Deleuze, the ontology of equivocal being informs the philosophy of representation. In this ontology, whose origins he discovers in Aristotelian logical metaphysics, being cannot be said in the same way of all beings; there is a difference between the being of finite and infinite being such that the concepts for one can only be used equivocally of the other.[2] One of the consequences of the equivocal conception of being for Deleuze is the emergence of a philosophy of transcendence which, in the words of the later Spinoza book, 'always has an additional dimension; it always implies a dimension supplementary to the dimensions of the given' (Deleuze 1988: 128).[3] This supplementary dimension – infinite as opposed to finite being – permits the exercise of judgement or the 'proportioning [of] the concept to the terms or to the subjects of which it is affirmed' (Deleuze 1994: 33). This is made possible by means of the 'two essential functions' of judgement, namely *distribution* and *hierarchization*. These functions characterize for Deleuze 'every philosophy of the categories', but above all the work of Kant, Hegel and their successors.

The distribution and hierarchy of equivocal being is later specified in terms of a 'dividing up of that which is distributed', a division which 'proceeds by fixed and proportional determinations which may be assimilated to "properties" or limited territories within representation' (Deleuze 1994: 36). Such distribution within a demarcated field is sovereign and thus hierarchical; its principal characteristics are best conceived in accordance with the definition of the plan of transcendence given in the later Spinoza book:

> Any organization that comes from above and refers to a transcendence, be it a hidden one, can be called a theological plan: a design in the mind of a god, but also an evolution in the supposed depths of nature, or in a society's organization of power . . . it will always be a plan of transcendence that directs forms as well as subjects, and that stays hidden, that is never given, that can only be divined, induced, inferred from what it gives.
>
> (Deleuze 1988: 128)

This form of distribution of 'limits and lots' is contrasted with another form of distribution which Deleuze aligns with a univocal definition of being. In this tradition, which Deleuze traces back to Duns Scotus, there is no distinction between finite and infinite being – both are spoken of in the same way. Univocal being is unitary and immanent, in contrast to the divided and transcendent equivocal being. It is this concept of univocal being which for Deleuze informs the philosophy of difference/repetition, and makes possible a pattern of distribution other than the plan of transcendence of equivocal being.

The 'completely other distribution' is described by Deleuze as 'nomadic'. In this distribution 'there is no longer a division of that which is distributed but rather a division among those who distribute *themselves* in an open space – a space which is unlimited, or at least without precise limits' (Deleuze 1994: 36). In such a distribution there is no 'additional dimension' which could found a sovereign plan of transcendence (and its appropriate topology), but an immanence which resists the forms of representation:

> It is an errant and uneven 'delirious' distribution, in which things are deployed across the entire extensity of a univocal and undistributed being. It is not a matter of being which is distributed according to the requirements of representation, but of all things being divided up within being in the univocity of simple presence (the One-All).
>
> (1994: 39)

In this distribution of being, the categories which order representation, such as those of quantity, quality, relation and modality, are succeeded by an 'enveloping measure' which is the 'same for all things'.[4] In place of the sedentary hierarchy of equivocal being, 'Univocal being is at one and the same time nomadic distribution and crowned anarchy.'

Deleuze proposes three moments in the history of univocal ontology – Duns Scotus, Spinoza and Nietzsche. Spinoza is thus in a crucial position between Scotus' still theological (Franciscan) conception of univocal being thought in terms of a divine immanence in nature, and Nietzsche's Godless conception. Spinoza's presentation of the substance, attributes and modes of being maps a distribution of being in which each is folded upon the others in an 'enveloping measure' which resists any hierarchization:

> Any hierarchy or pre-eminence is denied in so far as substance is equally designated by all the attributes in accordance with their essence, and equally expressed by all the modes in accordance with their degree of power.
>
> (Deleuze 1994: 40)

Yet at this stage Deleuze finds that Spinoza's topology of univocal being is still afflicted by an inequality between substance and its modes and attributes: the latter stand in an asymmetrical relation of dependence to the former. This inequality results from a decision to privilege substance within the plan of immanence, one which marks a selection prior to distribution. Nietzsche, however, folds even this selection into the plane of immanence with the test of eternal return[5]:

> Repetition in the eternal return, therefore, consists in conceiving the same on the basis of the different. However, this conception is no longer merely a theoretical representation: it carries out a practical selection among differences according to their capacity to produce – that is, to return or to pass the test of the eternal return. The selective character of eternal return appears clearly in Nietzsche's idea: it is not the Whole, the Same or the prior identity in general which returns. . . . Only the extreme forms return – those which, large or small, are deployed within the limit and extend to the limit of their power, transforming themselves and changing one into another.
>
> (Deleuze 1994: 41)

Here the selection which informs the distribution of being is wrapped into being itself, but not in the name of a principle or privileged instance, but rather in the name of a test of becoming – in Deleuze's words, 'production of repetition on the basis of difference and selection of difference on the basis of repetition' (1994: 42).

It is at this point that Deleuze's text is in close proximity with Darwin, for whom 'Any variation which is not inherited is unimportant' (Darwin 1993: 115). Such differences have failed the test of selection and have been unable to repeat or reproduce themselves.

The importance of selection within a philosophy of difference/repetition operating within the plane of immanence of univocal being is acknowledged in Deleuze's brief discussion of Darwin in *Difference and Repetition*. This moment, in chapter 5, 'Asymmetrical Synthesis of the Sensible', marks a possible transformation of Nietzsche's thought of the eternal return into a biophilosophy. Here Deleuze initially recognizes the 'essential role' of natural selection as 'the differentiation of difference (survival of the most divergent)' but then loses sight of the implacable rigour of Darwinian Selection by conceiving of moments when 'selection does not or no longer occurs'. This allows him to regard difference as either the 'primary matter of selection or differenciation' or as 'indeterminate variability' (1994: 148). Consequently, while acknowledging the 'Copernican Revolution of Darwinism' Deleuze misses the at once radically immanent and exterior character of its concept of Selection.[6]

The reasons for Deleuze's underestimation of Darwinian natural selection are diverse, but prime among them is his approbation of the work of the pre-Darwinian Etienne Geoffroy Saint-Hilaire. Darwin himself criticized Geoffroy's emphasis upon the '*mode ambiant*' as the cause of change of an organism, and by implication of the role played by the reciprocal relation between the composition of the organism and the environment. Deleuze, however, discovers a possible rapprochement between Geoffroy and Spinoza through the latter's concept of the 'common notions'. He concludes *Difference and Repetition* by repeating the call for a combination of Spinoza's topology of the distribution of univocal being with Nietzschean selection, but without fully specifying the character of this topology of selection:

> All that Spinozism needed to do for the univocal to become an object of pure affirmation was to make substance turn around the modes – *in other words, to realise univocity in the form of repetition in the eternal return*.
>
> (Deleuze 1994: 304)

Yet this turn folds selection back into distribution, retreating from a Darwinian to a pre-Darwinian biology. To turn substance around the modes through eternal return is precisely to obscure the character of difference and repetition as a succession through the test of selection. It modulates the thought of selection into one of distribution by means of a formula, obscuring the law of distribution through selection by an appeal to the 'crowned anarchies' of 'nomadic distribution'.

It is in the complementary *Expressionism in Philosophy: Spinoza* that Deleuze establishes the conditions for his collapse of selection into a topology of distribution. This study of Spinoza further develops the univocal ontology informing *Difference and Repetition* through the concept of expression. Expression offers the condition of the possibility for a topological analysis of the distribution of being since it 'involves and implicates what it expresses, while also explicating and evolving it' (Deleuze 1990: 16). The complicated folds which express univocal being resist any move to transcendence; they define what Deleuze will later call a 'plane of immanence'. In the words of *Spinoza: Practical Philosophy*, the plane of immanence 'has no supplementary dimension; the process of composition must be apprehended for itself, through that which it gives, in that which it gives' (Deleuze 1988: 128). Expression, or the 'process of composition', is not a form applied to matter, but a 'composition' or 'structure' of being, the mode in which it distributes itself.

Deleuze's careful description of the Spinozan machinery of expression – substance, attributes and modes – culminates in an analysis of the 'common notion' or 'idea of a similarity of composition in existing modes' (Deleuze 1990: 275). The 'common notions' in Deleuze's reading are not abstractions such as 'transcendental terms' or 'universal notions' but the structural constituents of bodies, their 'composition' (1990: 277–8). Deleuze argues that 'Spinoza's "common notions" are biological rather than physical or mathematical Ideas. They really do play the part of Ideas in a philosophy of nature from which all finality has been excluded' (1990: 278). The 'common notions' are expressions of a univocal being, providing, in Deleuze's words, the beginnings of a topological analysis of 'the great principle of compositional unity' in which 'Nature as a whole is a single animal in which only the relations between the parts vary' (1990: 278). The analysis of the 'common notions' is accordingly immanent, a description of the dynamics of 'the laws of production of essences' and the kinetics of 'the laws of compositions of relations' (1990: 293) of univocal being.

At a crucial point in his analysis of the obscure 'common notions' Deleuze describes Spinoza as 'a forerunner of Geoffroy Saint-Hilaire'. He expands on this comment in a significant footnote which reveals the pre-Darwinian character of his biophilosophy. He applauds Geoffroy Saint-Hilaire's anti-Aristotelian method, which for Deleuze proposes:

> a determination of the variable relations between fixed anatomical components: different animals correspond to variations of relation, respective situation and dependence among those components, so that all are reduced to modifications of a single identical animal as such. For resemblances of form

> and analogies of function, which must always remain external, Geoffroy thus substitutes the intrinsic viewpoint of compositional unity or the similarity of relations.
>
> (1990: 393)

Yet while this view of nature is consistently immanent, seeing 'animals' as modifications of 'single animal' it still conceives of these modifications in terms of distribution, namely, 'variations of relation', 'respective situation' and 'dependence'. The implications of this *adaptive* view of the 'common notions' are spelt out more fully in *Spinoza: Practical Philosophy*, as is their link to a bio-ethics and politics. There each body is defined as a relation of motion and rest; different bodies compose new relations with other bodies in their environment. The 'common notion' is accordingly 'the representation of a composition between two or more bodies and a unity of this composition' (Deleuze 1988: 56). Through the 'common notions' it is possible to apprehend the composition of bodies

> as they are, that is, as they are necessarily embodied in living beings, with the variable and concrete terms between which they are established. In this sense, the common notions are more biological than mathematical, forming a natural geometry that allows us to comprehend the unity of composition of all of Nature and the modes of variation of that unity.
>
> (1988: 57)

This focus on the modes of variation – the pattern of their distribution – is indebted to both Geoffroy and Spinoza, and forms the basis not only of Deleuze's ethology, but also of a bio-ethics and politics.

In their encounters with each other, bodies agree or disagree with each other, leading to the augmentation of the bodies' composition or its destruction. Deleuze reads from these vivifying or destructive relations the affects of joy or sadness, a move which allows him to make with Spinoza the passage from a biophilosophy to a bio-ethics and politics. The purpose of such a bio-ethics and politics is to select joyful encounters, and accordingly in both Spinoza books such selection/composition of joyful encounters is central. In *Expression in Philosophy: Spinoza* Deleuze describes four stages in the formation of an ethics of active joy. The first stage, passive joy, follows from desires and passions based on inadequate ideas; this stage issues in the formation of 'common notions', which form the basis of the active joys which in the fourth stage combine with the passive joys in an affirmative joy of reason (1990: 284). Crucial to the formation of active joy is the concept of selection, as becomes clear in the subsequent discussion of the passage through the stages of joy.

The passage from the first to the second stage of active joy – the formation of 'common notions' – is encouraged by the joy produced by our body encountering 'another body that agrees (or some other bodies that agree with it)' or impeded by 'the sadness or opposition produced in us by a body that does not agree with our own' (1990: 287). The passage from the second to the third stage – action according to 'common notions' – is accomplished by the selection of joyful and the avoidance of sad encounters. In the passage from the third to the fourth stage, selection is raised a power by the realization that sad encounters cannot necessarily be avoided, but can be experienced selectively as occasions for the active joy that understands their necessity. The 'common notions' are thus biological – concerning the encounter of bodies with each other – and selective, permitting the choice of joyful or sad encounters.

Such a concept of selection fuses biology and philosophical ethics and politics, but perhaps in a way that sentimentalizes selection. Darwinian Selection is not an analogue of judgement, replacing truth and falsity with joy and sadness, but is an implacable selection of those bodies capable of repeating or reproducing themselves. The distance between this concept and Deleuze's concept of selection may be shown by means of a brief conspectus of Darwin's concept of selection, which shows that the topology of selection is more complete than that entertained by Deleuze. Selection is immanent for Darwin, but implacably exterior, favouring a 'law' which admits no exception.

The Law of Selection

In the first sentence of the introduction to *On the Origin of the Species by Means of Natural Selection* (1859) Darwin remembers how 'When on board H.M.S. "Beagle" as a naturalist, I was much struck with certain facts in the distribution of the inhabitants of South America, and in the geological relations of the present to the past inhabitants of that continent'.[7] This opening, of extraordinary economy and beauty, locates the observer at a specific time and place within a vast spatio-temporal continuum. What is observed from this point is a number of facts about 'geographical distribution' and 'geological succession' that together pose a question about the link between the present and past patterns of distribution. The question posed by these facts is then claimed to throw light on the 'mystery of mysteries' that is the 'origin of species'. The answer to the question of the linkage between present and past distributions is to be found neither in an act of creation nor in adaptation to the environment, but in Selection.

For Darwin, Selection links the spatial order of distribution with the temporal order of succession. This linkage is conceived in two ways – through an analogy between 'domestic' and 'natural' selection or through the analysis of those characteristics proper to natural selection. Darwin sees in the argument by analogy 'the best and safest clue' to understanding natural selection, but solely in terms of the insight it gives into the accumulation of successive (and irreversible) variations. The fascination with the patterns of distribution created by the accumulation of successive, infinitesimally small changes was already evident in Darwin's work on the geology of coral reefs. His book of 1842 – *The Structure and Distribution of Coral Reefs* – begins in the same way as the *Origin of the Species*, that is, by explaining the origins of the forms of coral reefs from the observation of their distribution.[8] The 'species' in the book of 1859 are like the 'coral reefs' of 1842 not only in terms of the link between the two being conceived as the accumulation of infinitesimally small changes. The polypifers whose remains accumulate to form the coral reefs map by analogy onto the individuals whose accumulated variations accumulate into the species.[9]

It is the accumulative aspect of selection that constitutes the analogy between domestic and natural selection, and not the teleology of domestic selection. The latter is but the human attempt to channel an inhuman process, or in Darwin's words: 'nature gives successive variations; man adds them up in certain directions useful to him' (Darwin 1993: 127). Yet after establishing this analogy in chapter 1 of the *Origin of the Species* Darwin totally destroys it in chapter 4 on 'Natural Selection'. Here he dissolves human actions into the inhuman Selection that he calls nature. What is more, he regards this Selection as more rigorous and implacable than any that can be conceived of by analogy to human schemas and purposes. It cannot, for example, be understood in terms of the execution of a ruthless law, since even this analogy would qualify the immanence of nature by a transcendent law or teleology which nature merely executes. Darwin reduces the significance of human interventions by comparing the time of human with that of geological selection: 'How fleeting are the wishes and efforts of man! how short his time! and consequently how poor will his products be compared with those accumulated by nature during whole geological periods.' Such Selection exceeds human understanding not only in terms of its quantity but also in terms of its rigour. Darwin continues:

> It may be said that natural selection is daily and hourly scrutinising, throughout the world, every variation, even the slightest; rejecting that which is bad, preserving and adding up that which is good; silently and insensibly working, whenever and wherever opportunity offers, at the improvement of each organic being in relation to its organic and inorganic conditions of life.
> (1993: 162)

'We' can only imperfectly perceive the results of these changes; we cannot, however, have full insight into the combination of chance and necessity that makes up Selection. The infinitesimally small variation that will pass the scrutiny of Selection and be bequeathed to successive generations cannot be perceived or predicted by human understanding. Selection, indeed, is rigorously exterior to human purposes, and yet also immanent in them and nature.

What is important for Darwin is not so much the patterns of distribution – whether they be those of coral reefs or of species of animals – but the incremental process of selection through which they are formed. In selection, a minute variation is put to the test of its environment and bequeathed or negated if successful; adaptation is consequently a long-drawn-out play of chance and necessity, one far beyond the time and the purposes of human beings. Consequently it is temporal succession through selection which ultimately determines spatial patterns of distribution. Deleuze, on the contrary, follows the pre-Darwinian Geoffroy Saint-Hilaire in focusing on patterns of distribution and composition rather than upon selection. In his ethology, distribution would determine selection, except that as Darwin had already observed in his critique of Geoffroy, selection returns to test all patterns of distribution.

The Eternal Return of Selection

Deleuze's biophilosophy seeks systematically to replace concepts with affects, a programme for which Spinoza's work provides a powerful precedent. Spinoza is situated by Deleuze in a 'great lineage that goes from Epicurus to Nietzsche' (Deleuze 1988: 72) in which the order of concepts such as good and evil is subordinated to an order of active and passive affections. The latter order produces a distribution of organisms whose folds and convolutions are mapped by ethology (1988: 27). Yet the stress upon the biological character of active and passive affections maps awkwardly with the ethical motif of maximizing active and minimizing passive encounters. Deleuze writes with great philosophical pathos that

> It is a disgrace to seek the internal essence of man in his bad extrinsic encounters. Everything that involves sadness serves tyranny and oppression. Everything that involves sadness must be denounced as bad, as something that separates from our power of acting; not only remorse and guilt, not only meditation and death (IV, 67), but even hope, even security, which signify powerlessness.
>
> (1988: 72)

While the rhetoric is perhaps admirable, what it hides is the fact that a bio-ethics or politics does not consist in choosing encounters that encourage active affections. For Darwinian biology, such affections would be the result of passing or failing the Selection, and not a criterion of that selection itself.

In *Expressionism in Philosophy: Spinoza*, Deleuze presents what can only be described as a humanized account of selection. In the concluding paragraph of his chapter on 'Beatitude' he appears to align Spinoza with a Darwinian naturalism, saying 'There are no such things as the moral sanctions of a divine Judge, no punishments or rewards, but only the natural consequences of our existence' (Deleuze 1990: 319). Existence for Deleuze as for Darwin is a test, but for the latter this test is an implacable test of fitness to reproduce, while for the former the test of existence consists in the ethical requirement that 'while existing we must select joyful passions'. The implication of choice and value in Selection persists even in the harder account of selection given in *Spinoza: Practical Philosophy*. There, as already mentioned above, each 'thing' in nature 'selects what affects or is affected by the thing, what moves it or is moved by it'. Deleuze gives as an example the selection pursued by an animal in the world.

> What does it react to positively or negatively? What are its nutrients and its poisons? What does it 'take' in its world? Every point has its counterpoints: the plant and the rain, the spider and the fly. So an animal, a thing, is never separable from its relations to the world. The interior is only a selected exterior, and the exterior, a projected interior.
>
> (Deleuze 1988: 125)

Here selection is clearly understood in terms of positive and negative affections, a philosophical perspective far from that of natural selection in Darwinian biology. It is a perspective which humanizes nature, at the same time as brutalizing human ethics and politics. The biological and the human orders cannot be so quickly confused without the risk of reducing ethics and politics to the image of a humanized nature.

Deleuze's ethology in the final analysis employs a biological rhetoric to evoke an anti-human, anti-ethical, anti-political, anti-philosophical pathos which sentimentally avoids the implications of biological selection. The immanence of the *Origin of the Species* remains far more rigorous and implacable than that of *Difference and Repetition* and *A Thousand Plateaus*. These texts moralize selection, linking it with the active or passive affective relations of an organism to its environment. They provide by default a strong case for maintaining the separation of the biological and the philosophical, especially in respect to their use of the concept of selection. Indeed, there is no place for philosophy with its active and passive capacities and relations within a rigorously defined Darwinian world. Any biophilosophy, consequently, will reduce not only the philosophical to the biological, but also the biological to the philosophical. Certain conceptions of action and classification will be applied to nature, and then refracted back into philosophy. In an earlier version of biophilosophy these conceptions were those of race and fitness, while now they are those of passive and active affections. In both cases, nature and politics are sentimentalized and brutalized. By refusing the full rigour of Darwinian selection, Deleuze is left with a sentimentalized nature and a brutalized ethics and politics.

Notes

1 This discussion forms the kernel of the immediately following collaborations with Guattari – *Anti-Oedipus* and *A Thousand Plateaus*. Both texts are notable for their philosophical *timidity*, for in spite of their rhetorical radicalism each avoids a full reckoning with the implications of Darwinian Selection, preferring to luxuriate in a thematics of distribution.

2 In *Expressionism in Philosophy: Spinoza*, Deleuze elaborates upon equivocation and its two species – eminence and analogy. In the former, infinite being is defined in terms of its excess over finite being, while in the latter it is defined in terms of an internal similarity of relation between the two beings.

3 The opposition of the 'plan of transcendence' and the 'plan of immanence' in this text is the apparent heir to the earlier distinction between the philosophies of representation and difference/repetition.

4 The contour of this 'enveloping measure' will subsequently be traced through the kinetics and dynamics of Deleuze's ethology.

5 *Editor's note*: As Robert Hurley, the translator of Deleuze's 'little' *Spinoza* book, points out, the French word *plan* covers nearly all the meanings of the English words 'plan' and 'plane'. Hurley proposes that 'plane' should be used only for Deleuze's *plan d'immanence* and *plan de consistance*, not for the notion of *plan de transcendance* or *plan d'organisation*, since the word 'plane' is suggestive of the kind of conceptual-affective continuum that Deleuze has in mind when writing of the *plan d'immanence*. The reader might wish to bear in mind this distinction in navigating the trajectory of Caygill's reading of Deleuze on Spinoza.

6 'Selection', like 'God', is always capitalized by Darwin.

7 From the introduction to the first edition reprinted in Darwin 1993: 107. By the sixth edition, the 'inhabitants' had become 'organic beings inhabiting' – see Darwin 1956: 17.

8 'The object of this volume is to describe from my own observation and the work of others, the principal kinds of coral reefs, more especially those occurring in the open ocean, and to explain the origin of their peculiar forms. I do not here treat of the polypifers, which construct these vast works, except so far as relates to their distribution, and to the conditions favourable to their vigorous growth.' Darwin 1993: 72.

9 Darwin himself uses the analogy at the end of the fourth chapter of the *Origin of the Species*: 'As buds give rise by growth to fresh buds, and these, if vigorous, branch out and overtop on all sides many a feebler branch, so by generatio I believe it has been with the great Tree of Life, which fills with its dead and broken branches the crust of the earth, and covers the surface with its ever branching and beautiful ramifications' (1956: 194).

References

Darwin, Charles (1956) *The Origin of the Species*, ed. W. R. Thompson, London: Dent.

—— (1993) *The Portable Darwin*, Harmondsworth, Middlesex: Penguin.

Deleuze, Giles (1988) *Spinoza: Practical Philosophy*, trans. R. Hurley, San Francisco: City Light Books.

—— (1990) *Expressionism in Philosophy: Spinoza*, trans. M. Joughin, New York: Zone Books.

—— (1994) *Difference and Repetition*, trans. P. Patton, London: Athlone Press.

10

Contagium Vivum Philosophia

Schizophrenic Philosophy, Viral Empiricism and Deleuze

Robert O'Toole

Schizophrenic Philosophy

> The three disciplines [art, science, philosophy] advance by crises or shocks in different ways, and in each case it is their succession that makes it possible to speak of 'progress'. It is as if the struggle against chaos does not take place without an affinity with the enemy, because another struggle develops and takes on more importance – the struggle develops *against opinion*, which claims to protect us from chaos itself.
>
> (Gilles Deleuze and Félix Guattari 1994: 203)

An epoch is defined, following Bergson, as a hyperplane of variable speeds, or a field of *contraction–expansion*. Contraction is the overall multiplication of connections in a network-system (rhizome), or more specifically, the familiar heating-up of activity/intensity (the difference that each difference makes) that occurs as combinatorial explosion, determined by the *power-rule* for the movement. Activity is a property of this explosion, and as will be argued, may only be specified at the level of populations. The operation of individuals, on the other hand, is defined as 'passive synthesis', or 'a search in the void' (Deleuze and Guattari 1984: 8). Active synthesis and passive synthesis are said to be two distinct and non-decomposable aspects of the real: *wave* and *particle*. The active movement is determined not through an algorithm, but rather a transfinite set of non-computable constraints/immobilities that are active as the so-called 'engineering agency'[1] or plane of immanence of the contraction, a *singularity*: 'Molloy and Moran no longer designate persons, but singularities flocking from all sides, evanescent agents of production' (Deleuze and Guattari 1984: 77) – this flocking together of a population designates the epoch:

schizos out in the park, pores exploding in the solar flame, energy, connected with all of nature, or the schizophrenic compositions of HIV positivity. Migrations of populations relative to each other are the constitutive elements of a contraction. And they are really distinct and non-decomposable populations passing across a threshold or singularities, incapable of genetic transmission (celibate machines, as they are termed in *Anti-Oedipus*):

> a schizophrenic experience of intensive quantities in their pure state, to a point that is almost unbearable – a celibate misery and glory experienced to the fullest, like a cry suspended between life and death, an intense feeling of transition, states of pure naked intensity stripped of all shape and form.
>
> (Deleuze and Guattari 1984: 18)

That celibate machines are productive, and worse still, that they are *the* immobile motors of production, is a heresy against linear history (of lineages). Dependencies are cut across laterally, obscuring property inheritance and syllogistic deduction. Both creationism and transformationalist Darwinianism[2] are unable to cope with the implications of non-linearity: non-anthropomorphic, cross-species production, in which: 'the components of the system are not permanent. . . . It is component productivity that is of primary importance' (Kampis 1991: 277), and information resides between the lines. Catastrophes are not assimilable to verticality, and as 'Every typology is dramatic, every dynamic a catastrophe' (Deleuze 1994: 219), morphology cannot truly be explained from within the linear paradigm. A *dynamical molecular Darwinianism is required*. Deleuze arrives at this conclusion concerning scientific analysis through a critique of the naive understanding of linearity. Such institutional history, as a strategic process, and its logic of succession, is ontologically conservative, positing the One and its divisions against the Multiple and its multiplicities. Its procedure is that of realizing potentials through factorial integration. This procedure is a function of Good Sense, or the harmonic alignment of distinct faculties that may be decomposed into its procedure. However, as Deleuze argues in *Difference and Repetition*:

> Good sense is by nature eschatological, the prophet of a final compensation and homogenization. If it comes second, this is because it presupposes mad distribution – instantaneous, nomadic distribution, crowned anarchy or difference.
>
> (Deleuze 1994: 224)

Linear history is incapable of dealing with its conditions of possibility, the enemy (contraction-time), and is incapable of writing its own story; time lost in doing so is irrecoverable. Philosophy is an attempt to write lost time, and therefore its relationship with history is intimate. The history of philosophy as a lineage of concepts and personae defines strategic relationships in which the faculties harmonize or are subordinated (diplomacy or conquest):

> the Kantian definition that posits God as the *a priori* principle of the disjunctive syllogism, so that all things derive from it by a restriction of a larger reality (*omnitudo realitas*): Kant's humour makes God into the master of *a* syllogism.
>
> (Deleuze and Guattari 1984: 76)

Scholasticism imagines a world in which God must procreate with himself, forming a lineage of creatures, and of concepts for the distribution of that lineage. But the Critical turn pushes philosophy across a threshold which brings into relief the conditions under which time enters this history; the fold between understanding and sensation, between the active operating over the passive, and the passive presenting the active to itself, through the loop called Transcendental Apperception. The uncertainty of the point of return of this loop, the re-presentation of the activity of representation to itself, encountered in dreaming, sickness, death, amnesia, scepticism and madness (which now become key objects in philosophy – areas in which time is lost), produces a bifurcation point at which one is forced either to have faith in the sexual continence of the procreating divinity (still sought today in genetics) or to face confusion in chaos. The Kantian epoch is thus marked by a singularity (how to decompose nature as chaos – temporality, and nature as cosmos – sensation, into one chaosmos). But more interestingly, it is marked by an influx of systems (philosophical, mythological, social), leading right up to psychoanalysis, that construct chaosmologies through strategic arrangements – that is to say, by paranoiacally denying the disruptive imposition of time while simultaneously feeding off that same force. Linear history has thus not sufficiently understood the determination of its own condition because it has not reconfigured itself beyond the mode of understanding that determined its condition – it is caught in a vicious negative feedback loop. However, the Kantian belief expressed in the latter stages of the *Critique of Pure Reason*, that what will follow those pages is merely interpretation of the system, is quite telling. Understood in a non-linear Bergsonian way, the Kantian critique and its interpretation build up the explosive dynamics that allow for the interminable loop to be broken. Philosophy has, at least partially, understood that writing is itself the loss of time, that writing is diseased, entropic. But worse, it stands terrified at that thought, which seems to be an abyss, and is unable to progress to a positive affirmation of entropy as production. The difficulty is in passing across the singularity at which this positive affirmation is selected. The multiplication and diversification of systems at the philosophical level, as well as the multiplication and diversification of passive re-presentations of representation in the manifold (concepts themselves have an empirical/material presence), results in a contraction in which the hyperplane of philosophy becomes a densely filled schizo-matter, obeying the dynamics of such a volume, rather than determining those dynamics from outside. Each non-decomposable space in the hyperplane is filled with a transfinite series of bifurcations or intensities, as attempted resolution merely results in further complication. Philosophy starts to scream; an anonymous and schizophrenic scream, it is being tortured by something terrible, its own engineering agency. As Manuel De Landa states in his non-linear history of machines:

> Instead of leading to the achievement of total certainty, centralized schemes lead to 'information explosions' which increase the amount of overall uncertainty.
>
> (De Landa 1991: 61)

Furthermore, philosophy has no recourse to its old metaphysics, for that is the instigator of the torture. The gap between chaos and cosmos seems greater than ever – the sublime returns, again and again. But a strange emission from this spiralling loop generates a novel direction, like a bastard child with a dice-game. Deleuze and Guattari write: 'In truth, there are never contradictions, apparent or real, but only degrees of humour' (Deleuze and Guattari 1984: 68). The operation of this black humour, of the machinic phylum that fills up matter and makes it break, of non-linear history, itself becomes a determining trend in the development of philosophy. The complex 'becoming' of history is now seen in its second aspect, as the motor of its own movement, or rather, the tension between these two aspects is the immobile motor at the heart of the movement, in an 'asymmetrical synthesis', as described in *Difference and Repetition*:

> Every phenomenon refers to an inequality by which it is conditioned. Every diversity and every change refers to a difference which is its sufficient reason. . . . Disparity – in other words, difference or intensity (difference of intensity), is the sufficient reason of all phenomena.
>
> (Deleuze 1994: 222)

The problem comes at the end, not at the beginning, and is no longer a matter of realizing potentials. The distinction between the possible and the real must be replaced by the distinction between the real virtual and the real actual:

> For a potential or virtual object, to be actualised is to create divergent lines which correspond to – without resembling – a virtual multiplicity.
>
> (Deleuze 1994: 212)

The solution does not solve a problem; rather, it differentiates it. This new movement, this progress by 'crises and shocks', by complication and tactical alliance (coming together in machinic assemblage), may be envisaged as a collapse of the old strategic order. And indeed paranoiac philosophical institutions will call us mad (but of course they cannot, by their very constitution, give a definition of that category). But it may also be envisaged as the development of a new technical possibility. The epoch was always a technology in the organization of the intellect. The chaos of the brain is epochal:

> The forces of attraction and repulsion, of soaring ascents and plunging falls, produce a series of intensive states based on the intensity = 0 that designates the body without organs.
>
> (Deleuze and Guattari 1984: 21)

– just as the loop of Transcendental Apperception defines its epochs. Indeed, Transcendental Apperception may be understood of as a *community of decay* between the empirical *communis* and the transcendental *communis*: 'A broken Earth and a fractured sky' (Deleuze 1994: 284), *tragic community*. But the engine of production was always mysterious and distant, and hence our epochs always seemed to be solutions computed to the specification of problems defined elsewhere. Kant is accused of posing a false problem: an abstract *extension* or the logical ideal of geometrics, in need of *intension*, a subject *lacking* a sublime (Deleuze 1994: 224). Now that the epoch has been unveiled in its dual capacity, as both solution and engine, phenomena and noumena, exploded and explosive, we lose ourselves to the process, but discover that the process is ourselves. It no longer matters whether one says 'I' any more, merely that one is *dynamite*. To explore this further, it will be necessary to look into the pyrotechnics of the immanent process, and then to diagram the most intense site of its operation: the brain and its science, demonstrating how they have become differentiated into the production of tactical alliances.

To avoid confusion, understand the contraction of an epoch as the distribution of the probable states of a system across an increasingly dense set of modalities, such that the probability of any given state decreases with the contraction of the system away from the actual towards the virtual (i.e. towards the non-communication/incompossibility of the content of each state, or the disappearance of the content of each state, as the system is attracted towards the full Body without Organs upon which communication equals instantaneous rupture equals chaos equals non-communication – the sublime as such is a supersensible communication without communication, or pure expression). This first aspect of contraction defines its trope as moving away from extensive determination in the actual (selection of states or *extension/perception* on a single affective plane) towards the intensive diversity of the virtual; as if moving from the point of a cone downwards. At the tip, the memory (or phase space) of the system is encapsulated in single determining states. As one proceeds away from the tip, the memory (or organization) is increasingly determined as a cumulative property distributed across the entire plane of the conic section. Each individual state of the assemblage expresses itself as a suspension of the movement of the assemblage, like the motion of schizophrenic expressions, or of Klossowski's suspended bodies (Deleuze 1990: 285). Intensity or difference here seems to be sterile, in its passive phase: 'Intensity is suspect only because it seems to rush headlong into suicide' (Deleuze 1994: 224). But death occurs only within the aspect of *passive synthesis*, the void in which life was not present from the outset. But this does not freeze the system up, but rather causes the system to become more animated. A *static genesis* or *immobile motor* is in operation (Deleuze 1994: 183). This suspension should not be interpreted as the operation of randomness in the system (as evolutionary biology would have us believe) – genetic mutations are not random, but rather are the deterministic product of the interaction of many equally deterministic systems which *transversally construct* an 'excitable medium', as George Kampis has argued: 'It has to be understood that what is not deterministic need not be random. The solution is the existence of a new type of causality' (Kampis 1991: 257). Randomness is only posited as a causal force when a discipline requires computational completeness but is unable to specify all the initial conditions necessary and all the component-systems that may be produced. It is one of the last remaining metaphysical components in science, and the first to go as the singularity is crossed. Following its trajectory of transversal construction, the assemblage progressively becomes more indeterminate and contains more degrees of freedom, more engineering agency, more processing power, more life, composed of more excitable media, and ultimately more non-linearity. The importance of the A-Life technique known as Genetic Algorithms lies precisely in this property: a massive distribution of sub-optimal 'genes' is a real dynamic force. Contraction provides a massive influx of *solution states*, but it has another aspect or dimension, its twin, its *problematics*, its incompossibility.

Expansion or stratification (cooling down of complexification, or the relative absence of non-linearity) is commonly taken to be definitive of the epoch; the question arises alongside a stratification: *what should we do with it?* – the defining question of an age. The power of the masses is commonly seen as the defining problem of the twentieth century, and its solutions mapped as fascism, global war, mass-production, Fordism, consumerism, etc., all supposedly genetically related ideologies. Matter, for example, appears pointless and hence subject to the will as a gadget. In an act of mutual emergence, this pointless sub-object or stratum demands the will to take itself in hand, resolute. It can then be formed and differentiated at will, to the extremes of even the most 'fallen' of projections, but must in the end not be allowed to get out of hand – time is called, and the excess, which is 'liquidized' by the metaphysical origin, is unveiled as unreal(izable). Resolute action separates matter from time in a most fundamental way, positing the problem as atemporal and the solution as the giving of time (from where?). But this is merely the false problem of phenomenology (again), and one should not be led astray by it. The twin concepts of 'discovery' and 'invention' play an important role in this process, and are in fact the twin pillars of metaphysics. Mass society was discovered as a problem to be solved, and is conceived of as a tool without dynamics. Postmodernist discourse gets terribly confused as to whether it is a good thing or not, but that's missing the point quite significantly: it is not a problem in the sense of good or bad, or of good uses and bad uses; rather it is a threshold to be differentiated from, a navigational marker, not a moral question-mark. Mass society is a solution, *and* a motor for change. It is a virtuality, a threshold crossed by many lines simultaneously. Problems are not constitutive; they are residual states, differentiated crossings. The actual is related to problems by differentiation, and is differentiated from them: 'Actual terms never resemble the singularities they incarnate' (Deleuze 1984: 212). We should not seek a secret alliance given in abjection, a dialectic between slave and master. Deleuze and Guattari deploy the example of the telephone exchange, which perhaps can now be replaced by the Internet, as a system 'discovered' by the State for the ordering of its lines of command, and then employed surreptitiously for the pleasure of individuals. But did the State invent the network to satisfy its needs, or was there a more complex and non-linear genesis in which local tactical alliances between military command and personal pleasure form the discovery of this military need? To what extent was Freud used by his patients? There are no clear points of contact between the strategic delineations because they are merely the product of complex local differentiations and tactical alliances. The schizo can play the analyst's game quite happily, laughing and screaming to the tune of mommy–daddy–me, while making more and more intensities flow. Similarly, we can use our black-humour tactics.

Before reaching the full Body without Organs, content (history or vertical lines of dependence) must be annihilated, that is to say, the vector must release itself from the tyranny of more probable states, or of the repeated selection of a small set of dominant states. The memory of the system should progressively move to being held as a property of the dynamics of the system as a whole, rather than as a property of a few 'royal' states. The thermodynamic hypothesis seems at first to contradict this, with a movement from low probability to high probability being described. As Deleuze notes, Boltzmann sought to ground good sense in the entropic rule (Deleuze 1994: 225). However, we can see that the dissipative structures that are formed in an open thermodynamic process are less probable selections at the fulcrum of the interaction of many systems together, causing local streamlining of process as well as local turbulence (dissipative structures being defined as both efficient and turbulent depending upon the point-of-view). There is thus a virtual increase in complexity: as the memory of the system moves towards being critically responsive to the fluctuations of its environment, it becomes *intelligent* towards its interactions, and the emergence of feedback loops routing its dissipators into its field of problems may define it as having a metabolic characteristic in its morphogenetic development. And yet the complexity increases, as if this metabolic persona were a wave of complexification surging through the world. The resolution of compatible states into non-compatible states frees up the degrees of movement. As the complexity of input and feedback into the system increases, so does the density of possible states, the activation of which becomes less certain. As Manuel De Landa has argued: 'The most successful command systems in history have been the ones that manage to 'dissipate' uncertainty throughout the hierarchy' (De Landa 1991: 60). These systems rely upon unplanned local tactical interactions to 'make redundant' local resistances to the overall movement. Thus uncertainty is eliminated, and the commander no longer needs to make many decisive commands during battle. However, uncertainty at a lower level allows for the possibility of the army getting caught in a headlong rush towards the full Body without Organs, and hence opening itself up to being 'caught' by a singularity that is not the one that the commanders and politicians had in mind. De Landa argues that the command structure is reinforced with the use of radio and computer communications. However, recent conflicts have shown that semi-autonomous soldiers may be caught in an unforeseen delirium and begin to re-engineer the overall strategy of the mission (trigger-happy A-10 pilots, etc., and of course the many strange waves that passed through Vietnam – what was that war about?). Intelligence, in this context, becomes a difficult concept – which systems are more intelligent: the ones that are able to obey commands despite uncertainty, or the ones that are able to modify their plans completely, in dynamic relationship with the world (i.e. learn, adapt)? Already we have seen how the Kantian crisis developed from the threat which the dynamics of the intellect posed to strategic delineations. The tendency of strategy is to abstract dissipative structures (selected less probable states) and attempt to transfer them to the tip of the intensive cone – to install them as institutional memories, and attach all other states to them in lines of dependence. This is precisely how signification operates, as a despotic body. But strategy only gets us so far. Similarly, *computational* models of intelligent processes rely upon a strategic platform – global purpose, objective function or problematics – and expression is understood as the realization of a secret plan thwarted by a globally specific randomness. When the gadgets and the best-laid battle plans break down, complexity returns, a tactical retreat, a negotiation . . . etc. DNA as a computational system is not a good model. It is strategic, and without the inclusion of local processes, local alliances, its full reality as a plane of excitable media (with proteins etc.) will not be understood. Embryology, as Deleuze foresaw, is now a science of local tactical alliances, of thresholds and complexities, of excitable media as epochs. As the biologist Brian Goodwin has stated: 'DNA on its own can go nowhere but towards greater simplicity. In order for evolution of complexity to occur DNA has to be within a cellular context; the whole system evolves as a reproducing unit' (Goodwin 1994: 34). And hence the radical proposal which pushes biology across the singularity: 'We could, if we wished, simply replace the term natural selection by dynamic stabilization, the emergence of the stable states in a dynamic system. This might avoid some confusion over what is implied by natural selection' (Goodwin 1994: 51). This journey towards the full Body without Organs takes us to the threshold of the epoch, to the epoch in which time as immanent process is fully actualized in a machinic assemblage: dynamic intelligence, schizotechnics, complexity diagrammatics. Singularities free us from the past: 'A universal point at which everything becomes ungrounded' (Deleuze 1994: 200). But crossing this singularity accelerates our progress across more and more thresholds, as activity becomes directed less by the strategic concerns of the pre-Kantian notion of intelligence and agency, and more by the expression of the machinic phylum within us. We become exploratory self-modifying systems.

On two levels this singularity can be seen to be operating at present, although these two levels of analysis are intermeshed with an increasing intimacy. With strategic military blocks as the determining presence of economic development and the development of technology, the research and production of intelligent systems (people, economic and social units, computers, etc.) was directed towards the fulfilment of distinct computational ends. Economic development remained closely marshalled by computation. But the relationship between the objective function of command and the actual functioning of machines became increasingly difficult to specify at the production stage and subsequently to discipline in the field. Thus experiments with total control were tried and failed (Kant, Stalin . . .). And then more autonomy was passed down to the operatives in the field. Intelligent systems further and further from equilibrium were developed in the hope that some 'common sense' would emerge amongst them in line with the strategic 'truth' of the command structure. In Artificial Intelligence and computation the grounds for a new type of involvement with the world was being tested in the hope that autonomous robots would emerge. Rod Brooks of MIT has experimented with supposedly 'situated' and 'emergent' robot intelligence, but as yet has failed to progress beyond the strategic paradigm.[3] Meanwhile, autonomous processes created waves of desire through the cultures and economies constituted by the military economy. The command system starts to change; it is confused. Who decides strategy? The purpose of a State now seems to emerge from the local desiring-production of its heterogeneous population. And that population is increasingly discovering that it has an intelligent relationship to the State: *it can play with it*. Münchhausen's Disease by Proxy, a condition in which 'sufferers' (who are far from unhappy) seem to fake illnesses so as to enjoy all the free high tech and dramatic attention provided by the State, is an example of people treating the State as a toy. Similarly, free or cheap drugs provide a new route to entertainment. People even commit crimes to experience the high drama of justice. Sado-masochistic fantasies proliferate. Simulacra generals and slave-masters are everywhere. To resolve the question of the State's purpose, the newly developed technologies, first radio then television, and ultimately computer intelligence, virtual reality and networking are deployed to the people, techno-democracy. A fatal error for command. The threshold is passed. The technology to play with reality in unknown and experimental ways passes out of the hands of the command centre, and production becomes orientated wholly towards the new entertainment/experiment ethos. The Sega-rization of planetary capitalism is the reconfiguration of Transcendental Apperception from strategic integration to tactical experimentation. The micro-war(s) of the entertainment economy and of conceptual ballistics replace(s) the strategic war of philosophical lineages and interpretation. Science itself has passed across the singularity, reconfigured into new tactical alliances with art and chaos. Artificial Life, perhaps science's closest vector to pure entertainment, seeks an experimental toolkit of molecular componentry for the emergence of novel circuitry. As Chris Langton states:

> A different approach to the study of nonlinear systems involves the inverse of analysis: *synthesis*. Rather than start with the behaviour of interest and attempt

> to analyze it into its constituent parts, we start with constituent parts and put them together in the attempt to *synthesize* the behaviour of interest.
>
> (Langton 1989: 41)

A-Life experimentation should not proceed by analysing problems into the analytic parts that they constitute, but should rather let components *synthesize* virtualities in the manner described by Deleuze and Guattari. What has been activated in crossing the threshold is a new creativity, a positivity at the heart of AI. As Langton states:

> *Behaviours themselves* can constitute the fundamental parts of nonlinear systems – *virtual parts*, which depend on nonlinear interactions between physical parts for their very existence. Isolate the physical parts and the virtual parts cease to exist. It is the *virtual parts* of living systems that artificial life is after; the fundamental atoms and molecules of behaviour.
>
> (Langton 1988: 41)

Artificial life is a schizotechnical science of Virtuality.

Viral Empiricism

Artificial life marks the crossing of a singularity and the actualization of a new understanding of intelligence. It also serves as a technical catalyst in developing that understanding. It is a self-assembling force, virtually present, which transports us across a threshold, but always in tactical alliance with other forces, of which the concept of intelligence in molecular biology is another significant vector. The result that has had the most widescale effect is the development of our understanding of the intelligence of the brain – now closer to the 'pure computer' of *expression*, evoked by Deleuze and Guattari, than the systems developed by military science (Deleuze and Guattari 1988: 57). Brain science was pulled across the singularity in cumulative assemblage with many forces. For example, in the study of viruses, the replacement of Beijerinck's hypothesis of the *Contagium Vivum Fluidum* – or intelligent fluid – as an explanation for the intelligent behaviour of disease-causing fluids (in which the agents that specify the behaviour of the disease could not be located) by the notion that many micro-molecular processes act in cooperation to stabilize as a viral metabolism was a forerunner of the idea that the brain might be such a micro-molecular distributed metabolism producing concepts – a *Contagium Vivum Philosophia*. The task that the new neuroethology sets itself is to diagram the modular interactions and metabolisms of transformations in the brain, or in its properly developmental instantiation, of the brain itself as a plane of consistency. Its object is a complex assemblage that is itself constituted from the specific deterritorializations of the brain through entropic fields of interference and zones of economic/computational instability in which consistency is subject to an irrecoverable loss (the *problematics of singularities*): lesions in the essential neuronal fabric, the rhizomic plasticity of neuronal development (see, for example, J. T. Schwartz's *The New Connectionism* for a description of these processes[4]), chemical and mineral restrictions upon its morphology, non-bial and bial alien vectors establishing lines of transverse disruption from 'non-human' agents, the vastly complex dynamics of neuropeptide production and interactivity, and so on. It is, in fact, an ethological study of brains as distinct singularities, as non-normative diversities, and hence as problems for synthetic understanding. The brain will now be studied not as a uniform computational set of states, with definite input–output objective functions, but rather as exploded and explosive. The plane that constitutes the brain is, as Deleuze argued, one which passes outwards to delirium and back again, through the Transcendental Imagination:

> It is imagination which crosses domains, orders and levels, knocking down partitions coextensive with the world, guiding our bodies and inspiring our souls, grasping the unity of mind and nature; a larval consciousness which moves endlessly from science to dream and back again.
>
> (Deleuze 1994: 220)

Now that we have a science of the larval consciousness, the imagination is no longer a distant and mysterious force. The operation of the singularity in brain science gives us a new tactical alliance between molecular-biological intelligence and our ability to operate in the environment called the brain, populated by concepts, which now take on viral characteristics. Daniel Dennett describes this environment in *Consciousness Explained*:

> Memes now spread around the world at the speed of light, and replicate at rates that make even fruit flies and yeast cells look glacial in comparison. They leap promiscuously from vehicle to vehicle, and from medium to medium, and are proving to be virtually unquarantinable . . . persisting in the face of the Second Law of Thermodynamics.
>
> (Dennett 1993: 205)

And these viral concepts multiply not by means of anthropomorphic familialism, but by far more devious and cunning processes. Concepts, like the schizophrenic, are universal agents of production – *celibate machines* – which produce at such a rate, changing constantly (close to the fBwO), that the category of causation becomes confused, inoperable, leaving only a contiguity of affects, a density of empirical detritus, and a techne of Viral Empiricism. The notion that schizophrenia, the condition of akrazed concepts, might be *caused* by a virus has recently been suggested. This, as will be demonstrated, is a misunderstanding produced by strategic power's inability to cross the singularity. I shall, on the contrary, argue that schizophrenia *is* viral, that it is the very nature of virulence, empiricism, and hence the true nature of the brain. A report in the *British Journal of Psychiatry* describes the activities of two men on the discovery that they are HIV positive (the idea being that exposure to HIV occurs simultaneously with exposure to other viruses):

> For seven days he locked himself in his flat with a friend. They spent their time holding pseudo religious services and daubing the walls with poems and prayers, which they then photographed because they were laden with significance. They lit candles which, when the last one went out, they thought would signal the start of Armageddon. This culminated in the subject running to a friend's house to escape Satanists who, he believed, had broken into his flat. He began tampering with the electrics with one hand while touching the water tap with the other, and the police were called. On admission he was neat and tidy but barefooted. He was not elated but was excited, suspicious and unpredictable, and no rapport was possible. There was pressure of speech. The thought content was poorly formed and he was unable to account for himself. He spoke continuously and monotonously. He falsely claimed to have three university degrees. He believed that two Christs would come and expounded at length on philosophical matters. He was controlled by messages from New Zealand which were linked to TV and radio. He said that 'spiritual things are happening in my body'. He denied auditory hallucinations.[5]

But spiritual things *are* happening in his body. Ideas, Deleuze argues, are the virtualities or larval swarms that writhe in the flesh. These virtualities occur when a swarm of vectors passes a singularity, when a transversal synthesis occurs between distinct elements. Culture and molecular biology, a cultural expression of HIV and a biological expression of culture and . . . and . . . and . . . in complex feedback. The psychiatrist's relation to the expression is strategic, uninvolved. The components of the behaviour of the schizo-HIV positive assemblage must be analysed down and the problem reduced from them. But, the schizo stands there before him; the relationship is one of pressure and escape. The psychiatrist morphs into the bars on the cell wall; his skin unwraps like a snake and strangles the cop who watches in disbelief. And transforms. The State, the body, the capital becomes a thousand distributed signs that vomit from the psychiatrist's mouth and swarm through the atmospheric volume of the jail, at first just a mist of vague insect forms, then more densely, a choking fog; asthmatically he coughs – the pressure of surplus code filling his lungs, expanding the fibrous arborescent interior with an irritating pressure. He gets the idea that they want to fry him Texas style; suddenly he feels the words lacerating his throat – 'they are Satanists'. He feels the pressure of speech. The more he struggles to instantiate control, the more the system becomes clogged with white noise. The pressure builds. 'It is by headlong flight that things progress and signs proliferate. Panic is creation' (Deleuze and Guattari 1988: 73). In some important sense he is above it all, out of the body, and not experiencing, more like the feeling produced by his DIY electrics – connect-I-cut. That's what it is. And he may eventually appear as catatonic; a storm of collapse may disable the system down to intensity = 0 – he may become botched, not be able to account for himself. But only as a result of the inquisition, the recurrent posing of cold questions by his interrogator, building massive redundancy and dissipating his energy. Schizophrenizing may be turned into the schizo. The eventual fate of the HIV positivists in this case is not given, but one can imagine that they were prevented from *becoming-into* a post-singularity phase: the schizophrenizing forces of their condition, the invisible-schizo, trans-migrating from one plane to another, defining that complex line – the hyperplane across the cone. Who knows what delirious textures they would have been able to inscribe had they been allowed to proceed? The psychiatrist cannot allow the development of such local tactical alliances; he prevents their delirium from schizophrenizing out into the *chaosmos*. Learning is incapacitated; exploration of an unknown space is prevented. The singularity cannot be crossed.

Deleuze

In opening himself up to tactical alliances between the different concepts and conceptual personae of philosophy, as well as lines that move across the disciplines of art, science and philosophy following a sometimes *mad distribution*, Deleuze has been the site of an assemblage which has dragged philosophy across the singularity, and thus made the assemblage of that site actual. A new image of thought has resulted: Viral Empiricism. And a new practice of philosophy has emerged, along with the destruction of traditional philosophical institutions and lines of dependence. Strategic philosophy could not possibly make it to the other side, and hence philosophy seems to be in crisis (from an institutional perspective), under constant threat from new disciplines such as AI, A-Life, Complex Systems, etc. But the truth is that it is the very notion of institutional thought that has not passed across the threshold. Philosophy finds itself exploded. But as a practice which is now disseminated into a thousand new fields, many more circuits of Ideas, it is thus also more *explosive*. The psychiatrist, through his strategy, confined the philosophical expeditions of the HIV positivists to fantasy – they 'expounded at length on philosophical matters' – but nothing was deemed worth reporting. Philosophy has escaped from this, and conceptual activity is spreading, to be found at the site of all crises in intelligence, and hence all intelligence. It would perhaps be apt to rerun the philosophical experiment of the HIV positivists, at least to attempt to realize the expressive fields that they hoped to cross, with Deleuze and the (non-linear) history of philosophy:

The philosophers sat in their room, candles miraculating lines of divine combustion drifting to the outer limits of their inclusion – this room, *baroque* volume, completely enclosed to light but open all the same – apocalyptic time enclosing, being sucked-in upon them, along the trajectory of the candle's disappearance *in reverse*. They talked of an Armageddon – but was it really a black-hole? Visualized in the wall-poetry with which they decorate the surface of their inclusion like so many permutations of the Torah, so many divinities, or death-camp serial numbers – textures built up from painting white upon white. They photograph the walls, capture the face of death again and again, reel after reel of film, images multiplying; scrambling the symbols like animal bones on charred earth, they focus in upon the object of their fascination. Seven days of expectation, of revelations and moments of incredible pleasure. Joyfully they chant their *momento mori*, their hope. Blindly, eyes burnt out by an excess of vision, intoxicated visions. As if they could through this gesture move the arrow of time, the arrow that designates the entropic depense that dissipates force into relations of forcing, turned back into itself. Meanwhile a machine is assembling, a transmission machine; something spiritual is happening in their bodies. They are being carried across the planes in the chariot of the sun goddess – Parmenides and Heraclitus are watching them burn. The retrovirus is hacking across incompossible matters – its force operates as a transversal deterritorialization, redistributing organizations, provoking non-linear reactions. Infecting, it opens up the skin; new liquids are released. Terrifying episodes of panic and beautiful forms are ripped from pupae-inclusions like a swarm of butterflies, white textures upon white. HIV positivity now expresses itself culturally, artistically, philosophically; it decorates the interior that is carved out from The Skin – Nietzsche's *sea of many-hued fishes*. Events are formulated as delirious practices, and come to pass like sub-atomic particles skipping across the void. The arrow narrows down to a point, the point a line. Incompossible planes connect and communicate, resonate, upon a more intense plane in which the transversal flows are actualized, now so real, that they are no longer even flows but once again singularities. The arrow narrows not to disappear, but to become intense, to become intensity, to be all the stars in the sky, all the burning suns of desire. They reach out and touch the full Body without Organs.

Notes

1 This excellent term is used by Deleuze and Guattari in their essay 'Balance Sheet Program for Desiring Machines'.

2 It is not the case that Deleuze and Guattari wish to deny the existence of an abstract line resonating between content and expression, such as the linearity of the nucleic sequence. Rather, they wish to demonstrate that: '*linearity* takes us further in the direction of *flat multiplicities*, rather than unity' (Deleuze and Guattari 1988: 59). Markov chains, synergistic and correlative deterritorializations (Deleuze and Guattari 1988: 61), invariant reproduction (Monod 1972: 23), etc. are all to be undertsood as emergent properties of the invariance of the immobile motor of entropic interference (fBwO).

3 See, for example, the essay (well respected amongst AI workers) 'Intelligence Without Representation', *Artificial Intelligence* 47 (1991), 139–59.

4 J. T. Schwartz, *The New Connectionism: Developing Relationships Between Neuroscience and Artificial Intelligence* (Graubard, 1988), pp. 123–41.

5 *British Journal of Psychiatry* 153: 618–23.

References

Deleuze, G. (1990) *Logic of Sense*, trans. M. Lester and C. Stivale, New York: Columbia University Press.

—— (1991) *Bergsonism*, trans. G. Burchell, H. Tomlinson and B. Habberjam, New York: Zone Books.

—— (1994) *Difference and Repetition*, trans. P. Patton, London: Athlone Press.

Deleuze, G. and Guattari, F. (1984) *Anti-Oedipus: Capitalism and Schizophrenia volume 1*, trans. R. Hurley, M. Seem and H. Lane, London: Athlone Press.

—— (1988) *A Thousand Plateaus: Capitalism and Schizophrenia volume 2*, trans. B. Massumi, London: Athlone Press.

—— (1994) *What is Philosophy?*, trans. H. Tomlinson, London: Verso.

Dennett, D. (1993) *Consciousness Explained*, London: Penguin.

Goodwin, B. (1994), *How the Leopard Changed its Spots*, London: Phoenix.

Graubard, S. R. (1988) *The Artificial Intelligence Debate: False Starts; Real Foundations*, Cambridge: MIT Press.

Kampis, G. (1991), *Self-Modifying Systems in Biology and Cognitive Science: A New Framework for Dynamics, Information and Complexity*, Oxford: Pergamon Press.

Landa, M. De (1991) *War in the Age of Intelligent Machines*, New York: Zone Books, MIT Press.

Langton, C. (ed.) (1989), *Artificial Life VI*, Santa Fe Institute Studies in the Science of Complexity, Boston, MA: MIT Press.
Monod, J. (1972) *Chance and Necessity: An Essay on the Natural Philosophy of Modern Biology*, trans. A. Wainhouse, London: Collins.

11

Viroid Life

On Machines, Technics and Evolution

Keith Ansell Pearson

> The possibility of metaphor is disappearing in every sphere. This is an aspect of a general tendency . . . affecting all disciplines as they lose their specificity and partake of a process of contagion – a viral loss of determinacy which is the prime event of all the new events that assail us.
>
> (J. Baudrillard 1993: 7)

> *This* is evolution: the use of new technics. There is no such thing as 'biological evolution'. . . . The most terrible mistake of the nineteenth century: the abandonment of creation theory was based on a biological rather than a technical-artificial foundation. We are the children of the consequences of this mistake. Instead of technical practices, we inherited the master-race as our God-function. As good children of the master-race elders, 'we' believe (*green* as we are) that we can protect ourselves against fascism with 'nature' (instead of realizing that only technics can abolish fascism.
>
> (K. Theweleit 1992: 260)

> It is less a question of evolution than of passages, bridges, and tunnels.
>
> (Deleuze and Guattari 1988: 322)

1. Modernity is haunted by the threat of the eternal return of the same and captivated by the promise of the arrival of the new, the unique and the singular, an experience of time that is ecstatic, explosive and aeonic. If we are to gain a critical purchase upon it, Deleuze's philosophy, considered as a philosophy of difference and repetition from his early 'Bergsonism' to his later attempts with Guattari to map the 'reality of the creative', needs to be situated within the general problematic of

philosophic modernity. Philosophical modernism is born of the failure of representation, of the corrosion of identities, and of the discovery of non-human forces that operate under the representation of the same and the identical (the 'pre-human soup' that immerses us). 'Man' does not survive the death of God, and the postulates of pure practical reason do not escape the vortex of nihilism that exposes their nakedness, while the identity of the subject cannot survive the de-reification of the notion of a permanent substance (even a substance that becomes a subject). Identities, and matters of life and death, are simulations, masks produced as an optical effect of the more profound game of difference and repetition. A thinking of difference and repetition generates itself at the point in history when the most stereotypical and mechanical repetitions appear to have taken over life completely and subjected it to a law of entropy (homogeneity, abstract equivalence, neutralized differences, etc.). The dominant logics of modernity from the death-drive to capital all partake of a transcendental illusion that any radical philosophy of difference must seek to expose. Otherwise there is only the guarantee of the eternal return of the same, of the same old death. But, once thought has emancipated itself from its anthropocentric naivety, this cannot be done in the name of man or spirit, but only in that of the alien and the inhuman, or the non-organic and machinic. Thought moves *outside*: 'one cannot write sufficiently in the name of an outside', an outside which has 'no image, no signification, no subjectivity' (Deleuze and Guattari 1988: 23). This is a mode of thought that stands in contradistinction to Cartesian/Hegelian modernity with its emphasis on the interiority of philosophical reflection and the positivity of knowledge (see Foucault 1990: 16). Outside thought does not invigorate our powers or enhance our mastery of the world, but annihilates them. There are only insecurity systems from now on. The antinomies of bourgeois thought will not be overcome through the invention of new organic social relations, by praxially transforming ourselves into rounded wholes, transparent and self-fulfilled persons harmoniously labouring away at the negative. The critical and historicist philosophies no longer hold any charm for us, only the promise of the same. We shall not 'make' history. Let's go outside . . .

2. Current continental philosophy contends that the human is necessarily bound up with an orginary technicity: technology is a constitutive prosthetic of the human animal, a dangerous supplement that enjoys an originary status.[1] That is, the origin of the 'human' as a species and a *Dasein* is radically aporetic since what lies at the origin of the making of man is the *lack* – or excessiveness, depending on one's perspective – of origin. History appears to have reached the weird point where it is no longer possible to determine whether technology as an extended phenotype is an expression of the desire of our genes or a sign of nature's cultural conspiracy. As

Lyotard has put it: the 'truth' of the time of technics is not a 'revelation' but a 'betrayal' (Lyotard 1991: 52). The task of the new technologies is to unblock the 'obstacle' constituted on earth by human life. However, this collapsing of bios and technos into each other is not only politically naive, producing a completely reified grand narrative of technology as the true agent and telos of natural and (in)human history; it also restricts technics to anthropos, binding history to anthropocentrism, and overlooks the simple fact that the genesis of the human is not only a technogenesis but equally, and more importantly, a *bio-techno*genesis. The phenomenon of symbiosis provides the clearest demonstration of this thesis, presenting a genuine challenge to the entire Occidental tradition of speculative thought and suggesting the urgency of adopting a rhizomatic praxis. The image of the tree has dominated 'all of Western thought from botany to biology and anatomy, but also gnosiology, theology, ontology, all of philosophy' (Deleuze and Guattari 1988: 18). These new anthropocentric readings of history lead to the entirely spurious claim that with the coming of computers and the arrival of robot intelligence the planet is now entering a 'silicon age'. What this ignores is the fact that metallurgy has an ancient pre-human history, with human metalworking following the bacterial use of magnetite for internal compasses by almost three thousand million years (Margulis and Sagan 1995: 194). Moreover, symbiosis has a filthy lesson to teach us: the human is an integrated colony of ameboid beings, just as these ameboid beings (protoctists) are integrated colonies of bacteria. Like it or not, your origins are in *slime*. Biologists have established that the nucleated cell of eukaryotic life evolved by acquisition, not of inherited characteristics à la Lamarck's model of evolution, but of inherited bacterial symbionts, in which 'amid cell gorgings and aborted invasions, merged beings that infected one another were reinvigorated by the incorporation of their permanent "disease"' (Margulis and Sagan 1995: 90). There is thus no need to search for alien intelligent life since it is already deep within us. The case of viroid life is a little more strange, it has to be admitted, since this 'life' is a virtual, abstract machine that exists both within and without us in a state of suspension – insisting on existing between life and non-life, and between virtuality and actuality.

3. The attempt to develop a general theory of evolutionary systems is entirely dependent on the kinds of problems being set up. To consider the nature of species, organisms and evolution itself, independently of the cognitive framing and mapping of theoretical inquiry – and all theory needs to be understood as a praxis (Reuleaux 1876/1963: introduction) – is to produce nothing but reification. As Bergson pointed out in his thinking of 'creative evolution' in 1907, our science is contingent, relative both to the variables it selects and to the order in which is successively

stages problems (Bergson 1983: 219). Conceptions of 'evolution' only make sense in relation to time-scales within which they are framed. For example, from the perspective of 'universal evolution' species and organisms cannot be treated as fixed or static points of reference or interpreted as the end points of life's novel activity of invention. The boundaries between species are constantly shifting, mobile and porous, while geographical landscapes harbour only extrinsic harmonies of an order of ecology in which any equilibrium between populations can only be regarded as temporary. Indeed, on a certain model one could legitimately claim that the 'success' of a species is to be measured by the speed at which it evolves itself out of existence. Deleuze and Guattari's most radical gesture is to suggest that there has never been purely 'biological' evolution, since 'evolution' is technics, nothing but technics: 'There is no biosphere or noosphere, but everywhere the same Mechanosphere' (Deleuze and Guattari 1980: 89; 1988: 69) (on the noosphere see de Chardin 1965; on the biosphere see Vernadsky 1945, and Margulis and Sagan 1995). All systems from the 'biological' to the 'social' and economic are made up of machinic assemblages, complex foldings, and movements of deterritorialization that serve to cut across and derange their stratification. This explains why for them 'pragmatics' (or 'schizoanalysis') becomes the fundmental element upon which everything else depends. Deleuze and Guattari are most keenly interested in the differential rhythms and affective intensities of evolution, the 'invisible' becomings of non-organic life that can only be effectively navigated and mapped when situated on the plane of abstract machines which consists of non-formed matters and non-formal functions (1980: 637; 511). Time to go outside and 'get Real'.

4. *Explosions fall upon deaf ears*: In *Difference and Repetition* Deleuze deploys biological thinking in the service of a philosophy of internal difference. He approaches 'evolution' on the level of a philosophical embryology ('the world is an egg'), insisting that 'Evolution does not take place in the open air' since 'only the involuted evolves' (Deleuze 1994: 118). Embryology demonstrates, for example, that there are vital movements and torsions that only the embryo is able to sustain, and which would tear apart an adult. This means that there are 'spatio-temporal dynamisms' which can only be experienced at the borders of the liveable: 'Something "passes" between the borders', he writes; 'events explode, phenomena flash, like thunder and lightning' (1994: 118). Moreover, in this work Deleuze is already articulating the kind of 'molecular Darwinism' that characterizes Deleuze and Guattari's joint work and their utilization of population thinking in modern biology with its attack on typological essentialism. Deleuze does not read natural selection as a theory about the evolution of 'species'; rather, for him, what is primary is the play of the individual and processes of individuation, in relation to

which the evolution of species is only a transcendental 'illusion' (Deleuze 1994: 250).[2] In *A Thousand Plateaus* Deleuze and Guattari argue that neo-Darwinism's emphasis on populations over types, and differential rates and relations over degrees, makes for a vital contribution to an understanding of biology as nomadology, steering the logic of life in the direction of a *science of multiplicities*. In the former work Deleuze will reverse the relationship between ontogeny and phylogeny as classically depicted in biological thought, such as Haeckel's famous biogenetic law, insisting that it is not the case that ontogeny simply recapitulates phylogeny but rather that it *creates* it;[3] while in the latter work Deleuze and Guattari make the identical point, speaking of the relationship between embryogenesis and phylogenesis as one that involves the virtual becoming of a creative 'universal evolution': 'the embryo', they write, 'does not testify to an absolute form preestablished in a closed milieu; rather, the phylogenesis of populations has at its disposal, in an open milieu, an entire range of relative forms to select from, none of which is preestablished' (Deleuze and Guattari 1988: 48). One can only insist on the irreducibility of the forms of folding.[4] The antinomies of modern biological thought – individual/species, selector/selectee, organism/environment, variation/selection, and so on – are fully caught up in the antinomies of bourgeois thought and are at play in Deleuze's 'Bergsonism'. In *Difference and Repetition*, I would argue, Deleuze too readily assimilates natural selection into the project of thinking difference and repetition at the level of philosophical embryology and morphology. He claims that selection works in favour of guaranteeing the survival of the most divergent (Deleuze 1994: 248). In this work Deleuze conveniently ignores Nietzsche's critique of Darwin, where the critical focus is on the reified notion of 'fitness'. On Nietzsche's understanding, natural selection may well be a machine of evolution, but it functions in accordance with a specific entropic principle, namely, 'survival of the fittest' (see Nietzsche 1968: sections 684, 685).[5] It can thus not be so easily regarded, as it is in Deleuze as a positive power of differenciation (a 'differenciator of difference'). Indeed, the term 'natural selection' is something of a misnomer since nature does not at all *select*; rather, it operates as an arbitrary force of *extermination*, resulting in the differential loss of differently constituted individuals. Nature does not so much select the fittest as exterminate the ill-fitted, adapting forms of life to the environment slowly and imperceptibly in an entirely mechanistic, algorithmic fashion. Thus, we find in *Difference and Repetition* major tensions emanating from the uneasy alliance Deleuze makes between the competing claims of 'complexity' and 'selection'. In the work with Guattari primacy is clearly given to 'involution' over 'evolution' and to modes of deterritorialization, that is, to the power of endogeny over that of exogeny: 'The more interior milieus an organism has . . . assuring its autonomy and bringing it into a set of aleatory relations with the exterior, the more deterritorialized it is' (Deleuze and Guattari 1988: 53–4). It is precisely the 'creative' reality of deterritorialization that Deleuze was articulating in *Difference and Repetition* in such novel terms and which serves to link the work up with current complexity theory in philosophical biology. For example, in *Difference and Repetition*, the 'formula' for 'evolution' (Deleuze has the word in scare quotes) is given as: 'the more complex a system, the more the *values peculiar to implication* appear within it' (Deleuze 1994: 255).[6] It is the 'centres of envelopment' that function as both a 'judgement' of the complexity of any given system and as the differenciator of difference. For example, we know today that the difference between humans and chimpanzees consists not in their genetic difference, which is minimal anyhow, but in the spatial organization and folding of their cells. Such an insight counters the reductionism of those biologists who place the emphasis on the determination of genes and so erase the trace of genetic indetermination. It is precisely the endogenous powers of spatio-temporal rhythms and intensities that Deleuze is privileging in *Difference and Repetition* as a model of 'evolution' over the strictly exogenous mechanism of selection.[7] This thesis is now supported by leading complexity theorists such as Stuart Kauffman who argue that many of the highly ordered features of ontogeny are not to be regarded as the achievements of selection, but rather as the self-organized behaviours of complex genetic regulatory systems. Moreover, the properties of self-organization are so deeply immanent in these complex networks that '*selection cannot avoid that order*' (Kauffman 1993: xvii). On this model selection can in no way be regarded as the sole or primary generator of evolutionary order and composition. When in *Difference and Repetition* Deleuze calls for a 'kinematics of the egg', insisting that what is seminal in embryology is not the division of an egg into parts, but rather the morphogenetic movements, such as the 'augmentation of free surfaces, stretching of cellular layers, invagination by folding', and in which 'transport is Dionysian, divine, and delirious, before it is local transfer' (Deleuze 1994: 214), he is anticipating the turn to questions of embryogenesis and morphogenesis that characterizes current attempts amongst biologists to move beyond the hegemonic neo-Darwinian paradigm. Here the focus is on the production of spatial patterns that are explicable not in terms of the nature of the components involved, such as cells, but rather in terms of the way the molecules interact in time and in space (their relational order). Deleuze goes further in insisting that these processes involve the creation of a space and a time that is *peculiar* to that which is actualized. On this model of a philosophical embryology, time and space are no longer treated simply as universal *a priori* forms of sensible intuition, but rather are understood as components in the *production* of variation and difference. As one eminent neuroscientist who works on embryology has recently put it: 'Diversity must inevitably result from the *dynamic* nature of topobiological events' (Edelman 1994: 64). In short, what Deleuze does not appear to appreciate is that his thinking of difference and repetition, in terms of a thinking of the creation of the new and the different, along the lines of a philosophical embryology and morphology, presents a fundamental challenge to the core tenets of Darwinism.[8]

5. A strand of contemporary biology has sought to move away from the genetic reductionism of ultra-Darwinism – best typified in Richard Dawkins' Schopenhauerean-styled theory of the selfish gene – insisting that questions of form cannot be reduced to those of simple adaptation, since the organism enjoys an integrity and autonomy of its own and has to be treated as a self-organizing structural and functional unity (see Goodwin 1994). But this move from genetic reductionism to organismic holism in complexity theory is by no means a straightforwardly progressive one. The 'organism' is always extracted from the flows, intensities and pre-vital singularities of pre-stratified, non-organic life in order to produce, through techniques of normalization, hierarchization and organization, a disciplined body, a controlled subject and a subject 'of' control. The organized body of both biology and sociology is an invention of these techniques of capture and control. It is the judgement of theos: 'You will be organized, you will be an organism, you will articulate your body – otherwise you're just depraved' (Deleuze and Guattari 1988: 159). This explains why it becomes necessary to think about machines, about the reality of parts and wholes, about machinic modes of 'evolution', and about a 'machinic surplus-value' that produces an excess which cannot be located within a 'subject' since it lies *outside*.

6. Evolution, like the egg, does not take place in the open air: invention in evolution takes place not simply in terms of a process of complexification, say from a less to a more differentiated state, but rather in terms of a process which Deleuze and Guattari call 'creative involution'. The word 'involution' should not be confused, as it is in Freud, for example, with regression, but suggests the emergence of a symbiotic field that allows assignable relations between disparate things to come into play. It is this 'block of becoming' that represents the 'transversal communication' between heterogeneous populations, making becoming a rhizome and not a classificatory or genealogical tree. The 'tree' model of evolution is highly ambiguous, being both genealogical (the tree of the family man) and the tree of non-human nature that shows no particular concern for man. As one commentator has also noted, it is both an oppressive colonial image and an organic image (Beer 1986: 239). Becoming is to be conceived neither in terms of a correspondence between relations or identities nor in terms of progression or

regression along a series. This is to posit evolutionism as linearism (Deleuze and Guattari 1980: 292; 1988: 238–9). It thus becomes necessary to think of a reality that is specific to 'becoming'.

7. The important role played by symbiosis in the history of technology, in which previously disjoint and unconnected technologies merge, is widely recognized (Sahal 1981). In biology symbiosis has had a curiously awkward history which reveals much about the anthropocentric determination of the subject and about hominid fears of contamination. It has played, and continues to play, a subversive role in biology since it challenges the boundaries of the organism.[9] Indeed, it has been argued by one commentator that it was not until 1950, when geneticists extended their field of study to micro-organisms, that biology recognized that there were means other than sex for transmitting genes, such as infections and symbiotic complexes. Prior to this it was the institutionalized boundaries of the life sciences themselves, such as zoology, botany, bacteriology, virology, genetics, pathology, etc., which prevented the synthetic studies of symbiosis from being properly assessed (Sapp 1994: 208–9). The importance of symbiotic bacteria in the 'origin of species' – repeated bacterial symbioses result in the emergence of new genes – is now widely appreciated, but must ultimately be disturbing to our anthropocentric claims upon life (and death). The detailed structure of the organelles in eukaryotic cells, such as the mitochondrian, and the composition of the DNA in those organelles, shows that crucial evolutionary processes were not the result of slow accumulation of random changes (mutations) in the genes of ancestral prokaryotic cells. Rather, it seems highly probable that they were the result of intracellular symbiosis in which some cells incorporated into their own cell contents partner cells of another kind that had different metabolic abilities. Over time the genetic and metabolic organizations of host and guest cells fused to the point where it became impossible to distinguish where one cell began and another finished. The strength of this hypothesis lies in the fact that it offers the most convincing explanation as to why both mitochondria and chloroplasts contain their own ribosomes and DNA. The case of multicellular organisms is now part of the 'orthodoxy' of contemporary biology, but there are other more disturbing examples of the transversal character of genetic lineages such as viruses ('poisons'), for example. Modern biology has identified not only 'bacteroids' as playing a crucial role as symbionts in certain metabolic processes, but also symbiotic 'viroids'. Indeed, a leading researcher in the field in the 1940s postulated the idea of a distinct kingdom for such viroids, the *Archetista*, arguing that within evolution they have acted, on account of their small size, as highly adaptable intracellular symbionts, so supplying from 'amoeba to man' a virtual 'reservoir' for viruses in the course of evolution (Sapp 1994: 151–2). More recently, Dennett has

referred to these pioneers of evolution as 'macros', which is the name given by computer programmers to cobbled-together fragments of coded instructions that perform particular tasks, in order to draw attention to the similarities between the machinery of 'natural' viruses and 'artificial' viruses such as computer viruses. Both are 'bits of *program* or *algorithm*, bare, minimal, self-reproducing mechanisms' (Dennett 1995: 156–7). Standing as they do at the border between the 'living' and the 'non-living', and *virtually real*, viruses serve to challenge almost every dogmatic tenet in our thinking about the logic of life, defying any tidy division of the physical, such as we find in Kant, for example, into organisms, the inorganic, and engineered artefacts (for further insight see Eigen 1992: 101–6). Creative evolution on Earth would have been impossible without the intervention of the genetic engineering that characterizes viroid life.

8. The scientific work that was carried out on genetic engineering in the 1950s, which today provides the basis for recombinant DNA technology, derived from observations of the mechanisms of recombination in bacteria. The emphasis was on 'transformations', such as 'conjugation' and 'transduction', which involve the transfer of genetic material from one cell to another by a virus (Sapp 1994: 158). This research, however, must necessarily lead to a fundamental revision of dominant models of evolution. If it is the case that viroid life is one of the key means by which the transferral of genetic information has taken place, then it is necessary to entertain the idea that there are cases where this transfer of information passes from more highly evolved species to ones that are less evolved or which were the progenitors of the more evolved species, with the result that reticular schemas would have to be substituted for the tree schemas that dominate almost all thinking about the logic of life. Transversal communications between different lines serve to 'scramble the genealogical trees' (Deleuze and Guattari 1988: 11). The existence of complex phenotypic traits in organisms has long been recognized as a problem for Darwin's theory of evolution by natural selection, but recent research in biology seeks to show that the paradigm of symbiosis can be used to explain how novel phenotypic traits can come about through the association of organisms of different species. One example given of a symbiotic phenotypic trait, in which these traits only exist by virtue of the association of the partners, is the leghemoglobin protein of the root nodules of legumes, which are coded in part by the *Rhizobium* genome and in part by the leguminous host (Law 1991: 58). The boundaries which ensure the evolution of separate identities begin to collapse and a machinic mode of evolution comes into play. This is a perfect illustration of the rhizomatic evolutionary schema proposed by Deleuze and Guattari, who themselves supply the example of the type C virus with its double connection to baboon DNA and that of

certain domestic cats. Here we have taking place an '*aparallel evolution*' in which there is neither imitation nor resemblance. The becoming-baboon which characterizes the cat does not mean that the cat is imitating the baboon, but rather denotes a rhizomatic becoming which operates in the zone of the heterogeneous (a zone of invention as opposed to imitation) and the connection of already differentiated lines: 'We form a rhizome with our viruses, or rather our viruses cause us to form a rhizome with other animals' (Deleuze and Guattari 1988: 10). Or: *the organism unbound*.

9. Like philosophy, the field of biology is full of born Platonists, but symbiosis shows that the delineation of 'organic units', such as genes, plasmids, cells, organisms and genomes, is a tool of a certain mode of investigation, not at all an absolute or ideal model. It challenges notions of pure autonomous entities and unities, since it functions through assemblages (multiplicities made up of heterogeneous terms) that operate in terms of alliances and not filiations (that is, not successions or lines of descent). The only unity within an assemblage is that of a plural functioning, a symbiosis or 'sympathy' (on the importance of sympathetic relationships in creative evolution see Bergson 1983: 173–4). An animal, for example, is best defined less in terms of genus, species and organs, and more in terms of the assemblages into which it enters (man–animal symbiosis, animal–animal symbiosis, plant–animal symbiosis). In all cases a clear establishment of distinct kingdoms is rendered problematic and what becomes important is a 'machinic' phylogenetic becoming. Symbiosis also challenges the notion of informationally closed systems, and corresponds to the function of the idea of the 'rhizome' in the work of Deleuze and Guattari, in which evolution is removed from the limits imposed by filiation. A rhizome operates as an open system, both entropically and informationally, designating, in the words of one commentator, 'a constructive feedback loop between independent information lineages', whether they be cultural, linguistic or scientific lineages or biological germ lines (Eardley 1995) (an essential part of the history of symbiosis will be to formulate germs not simply as 'disease-causing' but as 'life-giving' entities). As opposed to conventional phyletic lineages, rhizomatic lineages serve to demonstrate the extent to which exclusively filiative models of evolution are dependent on exophysical system descriptions that are simply unable to account for the genuinely creative aspect of evolution (machinic becomings). If the organism is a function of the frame within which the science of biology encodes it, then it is necessary to recognize that the frame captures only a small part of the possible information that assemblages are able to express. A code is inseparable from an intrinsic process of decoding (no genetics without genetic drift, as Deleuze and Guattari pithily express it). Modern

work on mutations shows that a code, which is necessarily related to a population, contains a margin of decoding. This decoding takes place not only through the 'supplement' that is capable of free variation, but also within a single segment of code that may be copied twice with the second copy left free for variation. In utilizing the notion of a 'surplus value of code' – codes are always paralogical, always beside – to account for the transferral of fragments of code from the cells of one species to those of another, Deleuze and Guattari insist that this is not to be understood as a process of 'translation' (viruses are not translators), but rather in terms of a singular process of 'side-communication' (*communication d'à-côté*) (Deleuze and Guattari 1980: 70; 1988: 53).

10. In accordance with this new model of machinic evolution, becoming is to be conceived neither along the lines of a correspondence between relations nor in terms of a resemblance or an imitation. This is not to think becoming but to reduce it to the given. There are no series or stages involved in becoming, whether regressive or progressive. What is actual in becoming is the 'block of becoming itself' and not the fixed terms through which becoming passes. This is the force behind Deleuze and Guattari's idea that 'becoming is not an evolution' (1980: 291–2; 1988: 238). That is, not an evolution if evolution simply denotes descent, heredity or filiation along an axis of linear or genealogical becoming.[10] The only veritable becomings present in evolution are those produced by symbioses which bring into play new scales and new kingdoms. Only involution breaks with filiative evolution by forming 'blocks' which allow things to pass through and freely become. Involution is difference conceived not on the order of filiation or heredity but excessively in terms of the surplus value of code. Involution is genuine freedom, the rhizome as opposed to the genealogical tree. The model of becoming that the rhizome brings into play has obvious affinities with recent attempts within feminist and postcolonial theorizing to go beyond the genealogical prejudices of an autochthonic politics of identity. Hybridization, however, takes us only so far away from arborescent schemas. Hybrids involve the connection of points, but they do not facilitate the passing *between* points. A point remains wedded to a point of *origin*. In rhizomatic-styled becomings becoming denotes the movement by which the line frees itself from the point and renders points indiscernible. *Machinic* 'evolution' refers to the synthesis of heterogeneities, whereas hybridization is still tied to the idea of there being elements that are pure and uncontaminated prior to the mixing they undergo in hybridism. The difference is crucial and enables Deleuze and Guattari to posit 'ethology' as a privileged *molar* domain on account of its demonstration of how the most varied components – from the biochemical, the hereditary and acquired, to the social – are able to crystallize in assemblages that do

not respect the distinction between orders. What holds the various components together are 'transversals', in which the 'transversal' itself is to be understood as the *deterritorialized* component within the complex adaptive system, that is, as the non-subject 'agent' of the evolution of complexity (Deleuze and Guattari 1988: 336). In this novel conception of ethology the 'assemblage' is being privileged over the classical emphasis on 'behaviour'. This means that we must arrive at a much more complex understanding of 'evolution' than is facilitated by the Darwinian emphasis on adaptation to external circumstances, which ultimately rests on a reified and unmediated notion of the 'environment'. On Deleuze's ethological model an animal or life-form is never separable from its rapport with the 'world' and its relations with it, but that world is never just 'given' or simply passively adapted to. 'Evolution' involves learning. In nature there is invention (technics): 'Artifice is fully a part of Nature' (Deleuze 1988: 124). An originary technics thus informs Deleuze's so-called *Naturphilosophie*.

11. Within philosophy the machine has been classically defined in contra-distinction to the organism along the following lines: an organism is a self-organized being in which the parts are reciprocally cause and effect of the whole, forming not just an 'aggregate' or an 'assemblage', but a 'unity'. According to Kant, only organisms display 'finality' (purposiveness), that is, a self-organizing capability (for example, in its genus, *Gattung*); a tree produces nothing other than itself, and so preserves itself 'generically'. By contrast, a machine is entirely lacking in (self-propagating) *formative power* (*fortpflanzende bildende Kraft*), and so is unable to self-produce, reproduce and self-organize. The efficient cause of the machine lies outside the machine in its designer. The only power given to the machine is a 'motive power' (*bewegende Kraft*) (Kant 1974, 1982: section 65).[11] On Kant's model an 'organized' being is one in which each part has been trained and disciplined to exist '*for the sake of the other*', so that all the interacting parts exist for the sake of the whole which is ontologically prior and primary (Kant 1995: 60). It cannot be simply a question of inverting the dualism of machine and organism which has structured the history of metaphysics. Rather, the mapping of machines can be constructed in novel ways to the point where the fixity and certainty of techno-ontological boundaries and distinctions begin to destabilize and break down in true machinic fashion. The idea that when we speak of living things as machines we are being merely metaphorical also needs to be contested (Emmeche 1994: 50), since again such a view rests on little more than an anthropocentric bias, which itself is not 'natural' but 'artificial', the product of a certain historical formation and deformation of the human animal/machine.

12. For all its good sense, this philosophical determination of the machine rests on

the privileging of notions of unity and finality that then allows for the strict partition between organismic and non-organismic life. Dawkins has conceded that the concept of the organism is of dubious utility precisely because it is so difficult to arrive at a satisfactory definition of it. Much depends on the hierarchy of life which we are seeking to establish. To plant biologists, for example, the leaf may be a more salient 'individual' than the plant, since the plant is a 'straggling, vague entity for whom reproduction may be hard to distinguish from what a zoologist would happily call "growth"' (Dawkins 1982: 253). For Nietzsche, the organism is not to be reified as a monadic entity but is to be viewed as a 'complex of systems struggling for an increase in the feeling of power' (Nietzsche 1968: section 703). Moreover, there are only 'acentred systems' (1968: section 488). The 'organism' enjoys a largely semiotic status and cannot be conceived independently of our cognitive mapping of systems and their boundaries. In his 1867 speculations on teleology since Kant, Nietzsche questions the extent to which Kant demonstrates that only organisms can be viewed as ends of nature, arguing that in nature 'a machine would also lead to underlying final causes'. Human thought can only reify the 'eternally becoming' (*ewig Werdende*) of life by grasping living things solely in terms of their forms. In an insight that anticipates the Bergsonian-Deleuzian understanding of creative evolution, he argues:

> our intellect is too dull to perceive continuing transformation: that which it comes to know it names form. In truth no form is given, because in each point sits infinity (*Unendlichkeit*). Every thought unity (point) describes a line. A concept similar to form is that of the individual. We call organisms unities, as centres of purpose (*Zweckcentren*). But unities only exist for our intellect. Each individual has an infinity of living individuals within itself.[12]

In spite of everything Kant seeks to do with the notion of teleology, Nietzsche insists that the standpoint of reflective judgement is utterly whimsical and arbitrary (*willkürlich*). The move Kant makes, in which the end of the 'real existence' of nature can only be discovered by looking beyond nature, amounts to a violent (moral) subordination of nature to human reason. Today, he argues, as we undergo the experience of morality's self-overcoming (the self-overcoming of the will to truth), we are compelled to recognize that man has become an animal whose existence in the visible order of things appears as 'arbitrary, beggarly, and quite dispensable' (Nietzsche 1994: II, section 25). It is no wonder that the issue of teleology so often appears as little more than the refractive influence of provincial human interests.

13. Nature is not impossible; it is simply becoming-artificial. Darwin's attempt to resolve the tension between the purposive artistry of breeding and the purely mechanical evolution of natural selection results in his writings in an almost

undecidable play between nature and art, or artifice. Ultimately he shifts away from his initial perspective, in which art is posited as inferior to nature, to endorsing a thoroughly 'technological', or artificial, conception of the operations of nature (Cornell 1984: 303–44). A techno-philosophy of the machine would begin by recognizing that the machine 'is' *not*, since it does not exist in itself but only through alienation. As Deleuze and Guattari point out, an abstract machine is destratified and deterritorialized with no form of its own. An abstract machine in itself, that is, viewed from inside according to its intelligible (virtual) character, is neither physical nor corporeal. It is not semiotic but *diagrammatic*, operating by matter, not by substance (too hard), and by function, not by form (too unelastic). In other words, the abstract machine is 'pure Matter–Function' that exists independently of the forms and substances it brings into play and distributes. A critique of the machine in terms of a machine's inability to replicate and reproduce itself does not begin to touch on the problematic of machinic heterogenesis. As Butler points out, it is illegitimate to declare that the red clover has no reproductive system simply because the bee must aid and abet it before it can reproduce. He writes: 'Each one of ourselves has sprung from minute animalcules whose entity was entirely distinct from our own, and which acted after their kind with no thought or heed of what we might think about it. These little creatures are part of our own reproductive system' (Butler 1985: 211).[13] The notion of machinic evolution, therefore, does not refer specifically or exclusively to human contrivances, gadgets or tools, but rather to particular modes of evolution, such as symbiosis and contagion, and is not specific or peculiar to the human–machine relationship, since it also speaks of the machine–machine nexus and alterity. The 'machinic' is the mode of evolution that is specific and peculiar to the 'becoming' of alien life. A machine can only exist through exterior elements. It thus enjoys an existence in terms of being a complementarity, and not simply in terms of its relationship to human design or a designer. A machine lives and dies in connection with other virtual and actual machines, suggesting 'a "non-human" enunciation, a proto-subjective diagram' (Guattari 1992: 59; 1995: 37). An assemblage works through invention, and does not imply a relationship of anastomosis between its components. Rather, it connects and convolutes things in terms of potential fields and virtual elements, crossing ontological thresholds without fidelity to generic or species' relation (Guattari 1992: 56; 1995: 35). The logic of life displays an infinite virtuosity, but, in truth, all that is happening is the transformation of seemingly determinate points into indeterminate lines. In his 'book of machines' Samuel Butler demonstrates, in an unnerving insight into the animal–machine nexus and the human–machine nexus, how it becomes virtually impossible to declare with any ontological certainty who is the host and who is the parasite. The transhuman imagination is one which does not rest content with anthropocentric prejudices about machines, but invents new ways of communicating with them and tapping into their non-human enunciation. Life is a universal technical – prehuman and transhuman – phenomenon. Evolution has always been about the becoming of alien life and intelligence (cutting-edge research today shows that the origins of terrestrial life are *extra*-terrestrial, with photosynthesizing cells evolving in outer space before landing on Earth).

14. In an essay on 'The Organization of the Living' Humberto Maturana and Francisco Varela set out to define, working from within an assumed non-animistic perspective, living systems as machines. They confess that they are attracted to the word 'machine' because of its decisive dynamic connotations. Entities are defined as unities with the power to reproduce and by their capacity for autonomy. 'Autonomy' is conceived as the 'self-asserting capacity of living systems to maintain their identity through the active compensation of deformations' (Maturana and Varela 1980: 73). This definition succeeds in capturing the essentially cybernetic nature of self-regulating systems in which feedback plays the crucial role. The question, however, is whether in their conception of the machine Maturana and Varela simply take 'unity' as given, with an underdefined deformation and 'reproduction' being posited in naive and essentialist terms (since things don't just reproduce themselves). In seeking to define a 'living system', Maturana and Varela contend that evolutionary thought has ignored the autonomous nature of living entities. 'Organization' is the principle that is best able to account for the 'unitary character' of living systems. If living systems are 'machines', then they need to be understood in terms of 'relations' and not of component parts. Only in this way is it possible to generate the desired notion of dynamism (*entelecheia*). The usual view of machines is that they are concrete hardware systems, defined by the nature of their components and by the purpose they fulfil in their operations as man-made artefacts. But this view says nothing about how they are constituted. Maturana and Varela are concerned with relations, not components; the latter can be any, so it is the organization which is crucial and constitutive. The organization of machines can then be described as autopoietic. Such machines are homeostatic, and all feedback is internal to them. What is peculiar to such machines, however, is not this feature but the fundamental variable which they maintain constant. Such a machine is organized as a network of processes of production (transformation and destruction of components) that produces the components which (a) continuously regenerate and realize the network of processes (relations) that produced them through their interactions and transformation; and (b) constitute the machine as a concrete unity in the space in which the components exist.

15. An autopoietic machine, therefore, is one which continuously generates and specifies its own organization through its operation as a system of production of its own components. It does this in terms of an endless turnover of components under conditions of continuous perturbations and compensation of perturbations.

Organization is the fundamental variable which it maintains constant. In other words an autopoietic machine is not defined in terms of the components or their static relations, but by the particular network of processes (relations) of production. The relations of production of components are given only as *processes*; if the processes 'stop', then the relations vanish. Therefore, machines require regeneration by the components they produce. An autopoietic machine has no inputs and outputs, although it can be 'perturbated' by independent events which cause it to undergo internal structural change. The claim that autopoietic systems are organizationally 'closed' can be misleading if it is taken to imply that these systems do not interact with their environment. Such systems are closed simply in the sense that the product of their organization is the organization itself. Internal changes which take place are always subordinated to the maintenance of the machine organization. A relation between these changes and the course of perturbations which can be pointed to, pertains to the domain within which the machine is observed, and not to its organization. An autopoietic machine can be treated as an allopoietic machine, but this will not reveal its particular organization as an autopoietic machine. An autopoietic machine, therefore, is one which maintains as constant certain relations between components that are in continuous flow or change, and it is this which constitutes its *modus operandi* as one of 'dynamic stability'. The actual manner in which the autopoietic organization is implemented in physical space varies according to the nature, or properties, of the physical materials which embody the structure of the machine in question. Although there are many different kinds of autopoietic machines in physical space, all of them are organized in such a way that any 'interference' with their operation outside their domain of compensations will result in their disintegration. Maturana and Varela reach two principal conclusions concerning the machine: firstly, if living systems are machines (physical autopoietic machines), which transform matter into themselves in a manner such that the product of their operation is always their own organization, then the converse is also true: if it is autopoietic then a physical system is living; secondly, from this, it follows that the distinction between machine (automaton) and living (spontaneous) becomes untenable and must break down. The classic view is that machines are man-made artefacts with completely deterministic properties and perfectly predictable. Contrariwise, living systems are deemed to be *a priori* autonomous, unpredictable systems. The prejudice is that man could not manufacture a living system but 'only' a machine. As a result of these redefinitions, however, certain distinctions begin to break down and certain prejudices get supplanted.

16. In spite of the progressive character of the last insight, a fundamental metaphysical opposition operates deep within the so-called machinic thinking of the school of autopoiesis. Maturana and Varela's conception of the machine as a self-referential, self-reproductive monadic entity rests on the positing of an opposition between pure autonomy (self-maintenance and self-preservation), on the one hand, and impure heteronomy (invasion) on the other. They do not see that a genuinely machinic thinking of the 'entropy/evolution' problematic must lead to a corrosion of molar-organized unities and identities, leading to the construal of a fluid relationship between 'inner' and 'outer', between autonomy and heteronomy, and between nature and artifice. Autopoiesis cannot allow for transformation except in terms of a highly restricted economy, presenting us with a stark either/or choice: *either* entropy *or* perfect performance. It is guided by a whole conservative metaphysics of living systems, and presupposes a paranoid machine. This is evident in the emphasis it places on systems as closed and recursive unities that are guided by, above all else, the maintenance of stability. To claim, as they do, that organization is an invariant of a component system is to equate change with simple destruction, and to reify organization as something 'over' physical reality rather than 'to' it. In contradistinction to Maturana and Varela, Vilmos Csanyi and George Kampis maintain that if new components endowed with new functions come into existence in a system, then the organization of that system cannot remain invariant. Moreover, change in a system's organization, as a result of the emergence of new components, does not result in the disintegration of that system. This must mean that the 'autonomy' of the individual organism is 'always relative' (Csanyi and Kampis 1985: 306). For them the main problem with an autopoietic model of evolution is that it fails to appreciate that if a system were to be driven by the desire for perfect autonomy it would get trapped in an evolutionary deadlock, unable to form further relationships and connections. Exactly the same point was made by Bergson, in the context of a different debate, who argued against a vitalist position which rested on the assumption that nature evolved in terms of a purely internal finality and absolutely distinct individualities (Bergson 1983: 42). It is impossible, he argued, to determine with any degree of fixity where the vital principle of the 'individual', or autonomous machine, begins or ends.

17. In the three sections on 'The book of the machines' which make up his fiction *Erewhon* of 1872 Samuel Butler challenges the way in which lines are drawn between machine life and animal life:

> Where does consciousness begin, and where end? Who can draw the line? Who can draw any line? Is not everything interwoven with everything? Is not machinery linked with animal life in an infinite variety of ways? The shell of a hen's egg is made up of delicate white ware and is a machine as much as an egg-cup.
>
> (1985: 199)

As Deleuze and Guattari argue, Butler's reflections do not simply contrast two common arguments, one according to which organisms are only more perfect machines, the other according to which machines are never more than extensions of the organism. Butler is not content merely to claim that machines extend the organism (the pre-established unity), or that organisms are machines; rather he wishes to show that (a) the field of evolution is thoroughly machinic from the outset, and (b) organisms can be compared to machines in terms of the sophisticated engineering which integrate their distinct parts (desire *is* engineering) (Deleuze and Guattari 1972: 337–8; 1984: 284). As a result, Butler destroys the vitalist argument by calling into question the alleged personal unity of the organism, and, by the same token, he undercuts the mechanist position by calling into question the alleged structural unity of the machine. If 'life' can be conceived along the lines of a 'desire-engineering', then there can be no pre-established boundaries and no fixed determination of what constitutes the parameters and identities of individuated entities, such as organisms or machines. The mistake is to view complex machines as single entities whose individuated existence is pre-given. In truth, every complex machine, Butler maintains, is to be regarded as a city or society. Like organisms, machines reproduce themselves through an integrated network of co-evolution (as in the well-known example of the red clover and the bumble bee). Butler's reasoning forces us to question the fixity of Kant's distinction between motive and formative powers. In Deleuze and Guattari's terms the motive power of the technical machine requires the formative power of the social machine for its actualization and reproduction. The human animal enjoys no autonomy from nature and from technics. Like everything else it too is caught up in the 'surplus value of code', which denotes an excess that refers to a process when part of a machine captures within its 'own' code a code fragment of another machine and, as a result, owes its reproduction to a part of another machine. It is thus the always excessive desire of machinic becomings that deterritorializes the evolutionary lineages of all phenomena, and which enables us to privilege alliances over filiations, heteronomous assemblages over autonomous entities. It becomes possible to appreciate the compound nature of Deleuze and Guattari's formulation 'desiring-machines', in which the machine passes to the heart of desire and the machine is desiring desire, 'machined': 'Desire is not in the subject, but the machine in desire.' Desiring-machines are truly formative machines, but whose formativity is possible only through functional misfirings; that is, formation requires deformation, and what makes evolution a machinic process is the fact that it takes place through cuttings, breakages, slippages, breakdowns, and so on. Structural unities and mass phenomena (such as molar aggregates) conceal the intrinsic direction of singular multiplicities (interpenetration, direct communication), and force us to lose sight of the multitude of small machines which are dispersed in every organism, which itself is no more than 'a collection of trillions of macromolecular machines' (Dennett 1995: 206). Ultimately, at the point of 'dispersion', where techno-ontological boundaries break down, it becomes immaterial whether one describes machines as organs or organs as machines: 'A tool or a machine is an organ, and organs are tools or machines' (Canguilhem 1992: 55). Canguilhem also points out that the mechanistic conception of the body posited by Cartesianism is no less anthropomorphic than a teleological conception of the physical world. He shares Nietzsche's view that machines can be considered to be purposive in their endeavour and activity. Indeed, 'man' is only able to make himself the master and proprietor of nature to the extent that he denies any finality or purpose to what lies 'outside' him, such as nature or machines, which are then treated solely as means to serve his hubristic *Zwecken*. Nature and technics take their revenge when the realization dawns that the entire evolution of what we take to be 'spirit' is, in actuality, the becoming of something altogether different than what appears in consciousness and reason, namely, the body: 'In the long run, it is not a question of man at all, for he is to be overcome' (Nietzsche 1968: section 676). Only now, today, not tomorrow, is it possible to appreciate that the riddle of the *Übermensch* is of universal significance, and not simply the monstrous vision of some *fin-de-siècle* madman from Röcken who sported a highly dubious-looking moustache.

18. If the idea of autopoiesis is to retain any useful function it has to be thought in relation to entities which are evolutive and collective, and which sustain diverse kinds of alterior relations, as opposed to being implacably closed in upon themselves and maintaining their autonomous existence at the expense of casting out and dissipating anything external that would contaminate their inner purity (the machine as beautiful soul). In the case of the machine, entropy and evolution need to be viewed as co-extensive and mutually informative. The 'man–machine alterity' is inextricably linked to a 'machine–machine alterity'. As Guattari points out, machines already 'talk' to each other before they talk to us. The reproducibility of machines is not a pure, programmed repetition, but precisely an evolution.

Difference is introduced at this point of breakdown/evolution and is both ontogenetic and phylogenetic. There is no simple or straightforward univocal historical causality since evolutive lineages present themselves as 'rhizomes', meaning that 'datings' are not synchronic but heterochronic (on the crucial role played by heterochrony in the developmental processes of ontogeny, see Raff and Kaufman 1983: 173ff.). The tectonic movements of history have to be understood in terms of singularities which themselves have to be mapped out in terms of a virtual plane of rhizomatic and associative becoming. Such becomings take place 'in' history but are not reducible to, or identical with, it. Guattari has rightly insisted that the question of the ontogenetic evolution of the machine, for example, is not reducible to the 'linear causalities of the capitalistic apprehension of machinic Universes' (Guattari 1992: 79; 1995: 52).

19. In machinic heterogenesis it is less a question of the identity of a being that retains its heterogeneous texture while traversing different regions, and more of an 'identical processual persistence'. We are speaking neither of a Platonic whole nor of an Aristotelian prime mover, but rather of transversal creatures that 'appear like a machinic hyper-text' (Guattari 1992: 151; 1995: 109). Guattari's insight into this universe of machinic heterogenesis requires a fundamental reconfiguration of ontology. An ontology informed by an appreciation of the machine would neither place qualities or attributes as secondary in relation to substance, nor conceive of being as a pure and empty container of all possible modalities of coming-into-being. Rather, it would conceive being as first and foremost 'auto-affirmation' and 'auto-consistency' which actualizes itself through virtual and diverse relations of alterity. This would mean that we would cease viewing existence-for-itself and for-others in terms of the privilege of one particular 'species', such as *man*kind, and appreciate that everywhere 'machinic interfaces engender disparity and, in return, are founded by it' (Guattari 1992: 152; 1995: 109). 'Being' ceases to be a general ontological equivalent and becomes modelled along the lines of 'generative praxes of heterogeneity and complexity' (1992: 152; 1995: 109). Evolution by symbiosis – the vitality of viroid life – and rhizomatic becomings constitute an essential part of this heterogeneity and complexity.

20. In terms of the question of technology, there is no reification of technical machines in the work of Deleuze and Guattari since they readily appreciate that technical machines are only indexes of more complex assemblages that bring into co-evolutionary play material forces in which the role played by the social machine is decisive. One is not 'oppressed' by a technical machine but by a social machine which determines at any given moment what is the usage, extension and comprehension of technical elements (compare Braudel 1981: 431: 'there is no

technology in itself'). Technical machines are not an economic category but always refer to a socius or social machine that is distinct from them. This is akin to Marx's view that machinery is no more an 'economic' category than is the ox which draws the plough. Deleuze and Guattari insist that assemblages are never purely technological. Tools always presuppose a 'machine' and the machine is always social 'before' it is technical (compare Ellul 1965: 4–5, in which the question of the machine is reduced entirely to a question of mechanized 'technique'). As one commentator has noted, in relation to the new cybernetic machines, in no arena will the technologies themselves be determining (Nichols 1988: 45). In other words, questions concerning cybernetic technology can only be adequately attested to when they are articulated in terms of a social theory of the microphysics of power. One of the reasons given for the primacy of the social machine by Deleuze and Guattari is that technical machines do not contain the conditions for their reproduction, but require the social machine to organize and limit their development. There is no attempt made in their work to biologize crudely the technical-social; both a biological reading of human history and an anthropological reading of natural history must be avoided since the dangers of either strategy are all too obvious. The social is already artificially biologized. The terms of political theory, for example, are terms of capture and regulation, in which the evolution of societies is referred to as 'embryonic', 'nascent' and 'under-developed', and that of Third World societies as 'foetuses' and 'abortions' of culture and civilization. In challenging the reified conception of the organism found within a variety of discursive practices one is not advocating a retreat into a pre-social biosphere, but rather presenting a challenge that operates on myriad fronts. A politics of desire – the machinic assemblage of new solidarities and formations – comes into play when it is recognized that technocracy and bureaucracy (the functioning of the social machine) can never be reduced to being simply the operation of technical machines along the lines of a perfectly run cybernetic machine. In the 1960s Vaneigem argued that, 'by laying the basis for a perfect power structure, the cyberneticians only stimulate the perfection of its refusal. Their programming of techniques will be shattered by the same techniques turned to its own use by another kind of organization' (Vaneigem 1994: 85). In truth, the situation is now infinitely more complex than the likes of Vaneigem could ever entertain, since the 'outside' – virtual futures of all kinds – has been captured. Capitalism, having embarked upon a programme of endocolonization, has become a *futures* market on every level one cares to think. 'Nothing is true, everything is permitted' is no longer the slogan of the revolutionary nihilist but that of established powers of capture. The revolution *will* be televised (and already has been). This is the force, for example, behind

Umberto Eco's astute insight into (post)modern terrorism: terrorism is not the enemy of the great systems but their natural counterweight, both accepted and programmed (Eco 1986: 116). If the great systems function as headless systems, having no protagonists and not living on individual egoism, then they cannot be struck by killing the king: 'if there exists a completely automated factory, it will not be upset by the death of the owner but rather by erroneous bits of information inserted here and there, making hard work for the computers that run the place' (Eco 1986: 115). It is no longer sufficient to ponder Marx, he suggests; one must also ponder Norbert Wiener. Capital renders Marx's great insight into history null and void: the history of all hitherto existing society is the history of class struggle *except for the 'history' of (late, always late) capital*! Forever the great cynic, capital cannibalizes all negativity, 'parodistically going beyond its own contradictions' (Baudrillard 1994: 52).

21. Technology's powerful illusion of independence is part of its immense entropic and imperialistic success: the essence of technology is nothing technological, but it *appears* as if it is. Fetishism of technology is an essential – and *vital* – part of capital's transcendental illusion. But the social definition of what is technologically feasible or desirable is not external to technology but intrinsic to it. A distinction between the 'economic' and the 'technological' is arbitrary and unintelligent (see Hornborg 1992). Capitalism rests on a particular conjunction of technical and social machines. As a distinct social formation it functions by turning the technical machines into constant capital attached to the body of the socius (as opposed to 'human machines', which are made adjacent to the technical machines). The social axiomatic extends its limits through the 'non-technical' means of administration and inscription. Culture works as a mechanism of selection, inventing through inscription and coding the large numbers – organisms and complete whole persons – in whose interests it acts. This explains why 'statistics is not functional but structural', concerning 'chains of phenomena that selection has already placed in a state of partial dependence. This can even be seen in the genetic code' (Deleuze and Guattari 1984: 343). The State exists to regulate the decoded flows unleashed by the schizzo-tendencies of capitalism. While capital melts down everything that is solid and profanes all that is holy, bourgeois society guarantees that the productive forces of change are rendered equilibrial through the territorially fixed and juridically invariant structure of the modern State (Balakrishnan 1995: 56–7) (and news of its death are premature). Moreover, through State regulation and control the decoding practices of science and technics are subjected to a social axiomatic that is more severe than any putative 'scientific' axiomatic. The social and cultural revolution of postmodernity is about the potential liberation of technical

machines from monopolistic and scientistic control by the molar forces of capture that characterize the modern capitalist State, a bifurcation point at which capitalism is no longer able to monopolize for itself technical machines as the constant capital attached to its social body. The critical task of an alien thought-praxis, therefore, can only be that of decoding and deterritorializing the prevailing administrative and regulatory machines – in the State, in philosophy, in science, in culture and information – that have defined and restricted the present by despotically blocking the free flow of energy and knowledge throughout the social machine. Forces of resistance – and *attack* – are not simply, or only, human. Time to get artificial.

22. Grand narratives, it would seem, are coming back into fashion, and with a vengeance, assuming a distinctly inhuman character, in which we are offered a plethora of apocalyptic scenarios concerning an alleged phase-space transition to a new, 'higher' level of evolution based on machine intelligence, resulting in a genetic take-over of carbon life by soft machines (robots and computers) (for two accounts of our neg-entropic destiny from vastly different thinkers, see Lyotard 1991 and Tipler 1995). But this depiction of neg-entropic destinies, in which the human plays the role of a mere conduit in the inhuman process of complexification, can only provide simple options that are not options at all, such as a retreat into a new ethical purism (mourning the event, bearing testimony to the Event), futile Ludditism, or vacuous cyber-celebrationism. The dangers in conflating biology and technology are immense. Today palaeoanthropologists speak of life on earth taking place in terms of the evolution of techno-organic life that has cultivated positive feedback loops between 'intelligence' and biology resulting in an accelerated evolution, with the increasing hegemony of artificial life over natural life being understood as a Lamarckian invasion and take-over of so-called dumb and blind Darwinian natural selection (see Schick and Toth 1993: 315–16). A new mythology of the machine is emerging and finds expression in current claims that technology is simply the pursuit of life by means other than life.[14] This dubious neo-Lamarckism, which has recently reached an apogee in Kevin Kelly's bald assertion that the advantages of a Lamarckian style of evolution are so great that *nature herself* has found ways to make such an evolution possible, is not only philosophical idiocy, but also politically naive, resting on a highly vertical and perfectionist model of bio-technical evolution. He constantly speaks of 'what evolution really wants', as if evolution wanted anything, and as if one could easily speak of 'evolution' in terms of a global entity, as in the following gross assertion: 'Evolution daily scrutinizes the world not just for fitter organisms, but to find ways to increase its own ability. . . . Evolution searches the surface of the planet to find ways to speed itself up, to make itself more nimble, more evolvable – not because it is anthropomorphic, but because the speeding up of

adaptation is the runaway circuit it rides on' (Kelly 1994: 361). Such 'searching' on the part of evolution, we are told, results in the human brain providing the 'answer' to the problem of how evolution can gain the complexity necessary in order to peer ahead and 'direct evolution's course'. In the process of this ridiculous anthropomorphism questions concerning the utilizations and abuses of A-life and bio-engineering for life are rendered completely uninteresting, since, as Bergson would have put it, 'all is given'. In effect, what is happening in this kind of depiction of evolution is a blind, and dumb, reading of the dynamics of contemporary hyper-colonistic capitalism – Kelly's identification of speed with simple acceleration illustrates this – back into the mechanics of the biosphere, resulting in a biological justification of entropic modernization in its most imperialistic guise (speed is irresistible).[15] There are other reactive forces at play in recent paeans to the rise of machine intelligence. As Baudrillard has pointed out, having lost our metaphysical utopias we now build prophylactic ones in which our immortality is guaranteed (you can download your brain!). If in the past it was the dead that were embalmed for eternity, today it is the living that are being embalmed alive in a state of survival (Life owes me a right *not* to die!) (Baudrillard 1994: 87–8).

23. *Research has pierced all extremes of my sex (call it a day)*: Recall: everything is political, but every politics is simultaneously macro and micro, while it is the molecular that always makes or breaks it (Deleuze and Guattari 1988: 213). What we are witnessing at present within the discernible logic of postmodernity is a transition from the thermodynamic machines of industrial capitalism to the cybernetic machines of contemporary information societies that govern through intelligent control. But this is still a mutation within entropic (post)modernity in which the development of new forces of production outstrip existing relations of production but in no way guarantee their radical transformation or liberation from social control and molarization. Society – and 'we' who exist outside – are becoming more like snakes every day. Did the 'political' die with the collapse of the great empires, including the great empires of thought (-control)? Today the life of the great empires has assumed a retroviral form, fragmented and peripheral, genetically infecting their wastes and by-products, their basic cells and ugly growths, no longer on the order of the political but of the *trans*political whose passion, notes Baudrillard, is that of the interminable work of mourning, lost in 'the melancholy of homeopathic and homeostatic systems', in which evidence for the death of *the* political is impermissible since it would 'reintroduce a fatal virus into the virtual immortality of the transpolitical' (Baudrillard 1994: 51). Postmodernity (human, all too human) spreads the virus of voluntary servitude, an 'ecological micro-servitude, which is everywhere the successor to totalitarian oppression' (and how green were

those Nazi valleys). There is only the contagion of technics and the freedom of becoming imperceptible, invisible and ignoble (learn to growl, burrow and distort yourself).

24. In conclusion: it is necessary to show what cannot be demonstrated here, namely, that the questions which currently assail us – questions concerning technology, time, technics, matter, memory and machines – can only be adequately and properly addressed when they are posed in terms of the question of the fold. This is to speak of an 'outside' that always open onto an unknown future, and in which Nietzsche's great question of the overhuman can come home to us in all its strange, alien aspects.

Notes

1 As early as 1907, for example, Bergson was insisting that mechanical invention, as well as the technics of invention, had to be seen as constitutive of the kind of intelligent life-form we label 'human' since 'from the first' technics has been 'its essential feature' (Bergson 1983: 138). A powerful critique of twentieth-century schools of neo-Hegelian humanism for their forgetting of the technogenesis of the human, such as Debord's situationism, has recently been evinced by Regis Debray, who argues that these 'essentialist ontologies', which fantasize about a final reconciliation of essence with human existence, are based on delusions of historical transparency and effective historical agency that stem not only from their erasure of technological determination, but from their disclaiming of the 'hard labour of real mediations', such as 'political mediation', conceived as a structuring instantiation of collective existence, and 'technical mediation', conceived as a structuring instantiation of 'the hominization process'. See Debray 1995: 136–7.

2 For Darwin on the importance of 'individual differences' in selection see Darwin (1985: 101ff.). On neo-Darwinism see Mayr (1991), who writes that 'the discovery of the importance of the individual became the cornerstone of Darwin's theory of natural selection' (42); on the move to population genetics within evolutionary theory that characterizes the modern synthesis see Eldredge (1995: 10–30).

3 The inversion of Haeckel's law dates back to work done in the 1920s. For further information see Wolpert (1991: 185), who argues that the 'repetition' taking place in ontogeny is not that of phylogeny but simply of other ontogeny, that is: 'some embryonic features of ancestors are present in embryonic development'. For a comprehensive historical introduction to the problematic see Jay Gould (1977).

4 Deleuze suggests that the double helix of DNA should be treated in terms of the operations of the 'superfold'. See Deleuze 1988a: 132.

5 Nietzsche felt isolated in his 'contra Darwin' position, in which 'the error of the school of Darwin' became such a 'profound problem' to him. How could one see nature 'so badly'? he asks. In short, Nietzsche is maintaining that Darwinism is a biological theory shot through with assumptions of society and morality. 'I rebel against the translation of reality into a morality', he writes (1968: 685), while insisting that Malthus is *not* nature

(Nietzsche 1979: 75). Ultimately, the *Auseinandersetzung* becomes for Nietzsche a matter of *transvaluation* of so-called strictly 'biological' values. See, for example, the 'critical' denouement to essay 1 of *On the Genealogy of Morality*. For further insight into the topic see Ansell Pearson (forthcoming). The phrase 'survival of the fittest' appeared in the fifth edition of the *Origin of Species*. It is associated with the work of Herbert Spencer and was adopted by Darwin at the insistence of Alfred Russel Wallace, who considered it a better description of evolution than the misleading 'natural selection', with its anthropomorphic personification of nature. Throughout the *Origin* Darwin speaks of the 'economy' and 'polity' of nature, and there are places where it becomes undecidable whether he is talking of 'nature' or of industrial society. Marx, for one, saw 'civil society', the Hobbesian *bellum omnium contra omnes*, as playing a major role in Darwin's model of 'nature'. One should also note the extent to which a philosophy of 'good and evil' figures in his description of the animal kingdom, and at times he comes dangerously close to reading the text of nature through the lens of an anthropomorphic sentimentalism. The best example of this is his claim that natural selection acts solely for the good of each being, endeavouring to strike a 'fair balance' between the good and evil caused by each organ. It is because selection is not perfect, however, that it is possible to explain a bizarre phenomenon such as the sting of the wasp which when used in attack cannot be withdrawn, so resulting in the wasp's own death through the ripping out of its viscera (Darwin 1985: 230).

6 Compare Simondon (1992: 305), whose text on the genesis of the individual, published in France in 1964, exerted a major influence on Deleuze's philosophy of internal difference: 'The living being resolves its problems not only by adapting itself, which is to say, by modifying its relationship to its milieu . . . but by modifying itself through the invention of new internal structures and its complete self-insertion into the axiomatic of organic problems.'

7 It is interesting to note that Nietzsche also employs developments in the experimental embryology of his day to challenge the primacy accorded to the influence of external circumstances and the foregrounding of 'adaptation' (*Anpassung*) within Darwinian theory. In the crucial section 12 of the second essay of *On the Genealogy of Morality*, where Herbert Spencer is under attack, Nietzsche lifts the notion of 'form-shaping forces' (*die gestaltenden Kräfte*) directly from Wilhelm Roux, one of the founders of modern embryology, and his work of 1881, *The Struggle between Parts of an Organism* (*Der Kampf der Theile im Organismus*), notes from which first appear in the *Nachlass* in 1885. The notion critically informs his articulation of the fundamental activity of life as 'will to power', in which Nietzsche contends that adaptation to external circumstances is a secondary effect – a 'reactivity' – that takes place only *after* the activity of the spontaneous, expansive 'form-shaping forces' has had its effect. See Ansell Pearson (forthcoming) for further insight.

8 It is interesting to note that the major figure who appears after the cursory treatment of Darwin in *Difference and Repetition* is von Baer. It is von Baer Deleuze appeals to in order to show that the highest generalities of life point beyond species and genus in the direction of individual and pre-individual singularities (1994: 249–50). On von Baer's understanding of development as a process of 'individualization' and 'differentiation of the unique' see Jay Gould (1977: 52–9). It is clear that Darwin was unable to take on

board the full challenge of von Baer's stress on ontogeny over phylogeny since it would have fundamentally altered his theory of natural selection. At the time of Darwin's writing of the theory of descent embryology was undergoing a significant transformation in its own 'evolution', away from *Naturphilosophie* in the direction of modern epigenetic theory. Darwin's position on embryogenesis – that embryos mirror the history of the race by being similar to adult, though extinct, forms – is the one that Haeckel was later to advance in his biogenetic law, and which stands discredited today. For further insight into this crucial matter see Oppenheimer 1959 and, more recently, Lovtrup 1987: 150–65, who goes so far as to contend that to choose Darwin is to be contra von Baer and vice versa. Deleuze's work is unique in its suggestion that the work of Darwin and his so-called 'pre-Darwinian' predecessors, such as Cuvier, Geoffroy Saint-Hilaire and von Baer, can be held together to provide a more complicated conception of 'evolution', one that is not evolutionist. See Deleuze 1988a: 129, where it is argued that the tendency to diverge is produced through endogenous processes of folding. The same shortcoming which contemporary embryologists, such as Lovtrup, find in Darwin has also been identifed as a major weakness of the modern synthesis (neo-Darwinism). One commentator, for example, has argued that the modern synthesis is unable to generate a theory of ontogeny since it assumes individuality as a basal assumption (Buss 1987: 25).

9 The seminal text is Margulis 1970. See also Margulis 1981 and Jacob (1974: 311–12). Margulis has used her work on symbiosis to challenge the view that natural selection provides the prime explanation of evolutionary life. The fossil record and other evidence suggest that evolution from bacterial to nucleated cellular life did not occur by random mutation alone, but rather through ancient motility symbiosis. For an excellent introduction to the extensive use of models of symbiosis to account for a wide range of evolutionary phenomena see the essays in Margulis and Fester (1991).

10 It should be recalled that in the *Origin of Species* Darwin's account of evolution is a theory of 'common descent', what he calls 'descent with modification', which is genealogical identity in difference. The discussion of matters of embryology and morphology in the final chapter of the book, before the 'recapitulation and conclusion', takes place in the context of an examination of 'classification': 'community in embryonic structure reveals community of descent' (Darwin 1985: 427). Darwin does not understand genealogy in linear terms, but rather in terms of a 'branching' in which 'all living and extinct beings are united by complex, radiating, and circuitous lines of affinities into one grand system' (1985: 433). Darwin makes it clear, however, that what he is establishing with this model of genealogy are filiations of *blood*, in which the amount or value 'of the differences between organic beings' becomes ever more widely different in the course of evolution, and yet, 'their genealogical *arrangement* remains strictly true' (1985: 405).

11 Compare Hegel (1970: 198–202; 1980: sections 256–60), where the constitution of the organism is compared to the constitution of self- consciousness, as that which 'distinguishes itself from itself without producing any distinction'. This non-machinic conception of the organism as a functional and structural unity resulting from self-organization figures in the work of one eminent contemporary biologist, Brian Goodwin

(1994: 182–4). For another account of the difference between machines and living organisms see Serres (1982: 81).

12 This passage is taken from Nietzsche's 1867 dissertation outline on *Teleologie seit Kant* (not available in the *Kritische Studienausgabe*), *Historisch-Kritische Gesamtausgabe 3* (Munich, 1933–42), pp. 371–94. A German original and helpful English translation of this intriguing early piece can be found in the appendix to C. Crawford, *The Beginning of Nietzsche's Theory of Language* (Berlin and New York: Walter de Gruyter, 1988), pp. 238–67. In this chapter I have used my own translation, however.

13 Even this entrenched thesis on machines has been contested by Richard Laing (1979: 201–15), who has argued that deliberate explicit design is not the sole means by which machines come to exhibit complex behaviour, such as self-replication and self-repair. My aim in this chapter is limited to challenging the way in which we talk about machines and organisms by privileging wholes over parts, unities over multiplicities and autogenesis over heterogenesis.

14 Compare Deleule (1992: 205–6), where he writes: 'Life does not imitate the machine, nor is it reduced to a mechanical construct. It is the machine that actually simulates life. . . . Machines were not built in order to free humans from servile tasks. The function of machines is to increase the power of life itself, to enhance life's capacity for mastery and conquest. The machine does not in any sense replace life.' This so-called postmodern thesis on the machine was captured in its essential import by Samuel Butler in his strikingly titled essay 'Darwin among the Machines' of 1863, where he poses the question concerning the machine in quasi-Nietzschean terms, posing it as a question about 'the sort of creature' that will succeed man in the supremacy of the earth. His concluding opinion, not surprisingly, was that 'war to the death should be instantly proclaimed against them'. See Butler (1914). What perturbs Butler is the recognition that while machines have proven to be an indispensable aspect of human existence – 'man's very soul is due to the machines; it is a machine-made thing', he writes – in the future hegemonic evolution of machine intelligence the human may prove to be utterly *dispensable* as far as the desires of the machines are concerned (Butler 1985: 207).

15 Of course, the irony of Kelly's position is that he is a control freak. His opposition to natural selection is based on the fact that it *takes time*, time he does not have, he tells us.

References

Ansell Pearson, K. (forthcoming) 'Nietzsche contra Darwin', in D. W. Conway (ed.) *Nietzsche: Critical Assessments* (3 vols), London: Routledge.

Balakrishnan, G. (1995) 'The National Imagination', *New Left Review* 211: 56–69.

Baudrillard, J. (1993) *The Transparency of Evil: Essays on Extreme Phenomena*, trans. J. Benedict, London: Verso.

—— (1994) *The Illusion of the End*, Oxford: Polity Press.

Beer, G. (1986) '"The Face of Nature": Anthropomorphic Elements in the Language of *The Origin of Species*', in L. J. Jordonova (ed.) *Languages of Nature*, London: Free Association Books, pp. 207–44.

Bergson, H. (1983) *Creative Evolution*, trans. A. Mitchell, Lanham: University Press of America.

Braudel, F. (1981) *The Structures of Everyday Life: The Limits of the Possible*, London: HarperCollins.

Buss, L. W. (1987) *The Evolution of Individuality*, New Jersey: Princeton University Press.

Butler, S. (1914) 'Darwin among the Machines', *A First Year in Canterbury Settlement*, London: A. C. Fifield, pp. 179–85.

—— (1985) *Erewhon*, Harmondsworth, Middlesex: Penguin.

Canguilhem, G. (1992) 'Machine and Organism', in J. Crary and S. Kwinter (eds) *Incorporations*, New York: Zone Books, pp. 144–70.

Chardin, T. de (1965) *The Phenomenon of Man*, London: Fontana.

Cornell, J. F. (1984) 'Analogy and Technology in Darwin's Vision of Nature', *Journal of the History of Biology* 17(3): 303–44.

Csanyi, V. and Kampis, G. (1985) 'Autogenesis: The Evolution of Replicative Systems', *Journal of Theoretical Biology* 114: 303–21.

Darwin, C. (1985) *The Origin of Species*, Harmondsworth, Middlesex: Penguin.

Dawkins, R. (1982) *The Extended Phenotype*, Oxford: Oxford University Press.

Debray, R. (1995) 'Remarks on the Spectacle', *New Left Review* 214: 134–42.

Deleule, D. (1992) 'The Living Machine: Psychology as Organology', in J. Crary and S. Kwinter (eds) *Incorporations*, New York: Zone Books, pp. 203–33.

Deleuze, G. (1988a) *Foucault*, trans. S. Hand, London: Athlone Press.

—— (1988b) *Spinoza: Practical Philosophy*, trans. R. Hurley, San Francisco: City Light Books.

—— (1994) *Difference and Repetition*, trans. Paul Patton, London: Athlone Press.

Deleuze, G. and Guattari, F. (1972, 1984) *L'Anti-Oedipe*, Paris: PUF, *Anti-Oedipus*, trans. R. Hurley et al., London: Athlone Press.

—— (1980, 1988) *Mille plateaux*, Paris: PUF, *A Thousand Plateaus*, trans. B. Massumi, London: Athlone Press.

Dennett, D. C. (1995) *Darwin's Dangerous Idea: Evolution and the Meanings of Life*, London: Allen Lane.

Eardley, M. (1995) 'Deleuze and the Nonformal Function', unpublished dissertation, University of Warwick.

Eco, U. (1986) 'Striking at the Heart of the State', in *Travels in Hyper-reality*, trans. W. Weaver, London: Pan, pp. 113–19.

Edelman, G. (1994) *Bright Air, Brilliant Fire: On the Matter of the Mind*, Harmondsworth, Middlesex: Penguin.

Eigen, M. (1992) *Steps Towards Life: A Perspective on Evolution*, Oxford: Oxford University Press.

Eldredge, N. (1995) *Reinventing Darwin: The Great Evolutionary Debate*, London: Weidenfeld & Nicolson.

Ellul, J. (1965) *The Technological Society*, trans. J. Wilkinson, London: Jonathan Cape.

Emmeche, C. (1994) *The Garden in the Machine: The Emerging Science of Artificial Life*, trans. S. Sampson, New Jersey: Princeton University Press.

Foucault, M. (1990) 'The Thought from Outside', in M. Foucault and M. Blanchot, *Foucault/Blanchot*, trans. J. Mehlman, New York: Zone Books, pp. 7–61.

Goodwin, B. (1994) *How the Leopard Changed its Spots: The Evolution of Complexity*, London: Phoenix.

Guattari, F. (1992, 1995) *Chaosmose*, Paris: Galilée, *Chaosmosis: An Ethico-aesthetic paradigm*, trans. P. Bains and J. Pefanis, Sydney: Power Publications.

Hegel, G. W. F. (1970, 1980) *Phaenomenologie des Geistes*, Frankfurt: Suhrkamp, *Phenomenology of Spirit*, trans. A. V. Miller, Oxford: Oxford University Press.

Hornborg, A. (1992) 'Machine Fetishism, Value, and the Image of Unlimited Good: Towards a Thermodynamics of Imperialism', *Man* 27: 1–18.

Jacob, F. (1974) *The Logic of Living Systems*, trans. B. E. Spillman, London: Allen Lane.

Jay Gould, S. (1977) *Ontogeny and Phylogeny*, Cambridge, MA: Harvard University Press.

Kant, I. (1974, 1982) *Kritik der Urteilskraft*, Frankfurt: Suhrkamp, *Critique of Judgement*, trans. J. C. Meredith, Oxford: Oxford University Press.

—— (1995) *Opus Postumum*, trans. E. Forster and M. Rosen, Cambridge: Cambridge University Press.

Kauffman, S. A. (1993) *The Origins of Order: Self-Organization and Selection in Evolution, Oxford: Oxford University Press.*

Kelly, K. (1994) *Out of Control: The New Biology of Machines*, London: Fourth Estate.

Laing, R. (1979) 'Machines as Organisms: An Exploration of the Relevance of Recent Results', *Biosystems* 11: 201–15.

Landa, M. De (1991) *War in the Age of Intelligent Machines*, New York: Zone Books.

Langton, C. G. (1988) 'Artificial Life', in *Artificial Life: SFI Studies in the Sciences of Complexity*, Cambridge, MA: Addison-Wesley, pp. 1–46.

Law, R. (1991) 'The Symbiotic Phenotype: Origins and Evolution', in L. Margulis and R. Fester (eds) *Symbiosis as a Source of Evolutionary Innovation*, Cambridge, MA: MIT Press.

Lovtrup, S. (1987) *Darwinism: The Refutation of a Myth*, London: Croom Helm.

Lyotard, J. F. (1991) *The Inhuman: Reflections on Time*, trans. G. Bennington and R. Bowlby, Oxford: Polity Press.

Margulis, L. (1970) *The Origin of Eukaryotic Cells*, New Haven, CT: Yale University Press.

—— (1981) *Symbiosis in Cell Evolution*, San Francisco: W. H. Freeman.

Margulis, L. and Sagan, D. (1995) *What is Life?*, London: Weidenfeld & Nicolson.

Marx, K. (1976) *Capital: volume one*, trans. B. Fowkes, Harmondsworth, Middlesex: Penguin.

Maturana, H. and Varela, F. (1980) *Autopoiesis and Cognition: The Realization of the Living*, London and Dordrecht: D. Riedel.

Mayr, E. (1991) *One Long Argument: Charles Darwin and the Genesis of Modern Evolutionary Thought*, London: Penguin.

Nichols, B. (1988) 'The Work of Culture in the Age of Cybernetic Systems', *Screen* 29: 22–47.

Nietzsche, F. (1968) *The Will to Power*, trans. W. Kaufmann and R. J. Hollingdale, New York: Random House.

—— (1979) *Twilight of the Idols*, trans. R. J. Hollingdale, Harmondsworth, Middlesex: Penguin.

—— (1994) *On the Genealogy of Morality*, trans. C. Diethe, Cambridge: Cambridge University Press.

Oppenheimer, J. (1959) 'An Embryological Enigma in the *Origin of Species*', in B. Glass et al. (eds) *Forerunners of Darwin: 1745–1859*, Baltimore: Johns Hopkins University Press, pp. 292–323.

Raff, R. A. and Kaufman, T. C. (1983) *Embryos, Genes, and Evolution*, New York: Macmillan.

Reuleaux, F. (1876/1963) *The Kinematics of Machinery: Outlines of a Theory of Machines*, trans. A. B. W. Kennedy, New York: Dover.

Sahal, D. (1981) *Patterns of Technological Innovation*, Reading, MA: Addison-Wesley.

Sapp, J. (1994) *Evolution by Association: A History of Symbiosis*, Oxford: Oxford University Press.

Schick, K. D. and Toth, N. (1993) *Making Silent Stones Speak: Human Evolution and the Dawn of Technology*, London: Weidenfeld & Nicolson.

Serres, M. (1982) 'The Origin of Language: Biology, Information Theory, and Thermodynamics', in Serres, *Hermes: Literature, Science, and Philosophy*, Baltimore: Johns Hopkins University Press, pp. 71–84.

Simondon, G. (1992) 'The Genesis of the Individual', in J. Crary and S. Kwinter (eds) Incorporations, New York: Zone Books, pp. 297–319.

Theweleit, K. (1992) 'Circles, Lines, and Bits', in J. Crary and S. Kwinter (eds) *Incorporations*, New York: Zone Books, pp. 256–64.

Tipler, F. (1995) *The Physics of Immortality: Modern Cosmology, God, and the Resurrection of the Dead*, London: Pan.

Tudge, C. (1995) *The Day Before Yesterday: Five Million Years of Human History*, London: Cape.

Vaneigem, R. (1994) *The Revolution of Everyday Life*, trans. D. Nicholson-Smith, London: Rebel Press.

Vernadsky, V. I. (1945) 'The Biosphere and the Noosphere', *American Scientist* 33: 1–12.

Williams, R. (1994) 'The Political and Feminist Dimensions of Technological Determinsm', in M. R. Smith and L. Marx (eds) *Does Technology Drive History?*, Cambridge, MA: MIT Press, pp. 217–35.

Wolpert, L. (1991) *The Triumph of the Embryo*, Oxford: Oxford University Press.

12

Machinic Thinking

Alistair Welchman

The only thought adequate to the reality of the machinic continuum is a thinking that is itself machinic. It was through Deleuze and Guattari that machinism was first introduced into philosophy, with the publication in 1972 of volume 1 of *Capitalism and Schizophrenia: Anti-Oedipus* (Deleuze and Guattari 1972: 1ff.). According to this model machines themselves have two (inseparable) components: matter and engineering. The machinic continuum is material engineering and machines are engineered matter, although matter engineered by nothing other than matter itself.

The notion of a thinking that is plastic enough to be responsive to the unknown – empiricism – is by and large anathema to philosophy; even to philosophical empiricism. Although machinic thought contains components that are still approachable philosophically, it meshes these components with other machinic elements that are flusher with the real. Thus, the image of thought constituted by the model of recognition and reflection – characterized notably by the transitive nature of the construction of philosophical problematics, as in, for instance the philosophy *of* technology – cannot begin to comprehend the specificity of machinism.

It is true that the central elements of machinism – as the first part of this chapter shows – have indeed been misrepresented by the history of philosophy; and equally true that in order to liquidate such misunderstandings one can also refer to some philosophical machinery first erected by Kant; that is, as the second part of the chapter demonstrates, the weapon of critique. But such an account is not yet machinic in that it still presupposes a certain autonomy of the thought *of* the machine, rather than making thinking itself a machine.

To mechanize thought – a process considered in the third part of the chapter – is to go to the edge of philosophy, and, in the first instance to Nietzsche's genealogy.

Conceptual error does not occupy a space separate from the real; and critique is also a machine. On the one hand paralogisms occur directly in the real, and respond at least in part to the production of the real under certain determinate conditions; and, on the other hand, what conceptual errors remain are *themselves* also the result of the conditions of production, this time, of the conditions of production of cognition.

Whilst nothing real corresponds to the great and gross metaphysical concepts of philosophy – or indeed to their deconstructive refinements – there are real systems whose extensive structure may, on occasion, be grasped by simplified concepts related to those of philosophy.

The State, for instance, clearly has very few of the managerial powers ascribed to it, as a base assumption, by political theory; but it nevertheless has a real existence and real effects, although they are of rather restricted importance, and concentrating on them leads one to miss most of what *is* important. Correlatively, the cognitive misunderstandings by which the State is elevated into the transcendental repository of the law have their origins in a genealogical history – although one that Deleuze and Guattari argue must be extended to *geological* scales – and are not simply failures of rationality.

This extension is a broadening of Wilhelm Reich's question asked repeatedly in *Anti-Oedipus*: why do we love what oppresses us? As ideology is for *Anti-Oedipus* just the wrong question to pose; so for *A Thousand Plateaus* is the question 'why is transcendence a conceptual error?' simply inadequate. Both questions presuppose an autonomy of the intellect that is co-terminous with the over-valuation of consciousness characteristic of Western philosophy.

The last part of the chapter addresses the precise nature of the illusions that Deleuze and Guattari diagnose in the 'Geology of Morals' section of *A Thousand Plateaus*, and discusses the machinic thoughts of abstraction and deterritorialization.

* * *

The three terms most central to Deleuze and Guattari's machinism – engineering, machine and matter – have all been subjected to a curious antinomy in the history of representation theory. As Deleuze suggests, 'representation is the site of transcendental illusion' (Deleuze 1968: 265). In a structure that closely tracks the relation between Christian theology and evil, all three have been represented as essentially deprived and merely negative; but also at the same time as the source of a mysterious and often threatening positive power.

Engineering, as Dennett observes (Dennett 1995: 188), has not been considered worthy enough even to be the object of philosophy: there is no sub-discipline of the philosophy of engineering. Science, in this representation, wears the mantle of theoretical dignity; and engineering is merely the technical application of the results of science. The thought that philosophy actually *is* engineering – a thought at the core of Deleuze's writings – is catapulted beyond the objectionable into the simply not thinkable. It is several orders of magnitude more problematic than the already objectionable possibility that philosophy might be mistaken for or taken over by science (scientism).

On the other hand, almost from its inception, engineering has been associated with the development of the most threatening of technologies: the military. On the threshold of the industrial revolution, in *Paradise Lost*, it is Satan and his cohorts who mobilize a 'devilish enginery' (Milton 1667: VI, 553) of rebellious war. Indeed, in the middle of the seventeenth century the term 'engine' was reserved *only* for the military industrial: 'engine of war' is a pleonasm. The development of military technology has always operated on a level different from that of science: nomad rather than royal science (Deleuze and Guattari 1980: 367–8). Closely concerned not only with the practical and the pragmatic, but with a cunning born of accelerated decisions of survival, military engineering has been – and continues to be – less a matter of the materialization of scientific theorems than of patchwork and botching and *bricolage* and still somehow getting something right in the end, or if not, then not surviving to tell the tale. Machines similarly have been thought privatively by the tradition. This definition of the machine reaches a certain apogee with Kant's philosophy. For Kant a machine is a system with at best only motricity and not 'formative force or drive',[1] and is therefore a system that acts as the 'mere tool of external moving forces' (Kant 1786: 'Dynamics; General Observation'; Ak. 4: 532). Machines are the transmission site of an activity given from elsewhere, and are therefore deprived of any capacity to act themselves. Perhaps most significantly, for Kantian machines, systematicity is in the same position as motricity: external. Insofar as machines constitute systems at all, therefore, they describe the class of transcendent or intentional systems whose condition of unity is not to be found within them but elsewhere. It is this externality that prompts Kant to argue, with the tradition, directly from the existence of articulated artefacts to the existence of an artificer (the argument from design): 'vestigium hominem video' (Kant 1790: §64; Ak. 5: 370). Machines lack, and always stand in need of, something else: motor force or design force. On the other hand machines have also been seen as a major source of threat, despite their apparently merely privative character. Mechanization – a conversion into machines – is the dominant trope of reactionary rejection of economic industrialization. From Burke to Eliot the dissolution of the social under the impact of the economic has been thought through a series of terms orientated rhetorically around this concept of the machine: rationalization (Weber); calculation and *techne* (Heidegger); dehumanization; etc.[2] The conversion of the socius, which is contrasted to the organic – both in the dominant theoretical account of the machine in Kant and in the practical attempts at political intervention to 'save' the social – into a mere machine evacuates it of any intrinsic principle of unification. It follows from the dogmatic technical definition of the machine that attempts to resecure unity must be externally imposed; and the worst excesses of twentieth-century political management – both modernist and anti-modernist – follow in their turn from this. Again, a devalorized and negatively defined concept of representation is antinomically capable of positive, and positively threatening, activity.

The structure of this antinomy is, however, most clearly visible in the philosophical treatment of the thought of matter. Matter is *the* devalorized concept of the philosophical tradition; and its devalorization is repeatedly stamped with an absolute quality: matter is repeatedly defined *a priori* as what precisely does *not* have the qualities attributed to the non-material; matter is motionless, lifeless, incapable of knowing itself, etc. Locke, for instance, argues that:

> [I]t is as impossible to conceive that ever bare incogitative Matter should produce a thinking intelligent Being, as that nothing should of itself produce Matter. . . . Matter by its own strength cannot produce in itself so much as Motion.
>
> (Locke 1690: IV. x. 10)

Kant equally writes that:

> [W]e cannot even think of living matter as possible (The very concept of it involves a contradiction, since the essential character of matter is its lifelessness, *inertia*).
>
> (Kant 1790: §73; Ak. 5: 394)

And even Pascal – in an unsurprisingly rare moment of agreement – writes similarly of there 'being nothing so inconceivable as to say that matter knows itself' (Pascal 1670: §72–199).

It is paradoxically precisely this passivity of matter that can constitute a (theoretical) threat: Kant goes on elsewhere to suggest that even the possibility of living (i.e. active) matter 'would be the death of all natural philosophy' (Kant 1786: 'Mechanics', Proposition 3, Observation; Ak. 4: 544). But there is also a sense in which matter is not (or not only) the pure patient of monotheistic theology but also the pure (although unformed) *act* of Chaos. Chaos is matter as threat; and the neutralization of this threatening conception of matter is a condition of the installation of inert or dead matter. Milton's God performs a paradigmatic act in book VII of *Paradise Lost* when He is depicted by Milton engaging in a pre-creative act of the repression of the formless activity of Chaos, which is the condition of possibility of the creation as such. Milton's God's role is that of 'circumscribing/The universe' (Milton 1667: VII, 226–7), of simply containing and setting bounds to the limitless chaotic sea, of converting it into a reservoir of employable energy. Milton has God perform an act of binding upon the active materiality of the 'vast immeasurable abyss/Outrageous as a sea, dark, wasteful, wild' (VII, 211–12) whose *product* is dead matter, the matter of the tradition: 'matter unformed and void' (VII, 233). And this is the 'watery calm' (VII, 234) over which the spirit may now, and only now, move. For the creation even to appear that it occurs responsibly, there must, as condition, be a pre-creative move which serves primarily to repress (primary repression), stunt and constrain the irresponsible activity of the wilderness/ocean. It is only then that the creation may proceed according to its plan laid out in Genesis, and be provided with its now lethargic and receptive, patient and passive, primary matter.

In each of the three cases there is a transcendent evacuation of the terms. They are emptied of any possible content or effect; and something else is suspended above them, separating, guiding, controlling: 'a dead rat's ass suspended from the ceiling of the sky' (Artaud, cited in Deleuze and Guattari 1972: 124–5). They become impossible, uninhabitable philosophical terrains, which hardly even require the effort of refutation. Engineering is subordinated to a properly epistemological science as its mere application; the machine is subordinated to an external force, or equally to an external principle of systematicity, that acts as a transcendent *telos* for which the machine itself can only exist as a mere instrument; and matter is separated from what it can do and is a mere patient for form.

Equally, though, and again in each case, something remains, an insoluble remainder. In stark contradiction (antinomy) to the vacated inefficacy of the position of the term – mere application; mere instrument; mere patient – each also has a subterranean complexity, an ineradicable intransigence. 'Since World War II the discoveries that have changed the world were not made so much in lofty halls of theoretical physics as in the less-noticed labs of engineering' (Nicholas Metropolis, cited in Dennett 1995: 187). Purely instrumental machinery seems bent on prosthetic revenge. Matter produces an excrescence of complexity independent of form. '[T]he noumenon tends to appear as such in complex systems' (Deleuze 1968: 256).

* * *

Kant's method exhibits two great, and related, mistakes: aborting the specificity of the transcendental at the moment of its inception; and, whilst inventing critique, failing to take it far enough.

Firstly, the transcendental component of Kant's thinking fails to respect the autonomy of the transcendental (even though Kant was the first thinker to have opened up this transcendental field). The Kantian transcendental is, as Deleuze argues in *Difference and Repetition*, still merely empirical:

> It is clear that . . . Kant traces the so-called transcendental structures from the empirical acts of a psychological consciousness: the transcendental synthesis of apprehension is directly induced from an empirical apprehension, and so on. In order to hide this all too obvious procedure, Kant suppressed this text in the second edition. Although it is better hidden, the tracing method, with all its 'psychologism', nevertheless subsists.
>
> (Deleuze 1968: 135)

This psychological grounding is the basis of what Deleuze describes as the nexus of common sense and good sense (Deleuze 1968: 131–7; 223–7). It is the aim of critique precisely to call these uninterrogated presuppositions into question. Similarly, and this is the second point, the critical aspect of Kantianism fails to carry through the task that Kant nevertheless had himself invented. The objects of Kantian critique (World, Soul, God) are subject to an only apparent critique; after it they remain intact – indeed not only intact, actually immune to any further critique – but removed to a different level, that of practical and hence unquestionable revelation rather than theoretical cognition. Deleuze writes: 'We cannot accept that the grounded remains the same as it was before, the same as when it was not grounded, when it had not passed the test of grounding' (Deleuze 1968: 154). An effective critique eliminates its objects, and does not, like Kant's attempt, redeem them.

In fact the critical works represent a close collaboration of the traditional dogmatic understandings of engineering as mere application, of the machine as mere instrument and of matter as mere patient. Kant's commitment to a matter that is completely dead is clear. But this also ties closely into a thought of transcendental production that is dogmatically machinic, and engages Kant in a series of problems that are recognizable as engineering problems but that are also insoluble given the subordination of engineering to science.

Nature for Kant is a product, that is to say, ultimately it is engineered. This is his break with philosophical empiricism, which treats nature as simply given, and hence not engineered at all. However, his model for the engineering of nature specifically requires that the unity of nature be thought in exteriority to nature itself (this could serve as a definition of the transcendental). Indeed Kant appeals to one and the same model in characterizing the construction of nature and the externality of the controlling intention or concept in the use of machines: the model of an artisanal production, or what Kant importantly calls desire (Kant 1790: Introduction III note; Ak. 5: 177–8).

On this model, there is an engineering problem posed; but it is posed dogmatically, in terms simply of how to *apply* science (both in the more restrictive English sense and the more extensive German sense of *Wissenschaft*) to the world. The application of pure *a priori* geometry and mathematics to the world (i.e. the possibility of Newtonian dynamics, science in the English sense) is the problem that transcendental idealism sets out to solve. The answer (the synthetic *a priori*) is *Wissenschaft*: the pure concepts of the understanding, which are responsible for the construction of nature in accordance with nature construed as that which is described by dynamics. The result is a purely technical machinism: mathematically calculable science is presupposed; matter is thought transitively as the mere recipient of science; and engineering (Kant's primary term is schematization) is thought just as the application or one-to-one mapping of science to its material object domain.

It should be noted, however, that this residual engineering problem caused Kant no little difficulty; and his sensitivity to the difficulties of this project attest to his modernity. From the start Kant was unsure how science (a transcendental logic of concepts) could be *capable* of application; how the real could be made exhaustively characterizable in terms of science. The real always escaped conceptual determination (conceptual difference), as Kant's use of the paradox of incongruent counterparts shows: there is always 'a power peculiar to the existent, a stubbornness of the existent in intuition which resists specification by concepts no matter how far it is taken'; there is 'an always rebellious matter' (Deleuze 1968: 13–14; 264).[3] And consequently, Kant was always forced to suggest another impossible piece of machinery that could present the engineering problem of nature as the result of calculable conceptuality and science: he gives us two deductions; a schematism; the theses of time-determination; the theses of space-determination; the whole of the *Critique of Judgement* (a meditation on the conditions of possibility of application as such); and still has not satisfactorily solved the problem by the *Opus Posthumum*.[4]

Kant grasped the problem of the production of nature as a problem of engineering; but was simultaneously unable to solve it without appealing to uncritical or purely technical concepts of machinism. What is required is a critique of technical machines, a critique that demands that thinking itself become machinic. It is through Deleuze and Guattari that this critique is operated.[5]

* * *

Critique is also a history, a genealogy; and there is a whole material history or history of materiality that underlies this critique. Something was extracted from the continuum: the continuum was flattened out, and the something held on high above the flatness. Matter has been separated from what it can do and there is now a matter on which something else – representing a reactive focusing of activity into a central single point – may now act.[6] A dual performance repeated again and again on different levels: the separation of plasma into energy and matter; the agglomeration of matter into lumps (the Kant/Laplace hypothesis); construction of replicators and correlative production of an environment constituted as fuel, etc. The Despot resides in monotheistic religion, in individual consciousness ('God or the Self, it is the same thing' (Deleuze 1968: 203)), in the State, even in the genes. Once matter is patient, and any capacities it appears to have must be referred elsewhere, then machines have become technical (aggregates with external sources of design or motricity) and engineering has become sheer application (of external sources of energy/design to material aggregates).

Henceforth everything is dangerous. Every philosophical hypothesis is apt to be understood only in terms that are subsequent to and therefore presuppose this separation; every deterritorialization is apt to be reterritorialized. Take, for instance, the attitude of the tradition to matter. It is true that the 'inconceivability' of matter as act is susceptible of a positive reading; that the activity of matter is different in kind from the activity normally attributed to non-materiality. To this extent the inability of philosophy to think active matter is not *just* a symptom of the intensity with which the tradition repudiates immanent materiality. But it is nevertheless the case that the understanding of activity which is attributed (*per impossible*) to matter is perpetually in danger of being recast as the sort of activity that only comes after the separation of matter from what it can do. That is, the mode of material production is understood, uncritically, only on the basis of its *products*. In this way, immanent matter is persistently confused with hylozoism – the idea that matter is imbued precisely with that form of activity that is supposed to be characteristic of life. The kind of activity that is the *result* of draining out the distributed capacities immanent in matter and focusing them in a single point (subject or substance, structure or origin) is then *reprojected* out onto matter; and this is treated as the only possible understanding of the action of matter.

The absurdity of matter doing anything to the tradition is an analytic *a priori*: once action is *defined* as a singular focused point and once design is assimilated to intentional intelligence, then it is indeed inconceivable that just these could be distributed among matter. Hence, when the tradition even deigns to represent the kind of activity that matter can have, it is in terms of already previously separated activity: consciousness, thinking, intelligence, etc.

There is a rigorous conception of critique at stake here: that an account of activity or production cannot presuppose the constitution of its own products. The antinomies of materiality, machinism and engineering – that they are merely dead, merely technical, merely applicatory and at the same time active threats – are generated by a single basic paralogism according to which activity is concentrated into a single point that functions as its subject; according to which machines and their production are separated out into a dead machinism sourced from outside; according to which engineering is separated from its technologically generative capacities and subordinated to an externally acting science or theory. In each case products constituted through a long material history, and only under certain limited conditions, are projected backwards as the origin of what in fact produces them.

It is, however, a complex conception of critique. It involves both a conceptual component and a historical-genetic component. On the one hand, conceptual misunderstandings (paralogisms and their associated antinomies) are implicated to the extent that the functioning of real systems is confused with something that impossibly overhangs systems and controls them from the outside. On the other hand, systems that lend themselves to this misunderstanding are real configurations of machinically engineered matter, and as such have specific properties more (or less) amenable to analysis.

Deleuze condenses these two components of critique through his account of nineteenth-century thermodynamics in *Difference and Repetition*. There he suggests that 'not only are there sensory illusions, but there is also a transcendental physical illusion' (Deleuze 1968: 228). For Deleuze this illusion is of inevitable increase in entropy; in Freud's vocabulary, the working off of vital differences. Such an illusion represents a conspiracy of extensive physics with royal philosophy. Difference – one of Deleuze's early words for matter – is equalized into long-run identity as much by the technical outcome of statistical physical process as it is by the dictates of a pure reason.[7] As Deleuze writes, with thermodynamics '[t]he words "the real is the rational"' found a new sense, for diversity tended to be reduced in Nature no less than in reason' (Deleuze 1968: 224). There is a transcendental illusion; but one that is invested in the real:

> There is an illusion tied to intensive quantities. This illusion is . . . the movement by which difference in intensity is canceled. Nor is it only apparently canceled. It is really canceled, but outside itself, in extensity.
>
> (Deleuze 1968: 240)

There is a transcendental *physical* illusion; there *really* is stratification. This thought is vital to Deleuze and Guattari. Without it the machinic engagement of their texts would still retain a residual Enlightenment form: that of the criticism of conceptual errors, presupposing a backdrop of enlightened rationality (however complicated by its own internal torsions, as in Horkheimer and Adorno).

This is also the importance of Bergson to Deleuze. However much Bergson is carried off into the naivety of a kind of vitalism or specific hylozoism (and it is arguable exactly how much that is), he is always showing that our incapacity – always relative – to understand what kind of products we are is a result of our being the kind of products that we are (Bergson 1907: 1ff.). Machined by innumerable stratifications – material, biological, social – the human animal is engineered on the strata, feels at home there; but the strata just are (turned towards) the body without organs, the intensive continuum, immanence.

Equally important is the fact that this thought of transcendental physical illusion enables an understanding of Deleuze and Guattari's *prima facie* contradictory argument-pair that humans are machinically constituted, and at the same time chronically becoming-machine; subject to deterritorialization and overflow into the technically machinic. What is really immanent in transcendence – certain special-case systems exhibiting restricted capacities for interaction with the outside and characterized by self-sustaining feedback loops orientated towards homeostasis – is itself engineered and therefore already machinic; but the overall tendency of general-case engineering processes is towards the wastage of transcendence, and therefore the special-case systems are simultaneously becoming-machine. Machinism engineers both stratic transcendencies and perpetual destratification: the greatest strata are the result of great deterritorializing movements; the inauguration of the Despot is also a great schizophrenic levelling.[8]

There are a set of transcendental illusions (grounding paralogisms and consequent antinomies of matter, machines and engineering) constitutive of representation theory. These illusions, however, are grounded in the real, in the intensive continuum. Matter as intensity expresses itself in extensity (Deleuze 1968); the body without organs stratifies itself, without any help from anything else (Deleuze and Guattari 1980). These illusions are therefore transcendental physical illusions. To describe an extensive system is to arrange a genealogy of the materially engineered machines that contributed to its production as a stratified, but still immanent, system.

Cognition is itself such a system; perhaps, indeed, the *most* stratified feedback system; cognition was not engineered to understand its own conditions of production. Indeed, it was not engineered *for* anything: it was just engineered. There therefore remains the tendency to think transcendental physical illusions as constitutive of the real, ignoring their immanent basis. By-passing the immanent basis of transcendence in turn overlooks the perpetual instability of stratified systems: their tendency to degenerate, to deterritorialize.

Interestingly and perhaps surprisingly, the American analytic philosopher of mind Daniel Dennett develops a vocabulary to describe this situation: there are no skyhooks; there are only cranes (Dennett 1995: 74ff.). In general, cranes are immanent machinic accounts of systems that tend to be interpreted as transcendent, as skyhooks. More specifically, cranes are catalysts of (evolutionary or more generally auto-productive) processes; but they are accelerators that have their basis in the very processes they catalyse. Natural selection is perhaps the paradigm crane: a simple process that in itself contributes nothing to engineering design, but that makes possible a systematic selection of embryonic designs and, over geological time-scales, facilitates a relatively complex exploration of design-space.

Another, more interesting, example of a crane broached by Dennett is genetic engineering (even if understood only in the Darwinian sense of artificial selection).[9] Such engineering speeds up mutation rates, and sets new local optima for selection; but it 'is no miracle – *provided that genetic engineers . . . are wholly products of earlier, slower evolutionary processes* (Dennett 1995: 76–7, italic in original). Skyhooks are attempts to explain craning phenomena through the intervention of a mysterious transcendence that is problematic, but somehow necessitated, because one doesn't have the concept of cranes – skyhooks are dead rats' asses.

It is clear that we are not built to have the concept of cranes: it ranks as a perversion of thinking to have generated even the idea of them. The great tendency in biological thinking – initiated by Aristotle, and solidified into a recognizably modern form by Kant – has been to project the anthropomorphic characteristic of intentionality onto the biological world in the form of teleology. This tendency has been parodied by the ultra-Darwinians, who utilize a vocabulary of 'interests' explicitly to describe purely machinic processes: 'selfish' gene theory (set out most popularly in Dawkins 1976).

The vocabulary of intentionality and interests in the work of ultra-Darwinians has been badly misunderstood. They feel entitled to use such terminology – which was previously frowned upon in modern biology as symptomatic of a regression to theological or teleological biology – precisely because it is completely inappropriate. *Of course* genes do not have interests. And it is only when any residual tendency to think that they do has been ruthlessly expunged, that is, when one has an impersonal and machinic account of morphogenesis, that one can freely (but obviously ironically) use anthropomorphic terms, in the sure hope that no one will fail to get the joke.

Unfortunately there has indeed been a collective sense of humour failure amongst many of those responding to Dawkins' work. The situation is exactly akin to assimilating Deleuze and Guattari to a standard (rather than a technological) vitalism; or Schopenhauer's account of the world as will to a voluntarism. Intentions, vitalism and voluntarism are the names for activity after it has been paralogistically separated out from matter and projected into an imaginary point outside and transcending nature. Material activity immanent engineering, is what matter does to itself. One completely misconstrues machinism when one simply takes the concepts of transcendent activity, and applies them to matter (standard vitalism).

What is interesting is how much further Dennett is prepared to go than Dawkins about the result of this. Culture is a crane (Dennett 1995: 335f.); and the intentional resources of (say) genetic engineers, or artificial selectors, have the same status as the parodic intentions of selfish genes – they are ironic short-hand for sets of self-assembling machinic processes; cascading cranes (Dennett 1995: 75); unconscious engineering.[10]

> [H]ow could the products of our own 'real' minds be exempt from an evolutionary explanation? Darwin's idea thus . . . spread[s] *all the way up*, dissolving the illusion of our own authorship.
>
> (Dennett 1995: 63)

Where Dawkins hangs on at least to the idea that humans have interests, Dennett demolishes the basis for *any* interests. Rigorously thought, machinic materialism *must* also apply to primates, and our own ascriptions of intention must be as parodic as those of 'selfish' genes. Such an extension of machinism clearly goes further, to the *products* of primate activity, and that includes works of philosophy: machinic thinking.

Dawkins (1982) introduced the notion of the extended phenotype in a rigorous but consciously restricted manner. As an ethologist, he was quite comfortable because of his research speciality with the idea that genes could code for animal behaviour. The extended phenotype is merely the suggestion that it is essentially arbitrary (or dependent on some arbitrary variable like preferred zone of experimentation) where one decides to stop locating phenotypic effects: molecular biologists, for instance, might stop at specific protein constructs. The external boundaries of the organism are just as arbitrary. For a limited set of cases, building up from external morphology, through animal behaviour and animal artefacts (beaver dams and termite mounds) to phenotypic effects of one organism's genes on the behaviour and morphology of an organism of a different species (for example, *Leucochloridium* flukes and snails; Dawkins 1982: 213) to phenotypic action at a distance (in the Bruce Effect; Dawkins 1982: 228f.), Dawkins argues compellingly for a limited 'extended genetics' (1982: 203).

Dennett's argument has very considerably more scope: there is no rigorous way of thinking of the technical artefacts of the human species except as extended phenotypic effects. The 'unity of design space' (Dennett 1995: 135f.) demands that *all* artefact productions be viewed on the same level, as impersonal engineering programs.

Cranes are what is immanent in transcendence; skyhooks are transcendence, motivated by the limitations of primate cognition, limitations that themselves are produced by recursively craned engineering processes. But cranes do not stop getting built, and that they are already machines does not stop an increasing index of machinism.

* * *

Linguistics and abstract expressionism – the practical wing of formalism – develop the long obsession of philosophical abstraction with the conditions of representation into a recognizably modern form.

Guattari (1992: 39) criticizes (structural) linguistics both for being too abstract and for not being abstract enough. It is too abstract in the sense that it assures an all-too-easy inter-translatability of every one of the strata within language; everything must be represented in language. It is, on the other hand, too abstract to be able to encompass non-linguistic elements on the same level as language, what Guattari calls 'ontological heterogenesis'.

Deleuze similarly criticizes representation in general for not being abstract enough when he suggests: 'The theory of thought is like painting – it needs that revolution which took art from representation to abstraction' (Deleuze 1968: 276); but later he also criticizes abstraction (in painting) for being itself too abstract: 'One wants to say about abstract painting what Péguy said about Kantian morality, it has clean hands, but it doesn't have any hands' (Deleuze 1984: 67).

In 'The Geology of Morals', Deleuze and Guattari (1980: 39–75) describe a succession of destratifications and restratifications that correspond to the inorganic,

organic and cultural strata (Deleuze and Guattari's term for this last is 'alloplastic' (1980: 60)). Using a matrix of terms derived from Hjelmslev 'the Danish Spinozist geologist' (43), they characterize each stratum on the basis of differential distributions of content and expression. In particular, expression gains an increasing autonomy. Initially expression and content, although bound together, are separated only by orders of magnitude (the one molar, the other molecular). On the organic stratum, however, 'expression and content are both molecular *and* molar' and expression (forming nucleic acid sequences out of nucleotides) has become an independent line from content (forming proteins out of amino acids (59)). On the alloplastic stratum, finally, vocal signs achieve a superlinearity or temporal linearity whereby not only is expression independent of content, but *form* of expression becomes independent of substance of expression (62).

This huge deterritorialization is fraught with dangers: the 'imperialism of language', the overcoding of the Despot, the illusions of linguistics (62; 65). But it also begins to frame a thought of machinic abstraction that is of extreme importance to machinic thinking: abstract machines are increasingly implementation-independent or substrate-neutral non-computable programs (Dennett 1995: 82). '[Challenger's] dream was less to present a paper to humans than to propose a program for pure computers' (Deleuze and Guattari 1980: 57).

The deterritorialization that Deleuze and Guattari assign to the production of the alloplastic is itself generated by the increasing autonomy of forms of expression from forms of content, as well as of expression in general from content. Today it must be acknowledged that the organic stratum itself is undergoing a similar deterritorialization and abstraction. The forms of expression aligned with living entities are increasingly seen as capable of implementation in different substrates. This deterritorialization is demonstrated by Dennett's analysis of biological processes.

Dennett defines natural selection as an 'algorithmic process' (Dennett 1995: 48f.) and at least implies that it is a computable process; that is to say, he is in danger of identifying an open-ended and essentially unpredictable and problematic engineering process with a theorem of royal science. But what he is getting at is better thought of as an abstract machine for four reasons. Firstly, he explicitly includes 'heuristics' in his definition of an algorithm (Dennett 1995: 210), and heuristics or pragmatics are incapable of formalization as a computable function. Secondly, natural selection is a process only to the extent that it is randomly seeded with difference in the form of variation. The introduction of randomness also defies computational capacity. Thirdly, natural selection is not an algorithm *for* anything in particular; it is intransitive (Dennett 1995: 308). Fourthly, lastly and most importantly, it is *extremely* platform-independent.

An old but interesting problem in biology is that of the origin of replication. If construction processes are dependent on the existence of replicators, then it is difficult to see how replication could have got started, could have bootstrapped itself. That this has been a problem is an index of a failure of abstraction. Machinic replication can be implemented in multiple domains; and at least one compelling speculation as to the solution of this problem appeals to this abstraction. Cairns-Smith (1985), for example, argues that strictly biological replicators are the results of parasitic take-over of older and less sophisticated replicators embedded in a different substrate.

A machine deterritorializes, and becomes *more* abstract, when its codes spill over from one implementation (substance) to another. Carbon replication is already a deterritorialization; neural pattern replication ('memetic engineering') is another; computational replication – artificial life – another. It is important to disengage deterritorializing engineering tendencies from technical-scientific projects. This has always been the dream of the West: a pure despotism of knowledge; the West is, in a profound sense, technocratic: 'Transcendence [is] a specifically European disease' (Deleuze and Guattari 1980: 18).

The currently fashionable Human Genome Project is structured identically with the expert systems artificial intelligence programs of the 1970s. In both cases science attempts to construct a model of a complex object, and then treats engineering as a direct, point-to-point, remapping of the model. Thus, taking intelligence as its object, artificial intelligence attempted to produce a logical model, directly remapped into the gated logic of computer circuits; similarly, the Human Genome Project is attempting to construct a model of human embryological development that can be mapped one-to-one onto a database for patently technocratic reintervention in development. The complicity between these two attempts is not coincidental. The mapping of (complex) dynamical systems (like embryological development) onto formal logical systems is the essence of (royal) science, embodied in the Church–Turing thesis (Kampis 1991: v).

As Deleuze and Guattari never fail to emphasize, however, there is *no* 'correspondence or conformity' (1980: 44) between content and expression (for instance, between phenotypic proteins of content and nucleic acids of expression). Contemporary artificial intelligence (connectionism) and artificial life are pure Deleuzian engineering: deterritorialized intelligence and life implemented in new media and, in a phrase of Tom Ray's that could equally characterize a postmodernist aesthetic, 'search[ing] out the possibilities inherent . . . in the medium' (Ray 1995: 181).

This new alliance between Deleuze's machinic thinking and Anglo-American analytic engineering philosophy is of some importance. Deleuze's reception in the

Anglophone world has been, along with all the other French *maîtres à penser* since 1945, carried out mostly in conjunction with aesthetic preoccupations. But Deleuze's machinism breaks up the Saxon traditions of Humboldtian disciplinary 'separate but equal' Jim Crowism: *Geistes- und Naturwissenschaften* (rather palely reflected in Britain as the 'two cultures' debate). This academic division is the institutional realization of the philosophical antinomies already discussed; it reflects all the most questionable dichotomies of the West: value/fact; autonomy/heteronomy; non-determinism (understood juridically as responsibility)/determinism, etc.[11]

The simple aestheticization of Deleuze's work – its relegation to being a new tool for the production of critical texts in the humanities departments of universities – effectively neutralizes its critical bite. It does this in a way that directly follows the structure of other misunderstandings of Deleuze's work. Apart from being in such a context of clearly no more than instrumental – that is, uncritically machinic – use, its association only with the *Geisteswissenschaften* places Deleuze's work in the structural position of humanitarian anti-scientism.

This is why it is always important to insist upon Deleuze and Guattari's own repeated claim that desiring-machines are not literary tropes: 'Everywhere It [the id] is machines – real ones, not figurative ones' (Deleuze and Guattari 1972: 1). That would be the most obvious submission to the imperialism of the signifier.

Not that this is to argue that Deleuze and Guattari have *no* relation to aesthetics. In fact the aesthetic flows of German idealism were some of the first outpourings of the impersonal into Western thinking, the first thoughts of material morphogenesis. Indeed, it would be far from paranoid to argue that the organization of the university into its modern form, undertaken by von Humboldt, was directly a response to the threat of this incipient machinism.

If the current structure of the Academy was born as a bulwark against the convergent tendencies of the nineteenth century, and probably helped to exterminate them, then the deterritorialization of intelligence into silicon substrates currently underway demands a simultaneous deterritorialization of research, or the by-passing of the blockage. Machinic thinking cannot engage with two cultures.

Notes

1 Kant usually uses the term '*bildende* Kraft' in contrast to a machine's merely '*bewegende* Kraft' (see, for example, Kant 1790: §65; Ak. 5: 374), but he also cites – without criticism – the biologist Hans Blumenbach's rather stronger term '*Bildungstrieb*' (Kant 1790: §81; Ak. 5: 424).

2 This issue is covered in great historical detail in Williams 1963.

3 Deleuze argues that '[d]ifference can be internal, yet not conceptual (as the paradox of symmetrical objects shows)' (Deleuze 1968: 26). The argument is taken from Leibniz (Leibniz 1715–16: 26), and shows that an object and its mirror-image exhibit a difference – left-/right-handedness or cheirality – that cannot be thought conceptually. Kant's critical use of the paradox is supposed to be an argument for the transcendental ideality of space. But Kant also alludes to the same argument – with a purpose closer to that of showing that spatial intuition is irreducible to conceptual determination – in his *Inaugural Dissertation* (Kant 1769: 28).

4 Paul Guyer argues that the theses of time-determination (which pre-date the critical enterprise) are designed to perform the same task as the deduction(s); and, he suggests, the former succeed where the latter fail (Guyer 1987). Eckart Förster argues that the *Metaphysical Foundations of Natural Science* – which performs a task for space analogous to that performed for time by the analytic of principles in the first *Critique*; hence thesis of space determination – and the *Opus Posthumum* (with its continued problematic of the 'transition') are different solutions to the same problem of engineering (Förster 1987).

5 It should be noted that Kant's attempts to make an apparently irreducible intuition directly compatible with concepts are wholly reactionary; but it would be unfair not to note that the texts in which he makes these attempts (and most notably the *Critique of Judgement*) involve his tabling a number of extremely interesting ideas, and ones that were to have an important impact on the philosophical developments of machinism. A mode of production characterized by a *Zweckmässigkeit ohne Zweck*, for instance, pre-empts both Schopenhauer's and Nietzsche's conceptions of active matter.

6 See Deleuze's account of Nietzsche's critique/genealogy of reactive forces as forces separated from what they can do in Deleuze 1962.

7 It is by no means a trivial fact that nineteenth-century thermodynamics was initiated by an engineering-industrial investigation into the functioning of the processes – both technically and socially machinic – of the industrial revolution.

8 'Far from seeing in the [Despotic] State the principle of a territorialisation . . . we should see . . . the effect of a movement of deterritorialisation'; 'The Despotic State . . . forms a new deterritorialised machine'; 'the despotic sign . . . *the signifier is merely the deterritorialised sign itself*' (Deleuze and Guattari 1972: 195; 198; 206).

9 Dennett's other examples are sexual reproduction and the Baldwin Effect (Dennett 1995: 76f.).

10 Even Darwin noted (1859: 35) that artificial breeding can induce 'unconscious selection'.

11 Arguments about the relative scope of scientific methodology do nothing to alter this structure. The question there is merely where the dividing line should be drawn, even in the case where there is no space for the *Geisteswissenschaften*.

References

The dates given are those of original publication. The page references are to the pagination of the English translations where appropriate; except in the cases of Kant, where references are to standard divisions, and then to the *Akademie* edition; and of Milton, where references are to the book and then the line numbers of *Paradise Lost*.

Bergson (1907) *Evolution créatrice*, 7th edn, Paris: Presses Universitaires de France, 1949.

Cairns-Smith, A. G. (1985) *Seven Clues to the Origin of Life*, Cambridge: Cambridge University Press.

Darwin, Charles (1859) *On the Origin of Species by Means of Natural Selection*, London: Murray.

Dawkins, Richard (1976) *The Selfish Gene*, Oxford: Oxford University Press, 1976; 2nd edn 1989.

—— (1982) *The Extended Phenotype: The Gene as Unit of Selection*, Oxford: Oxford University Press.

Deleuze, Gilles (1962) *Nietzsche et la philosophie*, Paris: Presses Universitaires de France, trans. Hugh Tomlinson as *Nietzsche and Philosophy*, London: Athlone, 1986.

—— (1968) *Différence et répétition*, Paris: Presses Universitaires de France; trans. Paul Patton as *Difference and Repetition*, New York: Columbia University Press, 1994.

—— (1984) *Francis Bacon: logique de la sensation*, 2nd edn, Paris: La Différence.

Deleuze, Gilles and Guattari, Félix (1972) *Capitalisme et schizophrénie: 1. Anti-Oedipe*, Paris: Minuit; trans. Robert Hurley, Mark Seem and Helen R. Lane as *Anti-Oedipus*, Minneapolis: University of Minnesota Press, 1983.

—— (1980) *Capitalisme et schizophrénie: 2. Mille plateaux*, Paris: Minuit; trans. Brian Massumi as *A Thousand Plateaus*, Minneapolis: University of Minnesota Press, 1987.

Dennett, Daniel C. (1995) *Darwin's Dangerous Idea: Evolution and the Meanings of Life*, London: Allen Lane/Penguin.

Förster, Eckart (1987) 'Is There a "Gap" in the Critical System?' *Journal of the History of Philosophy* 25(4) (October): 533–55.

Guattari, Félix (1992) *Chaosmose*, Paris: Editions Galilée; trans. Paul Bains and Julian Pefanis as *Chaosmosis*, Bloomington and Indianapolis: Indiana University Press, 1995.

Guyer, Paul (1987) *Kant and the Claims of Knowledge*, Cambridge: Cambridge University Press.

Kampis, George (1991) *Self-Modifying Systems in Biology and Cognitive Science*, Oxford: Pergamon Press.

Kant, Immanuel (1769) *Inaugural Dissertation and Early Writings on Space*, trans. J. Handyside, London: Open Court 1926.

—— (1786) *Metaphysical Foundations of Natural Science*, trans. James W. Ellington in *Philosophy of Material Nature*, Indianapolis: Hackett Publishing, 1985, pp. 3–134; Ak. 4: 467–565.

—— (1790) *Kritik der Urteilskraft*, Stuttgart: Gerhard Lehmann, 1963; Ak. 5: 165–485; trans. James Creed Meredith as *Critique of Judgement*, Oxford: Oxford University Press, 1952; also trans. Werner S. Pluhar, Indianapolis: Hackett, 1987.

—— (1902) *Kants Gesammelte Schriften*, Berlin: Deutsche [formerly Königliche Preußische] Akademie der Wissenschaften, Walter de Gruyter & Co. and predecessors 1902–, 29 vols.

Leibniz, Wilhelm Gottfried von (1715–16) *Leibniz–Clarke Correspondence*, trans. S. Clarke, ed. H. G. Alexander, Manchester: Manchester University Press, 1956.

Locke, John (1690) *An Essay Concerning Human Understanding*, ed. J. W. Yolton, London: Dent, 1977.

Milton, John (1667) *Paradise Lost*, ed. Alastair Fowler, London: Longman, 1971.

Pascal, Blaise (1670) *Pensées*, Paris: GF-Flammarion, 1976.

Ray, Tom (1995) 'An Evolutionary Approach to Synthetic Biology', in Chris Langton (ed.) *Artificial Life: An Overview*, Cambridge, MA: MIT Press, pp. 179–209.

Williams, Raymond (1963) *Culture and Society: 1780–1950*, Harmondsworth: Penguin.

Part IV

ART AND WILDSTYLE

13

Deleuze on J. M. W. Turner

Catastrophism in Philosophy?

James Williams

> Turner's last watercolours do not only conquer already all the forces of impressionism, but also the power of an explosive line without contours. Making painting itself a catastrophe without equal (instead of romantically illustrating catastrophe).
>
> (Deleuze 1981: 68)

> But does not difference as catastrophe precisely bear witness to an irreducible ground which continues to act under the apparent equilibrium of organic representation?
>
> (Deleuze 1994: 35)

Introduction

It is argued here that Gilles Deleuze puts forward a world-view where catastrophe plays a positive role. This advocacy for catastrophe is most explicit in Deleuze's studies of art, in particular, in his work on J. M. W. Turner. There, the greatness of Turner's late paintings is seen to lie in their expression of catastrophe, that is, they allow catastrophe to become actual insofar as the works of art are catastrophes in themselves. In this case, artistic expression is in direct opposition to the representation of catastrophes. However, Deleuze goes beyond catastrophe and, more importantly, he avoids the accusation of destructive nihilism. For him, catastrophe is only a stage that allows us to express the differential changes that underlie identity in a world committed to identity and representation. Once these changes are expressed and understood our commitment to identity disappears and with it the need to relate to change purely in terms of the extreme violence of catastrophe. In its place, Deleuze puts forward the doctrine of counter-actualization, that is, the practice of expressing the catastrophic changes that come to constitute and destroy any actuality.

Catastrophism in Philosophy

For Deleuze disaster and destruction must be present in all things and must be put into motion in all great creations. Not only are all things overshadowed by catastrophe, but it is the task of great art to participate in this disaster. In his remarks on Turner, his 'oracle', Deleuze singles out the painter's absolute dedication to catastrophe. The English painter is not put forward as great simply for his early representations of Alpine avalanches and other awe-inspiring disastrous events.[1] He is great because, in the later works, the paintings become catastrophes in themselves and for those who view them.

This is no mistaken usage: the *Littré* and *OED* definitions are unequivocal. A catastrophe is a great reversal, a disaster and a deplorable end. Deleuze risks outdoing Voltaire's Pangloss–Leibniz by inviting rather than merely accepting the Lisbon earthquake: 'trente mille habitants de tout âge et de tout sexe sont écrasés sous les ruines. . . . – Quelle peut être la raison suffisante de ce phénomène? disait Pangloss' (Voltaire 1960: 147). Indeed, for Deleuze, catastrophe is to be affirmed and sought out in art and in life. His reasons are not simply millenarian or tragic in the sense of the final disaster or undoing; rather, in accord with the more abstract definition of the *OED*, his catastrophe is any event 'subverting a system of things'. The subversion of systematicity and identity is the attraction of catastrophe rather than the harsh lessons of its violence.

Deleuze's catastrophism, then, appears to be radical and thoroughgoing. Where, in geology, the term indicates a theory that explains changes on the earth's surface in terms of sudden catastrophic events, in his philosophy, catastrophe is ubiquitous and without fixed scale. From the smallest to the greatest state different catastrophic processes are at work (Deleuze 1994: 42). In Deleuze and Guattari's books, from *Thousand Plateaus* to *What is Philosophy?*, this geological catastrophism is expressed through the ever-present processes of deterritorialisation and reterritorialisation; no well-defined territory is safe or static: it is constantly undone and remade. The disappearance of familiar landscapes and the creation of an unfamiliar terrain in a volcanic eruption, tidal wave or earthquake are repeated in all things great or small.

Art – somewhat like time-lapse photography – can make these movements on different scales felt on others. For example, Le Corbusier uses vibration between colours or light and shade to animate a solid building; once coloured, static walls take on a dynamic quality that furthers the architect's project of making buildings into an active aesthetic experience. Motion and change take over from stasis.[2] Similarly, Peter Eisenman followed Deleuze in expressing movements in geology, urban planning and settlement, and communication in the folds of the structural designs for the Rebstockpark site in Frankfurt: 'The idea of the Rebstock Fold is to become this surface on which urban events would be inscribed with an intensive actuality' (Rajchman 1993: 119). Thus, according to Deleuze, every actual thing is subject to an infinite set of continuing and open-ended transformations and re-creations that can be expressed in art. There is no rule for the organisation of these processes. There also is no possible overview, or hierarchy; instead, the series is a multiplicity that cannot be totalized. Furthermore, this multiplicity is radically destructive insofar as the identity of things is not preserved in the transformation.

Here, the very concept of identity as ground is challenged: underlying any identity we find a set of destructive and creative processes. These processes are the transcendental condition for any actual identity. Deleuze owes this move from the empirical to the transcendental to Kant: 'Kant is the one who discovers the prodigious dominance of the transcendental. He is the analogue of the great explorer – not of another world, but of the upper or lower reaches of this one' (Deleuze 1994: 135). There can be no limited and clearly defined actual thing whose existence does not presuppose a set of past and future catastrophic changes. Though individuals and species become settled and attached to a particular form, they are the result of a series of dramatic changes and they are destined to be engulfed by further ones: identity must be understood in terms of a potentiality that can come to destroy it. Deleuze's favoured source in this respect is the work of the biologist Geoffroy Saint-Hilaire: '[the set of genes] constitutes a virtuality, a potentiality; and this structure is incarnated in actual organisms, as much from the point of view of the determination of their species as from the differentiation of their parts, according to rhythms that are precisely called "differential", according to comparative speeds or slownesses which measure the movement of actualization' (Deleuze 1994: 185). In this sense, life presupposes catastrophe and destruction as potentialities and the role of the philosopher, artist and scientist is to lift the illusion of settled identities and pure essences by expressing the processes that come to produce and undermine them.

This extreme nature of Deleuze's advocacy of catastrophe is unsettling, even distressing. In less radical versions, catastrophe in philosophy still leaves a place for redemption and reconciliation. It can be a sign of order and justice, where great disasters are in fact only lessons, purifications or selective events designed, in the end, to bring about the Good.[3] These possibilities are actively opposed in Deleuze's work, since they break with the belief in the omnipresence of destruction and re-creation. There can be no transcendent realm from which to explain and rationalize catastrophe. With this refusal of transcendence there is also the refusal of a transcendent ethical order: disaster cannot be redeemed by reference to a will outside this world. Deleuze's commitment to immanence and to a univocal philosophy is as strong as Spinoza's (Deleuze 1994: 40–1). Neither philosopher will exchange this commitment for the reassurance of a final cause and for the explanation of catastrophe through divine will. They despise those who do fall into this illusion: 'among so many conveniences in Nature they had to find many inconveniences: storms, earthquakes and diseases, and the like. These they maintain happen because the gods are angry on account of wrongs done to them by men' (Spinoza 1994: 111).

Deleuze and Turner

Deleuze's most important remarks on Turner appear in two passages of Deleuze and Guattari's *Anti-Oedipus*. Though the sections are relatively short, they are dense, and a careful reading allows a complex position to emerge. This density is a key factor of the style of the book: it is written to reflect the view, firstly, that all the possibilities that can occur and have occurred to an actual thing subsist in it as potentialities, and secondly, that the potentialities of any given actuality are the cosmos as a whole. In its most straightforward version this means that any Deleuzian actuality is the meeting point of all potentialities, or that any existent presupposes the subsistent world as a whole. It is important to note how this view departs from a statement such as 'God is fully present even in the smallest thing and all things are in God.' In the Deleuzian version, the identification of part and whole never takes place; rather, they are differentiated by the relation of actual to potential. It is for this reason that expression is an important function within his philosophy; it relates the potential to the actual. Passages from *Anti-Oedipus* therefore condense the book as a whole, and wide series of arguments and theories are found in concentrated form in extremely short passages.

In line with this property of Deleuze and Guattari's writing, the first passage on Turner from *Anti-Oedipus* will be unpacked into a series of points that cover wider Deleuzian arguments and ideas. The question 'Why does Deleuze come to develop a catastrophism in art and philosophy?' is the leading thread connecting these points. The key passage is:

> The visit to London is our Pythia. Turner is there. Looking at his paintings, one understands what it is to scale the wall, and yet to remain behind; to cause flows to pass through, without knowing any longer whether they are carrying us elsewhere or flowing back over us already. The paintings range over three periods. If the psychiatrist were allowed to speak here, he could talk about the first two, although they are in fact the most reasonable. The first are of end-of-the-world catastrophes, avalanches and storms. That's where Turner begins. The paintings of the second period are somewhat like the delirious reconstruction, where the delirium hides, are rather when it is on a par with the lofty technique inherited from Poussin, Lorrain, or the Dutch tradition: the world is reconstructed through archaisms having a modern function. But something incomparable happens at the level of the paintings of the third period, in the series Turner does not exhibit, but keeps secret. It cannot even be said that he is far ahead of his time: there is something ageless, that comes from an eternal future, or flees towards it. The canvas turns in on itself, it is pierced by a hole, a lake, a tornado, an explosion. The themes of the preceding paintings are to be found again here, their meaning has changed. The canvas is truly broken, sundered by what penetrates it. All that remains is a background of gold and fog, intense, intensive, traversed in depth by what has just sundered its breath: the schiz. Everything becomes mixed and confused, and it is here that the breakthrough – not the breakdown – occurs.
>
> (Deleuze and Guattari 1984: 132)

The first point to make is that the passage is a response to a key problem in Deleuze and Guattari's work. The problem has a political and moral side, and also has a logical aspect. Firstly, the break with identity and with the repression of desire as change (Deleuze defines desire as a movement rather than as a longing for a specific goal or object) risks descending into a chaotic, structure-less state. Secondly, in terms of logic and the philosophy of language, the question arises of whether there can be a radical break with rules without a collapse into nonsense. From the point of view of this revolutionary book written in the aftermath of May 1968, the political risk of anarchy and the moral risk of nihilistic destructiveness must be addressed. This is why we find the passage opening on the opposition between passing over the wall and remaining behind or allowing flows to pass through, but also to return. It is also why the passage closes on the opposition between a breakthrough and a breakdown. The analogies capture the tension between the escape from repression, escaping over the wall of the prison, the home or the State, and the need for an order, limitation and sense without which chaos would reign. They also capture the psychological, and more importantly, the mechanical tension between a breakthrough and a breakdown: the breakout from repression or from technical limits is energizing and life-affirming, but it is also the point of greatest danger in terms of complete breakdown or failure, whether psychological or machinic. Thus, the passage on Turner is situated exactly where Deleuze and Guattari consider the possibility of a terminally chaotic catastrophe in politics, psychology and, more generally, in any machinic set-up. Turner's paintings are a creative response to this problem.

Deleuze and Guattari deal with the response in terms of standard divisions in the critical understanding of Turner's work and a non-standard interpretation of those divisions. His work evolves from early picturesque paintings, through a historical and mythical period, inspired among others by Poussin and Claude, to his late, more abstract and now more famous paintings (for instance, *The Fighting 'Téméraire'*, 1838), where recognizable forms are disturbed or torn asunder in explosions of light and colour. This division into periods is not especially controversial, since it follows clear formal and substantive differences. However, given the integrity of Turner's work these distinctions are most often conflated according to overall interpretations. For example, Turner's work has been united under the theme of the romantic sublime according to which each of the periods of his work is related to the sublime relation of nature to man. For example, in conclusion to the notes on his major exhibition on the Turnerian sublime, John Wilton writes: 'As human beings we cannot avoid being responsive to the sublime in nature and in the works of man. We must still be responsive to it in works of art. This instinctive human response is what prompts much of our admiration of Turner' (Wilton 1981: 105). According to this view, Turner's art represents the power and beauty of nature as it exceeds mere human scales and values. More significantly, John Gage has developed a subtle interpretation that claims, after Ruskin, that Turner's art brings together a painterly concern with the role of colour and a concern with the romantic relation of man and nature. This union is achieved through a complex poetic symbolism where colour and forms represent themes in the relation of colour to sublime romantic themes: 'Turner in his art was less and less concerned to express chromatic harmony, but rather the conflict of light and dark; for him the primaries were emblematic not of harmony but of disharmony' (Gage 1969: 117).

Deleuze rejoins Gage on the theme of light and colour but breaks with his symbolism and romanticism. For him, Turner's art breaks with representation through colour and only the late paintings achieve this break: 'The canvas is truly broken, sundered by what penetrates it. All that remains is a background of gold and fog, intense, intensive, traversed in depth by what has just sundered its breath: the schiz.' In these different interpretations the theme of catastrophe is never far away, whether it be in the immeasurable power of a sublime nature, represented by Turner's obsession with storms and turbulent sea-scape,[4] or in the catastrophic explosion,[5] background[6] or veil[7] of light and colour in the late paintings as viewed by Deleuze. However, for Gage, catastrophe can be averted through the intellectual function of symbolic representation. For him, Turner brings together an understanding of the forces of nature, of the science of colour and of the romantic relation of man to nature:

> In the study of Turner's career as a colourist, Ulysses deriding Polyphemes is a central picture because it is as much about light and colour as it is about the Homeric story; and because it invites us both to look for a conception of natural forces underlying some of the earlier subject pictures which have often been considered as merely conventional, and to look forward to a mythology of colour infusing some of the later landscapes.
>
> (Gage 1969: 132)

Thus, for Gage and for Ruskin, the deeper truth that underlies Turner's sublime pictures lies in the possibility of making sense of the apparent immeasurable force of nature through mythical interpretations blended into the landscape with the aid of his supreme command of colour: 'the aim of the great inventive landscape painter must be to give the far higher and deeper truth of mental vision, rather than that of the physical facts' (John Ruskin cited in Wilton 1987: 222).

The importance of this intellectual capture of the forces of nature in the mythology of colour cannot be underestimated. Ruskin was working against severe popular attack on the inventive and surreal use of colour in Turner's late paintings. His use of an apparently unreal, though in fact scientific,[8] three-colour basis for painting and his reliance on yellow, over and above red and blue, caused revulsion and ridicule among some critics. Turner was seen as ruining the real beauty of nature through personal obsession. Indeed, the sensual catastrophe picked up upon by Deleuze was felt very early on, but only in negative terms as a sensual scandal. The *Morning Herald*, for example, launched an attack on the very painting that Ruskin and Gage view as central:

> This is a picture in which truth, nature and feeling are sacrificed to melodramatic effect . . . he has reached the perfection of unnatural tawdriness. In fact it may be taken as a specimen of colouring run mad – positive vermilion – positive indigo; and all the most glaring tints of green,

> yellow and purple contend for mastery on the canvas, with all the vehement contrast of a kaleidoscope or a Persian carpet.
>
> (Wilton 1987: 160)

The British Press went further in attacking Turner for the catastrophe he unleashed on the canvas and in the senses of the viewer:

> all is yellow, nothing but yellow, violently contrasted with blue. . . . Mr. Turner has degenerated into such a detestable manner, that we cannot view his works without pain . . . [we] would wish Mr. Turner turn back to Nature and worship her as the goddess of his idolatry, instead of his 'yellow bronze' which haunts him . . . in Mr. Turner's pictures we are in a region that exists in no quarter of the universe.
>
> (Wilton 1987: 146)

Yet, it is this sacrifice of represented nature that Deleuze and Guattari pick out as the most important aspect of the late paintings: 'Everything becomes mixed and confused, and it is here that the breakthrough – not the breakdown – occurs.' This is because, unlike Gage, they value the power of catastrophe in painting exactly because it disturbs the mental function of ascribing sense to nature even where nature is hidden or strange. So, for them, colour and light in Turner are primordial, and cannot be reinscribed into a mythology of colour. Rather, the explosiveness of Turner's use of light and colour expresses the potential violent changes that bring about and destroy any actual natural state. This is why Deleuze is attracted to Turner's use of colour against figure. The explosive, undermining and sundering effects of colour in the paintings disrupt figure. Shapes lose their determinacy, not in terms of an imagined event – a storm or an avalanche – but as sensual facts. This catastrophe is to be Turner's greatest and most truthful achievement:

> But at least something arose whose force fractured the codes, undid the signifiers, passed under the structures, set the flows in motion, and effected breaks at the limits of desire: a breakthrough. . . . We have seen this in the case of the painter Turner, and his most accomplished paintings that are sometimes termed 'incomplete': from the moment there is genius, there is something that belongs to no school, no period, something that achieves a breakthrough – art as a *process* without goal, but that attains completion as such.
>
> (Deleuze and Guattari 1984: 370)

Where Gage and Ruskin attempt to tame catastrophe through an appeal to Turner's conceptualisations, his 'wonderful range of mind', Deleuze and Guattari seek to inflate the role of catastrophe to the point where intellectual functions are stilled by pure sensual intensity.

However, Deleuze is drawn not only to the late paintings but also to some of the characteristics of their creator. One of the effects of the opposition to identity in Deleuze's philosophy is the critique of the role of the self as a reference point for the understanding of art. The artist's character and psychology are often seen as mirrors for the works and vice versa. In this sense, they represent one another in different ways and in different areas and thereby offer an alternative to Deleuze's view of art as the expression of intensities that escape identification. He is therefore drawn to the secrecy and duplicity of Turner's later life, 'the series Turner does not exhibit, but keeps secret'. Not only did Turner keep these paintings to himself (in poor conditions in his studio), but he also took on a second identity in order to preserve himself from his artistic fame. This is, to use Deleuze's term, Turner's becoming imperceptible: the artist disappears just as his art reaches its greatest intensity. In order to disappear, Turner took the name of his companion Mrs Booth and withdrew with her to a small house in Chelsea hidden from his fame and reputation as an artist ('there where he could gratify his desire to be completely incognito', Wilton 1987: 202). The importance of this imperceptible quality of the artist is to render psychological analysis redundant: 'If the psychiatrist were allowed to speak here, he could talk about the first two, although they are in fact the most reasonable.' This then allows the pure intensity of the works to take effect and escape capture within a psychological interpretation. Paradoxically, Turner's earliest picturesque work was sponsored by Dr Munro, consultant to George III during his attacks of madness. Munro believed that drawing picturesque landscapes offered an escape from melancholy madness. However, where the early works fit into a theory whereby the harmony of the landscape must return a disturbed mind to calm, the later works express the violent potential of light and colour at work behind any scape: 'art, as soon as it attains its own grandeur, its own genius, creates chains of decoding and deterritorialization that serve as the foundation for desiring-machines, and make them function'.

The key to Turner's work does not lie in curing the disharmony of man and nature, but in liberating light and colour as elements of desire in themselves. According to Paul Signac, Turner reached a kind of creative madness (pre-figuring abstract expressionism): 'From 1834, Turner frees himself from black and looks for the most beautiful colorations; colour for colour's sake. You would say he was mad. . . . The works of Turner prove to me that we must be free of all ideas of imitation and copying, and that hues must be created' (Rewald 1952: 279). For Deleuze and Guattari, Turner has unleashed the power of changes in the intensity of light and colour within the framework of nature and the human form. The intensity of Turner's colour as it flows through a painting such as *Norham Castle, Sunrise* achieves a breakout away from sense and the restriction of familiar identifiable forms. It also achieves a breakthrough in the expression of the role of an intense and uncontrolled light in sensation. The effects do not take place through the mediation of a reflection upon the paintings; rather, the cognitive command over the senses is overwhelmed in favour of pure sensual intensity. It is in this sense that there is a literal catastrophe in Turner's late paintings, as opposed to a represented catastrophe in his early picturesque or mythical work.

The Deleuzian Diagram

If Turner's greatest achievement is to have broken through figure and broken out of sense, does this mean that painting and other expressive creation must always tend to the most pure expression of intensity? Is the logical extension of Turner's actual catastrophes to turn away from any figure and sense and into twentieth-century abstract expressionism? Finally, does this catastrophism in painting find a parallel in a nihilistic philosophy that rebels against meaning and structure in favour of the destruction of any representations and identities? Deleuze considers these questions directly in his important book on Francis Bacon, in particular where he applies his concept of the diagram to painting.

For Deleuze, the diagram is the pre-figural preparation of the canvas, that is, the series of shades, colours, scratches and layers of material set down prior to the delineation of figure. Although the artist may have made a series of mental and draught preparations for a painting – sketches and ideas about figures, for example – after this preparatory work a non-figurative diagram must also prepare the way for figuration. In Bacon's case this consists of a series of haphazard lines, coloured spots and pitched paint. For Van Gogh, to give a familiar example, this preparatory work is the set of straight and bent strokes of paint that deform earth, trees and sky (Deleuze 1981: 66). This physical rather than visual act of painting puts down a ground that is in contradiction with the pre-planned figure. After visual preparation in the mind's eye or in sketches, there is an automatic and random production of non-figurative shapes and colours that threatens to engulf the figuration it is meant to prepare for. The diagram, then, is the physical catastrophe that underlies figuration in painting:

> It is like the sudden appearance of another world, because these marks, these lines are irrational, involuntary, accidental, free, driven by chance. They are

> non-representational, non-illustrative, non-narrative. But they are also not significant or signifying: they are asignifying lines. They are lines of sensation, but of confused sensation. . . . The hand becomes independent and passes into the service of other forces, tracing marks that do not depend on our will or on our vision. . . . The artist's hand has stepped in to exercise its independence and to smash a sovereign optical organisation: nothing more is seen, as in a catastrophe or chaos.
>
> (Deleuze 1981: 66)

The diagram allows Deleuze to define what he calls the 'haptic' aspect of painting, that is, the sense of a manual space given through coloured planes and the warmth and coldness of colours, rather than through perspective and light and shadow. In the diagram, an optical space organised according to the rigid geometrical coordinates above–below–far–near is replaced by a manual space organized according to the more fluid grasp of warm–cold–hard–soft. This means that instead of placing objects within a geometric grid, the painter gives a world that is sensed in terms of greater and lesser tactile intensities.

The concept of the diagram allows Deleuze to explain how Turner's paintings undermine conceptual and visual organisation through the intensity of colour, and, indeed, Turner's method fits this account very well on at least two counts. Firstly, Turner prepared his oil paintings with the rapid and instinctive ground that Deleuze describes. This preparation astounded his contemporaries. How could the sublime beauty of the finished work be the result of a random, chaotic act of painting?

> he began by pouring wet paint till it was saturated, he tore, he scratched, he scrubbed at it in a kind of frenzy and the whole thing was chaos – but gradually and as if by magic the lovely ship, with all its exquisite minutiae, came into being.
>
> (Wilton 1987: 114)

Turner's virtuoso performances on varnishing days at the Royal Academy confirm this description of his method. He would allow a hopelessly unfinished or dim painting to be hung with only days left before the opening of the exhibition. But this unsatisfactory state, this diagram, would be rapidly transformed by the addition of small details or colorations: 'Indeed it was quite necessary for him to make best use of his time, as the picture when sent in was a mere dab of several colours, and "without form or void", like chaos before the creation' (Wilton 1987: 177–85).

The Deleuzian answer to this critical astonishment is that the beauty of the paintings depends exactly on the chaotic intensity of the preparatory diagram that seems so at odds with the final figural sublimity. This point comes out more clearly in the second, and most important 'diagrammatic' aspect of Turner's work. Deleuze describes Turner's diagram in terms of a coloured 'line without contours'. What he means by this is that Turner's paintings are grounded on washes of colour with no clear boundaries. Patches of intense colour and light traverse the well-defined figures of the paintings.[9] These washes or lines without contours were indeed one of the most important preparatory aspects of Turner's late paintings; they were also the most striking feature of his watercolours. In Turner's late work, the sketching of figures is overtaken by astounding colour preparations or 'colour beginnings' where fluid patches of colour are put down in series in sketchbooks (see Wilkinson 1973). Draughtsmanship takes second place to the search for the perfect background colour wash for a given scene. In fact, in the last watercolours and some of the oils the background effaces the figure completely, for example, in the last watercolours of Switzerland. This is why Signac can claim Turner as the 'mad' painter of colour for colour's sake. It is also why he is seen as the greatest forerunner of abstract expressionism: the colour beginnings and late watercolours resemble nothing more than Rothko's abstract shadings and contrasts.

However, it is exactly when Deleuze discusses these last watercolours that he comes to question the extreme catastrophe that Turner brings to painting: '[In the diagram] the painter confronts the greatest dangers for himself and for his work.' Having argued that the diagram is a crucial part of any painting, he then considers three modern ways of acting out this fact: pure abstraction or a minimal, ascetic diagram as in the work of Mondrian; a maximal diagram, which is the most chaotic, as in Turner's last work and American abstract expressionism, Pollock, for example; and finally, a diagrammatic painting that saves line and figure by 'controlling' catastrophe, as in the work of Francis Bacon. The importance of this division lies in the set of remarks that accompanies it. Each of the three ways is a handling of catastrophe: the first minimalises the role of the diagram in favour of a pure spiritual vision; the second flirts with complete destruction in the chaos of catastrophe without sense or figure – this is a pure manual painting; the third, however, involves an explicit criticism of the first two: what it seeks to avoid is the loss of intensity, caused by a fear of chaos, in the pure vision of formal abstraction, but also the complete foundering of painting in manual confusion. For Deleuze, Francis Bacon's third way avoids the catastrophic dangers of the first two. It is necessary for there to be the risk of destruction by the diagram, but catastrophe has to be controlled. Against Turner's 'line without contours' Bacon aims to save the contour from catastrophe:

> To save the contour, nothing is more important for Bacon. . . . The Diagram must not devour the whole painting, it must be limited in space and time. It must remain operational and controlled. The violent means must not be unleashed and catastrophe must not submerge everything. The diagram is the possibility of fact, it is not Fact itself. All figurative facts must not disappear; and, above all, a new figuration must . . . emerge from the diagram and carry clarity and precision with it. To emerge from catastrophe . . .
>
> (Deleuze 1981: 71)

Conclusion

Thus, although catastrophe and Turner 'bear witness to an irreducible ground' (to use the expression from *Difference and Repetition*), the point is never merely to merge with that chaotic condition for identity. Deleuze's attraction to catastrophe is not a nihilistic rush towards collapse and chaos; rather, 'the diagram must remain operational and controlled'. The role of philosophy and art is to divulge the presence of the intensities that come to constitute actuality without plunging into pure intensity. This measured response to catastrophe is made most clear where Deleuze considers the Stoic response to catastrophic events in conjunction with closeness to disaster encountered in Anglo-American literature (a topic that he covers immediately after Turner's painting in *Anti-Oedipus*). The controlling response to catastrophic events is counter-actualization, that is, a doubling of the event where an artistic expression doubles the expression of differential changes in actuality. In counter-actualisation, the potentialities that are expressed in any actuality as destruction and creation are themselves expressed:

> The eternal truth of the event is grasped only if the event is also inscribed in the flesh. But each time we must double this painful actualization by a counter-actualisation which limits, moves and transfigures it . . . to be the mime of *what effectively occurs*, to double the actualization with a counter-actualization, the identification with a distance, like the true actor and dancer, is to give the truth of the event the only chance of not being confused with its inevitable actualization.
>
> (Deleuze 1990: 161)

Where Turner expresses the intensity of light and colour at work behind actual figures he achieves the counter-actualisation of the role of colour in actuality and helps us to live up to and live with the power of light and colour. But, if this expression takes over altogether from figures, then that achievement will be lost.

Notes

1 See J. M. W. Turner, *The Fall of an Avalanche in the Grisons*, 1810; *Snowstorm: Hannibal and his Army crossing the Alps*. R.A. 1812.

2 Le Corbusier developed the use of colour planes in architecture from his work on and in modern art:

> Walls are painted white, brown, grey and blue, and these activate the interiors still further. In 1923 there was an exhibition of de Stijl architecture at the Galerie Rosenberg in Paris, and it is possible that Le Corbusier was influenced by Neo-plasticist ideas for generating contrast and vibration between pure colour planes.
>
> (Curtis 1992: 72)

3 For a limit case of this view of catastrophe as an ethical burden see Llewelyn 1995: 209–13.

4 See *The Wreak of a Transport Ship*, c. 1807; *A Fire at Sea*, c. 1835; *Snowstorm – Steamboat off a Harbour's Mouth*, RA 1842.

5 See *The Burning of the Houses of Lords and Commons*, 16 October 1834, RA 1835; *Slavers Throwing Overboard the Dead and Dying – Typhoon Coming on (The Slave Ship)*, RA 1840, *Rain, Steam and Speed – The Great Western Railway*, RA 1844.

6 See *Keelmen Hauling in Coals by Night*, RA 1835; *Norham Castle, Sunrise* c. 1840–5; *Sun Setting over a Lake*, c. 1845.

7 See *Light and Colour (Goethe's Theory)*, RA 1843; the oils and watercolours of Venice, 1840–5.

8 Turner was enthusiastic about the three-colour theory put forward by Brewster against Newton. See Gage 1969: 122.

9 See *Sun Setting over a Lake*.

References

Curtis, William J. (1992) *Le Corbusier: Ideas and Forms*, London: Phaidon Press.

Deleuze, G. (1981) *Francis Bacon: logique de la sensation*, Paris: La Différence.

—— (1990) *Logic of Sense*, trans. M. Lester with C. Stivale, London: Athlone Press.

—— (1994) *Difference and Repetition*, trans. P. Patton, London: Athlone Press.

Deleuze, G. and Guattari, F. (1994) *Anti-Oedipus*, trans. R. Hurley, London: Athlone Press.

Gage, J. (1969) *Colour in Turner: Poetry and Truth*, London: Studio Vista.

Llewelyn, J. (1995) 'Genealogy as History Catastrophized', in *The Genealogy of Ethics*, London: Routledge.

Rajchman, J. (1993) 'Perplications', in P. Eisenman et al. (eds) *Re-working Eisenman*, London: Academy.

Rewald, J. (1952) 'Extraits du journal de Paul Signac', *Gazette des Beaux Arts* 39.

Spinoza, B. (1994) *Ethics* ed. E. Curley, Princeton: Princeton University Press.

Voltaire (1960) *Candide, ou L'Optimise*, in *Romans et contes*, Paris: Garnier.

Wilkinson, G. (1975) *Turner's Colour Sketches*, London: Barrie and Jenkins.

Wilton, A. (1981) *Turner and the Sublime*, London: British Museum.

—— (1987) *Turner in his Time*, London: Thames & Hudson.

14

Capitalism and Schizophrenia

Wildstyle in Full Effect

Robin Mackay

> Guerrilla dance, guerrilla musicality, coming from anywhere, taking what is needed.
>
> (Two Fingers and Kirk 1995: 191)

The increasing ubiquity of sound-recording technologies (essentially diagramming or stratigraphical systems) has, in transforming sound into stored material, deritualized and demystified the experience of music. Increasingly appreciated as much for abstract sonic qualities as for ostensible musical 'content', able to employ a vast range of sonic resources, 'performed' unceremoniously every day and everywhere, music is drawing nearer to an immanence with general ambient sound. At the same time, we are growing accustomed to the experience of absolutely synthetic sound, sound only made possible by the recording technologies themselves. Analysis of the production of *machinic surplus value* in such processes and the exact fate of such excess machinic production provides a key cross-section of the abstract machine of capitalist production and its future. On this route through the phylum of the sonic assemblage, *abstract matter* becomes not only a comprehensible and applicable term but an uncompromisingly tactile phenomenon. Beginning with *Capitalism and Schizophrenia*'s insistence that the diagram is never simply a tracing, or a representation, the key process of capitalist machinic abstraction and its enslavement to the docilizing powers of consumer capitalism can be approached through the sonic assemblage: the interaction between the human body and the fundamental molecular disturbance which constitutes sound, and the machines which interpose and mediate within it.

Hearing already presupposes a complex of syntheses, biological and mnemotechnical apparatuses of capture. The function of memory in the feedback loops of the simplest humanoid–sonic assemblage introduces the possibility of continually sophisticating circuits of reception and transmission, the exploitation of coded sound. Rhythmic disturbances become interpreted as traits of external phenomena in recognition patterns where meaning can already be analysed into signaletic frequency response:

> All that can be inferred from a signal may appropriately be called the 'meaning' of this signal. Depending on the complexity of an organism's nervous system, the meaning of a signal can vary from a simple initiation of a feeding response, that is, the signal means 'food', to a realization of the most complicated relationships in an environmental situation.
>
> (Foerster and Beauchamp 1969: 7)

This may primarily be made possible by the production of a reliable method of recording, for a stable storage system is necessary for such a process to take place. That there are biological, even inert, recording technologies is established by *Capitalism and Schizophrenia*'s '*Geology of Morals*'. Systems of Stratification, deducting similar elements from a material flow and arranging them in resonantly ordered compounds, produce stabilized, resistant matter. Therefore corporeal reality as such is constituted as a gigantic memory, densely embedded synthetic compounds differing in degrees of plasticity and modes of composition.

Although contemporary recording processes allow us consciously to treat sound as a synthetic assemblage, there have been few attempts to discuss music in terms of its machinic processing. Music would perhaps like to remain the stratified and secretive reserve of soulful artists. Pragmatically, however, the field of sonic production has provided an unparalleled fertility for strato-analytical procedures to emerge and develop. Given the preponderance of interpretative 'readings' of all manner of subjects, it is refreshing instead to be able to listen to strato-analysis in action. Writing more often than not provides a system of recording whose 'object of study', exploiting it parasitically, nonetheless surpasses it in terms of machinic connectivity (this piece being no exception). The written word proves redundant, disintensified and insufficiently plastic. An effective strato-analysis requires a system of recording which fulfils the required criteria immanently without pretending to a relationship of absolute objectivity, the theatre of representation, thus becoming the writing of the State. A writing is required which operates on vectors directly consistent with other matter. By listening to the strato-analysis achieved in the sonic assemblage, steps can be taken towards such a writing-machine.

* * *

The musical division of sound into pitch and duration (the stave) deducts audible vibrations, and folds the audible continuum at a threshold point (physically about nineteen cycles per second, although the threshold is rarely explored), to form two exclusive time-series which articulate sounds as complicit relations of content and form. Pitch assigns a signifying value (note) to cyclical transformations of molecular compression and rarefaction, and duration gives the metric length of the tone, which positions it in relation to other tones, or 'empty' spaces.

Even phonography freezes intensive differences into extensive surface inscription, disjoining intensity and duration. The recording made by a phonographic apparatus depicts sound as a waveform etched onto a moving surface, with time and amplitude (amount of molecular displacement) plotted perpendicularly. For any given sound, pitch rises as duration is shortened, and duration is lengthened as pitch is lowered (think of changing the speed of a record-player). Sounds become packaged objects for the clockspace of a mechanical duration, two measures in reciprocal presupposition, biunivocal time-series: one naming (pitch, amplitude), the other counting (time signature, recording speed). Compressive/extensive (content/expression). Double pincers locking into compensatory homoeostasis.

Vibrations are perceived through rapidly oscillating *differences* in pressure, the measure of amplitude, and consequently the sensation of acoustic intensity, being relative to a molecular equilibrium. The vibratory continuum plugs into the delta and theta waves of the brain, into bodily sensation and ultimately into temperature, at hyper- and sub-sonic values. Pitch slides into duration as it decreases, as harmony becomes monometric rhythm (the properties of consonance and dissonance result from the factorial resonance of combined frequencies[1]). And sound, on its broad peripheries, creeps out of the brain and into the body, then out of conscious sensation altogether. Since mechanical recording apparatuses know no such distinctions, human territorializations of the vibratory continuum on all levels – psycho-physiological, cultural and musicological – can only be relativized by the acute analysis of sound. Stratal schema are transcendentally deduced from experience. They map real memory systems, but these are only guaranteed sovereignty for as long as they are venerated as the final cause of the intensity which is articulated through them: fetishism (Pythagoras: 'Everything is number and harmony').

> The distinction between content and expression is *always real*, in various ways, but it cannot be said that the terms preexist their double articulation.
>
> (Deleuze and Guattari 1987: 44)

The reinforcement of material and conceptual stratifications of sound makes Western music a wasteland of redundancy. Sonic technology locking into the song as tragic-orgasmic structure, emotional engineering overlaid by the signifying power of words; the cultural fixing of molar arrangements of specific instruments (orchestra to rock band) with a certain predictable range of musical effects. Harmony and counterpoint limiting the sonic to a grid of resonant points. Harmonic and monometric form itself as Hellenic beauty, right through to the transcendental despotism of Kant's *Stimmung*, is endemic in Western art. In the Western tonal musical form, the tension of dissonance is always relieved by a consonant homecoming; this is implied even in the facetious mischief of the avant-garde.

Formed by these resonant coding systems, the reproduction of Western music has long been a specialized technique, its performance linked to ritualized spectator events and expressions of power and its graphism being the preserve of specialized cognoscenti. Mechanical recording makes these techniques entirely procedural, and the mode of production and reproduction of sound becomes an increasingly dispersed network. At the same time as it immanentizes music, speech and other 'noise', mechanical sound-recording potentially flattens the divide between musician and listener, allowing the latter a (perhaps modificatory) hand in the performance.

The digital manipulation of sound accelerates to the point of breakdown the loop between playing and recording, composing and listening and even between composer and sound. Summarized and abstracted in the circuits of digital sound manipulation are the obvious virtues and the incidental features of the entire history of sound-recording technologies. This latest stage of the abstractive vector of the sonic assemblage stands in relation to late 1990s capitalism as the phonograph stood to the industrial era.

The phonographic diagram, given its direct transduction of physical wave to mechanical impulse or electrical signal, provides a code both precisely reproducible and potentially editable. There is no need of specialized knowledge to interpret the phonographic record: where the score represents, phonography simply transduces and can evidently not be described as a system of *writing*, but only as a diagram, despite its inventors' wishes:

> (T)hey intended it as surface for the preservation of representation, in other words, a protector of the preceding mode of organization. It in fact emerged as a technology imposing a new social system, completing the deritualization of music and heralding a new network, a new economy and a new politics – in music as in other social relations.
>
> (Attali 1985: 89)

Sound remains stratified only to the extent that systems of observation and recording are the preserve of the powerful or wise, and their codes and territories appear as the divine presupposition of acoustic phenomena. But if the locking-in and conceptual reinforcement of such coding systems are inevitable, then also a very different process necessarily follows from the increasingly radical analysis and resynthesis of sonic material. The production of a sonic technology implies the construction of principles on the back of a deterritorialization (the production of an interruption or break in the assemblage at a certain point and the arbitrary repetition of redeparture from that point, transforming the conditions of possibility for sound production) and a decoding (rendering any regime of sound-ordering relative within a field of chromatically variable parameters) whose efficacy potentially releases, or releases the potential of, the matter of sound.

> [T]rends in the evolution of Western Music begin with Pythagoras and terminate – open-ended – with the theories and experiments of (electronic music). . . . What are these trends?
>
> They are most clearly understood in information-theoretical terms, namely as a gradual reduction in the redundancy in works of music or, expressed differently, as a continuous increase in the complexity of sound and composition, hence an increase in the amount of auditory information transmitted during a given interval of time. Redundancy reduction has been achieved over the last two millennia by a steady abolishment of constraints on three levels: specificity of waveforms, selection of frequencies, and rules of synchronism and succession.
>
> (Foerster and Beauchamp 1969: 9)

The sciences are incomprehensible apart from their combination with currency (communication): processes are only modelled in order to abstract and reproduce them on a more efficient basis, at will, or in bulk quantities. But concurrently, the street finds its own uses, and always produces strange offspring. In the middle of the processes of analysis and synthesis, the diagram or abstract machine of the assemblage at issue is seized upon by uninvited forces. Instead of simply reproducing, the diagram slowly yields its machinic surplus value.

As soon as the deterritorialization of sonic matter into vinyl abstracts it from the moment, and makes music into this random-access memory available time and time again, the sonic matter is susceptible to temporal mutation, warping, looping. The simple laws of selection and connection of elements within any medium used to store an abstracted signal produce a machinic surplus value anexactly proportional to the differential between its immanent logic and that of the 'original' medium, or its derangement of temporal normativity (deterritorialization). The contact between vinyl and hand, the technique of 'scratching', is an interface between temporal systems: rendering the abstract tactile (abstract *matter* is not a figurative or metaphorical term), this unplanned interaction makes audible more about the technology than even its designers were able or willing to realize.

The memory-system of a phonographic record could easily be (and was intended as) a simple archive, exerting a minimal derangement easily counterbalanced by the State-friendly effects of pseudo-propaganda (Edison envisaged us listening to stirring records of political speeches rather than music). Only in materially realizing the temporal derangement – the abstraction – which had taken place, by creating something new out of the record, was the machinic potential of the apparatus unlocked.

Despite the contemporary omnipresence of such abstract matter, a huge amount of energy is spent in preventing this from happening – docilizing consumers into using it simply as archival material, or as negative-feedback entertainment. However technology decodes human experience, redundant forms are tenaciously reaffirmed. Even in the age of digital technology, the production of a gigantic surplus value is suppressed or absorbed by the fetishistic packaging of ever-reproduced classical and 'classic' Western forms and the recording industry's strangely hypocritical (if not surprising) promises of authenticity and faithfulness.

> While decoding doubtless means understanding and translating a code, it also means destroying the code as such, assigning it an archaic, folkloric or residual function.
>
> (Deleuze and Guattari 1983: 245)

Bourgeois tragic pop culture revels in a retro-reactive fascination for these archaisms, building them back into the system at the level of ironic simulation, or as 'classics' – further strengthening the reflection-reproduction of a self-satisfied human interiority under the great weight of its own poignant degeneration. Nomads are more interested in migrating, investigating where else technological synthesis can take them, via the abstract, the diagram, the plane of consistency.

* * *

> A synthesizer places all of the parameters in continuous variation, gradually making 'fundamentally heterogeneous elements end up turning into each other in some way'. The moment this conjunction occurs there is a common matter. It is only at this point that one reaches the abstract machine, or the diagram of the assemblage.
>
> (Deleuze and Guattari 1987: 109)

Likewise the sampler places disparate sonic elements upon a plane of consistency without destroying their particular traits, the intensities produced in the sonic assemblage by their singular complex of rhythmic disturbances. Instead it enables these to be systematically diagrammed, edited, merged, manipulated as virtual entities, then reactualized. Sound becomes a series of partial objects for engineering, rather than an object of admiration for heavenly metaphorics. Even unassuming theorists who provide reconnaissance data for nomadic war upon the strata know to some extent what they're doing:

> I would hope that we could soon find whatever . . . excuse we still need to quit talking about 'mellow timbres' and 'edgy timbres', and 'timbres' altogether, in favor of contextual musical analysis of developing structures of vibrato, tremolo, spectral transformation, and all those various dimensions of sound which need no longer languish as inmates of some metaphor.
>
> (Foerster and Beauchamp 1969: 128)

> The plane of consistency is the abolition of all metaphor – all that consists is real.
>
> (Deleuze and Guattari 1987: 69)

It is truly the minority whose experimentation has begun to explore the full potential, the true alien nature of abstract matter. The question will be, what sort of tactics are most efficacious in the releasing of machinic potential (surplus-value)? And how is it that, speaking in terms of the sonic assemblage, the vernacular cybernetics of underground subcultures have already sent such vectors crashing through the strata?

* * *

> Lift the needle, bring it across, smooth, gliding, frictionless, cue it up and then let it delve into that 12 inch plane of existence.
>
> (Two Fingers and Kirk 1995: 37)

Hiphop, house, techno and jungle ('Hip hop with the last vestiges of 'natural' funk removed+house shorn of all humanist glitz/gospel evangelism+digitized reggae+ . . . metallic voodoo simulacra+' (Fisher 1995: 5)) as strains of clandestine anti-music.

> A machine may be defined as a *system of interruptions* or breaks. These breaks should in no way be considered as a separation from reality.
>
> (Deleuze and Guattari 1983: 36)

Breakbeats – cannibalized rhythmic segments of soul and funk records, looped and mixed endlessly, becoming dehumanized chunks of sound migrating from their function as a 'break' within the song. DJs invaded by turntable logic, forming non-organic circuits to produce another time. MCs overlaying breakbeats and misappropriated soundbites with street neologisms, comic-book mechanismo and afro-blag, and returning them to vinyl.

Planet Rock, Afrika Bambataa's rerouting of Kraftwerk's *Trans Europe Express* through the warzones of the South Bronx, provides the soundtrack to robotics and breakdance – a neo-industrial voodoo-tech somatics of the grey area between the white lines of neo-classical German synth-pop and the legacy of the black heroes of funk and soul.

Hip-hop, together with many other sources, recycled once (many times) more in dance tracks where, de/reterritorialized as digital signal, sound is redesigned and reprocessed and once again returned to vinyl for DJs to mix into complex layers and sequences, melding tracks together. At every stage of this sonic metallurgy, a complex feedback and slippage between the functions of crowd, musician and machine, where sounds produce and execute their own evolutive pressures. New strains emerge faster than you can count.

As LA's gangsta rap played uncomfortably upon black American youths' status as 'niggaz' and revitalized the memory of soul and funk pioneers, jungle, from the inner cities of the UK, recalls racist taunts, immigration policies, inner-city meltdowns, and the hybridities of dub, rave, jazz, ska and twotone. It synthesizes distorted patois gun talk, horror video samples, dubterranean sub-bass and accelerated razor-sharp rhythms digitally cut into precise flurries. The rhythmic eccentricity, anexact precision, and constant development of jazz lines shot through with the mechanical pounding of funk and house and the cavernous low-end of dub. Africa filtered through Diaspora, alienation, urban decay and techno-virtuality, the supposedly 'impossible combination of blackness and the future' (Fisher 1995) lethally injecting the colonial terror of the living jungle and its 'natives' with SF future-shock.

Sound is no longer experienced as whole, recognizable and familiar structures, associated with persons or instruments; it doesn't *signify*. Sounds could have come from anywhere, and can potentially go anywhere, mutating as they pass through multiple vinylurgical singularities (tracks). They engender their own vast, clandestine plane which is nothing apart from what moves on it but is nonetheless real, transversal, tilting though heaps of bastardized techno-junk, Cubasing across bedroom studios . . . swerving through clubland, into advertising . . . sinking back into James Brown and P-funk and Dub and Voodoo . . . diving through magnetic signal, vinyl, vibration, intensity . . . transmitting as cultural virus, pirate radio, illegal duplication . . . opening onto insomniac planes, fashion codes, violence and ecstasy, social disintegrations.

Composition by experimentation: the keys of the synthesizer keyboard have only a machinic relation to the sounds they trigger. Unlike the state-numerical system of the musical scale, the digital sequencer operates nomadically: number systems with no necessary hierarchical relations but available to be assigned for maximum functionality, references and designations reassignable and manipulable on every level, numbers working rather than signifying.

Samplers making time for the future: timestretching, a digital technique commonly used in jungle which elongates sounds without altering their pitch, demonstrates how the speed at which levels of acoustic intensity are digitally recorded (around 44,000 samples/second) means that a certain level of destratification is automatically accomplished. Since magnitudes (of acoustic intensity) are all that each sample bit contains, they can be manipulated so as to operate *underneath* the stratification of pitch/duration which depends on the differentiation of the relatively slow comprehensive temporality of cycles per second.[2] Designed to tune up samples of musical instruments, timestretching is employed as a means of creating periods of disorientating duration, impossible speeds and slownesses, realizing the temporal disturbance it is capable of. This is only to repeat again that acute analysis of strata presupposes sub-stratic sampling and so is tantamount to their dissolution, and the freeing of machinic potential. This principle also applies to sampling in the more usual sense, as the decontextualized use of pieces of recorded sound (and to similar techniques in other media). Most of the accumulated techniques of today's sonic engineers were acquired by chance, or as a response to some mechanical or economic limitation. That's the story of hip-hop, the cyberpunk history of a new sonic assemblage taking shape with neither metanarrative nor progressive urgency. Unexpected convergences during the *bricolage* of machine-sequenced sound count more than planned outcomes. Following the grain of sound, rolling with the rhythm. Distributed wildstyle jamming, describing polyrhythmic lines of metamorphosis which take in at irregular intervals sample, sequencer, composer, party crowd, DJ.

The much-vaunted connection between avant-garde movements such as serialism and *musique concrete* and hip-hop techniques needs to take account of the fact that, far from being an intellectual experiment, hip-hop has always been concerned with producing the maximum intensity where it matters: bodily sound, made for dancing, no interpretation necessary.

This reticular phylogenetic webbing of transcodings and deterriorializations marks out hip-hop and its progeny as the sound of superheated anthropo-technic circuitries, where decoded flows begin to leave meaning behind, and escape from molar commoditization by means of a constant flight underground. Uprooted shapes and sounds merge and rescript, break up and repermutate in the virtual machinery of the sampler whilst social fabric warps into localized chaosmosis. A subterranean diagonal which unconditionally migrates from its habitat: accelerating BPMs (no time to understand), reprocessed percussion (Neither harmony or noise), timestretching (violating the chronogenic homeostat of pitch/duration) and sub-bass (sound becoming uncompromisingly physical) retune the neuro-auditory apparatus to awesomely intricate and dense abysses of sound, and permeate the body as an amnesiac addiction. Becoming-sound.

> Freight weight bass rolling over me. The Rumblism in full effect. From back to front a wave of sound, heartbeat-stopping rumblism. . . . Jungle is me and I am the Jungle – no distinction, no separation.
>
> (Two Fingers and Kirk 1995: 101,109)

But why was it the bass and percussion breaks that set the ghettos alight, that demanded a line of flight out of the song? The operation of rhythm within the African socius involves physicality and communication, rather than signifying sound shut up in the soul of the music-lover, merely an adjunct to the harmony of the spheres. African rhythm is a body technology, a precise component, like African art which is assigned its function by *nommo*, power of the word (Jahn 1961: ch. 5), and discarded when it has been used, rather than being retained for eternity in the museum (a scandal which led the 'art-world' to have serious doubts about its value). *It is the Western art object which is the 'fetish'*; and it is logocentric Western world history which cannot understand the transitive voice of the drum.

Voodoo loa are rhythms, or traits immanent in the social machine, which manifest themselves in response to needs of that machine.[3] From where voodoo is, the Christian God is oppressively monometric and dysfunctional. When the Haitian authorities tried to force the slaves to convert to Catholicism, the slaves received a new god into their pantheon, wondering only why the white man lets just one (dull) loa ride him. For the divine nature of the loa is in their immanence and availability, not in a miraculous transcendence at once inutile and terrifying which despotically inscribes its disjunctions onto the social body, allowing no feedback. Even Bon Dieu is neither feared nor praised. 'Vodou isn't like that. . . . It isn't concerned with notions of salvation and transcendence. What it's about is getting things *done*' (Gibson 1993: 111). Voodoo drums call Legba, loa of the pathways, to remove the barrier (the black mirror) which seals the street of the loa off from the human world. Intoxicating polyrhythm calls the loa to ride the initiates, to possess them, to inhabit them with their trances, their traits, their dances. Sound experienced as bodily sensation, rather than spiritual recreation (Jahn 1961: 122) shows how African languages express non-visual intensity as tactile.

> The bassline. Bass it all. Going back to the beginning of everything. . . . The tribal notes, the lost civilization of drum and bass. Bass is the vanishing point on the horizon where all black music disappears back to.
>
> (Two Fingers and Kirk 1995: 100–1)

The climatic impracticability of an extensively developed writing system in early African history produced an asignifying semiotic which resisted the vertical flight of interpretability and signifiance. The drum functioned as immanent memory system and transmitter of cultural history, co-intensive with the intonation and percussion of African languages (a coupling still present now in hip-hop). The somewhat repellent *modus operandi* of the slave trade was to capture tribes, destroy the drums, and then claim disgustedly that Africa had 'no history'. Not that the ROM-museum of Western history could claim any filiation with the vastly distributed machinery of a communicative social machine whose resilience defies genocidal colonialism.

The virtual history of the drum gradually rematerializes, irrupting into Western music like a long-awaited revenge for its brutal silencing. Speaking for centuries in all outlawed musical forms, those which explored the virtual spaces of sonic assemblages rather than reciting texts, and currently in cyberflux digi-processed afro-futurist, it steals sounds and speaks them back in its own becoming-Creole (nommo is always a becoming-word and a word-becoming which does not signify but *(re-)invents* what it is applied to), its own complex of rhythms. The meme-grinder. Predator, indiscernible jungle warfare. All State authorities, like the Haitian plantation-owners, fear the materiality of sound, and the unintelligible, ungodly rites that surround it (sampled/sequenced music is the first form of music to have its performance specifically proscribed by an Act of Parliament). Again and again the drums are confiscated, but the Black Secret Technology continues. Voodoo, the practice of rhythmic contagion, is the tactile point of contact between the social body and the deterritorialized socius, proceeding by means of decoded sonic affect to reinsert the social into the pulsive maelstrom of matter-flows. Dahomian snake-becomings (plunging desiring-machines into the BwO) transform into distributed and refined subsocial programs under ascendant pressure from secured State molarity, travelling unnoticed by icebound damping systems.

* * *

The *Critique of Pure Reason*'s 'profoundly schizoid' (Deleuze and Guattari 1983: 19) theory maps reality as intensive magnitude, 'beginning in pure intuition = 0' (Kant 1933: 202 A166/B208), 'continuous' and 'flowing', the 'matter' of experience (Kant 1933: 204 A170/B211). Rational categories supplant the positivity of intensity with the ultimate and empty form of experience, zero intensity as negation, as the miraculous hypnostatic attractor of pure intuition. A complete stasis, an escape from 'that element which cannot be anticipated' (Kant 1933: 204 A170/B211), which brings us closer to the god of the disjunctive syllogism. The tautological death of pure form: a favourite trope of philosophy.

Capitalism and Schizophrenia's zero intensity is not a zero of absence or negation, but more like the zero of MIDI which designates the establishment of a plane of communication. The surface of a full body where intensity ebbs and shatters. Or think of the way morphing drum patterns glide and trip across the surface of their own momentum.

Disjunctive synthesis as primary is replaced in *Capitalism and Schizophrenia* by connective synthesis: '. . . and . . .'. The rational scaffold of Kantianism, the matter/form distinction together with the privileging of the latter, dismantled into the immanence of desiring-production, the machinic unconscious:

> [I]t is high time to replace the Kantian question 'how are synthetic judgements a priori possible?' with another question: 'why is belief in such judgements necessary?
>
> (Nietzsche 1973: 11)

Like Nietzsche's will to power, like Bataille's general economics, the machinic unconscious is a cipher for the dissembling force of critique whose runaway feedback loop consists of increasingly sophisticated analyses of its own stratification. *Capitalism and Schizophrenia* is a program for desirevolutionary autocritique, a toolbox for migrating (=) intelligence.

Reality production is described as a process of silting, mnemonic residue, stratification, the freezing, quantizing and subsequent coding and territorialization of sequences of intensities. So 'the question is not how things manage to leave the strata, but how things get there in the first place' (Deleuze and Guattari 1987: 56). Pragmatically the simulation or diagramming of strata is always the first task of stratoanalysis.

But reality consists also and contemporaneously in the circuit virtual–actual–virtual. The swoop to zero intensity and back, reinsertion into connective synthesis, the unfolding and metamorphosis of machinic potential into the experience of passage through its actualizations. Memory systems provide the spaces between which communication takes place, at the risk of their own dissolution. Schizophrenia-paranoia as the poles of desiring-production, the tensorial *polemos* which produces intensive gradients as frictional oscillation (Spinozan passion). Stratification is simultaneously cruel persecution and aboriginal reality. Repulsion – Attraction, Paranoia – Miraculation. Transcendental simulation. Reality as black humour (Deleuze and Guattari 1983: 11).

Mobilization: second task. To accelerate virtual-actual circuits; to constantly bring codes and territories as close as possible to their mutation or dissolution, prospecting for a new earth, new planes of communication, whose vast possibilities lie in lurker-space waiting for an escape/invasion. Memory-space is a necessary but not a sufficient condition for social or desiring-production. Intensive machinery is always in play, on transversal circuits.

Technology is an index of social sophistication since diagrammatic recording in the service of replication is precisely this impossible intimacy of stratification and communication. Digital communications technology is a hysterical stage in the history of this tension: its products must at once be invisible data-ducts *and* carry a trademark. So even 'late' capitalism still sees decoding equipment sold as, and in constant desperation to retain its identity as, sedentary consumer goods (digital publishing, home audio and video, communications, consumer credit, the Internet – one of the best examples being the lamentable familial-archival use made of camcorders).

Privatization coupled with deregulation in general involves a decoding of flows contrary to the establishment of a molar social machine. Capitalist social reproduction must domesticate intractable flows, although in the field of technical machines this function becomes almost automatic, the rate of technological dissemination necessitating great standardizations to ensure global compatibility. This techno-miraculative locking acts as a ratchet for intelligence, inscribing progressively sophisticated and autonomous coding systems upon the social body. Revolutionary systems which accelerate communication find commerce already waiting patiently for them, but because they lock into systems of resonance and redundancy under market pressure, their machinic potential is squeezed into sedentary structures which resist the drift of a deterritorializing socius. The embedding of these systems engenders an estrangement between the schizophrenic movements of the social unconscious and its corporeal reality. Darkside operates rhizomatically, spontaneously digesting complexification into its maelstrom and creating new monsters. Progressive ascendancy operates by heaping systems into functional axiomatics, reconstituting molarity where possible. They approach convergence in lurches, as disordered desiring-machines catalyse the molecularization of the social, reciprocally acquiring new influxes of estranged desire. The bombed-out schizophrenic is the one who takes this diagonal too far too soon, before the socius can digest it: Artaud binned by society, obsessively decoding vocal and/or logographical systems into the 'gasps and cries' of schizonautic BwO burnout, 'sheer unarticulated blocks of sound' (Deleuze and Guattari 1983: 9). The alphabet as an object of exploration, of machinic exploitation, an apparatus of migration. Consonants are break-cuts in a vowel-flow. Permutation hunts down potential. Various coding systems, some human, some unknown, emerge and are submerged in turn:

> katarsun
> dafrer
> urfru
> omprend unon
> non stop
> onmprend
> . . . tscharfukt
>
> (Artaud 1946: vol. 25: 193/216)

Not 'mistaking words for things', but using words as machine parts. Maximum slogan density – the delirious *opus postumum* of a psychotic advertising exec, short-circuiting the market to testify, alone and already a crowd criss-crossed by *nommo*, to the incarceration of machinic potential in 'natural' language. Using the frayed edges of words which connect like a hidden passageway to their milieu of exteriority to irradiate the whole system.

Playing de/coding apparatuses tactically against their fetishistic tendencies (solvent abuse) is a thoroughly schizoanalytic procedure – riding the cusp of cyberpositive commodification without turning into a shopkeeper, or rushing into black-hole deterritorialization. The perversity and ambivalence of capitalist production (exemplified by the advertising industry's enslavement of orphaned chunks of language-intensity to vapid consumerism) is the key to *Capitalism and Schizophrenia*, a justification in itself for that untimely coupling of cracked-up heads. But at its outer limit, the capitalist socius *is* the machinic unconscious. It clicks into desiring-production as decoded language clicks into rhythm.

Capitalization agitates for decoded communication, the abstract general equivalent, whilst performing a gross overcoding which dichotomizes monetary exchange as capital/cash, one mapping an intensive series, non-linear positive feedback, the other mapping extensive, linear and unproductive circles: investor/consumer. Cash is livestock for the capitalists' table. Keep the animals stupid, hand them little morsels and reap the profits, consumer spending constructed as an endlessly reconstituted lack expressed in molar units (financial psychoanalysis). Capital as a mysterious flow which is always intensifying, distributing and travelling.

But the double bind is not to be identified with contradiction, and besides, contra Marx, 'no-one has ever died of contradictions' (Deleuze and Guattari 1983: 151). The plication (stratogenesis) of capital and cash is a further manifestation of the twin tendencies of capitalism: a ceaseless expansion of its inner limits, and a labyrinthine flight from its outer limit – BwO. The clandestine channel of communication (cataspace) between investment (non-linear complication) and bovine consumerism (linear compliance) is the escape valve, the diagonal of the articulation: its covert presupposition and its greatest fear. The abstract currency/current which is always imagined as complicit (matter–slave–worker–woman–machine–money–data). But K-circuits inevitably tend towards positive feedback, accelerating each other. The circuits (even those of the black markets) *are* their own escalation, just as money *is* its circulation. The technological industries, in their tireless pursuit of efficiency and reproducibility (analysis), must retain increasing margins of decoding, cutting edges of deterritorialization, which are always exploited by vagabond science and guerrilla commerce, speeding reality circuitry into posthuman micro smear-cultures (catalysis – ARPANET becomes Internet, 303 becomes Acid Machine, car becomes ramraider, turntable becomes instrument, spraycan becomes paintbrush). There have always been hackers (because 'there was ice before computers' (Gibson 1993: 169)). The capitalist socius has always been (in) the process of disturbing its own striation, just as critique endlessly throws itself on its inner limits. And catalytic microcultures which induce BwO migration (lines of flight) are crucial to the cyberpositive surges which accelerate the process. *Anti-Oedipus*' synthetic process of desiring-production played out in macro feedback turbulence – '[T]he more it breaks down, the more it schizophrenizes, the better it works, the American way' (Deleuze and Guattari 1983: 151).

Code is viable currency only insofar as it exploits its margins of decoding. Internalism (and the separatism of hierarchized representational schemae) produces poverty. Trade barriers prevent development, and black marketeers always creep past the border guards. Decoding is always possible and usually inexorable. Successively decoded currents sweep through cold circuits, rendering them more conductive as they circulate. The circulation is the conductivity, the surplus value of code produced by/as desiring-production which renders territorial consolidation a volatile subcomponent of the material process. 'Stages' of capitalism are nomadic encampments. All currencies float on the full body of capital, and in their mobilization, mutate.

> [A] code is inseparable from a process of decoding that is inherent to it. . . . There is no genetics without 'genetic drift'. . . . Every code is affected by a margin of decoding due to the supplements and surplus values – supplements in the order of a multiplicity, surplus values in the order of a rhizome.
>
> (Deleuze and Guattari 1987: 53)

Will the margin of decoding and deterritorialization (a closed system's diagonal drip-feed) gradually widen until, as in the State's worst nightmare, in a cataclysmic spasm, the system is collapsed out of 'itself', irradiated by its own conditions of possibility? The nightmare of decoded flows, BwO? Always on the cusp of its own extropy, capitalism is a continually intensifying plateau which sweeps all of history along into its trail. And if it feels like it's gonna blow . . . you haven't seen anything yet . . . (of course Apocalyptic SF is one essential genre of 'late' capitalism).

> (C)apitalism has to deal essentially with its own limit, its own destruction – as Marx says, insofar as it is capable of self-criticism (at least to a certain point: the point where the limit appears, in the very movement that counteracts the tendency).
>
> (Deleuze and Guattari 1983: 140)

The 'limit' point which trips the fuse-switches of panoptic power, reterritorializing on all of the BwO's good work, ancillary State apparatuses trying to arrogate to themselves a share of the surplus value, or absorbing it just in order to endure. Crisis after crisis, the critical ambivalence appears in all its insane glory. The risible panic government of the post-Thatcher/Reagan State. The end of the family, of the social, interpreted by State priests as motives for consolidation, quiescence and/or despair. Fascist resurgences. Fetish marketing of consumer products under threat of pandemic anonymous black-market replication. Copyright clampdowns on sampling. Revival of the good old-fashioned pseudo-tragic pop-chart song as the response to decoded sub-scene sonic networks.

The tendency of code to drift and the consequent trade-off between migration and security, which at every subsequent stage must necessarily become less an option than an impulsion (hence the plasticity of the axiomatic), means that such illegitimate policing is a never-ending task requiring huge influxes of energy. Thus not only does a vast pool of machinic potential lie unexplored or become absorbed and neutralized, but regulators are constantly being assembled to prevent anything from escaping, overcoding and reterritorializing in a frenzy of xenophobic activity.

Illegitimate policing, coding to abolish migration, communication, external functionality, is an old story: Plato and the sophists, Kant and the nomads, psychoanalysis and schizophrenia. Confiscation of the drums and 'fetishes'. Eliminating all but the most impoverished *gestalt* transmissions, to create autonomous systemic reality-machines.

The State works so hard at its laziness, paying for the luxury of stasis with a general enervation and self-affirming sedentariness, revelling in its disengagement. In philosophy the schism between theory and practice (*arithmetica/logistica*), the intellectual's disdain for commerce and business (which is obviously reciprocated), developed into a perennial State trope on the basis of Hellenic slavery. The related love of static and ordered forms extends especially to the marriage of music and mathematics. The Pythagorean scale, which traps music in harmonic redundancy, geometry as a spatial overcoding of the social machine (*polis*), which freezes mathematics for centuries, deleting the problematic nature of Babylonian 'algebra' (*nomos*).

Such policing is eschewed by *Capitalism and Schizophrenia*, which instead assembles the tools necessary for micro-engineering stratoanalysis. *Capitalism and Schizophrenia* is a diagram of the highly schizophrenic assemblage of capitalist reality production, and hints at techniques for exploiting its suppressed potential, its ironic and critical movement, the process of its endless finalities and its artificial realities. Queer Mechanics. 'The schizoanalyst is a mechanic, and schizoanalysis is solely functional' (Deleuze and Guattari 1983: 322). Diagonalization invades/escapes stratification by producing apparatus which decouples reciprocal and vicious articulation-series. Finding again the intensities which are split (schiz-), in a process which of course includes further reterritorializations, further codes. A left-handed cartography in which, however, it is the *further* which takes precedence in a sinister divergence from the straight (State) line made of metric-spatial points.

> The diagonal frees itself, breaks or twists. The line no longer forms a contour and instead passes *between* things, *between* points. It belongs to a smooth space. It draws a plane that has no more dimensions than that which crosses.
>
> (Deleuze and Guattari 1987: 505)

In its insistence on the practicality of stratoanalysis (icebreaking), *Capitalism and Schizophrenia* plugs into the vernacular cybernetics of Gibson's street-voudu, emphasizing the power of minority microcultures whose pragmatic survivalism precludes for them the bourgeois marginality of the avant-garde or the heroic martyrdom of resistance politicos:

> [W]rite with slogans. . . .
>
> (Deleuze and Guattari 1987: 24)

Theory is already practice at the level of intensity; it is only by a conscientious disintensification that academia sends itself into the woods. Dislike of memetic transfer, popularity, becoming-style. Must keep it precious. . . . Heidegger singing peasant ballads on the folk-club circuit, the senescent Deleuze and Guattari's touching concern for the plight of philosophy in the age of advertising (Deleuze and Guattari 1995: 10–12).

HIT ESCAPE

Clandestine planes consist of technological (recording and reproductive) systems gradually escaping their instrumental definitions and designator-functionality to communicate through subterranean channels, between marginal non-agents, those excluded from the official processes of social recording and reproduction.

CONTROL DISABLED

Clandestine planes escape macro socio-theoretical and philosophical monitoring apparatuses because they operate transversally, without reference to molar categories or overcodings. No prescribed forms underlie the unfoldings and catastrophes of matter in such processes. No under-standing. Swarm. Hivelocity.

WILDSTYLE SOUND

Interference patterns and polymetric disturbances in a strange *milieu*, weaving, modulating and transcoding: temporary agglomeration and interplay, the track, or plateau. Writing-machine as remix, sample-heavy. If such an assemblage uses *Capitalism and Schizophrenia*, reactualizing its concepts (replication is not duplication, 'no genetics without genetic drift'), it is not as an object of veneration. As soon as the concepts 'deterritorialization' and 'decoding' leave the page they are already doing deterritorialization and decoding. Philosophical personae become irrelevant upon machinic engagement, and any misuse of terminology derives from schizoanalysis' nature as vague (vagabond) science: don't try and get it straight – bend it out of shape even more. Use the rough edges of the plateaus to slot them into others, creating new planes of consistency in a process which is not personal any more than hip-hop and jungle are the inventions of a benevolent music-lover.

ROUTES NOT ROOTS

Don't expect answers or origins, just lines twisting, converging and crossing as well as diverging; not arborescent but rhizomaniac. No original but always the *vershon*. Wildstyle like the graffiti that accompanied hip-hop – an unseen and unplanned alliance cross-fertilizing traits through the medium of the wall or the subway train, inciting unknown associates further and further into baroque foldings (aparallel evolution). The glistening surfaces of K-culture, videogames, advertising, twisted into Escher-space, projecting-probing-splitting and joining in unfathomable planes of colour until the word disappears beneath its own superfluity . . . neither really simple, nor really complex, but desimplified in the course of its production. Overlaid like a second skin onto the subway trains that criss-cross the subterranea of NYC, Wildstyle creates a clandestine cataspace, a mutant topology of unanticipated connections, at the same time eliminating the name in favour of the tag, the offhand flourish of the magic marker that stands for a multiplicity and its traits, something that once passed through here, leaving its art behind. . . .

> SPIRIT SUPERKOOL KOOLKILLER ACE VIPERE SPIDER EDDIE WOODIE 110 SHADOW 137
>
> the urban city . . . is the cut-up space of distinctive signs . . . [it] is a 'body without organs', as Deleuze says, an intersection of channelled flows.
>
> (Baudrillard 1993: 76–7, 79)

The city is becoming-wildstyle, and wildstyle uses capitalism's decoding equipment ('the terrorist power of the media . . . symbolic destruction' (Baudrillard 1993: 76–7) against the social and semiological reterritorializations of consumer capitalism.

> By tattooing walls, SUPERSEX and SUPERKOOL free them from architecture.
>
> (Baudrillard 1993: 82)

TRACKS NOT SONGS

The creation of the track as a singular coincidence of a swarmachine of sampled material, filter sequences, abstract gradients and resistances – the engineer tracking an anonymous and collectively constituted sonic phylum, actualizing it in the track as nomadic anarchitecture. Bass has no face, only a machinic probe-head which collects and connects, and is called on by means of a cthulic cipher:

> PHOTEK HYPE LEMON D TEK 9 A-ZONE FLYTRONIX SYSTEM X
>
> Urban style music. The city is a jungle.
>
> It's a whole new world under the cover of darkness, hiding from the beast, tuning up in anticipation of the dance. With flow of sound hanging thick in the air, crowding in and out of your lungs, becoming the oxygen you breathe, you realise that the youts in this for real.
>
> (Two Fingers and Kirk 1995: 4)

Clandestine in voodoo nights of microcultural mutation. Zero as machinic assemblages mash-up and cross-fade. Diagonal as markets lock into guerrilla commerce, ever-decamping nomad cultures, melting in the heat of the chase. Current.

> Beyond the face lies an . . . inhumanity . . . cutting edges of deterritorialization becoming operative and lines of deterritorialization positive and absolute, forming strange new becomings, new polyvocalities. Become clandestine, make rhizome everywhere, for the wonder of a nonhuman life to be created.
>
> (Deleuze and Guattari 1987: 190–1)

If it is inevitable that mnemotechnics should take hold of life in such a comprehensive fashion, it is only on the condition of a necessary and immanent indiscipline. The principal component of technological sophistication, analysis, is the progressive disintegration of corporeal machines into virtuality (catastrophe). Darkside influence functions as retroactive non-linearity (anastrophe), catalysing virtual components into new artificialities which reprocess the present through its machinic potential. Clandestine becomings plug the present into the future, looping virtual-actual into RAM-mutation, intersecting the black mirror which chronologizes non-linear temporal plurality. The history of the White Man Face will appear in Count Zero Vodou as a temporary dissipator for labyrinthine convergences, science fiction more alien than it ever dreamt it would be. 'The dark continent we're heading towards' (Fisher 1995). The living jungle, where to survive is to activate mutant lines, become-imperceptible in order to perceive, and follow diagonal paths marked out only by chromatic gradients of intensity (Schwarzenegger in *Predator*).

Jungle has nothing to do with a fetishistic 'primitivism', but signals a twofold movement whereby diasporic flows of abstract matter, alien(ated) forces, activate their potential irrespective of the apparently triumphant system of neutralizing, metabolic molarity. The micro-striation of the capitalist socius tends toward a smooth space whose inorganic zones of machinic detritus overwhelm the State apparatus, short-circuiting modernocratic optimism. Voodoo was already in cyberspace; it was just waiting for the Technics to arrive. Technologies less visible, less obvious than those of the West: forcibly virtualized on the Atlantic passage, ready for reactualization in local conditions, a vernacular cybernetics, a rhythmic contagion, local and specific, functional and asignifiant.

> The beats rolling over me, faster and more insistent, dark and dangerous, nebulous, underwater, slowing down time and interpretation.
>
> (Two Fingers and Kirk 1995: 190)

Stratoanalytical technique: sampling at substratic speeds and scrambling coding systems, feeding intensificatory experimentation back into the strata to optimize darkside convergence. Stratoanalysis is never distinct from its mode of operation: indeed certain modes of operation 'accidentally' invent stratoanalytic lines, or forgotten techniques suddenly resurface as tools of a new stratoanalytic practice.

Preliminary diagonalyses suggest that such so-called 'spontaneous phenomena' may result from the clandestine operation of photonic timestretching devices, steering junglist vectors from futurelooped loatronic encampments. Catalytic microcultures stretched across time, rhythms without sense assembling non-organic lives. As they touch us, we are immersed in new sonic assemblages where abstract matter becomes tactile. An into-body experience and a new model for thought that cuts through the grid-lines of acoustic, aesthetic, social and economic composition. The synthetic future, no longer enlightened, with a clear vision of the future and able to shut its eyes against the 'internal south', but coming from the dark spaces in the middle, when least expected. Disturbance of equilibrium . . . vibrations through the body; breaks and cuts.

> Music is prophecy. Its styles and economic organization are ahead of the rest of society because it explores, much faster than material reality can, the entire range of possibilities in a given code. It makes audible the new world that will gradually become visible.
>
> (Attali 1985: 11)

* * *

At a certain threshold, the experimental dismemberment of codes no longer just prevents us from complicitly saying what we didn't want to say, but arrives at a mobilization or a complication of flows which 'we' were never aware of, lines which emerge from another zone and meet in wildstyle on the darkside, in the jungle, in full effect.

It therefore remains for us to see how, effectively, simultaneously, these various tasks of stratoanalysis proceed.

Notes

1 This principle explains the Pythagorean discovery that ratios of natural numbers correspond to musical harmony thus: '(T)he ear resolves all complex sounds into pendular oscillations . . . and regards as harmonious only such excitements of the nerves

as continue without disturbance', i.e. tones whose frequencies are in factorial ratios and thus do not disrupt each other's cycles (Helmholtz 1954: 229).

2 This is also the reason one cannot slow down a CD in the same way as one can a record. This lack of tactile interaction explains the endurance (indeed resurgence) of such an apparently obsolete medium as the vinyl disc.

3 It is irrelevant to ask, as many sociologists and anthropologists do, whether initiates are really possessed, whether what is involved is mass hysteria, hypnosis, or playacting. This typical psychoanalytical move ignores the fact that the loa have no 'reality' apart from their immanence in the social machine, and therefore their desiring-manifestation (or machine-infestation) seeks no authenticating status over and above its active function within the social machine.

References

Artaud, A. (1946) *Oeuvres complètes*, Paris: Gallimard.

Attali, J. (1985) *Noise*, trans. B. Massumi, Minneapolis: University of Minnesota Press.

Bataille, G. (1992) *On Nietzsche*, trans. B. Boone, New York: Paragon.

Baudrillard, J. (1993) *Symbolic Exchange and Death*, trans. I. H. Grant, London: Sage.

Delany, S. R., Tate, G. and Rose, T. (1993) 'Black to the Future', in M. Dery (ed.) *Flame Wars: The Discourse of Cyberculture* (Durham, NC: Duke University Press).

Deleuze, G. and Guattari, Félix (1983) *Anti-Oedipus*, trans. R. Hurley, M. Seem and H. R. Lane, Minneapolis: University of Minnesota Press.

—— (1987) *A Thousand Plateaus*, trans. B. Massumi, London: Athlone.

—— (1995) *What is Philosophy?*, trans. G. Burchell and H. Tomlinson, London: Verso.

Deleuze, G. and Parnet, Claire (1983) 'Politics', in G. Deleuze and F. Guattari, *On the Line*, New York: Semiotext[e], 1983.

Eglash, R. (1995) 'African Influences in Cybernetics', in C. H. Gray (ed.) *The Cyborg Handbook*, New York and London: Routledge.

Fisher, Mark (1995) 'Black Noise', *** *collapse* 2.

Foerster, H. and Beauchamp, J. W. (eds) (1969) *Music by Computers*, New York: Wiley.

Gibson, W. (1993) *Count Zero*, London: HarperCollins.

Helmholtz, H. L. F (1954) *On the Sensation of Tone*, trans. A. J. Ellis, New York: Dover.

Jahn, J. (1961) *Muntu: The New African Culture*, trans. M. Green, New York: Grove Press.

Kant, I. (1933) *Critique of Pure Reason*, trans. N. K. Smith, London: Macmillan.

Métraux, A. (1972) *Voodoo in Haiti*, trans. H. Charteris, New York: Schocken.

Nietzsche, F. (1973) *Beyond Good and Evil*, trans. R. J. Hollingdale, London: Penguin.

Two Fingers and Kirk, James T. (1995) *Junglist*, London: Boxtree.

Select Discography

Dr Octagon *Blue Flowers Remixes*, Mo'Wax.

Ed Rush *Check Me Out*, DeeJay Recordings.

HeavyWeight *Oh Gosh*, Rogue Trooper.

Lemon D *Urban Flava Pt.1*, Metalheadz.
Marvellous Cain *Gun Talk*, Suburban Base.
Raekwon *Only Built 4 Cuban Linx*, RCA.
Remarc *In Da Hood*, Suburban Base.
—— *Menace*, Whitehouse.
Various *Drum & Bass Selection 1–6*, Breakdown.
—— *Platinum Breakz*, London/Metalheadz.
—— *Routes From The Jungle*, Virgin.
—— *Techsteppin*, Emotif.

. . . Thanks also to Switch, Turbofunk, Zc2 and Cur, who helped mix it.

Index